The Finnish

SS-VOLUNTEERS AND ATROCITIES

1941–1943

LARS WESTERLUND

THE FINNISH SS-VOLUNTEERS AND ATROCITIES

against Jews, Civilians and Prisoners of War in Ukraine and the Caucasus Region 1941–1943

An Archival Survey

Suomalaisen Kirjallisuuden Seura – Finnish Literature Society
Kansallisarkisto – The National Archives of Finland
Helsinki 2019

Steering Group
Permanent State Under-Secretary **Timo Lankinen**, Prime Minister's Office / Chair
Research Director **Päivi Happonen**, The National Archives of Finland
Director General **Jussi Nuorteva**, The National Archives of Finland
Legal Adviser **Päivi Pietarinen**, Office of the President of the Republic of Finland
Production Manager, **Tiina-Kaisa Laakso-Liukkonen**, Prime Minister's Office / Secretary

Project Group
Director General **Jussi Nuorteva**, The National Archives of Finland / Chair
Research Director **Päivi Happonen**, The National Archives of Finland / Vice-Chair
Associate Professor **Antero Holmila**, University of Jyväskylä
Dean of the Faculty of Law, Professor **Pia Letto-Vanamo**, University of Helsinki
Professor **Kimmo Rentola**, University of Helsinki
Academy Research Fellow **Oula Silvennoinen**, University of Helsinki
Docent **André Swanström**, Åbo Akademi University
Professor, Major General **Vesa Tynkkynen**, The National Defence University
Professor **Lars Westerlund**
Researcher **Ville-Pekka Kääriäinen**, The National Archives of Finland / Secretary

Publisher's Editor **Katri Maasalo**, Finnish Literature Society (SKS)
Proofreading and translations **William Moore**
Maps **Spatio Oy**
Graphic designer **Anne Kaikkonen**, Timangi

Cover: Finnish Waffen-SS troops ready to start the march to the East in May or early June 1941. *OW Coll.*

Kirjokansi 222
ISBN 978-951-858-100-3
ISSN 2323-7392

Kansallisarkiston toimituksia 22
ISSN 0355-1768

Printed: Hansaprint Oy, Turenki, Finland, 2019

CONTENTS

FOREWORD 9

1,408 FINNISH SS-VOLUNTEERS 12

The recruitment of the Finnish SS-volunteers originated in the Winter War experiences 13

The Finnish volunteers harboured strong Anti-Soviet attitudes 20

The Waffen SS-Division Wiking – Overview and Documentation 22

Composition of the Division **22** | Political views among the Finnish volunteers **26** | Efforts by the Finnish National Socialist organisations to enforce the recruitment of Finnish volunteers **30** | The illusion of an SS elite unit **33** | Involvement of Waffen-SS in atrocities **36** | SS-Division Wiking and atrocities witnessed by Finnish volunteers **41** | Atrocities by Danish, Norwegian, and Swedish volunteers **50** | Surviving archives of the Waffen-SS **54** | Other Archives **55** | The 76 diaries by the Finnish SS-volunteers **55** | Ten diaries by Dutch and Norwegian SS-volunteers **57** | Recollections by and biographies on Finnish volunteers **58** | Photo documentation **59**

THE UNITS OF WAFFEN SS-DIVISION WIKING AND THEIR COMMANDERS 61

The SS-Regiment Nordland 61
The SS-Regiment Westland 62
The SS-Regiment Germania 64
SS-Artillerie-Regiment 5 64
SS-Aufklärungs-Abteilung 5 66
SS-Panzerjäger-Abteilung 5 66
The Finnish SS-Volunteer Battalion 67
The Finnish contingent of the Waffen-SS 68
The Division Commander Felix Steiner 68
The Regiment and Battalion Commanders 73

THE HARSH GERMAN OCCUPATION POLICY IN POLAND, 1939–40 76

MASS KILLINGS IN UKRAINE IN 1941 77

Civilians **77**
Jews **78**
Partisans **82**
Soviet Prisoners of War **88**
Political Commissars **90**

NO PRISONERS WILL BE TAKEN 92

MASSACRES IN THE LEMBERG AREA, 1.–7.7.1941 98

Lemberg 1.7.1941: The Baptism of Shocking Scenes **98**
The Ukrainian nationalists **99** | The actions of Einsatzgruppe C **101** | The Wehrmacht City Commandant and German recollections **102** | A Dutch report **104** | Observations by Norwegian volunteers **104** | Experiences of Finnish volunteers **107**

Olszanica, 2.7.1941: The first shootings of Soviet POWs and civilians **111**
Novosilky, 2.–3.7.1941: Bloody revenge for the Regiment Commander Wäckerle **112**
Krivichi, 2.7.1941: The annihilation of a local community **118**
Slowita, 2.7.1941: Fire-raising, wild shootings, and executions **120**
Kurowice, 3.7.1941: 180 Soviet POWs were shot and some Jews **124**
Zolochiv, 3.–4.7.1941: Lieutenant-Colonel Groscurth restrains the brutality of SS-Division Wiking **125**
The atrocities in the recollections of the locals **125** | The Ukrainian nationalists **127** | Oberstleutnant Helmuth Groscurth **129** | The SS-Division Wiking **1230** | The minor role of Einsatzkommando 4b **132** | Actions by the Dutch and Norwegian SS-volunteers **133** | Experiences of the Finnish volunteers **133**
Zboriv, 4.7.1941: Further Massacre of Jews **134**
Ozerna, 3.–5.7.1941: 180–200 Jews killed, and two synagogues burned **135**
Nowiki, 3.–4.7.1941: Minor scuffles and the killing of stragglers **136**
Podhorylce, early July 1941: Two Finns shot two slaughter victims **138**
Urycz, 7.7.1941: At least 300 civilians were shot **139**

ACTS OF MASS VIOLENCE IN THE TARNOPOL AREA, 4.-6.7.1941 141

Tarnopol, 4.-5.7.1941: An urban massacre 141
The City Commandant Erwin Sander 141 | The Ukrainian nationalists 142
The Sonderkommando 4b 143 | Actions by the Dutch volunteers 143
Experiences of the Finnish volunteers 145 | The possible gauntlet of the Butchery Company 147
Mykulyntsi, 5.7.1941: The Berserk run of the Wikingers 148
The raids of the Ukrainian nationalists 149 | The actions of the SS units 150
Steiner is claimed to have ordered the execution of 200 Soviet POWs, 5.7.1941 151
Hrymailiv, 5.7.1941: Swift settlement in passing 152
Chorostków, 5.7.1941: Outrages against the Jews 154
Husiatyn, 6.7.1941: The mowing down of civilians and Soviet POWs 154
Recollections by Dutch volunteers 154 | Experiences of Finnish volunteers 155
Wehrmacht efforts to check the atrocities 157

VIOLENT EVENTS IN THE EASTERN AREAS, 11.7.1941 - JANUARY 1943 158

Proskurov, 11.7.1941: Mopping-up actions in the streets 158
Bila Tserkva, mid-July 1941: Shooting of Jews 159
The bridgehead of Dnipropetrovsk, August 1941: Shooting of civilians 160
Zhytomyr, mid-July 1941: The deathblow of a city 160
The Wiking round-ups 160 | Einsatzkommando 4b 161 | Cautionary hangings in the market square, 7.8.1941 162
Krementsug, 12.8.1941: The execution of a Soviet Lieutenant 163
Dniprodzerzhynsk: Suspect Russians shot, 22.8.1941 162
Village near Donskoye, 18.1.1942: Necessity to shoot the Ivans 163
Kabardinskaya, 26.9.1942:All the deserters were shot and two Russians hanged 164
Toldzgun, December 1942: Clearing the village 164
Metsentinskaya, January-March 1943: Shooting POWs 165

ATTITUDES TOWARDS JEWS AND REJECTION OF ATROCITIES **166**

Anti-Jewish sentiments among the Finnish volunteers **167**
SS-indoctrination on the race issue **172**
Feelings of sympathy for the suffering Jews **175**
Attitudes of indifference **180**
Rejection of atrocities and latent anti-German views among the volunteers **183**
Angry and understanding attitudes towards the Jews among Danish, Dutch and Norwegian SS-volunteers **187**

THE FINNISH INVOLVEMENT **190**

The number of victims **191**
The pattern of perpetrators **192**
The interlude of the Ukrainian nationalists **194**
The accompanying Einsatzgruppen **198**
The divided attitude of the Wehrmacht forces **199**
The Wiking atrocities as mission-focused tactics **200**
The Finnish volunteers were well aware of the atrocities **202**
The Finnish involvement **202**

Appendix **205**
Notes **212**
Archives **231**
Literature **236**
Index **245**

FOREWORD

On January 4th, 2018, Dr. Efraim Zuroff, the Israeli historian and director of the Simon Wiesenthal Center's Jerusalem office, sent a letter to the President of Finland Sauli Niinistö, requesting that Finland launch a comprehensive investigation into the role played by Finnish volunteers who served with the Waffen SS-Division Wiking between 1941 and 1943 in the murder of Jews in Ukraine and the Caucasus.

In his appeal to Niinistö, Zuroff cited an article by the Finnish historian Dr. André Swanström published in the 2017 Yearbook of the Finnish Society of Church History. Swanström's Finnish-language article was entitled *Fasismi ja uskonto suomalaisten SS-pastorien ajattelussa ja toiminnassa* ("Fascism and Religion in the Thoughts and Deeds of Finnish SS-Chaplains"), and it prefaced an extensive volume published in 2018 entitled *Hakaristin ritarit: Suomalaiset SS-miehet, politiikka, uskonto ja sotarikokset* ("Knights of the Swastika: Finnish SS-Men, Politics, Religion and War Crimes").

The Secretary-General of the Office of the President of the Republic Hiski Haukkala reported back to Zuroff on January 24th that Finland felt it would be important to produce an independent scientific report on the matter. Even in the case of difficult questions such as this, Finland sets great store by granting researchers liberal access to archive documents. Wartime registers and documents of all kinds have long been freely available to researchers.

On May 23rd, the National Archives of Finland was instructed by the Prime Minister's Office to deliver an independent archive-based survey of the Finnish SS-volunteers' participation in atrocities relating to Jews, prisoners of war, and civilians between 1941 and 1943. Professor Lars Westerlund was engaged to produce the report, and he and National Archives researcher Ville-Pekka Kääriäinen began work one week later. In spite of the considerable volume of material and work involved, the report itself was completed by the scheduled deadline of the end of November 2018, but it became clear that additional time was required to bring the project to a satisfactory conclusion, for extensive language checking, and for the printing and publishing of the final text. Consequently, the Prime Minister's Office decided that the report would be made public at the beginning of February 2019.

The Finnish volunteers served in the international Waffen SS-Division Wiking, which drew in volunteers from several other countries, including Sweden, Denmark, Norway, the Netherlands, Belgium, and Estonia. The commanding officers of the division and its subordinate units were mainly German Waffen-SS officers. Earlier research into the Finnish volunteers in SS-Division Wiking has leant almost exclusively on material residing in the National Archives and in the Military Archives that were integrated into the National Archives in 2008. This report has examined in detail the incidents and atrocities bearing on Jews, civilians, and Soviet POWs in those locations where Finnish SS-volunteers are known to have been during the extreme violence that took place. The work has taken account of material on the SS-Division that has been preserved in the archives of other countries. These documents have been used in earlier international studies, but hitherto they have not been widely exploited in Finland.

A great part of the international material has been drawn from various German archives (Bundesarchiv– Militärarchiv Freiburg, Bundesarchiv Berlin-Lichterfelde, Staatsarchiv Nürnberg, Ludwigsburg Zentrale Stelle der Landesjustizverwaltungen zur Aufklärung nationalsozialistischer Verbrechen). The material embraces wartime Waffen-SS documents, official reports and investigations dating from the post-war period, and documents pertaining to the war crimes trials. Useful material has also been sourced from the Netherlands (CABR and DANS in Den Haag and NIOD in Amsterdam). The United States National Archives and Records Administration (NARA) holds a vast body of records documenting German war crimes.

In the course of autumn 2018, the Finnish National Archives' Development Manager Prof. Dmitri Frolov has charted documents relating to the actions of SS-Division Wiking in Ukraine and the Caucasus that are preserved in archives in Russia, Belarus, and Ukraine. This is a considerable corpus of material. Given the tight schedule set for this report, it has not been possible to go through these documents in terms of content, but agreements existing between the National Archives and these other archives will permit the digitalising of the material and its use in further research, if separate funding is made available for this.

The Yad Vashem World Holocaust Remembrance Center in Jerusalem has gathered an extensive database of Shoah victims, and reference data linking to Holocaust-related documentary material held in archives and institutions in countries around the world. The Remembrance Center Archives also contain a huge body of photographic material. Similar material can be found in the United States Holocaust Memorial Museum (USHMM) in Washington D.C. The systematic utilisation of these sources will require further work.

The National Archives have been granted access to the archives of the *Veljesapu-Perinneyhdistys r.y.* Finnish Waffen-SS veterans' heritage association. In addition, some members of the association have provided the National Archives with material from their own personal collections. The diaries of SS-volunteers and other material, including photographs, have been received from Finnish individuals who have taken a documentary interest in the history of SS-Division Wiking. Many of these individuals have material of real importance in a research context. Among them, the most significant include the current *Veljesapu* Chairman Pekka Kääriäinen, Counsellor of Legislation, LL.D. Olli Wikberg from the Ministry of Justice, and the Chairman of the Board of Rauhala Yhtiöt Oy, Mika Hakanpää. They have freely given of their expertise in the clarification of numerous details pertaining to the project and the report. We also wish to thank Museum Amanuensis Jari Saurio of the Parola Armour Museum for his willing support.

The key corpus of original source material for the report is found in the 76 diaries that were kept by Finnish volunteers serving in SS-Division Wiking. Previous research has had access to 54 diaries. In addition, the research has examined Finnish files, both official and in private hands, correspondence, photographs, articles and clippings from newspapers and periodicals, personal memoirs, and research literature. The material received during the research has been digitalised. It will be added to the collections of the National Archives and will be available to researchers after the publication of the report.

In the course of producing the report, account has been taken of all the entries in the diaries of Finnish SS-volunteers that pertain to killings and violent actions in specific locations, to positive or disparaging remarks and attitudes towards Jews, local civilians, POWs, or Soviet partisans, and to comments on National Socialist ideologies and racial doctrines.

In terms of research literature as source material, the focus has been on international studies and JewishGen's Yizkor Book Project, produced by survivors and the descendants of survivors of Jewish communities destroyed in the Holocaust, and containing a mixture of religious texts, historical research, and personal recollections.

Professor Westerlund has forged an extensive international network of contacts and has reached out to SS-researchers around the world. The network has provided a great deal of useful information, hints on further literature sources, and documentary material.

The media have also followed the research project with some interest. The investigation has been the subject of articles and pieces in several European countries, and in Israel, the United States, and Japan. In December 2018, the National Archives and the Embassy of Finland to Israel arranged two press briefings on the subject in Israel. The Jerusalem Simon Wiesenthal Center director Efraim Zuroff spoke at both these events.

The research work has been supported by a Project Group established by the National Archives in June 2018 and by a Steering Group under the aegis of the Prime Minister's Office. The members of these two bodies are listed above. We are most grateful to them for their expertise and critical comments. The challenging task of checking the final language and of translating some additional texts from the Finnish was carried out in January 2019 by William Moore, who also showed an admirable grasp of the content and commented upon it. Katri Maasalo has served as the publishing editor for the Finnish Literature Society (SKS). We offer our gratitude for their efforts to all those who have taken part in the project.

FOR THE NATIONAL ARCHIVES OF FINLAND, 7.1.2019

Jussi Nuorteva
Director General, National Archivist

Päivi Happonen
Research Director, Adjunct Professor

1,408 FINNISH SS-VOLUNTEERS

In the years from 1941 to 1943, a total of 1,408 Finnish volunteers served in the Waffen-SS. Much is known of these individuals from around 50 studies, recollections, and popular works that have been released on the volunteers or published by them. Moreover, the extant newspaper and periodical articles on the subject run at least into the hundreds. This presentation will, however, focus on one issue of particular significance: the atrocities that may have been committed by the Finnish SS-volunteers in Ukraine and the Caucasus in 1941–43. Although this topic has been touched upon in many publications during the last eight decades, from 1945 onwards, this study will provide a systematic review of available documents on the Finnish SS-volunteers, and their possible involvement in atrocities.

Initially a short background section throws some light on the experiences of the Winter War (1939–40) between Finland and the Soviet Union as a platform for the attachment by the Finnish government to Nazi Germany in the fall of 1940 and during 1941. The SS-volunteers were recruited with the tacit though systematic support of leading national circles. The motives of the individual volunteers for entering service with the Waffen-SS are also touched upon. These were strongly influenced by anti-Soviet feelings that were only strengthened by the Winter War experiences.

The presentation includes an initial review of the SS-Division Wiking and its sub-units. This part will give the reader the institutional framework of the incidences of atrocities that occurred during the advance of the Division from Lemberg (Ukr. *Lviv*; Rus. *Lvov*; Pol. *Lwów*) eastwards, in particular in Western Ukraine during July 1941. This is all background information, presented briefly, and includes sections on the harsh German rule in Poland in 1939–41, which somewhat later was even more brutally reflected in Ukraine. The topic of racial indoctrination is likewise touched upon, because modest expressions of sympathy for the Jews are recorded among the volunteers.

What is common to the roughly two dozen geographical locations where atrocities took place is that the municipalities, towns, and cities were situated along the marching route of SS-Division Wiking, most particularly during the summer of 1941. However, the intention is not to provide a full picture of all the atrocities that occurred in these places. The presentation rather concerns only those atrocities associated with the Finnish SS-volunteers. In order to provide context, some comparative light is shone upon the atrocities in which Danish, Dutch, Norwegian and Swedish volunteers were involved. A chapter concerns the critical and condemnatory views of the volunteers on what they witnessed.

A section on the anti-Jewish sentiments among the Finnish SS-volunteers is also included, along with notes on their rejection and condemnation of the atrocities. Finally, the conclusions on the involvement in atrocities by the Finnish SS-volunteers will be noted.

The Soviet Union attacked Finland on 30.11.1939 in accordance with the secret protocol to the Molotov-Ribbentrop Pact, whereby Nazi Germany and the Soviet Union agreed that Finland would belong to the Soviet sphere of influence. Destruction from a Soviet air raid in Mikkeli, 5.1.1940. *SA-kuva.*

The recruitment of the Finnish SS-volunteers originated in the Winter War experiences

On 30.11.1939, Soviet forces invaded Finland with 21 divisions and bombed the capital, Helsinki. Soon after the Red Army had begun its advance, a Finnish Communist named Otto Ville Kuusinen, who had settled in Moscow after the 1918 Civil War, was pronounced head of the Finnish Democratic Republic (also known as the Terijoki Government). It was Joseph Stalin's puppet regime, through which he intended to rule Finland. A "Declaration of the People's Government of Finland" was issued in Terijoki on 1.12.1939, and a "Treaty of Mutual Assistance and Friendship Between the Soviet Union and the Democratic Republic of Finland" was signed by the Soviet Minister of Foreign Affairs Vyacheslav Molotov and Kuusinen in Moscow on 2.12.1939. The international community reacted strongly to the Soviet aggression. The League of Nations expelled the

Soviet Union from the organisation on 14.12. The expulsion was supported by seven of the Council's members, including France and the United Kingdom. In Finland it was generally understood that the Soviet Union intended to do to Finland the same as it had done to the Baltic States in September and October 1939, when they had lost their independence.

The Moscow Peace Treaty of 13.3.1940 brought to an end the Winter War between Finland and the Soviet Union. Under the terms of the treaty, Finland was forced to cede nearly 10% of her territory. Over 422,000 people, 12% of the total population, were evacuated inside the new border. Evacuation in progress in Särkisyrjä, 18.3.1940. *SA-kuva.*

The Soviet Union failed to achieve the goals it had set. Finland received political sympathy and some material support from many Western European countries and the war went on for over three months. Finally, a treaty was signed in Moscow on 13.3.1940. Under the terms of the Moscow Peace Treaty, Finland was forced to cede nearly 10% of her territory and over 422,000 people, 12% of the total population, were evacuated inside the new border.

The war had ended, but Finnish-Soviet relations remained extremely tense thereafter, and the Finnish Government was engaged in continuous efforts to counter further pressure from the Soviet Union. From the perspective of the leadership in Helsinki, the situation was complicated by the cooperation existing between the Soviet and German governments. This cooperation had started with the signing of the German-Soviet Non-Aggression Pact (the "Molotov-Ribbentrop Pact") and its secret protocol, on 23.8.1939. The Pact was basically an understanding on mutual neutrality, but a Secret Additional Protocol introduced spheres of either German or Soviet influence. Lithuania, Latvia, Estonia, and Finland and the eastern areas of Poland were deemed to belong to the Soviet sphere of interest. Both these agreements were upheld also during the Winter War and the months that followed the Moscow Peace Treaty. Germany had abstained from all support to Finland – her traditional ally.

However, from the viewpoint of the German leader Adolf Hitler, a new situation arose after the capitulation of France and after the German-French Armistice was concluded on 22.6.1940. As a consequence, the need for Soviet loyalty was no longer as urgent as it had been in the period from August 1939 to May 1940. On the contrary, as the threat to Germany in the West was now eliminated to a great extent, it became possible for Germany to start restraining the Soviet claims, because of greater freedom of movement for German policy in the Baltic sphere.

German forces invaded Denmark and Norway on 9.4.1940. Whereas the Danish government co-operated with the Germans, the pre-war Norwegian government escaped to Britain in June 1940 as the Norwegian armed forces laid down their weapons and the French, Polish, and British expeditionary forces were evacuated from Narvik. In late April 1940, the Reichskommissariat Norwegen under Reichskommissar Josef Terboven was established, and on 1.2.1942 a Pro-German puppet government was appointed with the Leader of the National Union Party (*Nasjonal samling*) Vidkun Quisling as Minister President. On 8.7.1940, Sweden signed an agreement on troop transports through Sweden to Northern Norway. As the German position in the West was secured after the capitulation of France in June 1940, this allowed Germany to grasp a more active role in the Baltic Sea area. Germany now also started to show concern at Soviet influence in the region. There was thus some scope for a German-Finnish rapprochement, and as the first outlines for the coming assault on the Soviet Union were drafted on 29.–30.7.1940, Finland was already vaguely included in the plans. At this time the German forces in Northern Norway were reinforced and plans were made for a possible occupation of the Finnish area of Petsamo, on the coast of the Barents Sea.[1]

A further step towards closer German-Finnish cooperation was taken on 17.8.1940 with secret German-Finnish negotiations on German arms

As early as August 1940, some former World War I Finnish volunteers of the Royal Prussian 27th Jäger Battalion raised a proposal to recruit Finnish volunteers to the German army, the Wehrmacht. General Leonard Grandell was one of the architects of the project, but the initiative did not lead to concrete results at this time. General Grandell (r.) with the then Minister of Trade and Industry Väinö Kotilainen at the War Finance Office in Helsinki, 1.3.1940. *SA-kuva.*

deliveries to Finland and the transit of German troops and military equipment through Finland to Northern Norway.[2] As the German plans for an attack against the Soviet Union gained more and more substance from late 1940 onwards, the representatives of the Finnish GHQ participated in informal negotiations with their German equivalents. Although the Finnish Government was keen not to conclude any agreement on common German-Finnish offensive operations, there was a mutual understanding on maintaining cooperative relations.[3] At the latest from August 1940, ideas of sending Finnish volunteers for training in Germany were raised among some leading Finnish officers and also the small Finnish National Socialist circles formed an informal SS-lobby. Finland would have preferred to attach the Finnish volunteers to the regular forces, the Wehrmacht, but Germany had already set as a goal the establishment of an international SS-Division. The purpose of this was to demonstrate how the German anti-Bolshevik policy was broadly supported also in other West European countries. By then, recruiting had already started in countries occupied by Germany. In March 1941, an understanding was reached also between the Finnish Government and the representatives of the SS-Hauptamt (SS-HA) on the recruitment of Finnish volunteers for military service in Germany. As a consequence, the former Chief of the Finnish State Police, Esko Riekki, was given the task of directing and carrying out the recruitment.[4]

However, as the recruitment violated Finnish neutrality[5], a non-governmental recruitment organisation was established. This employed the Engineering Bureau Ratas as a front organisation. Actually, it was only the inner circle of the government that was fully informed on the recruitment schemes and the various practical steps being taken. In particular, the Foreign Ministry under Minister Rolf Witting was involved. The Finnish GHQ was reluctant to have any formal role in the arrangements, although its background influence appears to have been strong. Hence Commander-in-Chief Carl Gustaf Emil Mannerheim recounted in his memoirs that in the spring of 1941 he was successful in limiting the recruitment of Finnish SS-volunteers to men not drafted into the forces. Thus the age cohort of 1941 liable for military service was excluded from those young men who volunteered for the Waffen-SS.[6] In actual fact the High Command informally supervised the recruitment, and the Conscription Office is likely to have given every single applicant accepted by the Ratas Bureau permission for recruitment as SS-volunteers.[7] One of the goals of the recruitment policy was to limit the number of ultra-right-wing candidates securing access to military training and possibly garnering a stronger position in the Finnish politics of the day. In his circular to the recruiters on 24.4.1941, the Recruitment Chief Esko Riekki rebuffed attempts at interference from the *Kansallissosialistinen Järjestö* (National Socialist Organisation, KSJ) and the *Vapaussodan Rintamamiesten Liitto* (the "Union of the Veterans of the War of Liberation", another far-right grouping, which had its origins in the White faction in the Civil War of 1918).[8] The GHQ also infiltrated several officers in among the SS-volunteers, with the task of working as informers.[9] All this must have happened with the tacit consent of the Commander in Chief, Field Marshal Gustaf Mannerheim.[10]

The main purpose of cooperation between the Finnish Government and the military leadership on the recruitment of SS-volunteers was to get German support against the perceived Soviet threat, i.e. to establish a German-Finnish war coalition. The Finnish side also strengthened the military-political cooperation that had emerged several months earlier. In the spring and early summer of 1941, the volunteers consequently acquired a pivotal role as a guarantee or 'pledge' for the de facto German-Finnish war coalition.[11]

The Finnish SS-volunteers can be characterised as a national, Finnish representative troop in German service – not dissimilar, for instance, to the *Corps Expéditionnaire Russe en France* in

1916–18. Finnish bodies carried out the recruitment and the volunteers entered SS service in accordance with the active support of the Finnish Government. Although the volunteers – or more precisely sizeable elements of them – were deployed continually on the Eastern Front from the summer of 1941, from a strictly military perspective the benefit for the Germans could not grow particularly impressive, owing to of the relative smallness of the Finnish force. Although this was basically a "flag" representative troop, the German propaganda on the Finnish SS-volunteers remained modest and rather understated. Only eight pieces on the Finnish volunteers are known to have been published in German newspapers, whereas Finnish newspapers published at least 350 articles.[12] One of the reasons for the low incidence of German writing on the subject is that the Finnish intermediaries did not wish any great publicity on the volunteers, as the Finnish government was inclined to take the mood and policies of the Western Allies into consideration. A strong propaganda emphasis on the SS-volunteers ran the risk of disturbing the Finnish relations to these powers. Keeping propaganda on the Finnish SS-volunteers at a muted level was also acceptable to the German side, which favoured pragmatic operational and mutual military cooperation with the Finnish government over emphasis on ideological issues and National Socialist aims. However, leading members of the SS-Hauptamt, such as SS-Obergruppenführer and General of the Waffen-SS Gottlob Berger, who was in charge of the recruitment policy, had set much stronger political goals for the foreign SS-recruits. His aim was to educate a Germanic elite that would share the views of the National Socialist Party of Germany and those of the SS. For the SS propagandists, an entire assortment of other national volunteers – Danish, Dutch, Norwegian, etc. – were nevertheless more easily available for efforts of that sort.

In December 1940, Nazi German policy appeared to be undergoing a change, and Finland started to seek support against an expected new attack on the Soviet Union. Finnish military attaché Col. Walter Horn in Berlin 1941 with German SS-officers and two civilians, most likely individuals who took part in Finland in the recruiting of the SS-volunteers. *OW Coll.*

SS-Obergruppenführer and General of the Waffen-SS Gottlob Berger was Himmler's right hand in creating the new structures of the SS. He started to recruit volunteers from annexed Austria and occupied Belgium, Denmark, Norway, and the Netherlands in 1940. For political reasons, Himmler and Berger also wanted to have Finnish volunteers joining the Waffen-SS rather than the Wehrmacht. *Bundesarchiv*.

Reichsführer-SS Heinrich Himmler was the supreme leader of the SS-troops and planner of the extermination of the Jews. He also supported the idea of recruiting troops from other European nations to the Waffen-SS to demonstrate that the doctrines about Jews and Communists in National Socialist ideology were shared by many others. *OW Coll.*

THE FINNISH VOLUNTEERS HARBOURED STRONG ANTI-SOVIET ATTITUDES

The main motives for the Finnish volunteers in joining the Waffen-SS were an ambition to receive the outstanding Germany military training, to benefit from the economic, material, and status advantages of the Waffen-SS, hopes of an individual position of power in the future and, in addition, as a means of fomenting anti-Soviet feelings and pro-German attitudes.[13] There is, however, no available method to properly measure the specific significance of these motives. Various researchers have stressed one or another motive as the prime one.

Nevertheless, what can be concluded is that the aforementioned motives were closely woven together. The desire to attain German military skills was directed particularly towards improving the ability to fight Soviet forces, and as this anticipated future German support, the fulfilment of the desire corresponded to a benevolent attitude towards the German forces and war aims. Moreover, the siren-call of the young men to German military training was based on economic factors. By attending military classes in Germany, the volunteers would have a chance to be entrusted with command positions with higher salaries and career prospects. A considerable number of the young men who joined the Waffen-SS were in the beginning of their working career or were pupils or students. The bulk of them had low positions and partly only occasional jobs with modest salaries. The simple act of joining SS-Division Wiking seems in many individual cases to have brought about an improvement in the economic situation of the recruits. The service advantages of the Waffen-SS were considerably better than in the other branches of the armed forces in terms of food, clothes, equipment, and quarters. Compared with the modest value of the Finnish Markka, the purchasing power of the Reichsmark was manifold. As a result, a good part of the Finnish volunteers saved their pay and sent it home to their family in Finland.[14]

A very strong motive for joining the Waffen-SS among the Finnish volunteers was their pronounced hostility towards the Soviet Union after the Winter War and the Moscow Peace Treaty of 13.3.1940. Although the Finnish military had successfully fended off many of the Soviet attacks and had acquitted itself well during the 105-day war, the fight was lost and some of the areas in the east and south-east had to be ceded. Moscow's peace terms were regarded as unjustified and unfair, and sparked in many the revanchist hope of an opportunity for recovering the lost territory in Karelia. In the fall of 1940, and particularly during the spring of 1941, a German-Finnish approach developed, which from late June 1941 took the form of a war of co-belligerents against the Soviet Union. This increasingly troubled Finnish-British relations, as Britain become a Soviet ally as soon as the German onslaught on the Soviet Union was launched on 22.6.1941. The recruitment of the Finnish SS-volunteers was only one element in this process.

Anti-Russian and anti-Soviet attitudes certainly had deep roots in Finnish society,[15] but these peaked during the Winter War, during the bitter peace interlude of 1940–41 and in the Continuation War of 1941–44. Many of the SS-volunteers went to Germany enthusiastically in the hope of merging into the German forces in what they saw as the inevitable forthcoming war with the Soviet Union. When the great German campaign against the Soviet Union started in June 1941, the highly-motivated Finnish volunteers joined in with the German units. A particularly violent expression of the anti-Soviet feelings of the Finnish SS-volunteers was their relative readiness to shoot Soviet POWs.

Although anti-Semitic opinions were to be found in Finland, particularly during the first half of the 20th century[16], racial doctrines did not gain any common support among Finnish-speaking circles. Jews had received full citizen's rights in 1918 and no anti-Semitic legislation was adopted in the 1920s and 1930s. The Finnish Jews served in the Finnish Army as every male citizen had to do. This alleged reluctance among the Finnish volunteers to liquidate civilians meant that a considerable number of them appear to have refrained from killing civilians and to have regarded atrocities of this kind as disgusting and regrettable. Nevertheless, a small number of the volunteers were – on the basis of documentation presented further below – involved in the atrocities that took place.

The main reason for a lack of support for racial doctrines in Finland was that the anthropologists and eugenics specialists in the 19th and 20th centuries commonly regarded the Finns as being descendants of Mongols and Asians. This patronising experience greatly dampened the enthusiasm for adopting race concepts.[17] As anti-Jewish legislation was introduced in Germany in 1933–35, the Reichsdeutsche members of the Waffen-SS became accustomed already in the pre-war years to the policy of suppressing Jews, to the stripping of their civil rights and rights as citizens, and to their eventual complete removal from German society.[18] The bulk of the Reichsdeutsche members of the Waffen-SS had probably also been members of the Hitler-Jugend, which by 1936 had a strength of 5.4 million youngsters before membership became mandatory in 1939.[19] Hence the Reichsdeutsche had for years been accustomed to anti-Jewish attitudes in a systematic way and differed clearly from the Finnish volunteers in this respect. The documented reluctance among the Finnish volunteers to shoot Jews during the march through Ukraine may therefore possibly

The 50-page pamphlet brochure *Der Untermensch* was published at the behest of Heinrich Himmler and Gottlob Berger from 1942. It was based on the racial theories of the National Socialists and aimed to support the reasoning behind the mass extermination in the East. *Private collection.*

be explained as a product of the relatively widespread non-agitational attitudes of the Finnish population as a whole.

THE WAFFEN SS-DIVISION WIKING – OVERVIEW AND DOCUMENTATION

Initially a brief overview of the SS-Division Wiking will be introduced. The presentation includes four main points: 1) the composition of the Division, 2) political views among the volunteers, 3) the general involvement by the Waffen-SS in the atrocities, 4) an overview of the atrocities committed by the SS-Division Wiking based on the research literature, and 5) preserved archives.

Composition of the Division

The SS-Division Wiking[20] was formed in December 1940 and was composed of three infantry regiments: the SS-Regiment Nordland, the SS-Regiment Westland, and the SS-Regiment Germania, but it also incorporated several other units of regiment- or battalion strength. The SS-Artillerie-Regiment 5 attained regimental strength, whereas five other units were only of battalion strength: the SS-Aufklärungs-Abteilung 5 (reconnaissance), the SS-Nachrichten-Abteilung 5 (communications, propaganda), the SS-Panzerjäger-Abteilung 5 (anti-tank), the SS-Flak-Mg-Bataillon 5 (anti-aircraft) and the SS-Pionier-Bataillon 5 (field engineering). There were also a few smaller units for sanitation, repair, support, and supply like the SS-Sanitäts-Abteilung 5, the SS-Wirtschafts-Bataillon 5, the SS-Instandsetzungs-Abteilung 5, and the SS-Nachschub-Abteilung 5.[21]

In the Finnish history writing on the subject, the 421 volunteers who served in these units in the summer and fall of 1941 are known as the 'Division Men' whereas the almost 800 others were called the 'Battalion Men'. During the same period in 1941, these men of the Finnish SS-Volunteer Battalion were trained in several places, but in particular in Gross Born in Poland, and they were not deployed at the front. In early 1942, the bulk of the 'Division Men', who by that stage numbered some 400 volunteers, merged into the Battalion.

In June 1941, the Division numbered 19,337 men, of whom 631 were Dutch, 421 Finns, 294 Norwegians, and 216 Danish. At that juncture, just one Swedish subject had joined the Division. By September 1941, the number of Dutch volunteers had risen to 821 and also 45 Dutsch-speaking Belgian volunteers were included. Eight Swedes were now registered in the ranks.[22] However, in the course of the war roughly 100 Swedish SS-volunteers eventually served in SS-Division Wiking.[23] After the establishment of the 11. SS-Freiwilligen-Panzergrenadier-Division Nordland in early 1943, one platoon was informally called the Schwedenzug.[24] By the spring of 1943, around 800 Norwegian volunteers had passed through the SS-Division Wiking.[25]

Initially, some 17,000 men, around 90% of the division strength, are likely to have been native Germans (*Reichsdeutsche*). The precise number of ethnic Germans (*Volksdeutsche*) is not known, but the contingent was probably rather small. These were recruits in great measure from Romania and Slovakia and they characterised only "a smattering" element of the total.[26] The numerous *Reichsdeutsche* of the Division were highly motivated men, having received an ideological education in the Hitler-Jugend units in their schools and other

SS-Obergruppenführer and Director of the Reich Main Security Office Reinhard Heydrich (front, centre) and Chief of the Gestapo Heinrich Müller (front, left) with other German officers visiting the Ekeberg German military cemetery in Oslo, Norway in September 1941. Heydrich had been in charge of building up the Einsatzgruppen units, who were in charge of the liquidation of the Jews and other "unwanted" elements during the campaign against the Soviet Union. Einsatzgruppe C was working together with the SS-Division Wiking. *National Archives of Norway.*

youth and sports organisations that were under strong National Socialist influence. Hence the Germans proper, over a period of several years, adopted Germanic racial doctrines and military values. They were also inclined to see their involvement in the Waffen-SS as an act of distinguished individual service and personal acknowledgement.

In broad terms, the strength of the Division steadily decreased, to 15,928 by 31.12.1942, and to 12,927 by 31.12.1943. By comparison with the situation in the summer of 1941, the Division's complement of men shrank by a third to the end of 1943. However, in February 1943 there were 790 Dutch volunteers serving in the SS-Division Wiking proper, 282 Finns, 209 Danes, 131 Norwegians, and 88 Flemish Belgians. A total of 1,326 representatives of these nations belonged simultaneously to the various replacement companies of the Division: 625 Dutch, 153 Flemish, 121 Norwegians, 209 Danes, and 219 Finns. In actual fact, in August 1943 the SS-Division Wiking did not number more than 11,254 members: 8,892 *Reichsdeutsche*, 715 *Volksdeutsche*, 664 Estonians, 619 Flemish Belgians, 177 Danes, 130 Dutch, 47 Norwegians, five Swedes, and one Finnish volunteer. However, these figures do not take account of the newly-formed II./SS-Panzer-Regiment 5. As 158 Dutchmen belonged to this unit, their total came to 288. At this stage, the share of the *Reichsdeutsche* soldiers had declined somewhat, to around 80%.[27]

Although wartime propaganda greatly promoted the SS-Division Wiking as an embodiment of the multinational Germanic European fighting force in action, the number of foreign volunteers actually decreased during its military advance until its relief from the frontlines in late 1941. The reason was that casualties and exhausted men outstripped the replacements. A total of 275 foreigners, mostly Danes and Norwegians, arrived as reinforcements for the SS-Regiment Nordland in December 1941. The Regiment Commander, SS-Standartenführer Fritz von Scholz, characterised the newcomers as generally good, although he regarded them "much too soft" and "cry-babies" compared with the earlier volunteers. The Finnish Volunteer Battalion eventually joined the Nordland Regiment.[28]

Of the Finnish SS-volunteers who served in the ranks of SS-Division Wiking in the summer of 1941, 372 or 88% of the total were enlisted in the SS-Regiment Westland, SS-Regiment Nordland, the Aufklärungs-Abteilung 5, and the Panzerjäger-Abteilung 5. However, small groups of Finnish SS-volunteers were also to be found in other units, such as the Nachschub-Abteilung 5, Flak-MG-Bataillon 5, SS-Regiment Germania, the Artillerie-Regiment 5, and so forth.[29] Hence the Finnish volunteers were unevenly distributed among roughly a dozen of the various sub-units of the SS-Division Wiking. The significance of this fact is that it is challenging to try to create an accurate overview of the Finnish involvement in the atrocities, since the archival documents, newspaper articles, and recollections are so dispersed.

In the summer of 1941, the smallest of the three German army groups – *Heeresgruppe Nord*, *Heeresgruppe Mitte*, and *Heeresgruppe Süd* – was the Southern Army Group *Heeresgruppe Süd*, under Generalfeldmarschall Gerd von Rundstedt. The operational task of von Rundstedt's Army Group was the conquest of Ukraine. Included in the Army Group was the 17th Army under General der Infanterie Carl-Heinrich von Stülpnagel, who was ordered to advance from his positions in the south-eastern part of the General Government of Poland (Ger. *Generalgouvernement*) through the Lemberg (*Lwów, Lviv*) area. The SS-Division Wiking was subordinated to the 14th Panzer Corps, which pushed forward between the 17th Army and the 6th Army under Generaloberst Ewald von Kleist, who also commanded the *1. Panzerarmee*. This *Panzergruppe Kleist* operated at the same level of command as the 6th and 17th Armies and initially between them.

As the SS-Division Wiking was less experienced in the field than the other German military forces, for a while the German High Command refrained from issuing it with demanding tasks. Consequently, the Division was held back for a week in the General Government in the southern part of Poland before it was deployed as a second-line unit in the immediate rearguard of the advancing front towards the east of Lemberg (*Lviv*). Initially, the SS-Division Wiking operated for the most part as a flanking guard unit, and for quite some time during 1941 it loaned its various regiments to other Corps for particular missions. Hence it was only elements of the SS-Regiment Germania and the SS-Artillerie-Regiment 5 that took part in the operations that started on 22.6.1941.[30]

SS-Division Wiking encountered some initial skirmishes after midday on 1.7.1941, while the first battle of any greater significance occurred in the Tarnopol (*Ternopil*) area in early July 1941. The Division's performance was at this point regarded as satisfactory. Thereafter, the Division was ordered to establish a bridgehead on the eastern shore of the Dnieper River. This position was exposed to fierce Soviet attacks. Nevertheless, the Division was able to hold its ground until the Soviet thrust ebbed away, and it could then march on to Rostov-on-Don.[31] In this presentation, the focus lies on this period, the actions of the SS-Division Wiking and its subordinate units from early July to September 1941.

The Division experienced a period of exhaustion in the late fall of 1941. During the hectic forced march east, Division Commander Felix Steiner had burned his candle at both ends, and after four months of intensive fighting and rapid movements the units were considerably worn down. Hence the 1st Battalion of SS-Regiment Nordland, the 1st Company of the SS-Aufklärungs-Abteilung 5, the 1st Battery of the SS-Flak-Abteilung 5, and the 1st Wirtschaftskompanie had been dissolved, and all units were exhausted and physically at the end of their tether. Moreover, the Division's vehicles were not up to active service in the field: the 1st Battalion of SS-Regiment Nordland had no vehicles to call on, and furthermore SS-Aufklärungs-Abteilung 5 had effectively been transformed into an infantry unit, as all the armoured reconnaissance vehicles (*Panzerspähwagen*) had been lost, along with 80% of the military motorcycles (*Kräder*). Only some parts of the artillery could be transported and only half of the radio vans (*Funkfahrzeuge*) were suitable for service, while the supply detachments could call upon no more than 30% of the original transport capacity (*Kolonnenraum*).[32]

The situation report for November 1941 notes that tactical movements could no longer be carried out without delay. As things stood, the Division Command did not have the capacity to lead operations in a timely and deliberate way, because the available forces and the condition of the fleet of vehicles caused severe transport risks. Hence it was concluded that "the Division is no longer deployable as a motorised troop. It must be completely furnished with new vehicles as all the available means are worn out and overstrained. The troops need rest (*Die Truppe ist ruhebedürftig, Die Divisions braucht … Ruhe*)."[33] In the spring of 1942, the re-supplied SS-Division Wiking continued its march and during the early summer entered the Northern Caucasus. There it was included in the *Fall Blau* (Case Blue), a strategic summer offensive targeting both the City of Stalingrad and the oilfields of Baku. This operation was carried out in the summer of 1942 in a surprisingly successful fashion. Within six weeks, the German forces, including the SS-Division Wiking, were able to push deep into the Caucasus as far south as the Terek River. Later, in the summer of 1943, the Finnish volunteers returned to Finland and the Finnish SS-Volunteer Battalion was disbanded.

Political views among the Finnish volunteers

The volunteer applicants filled in a form with questions on personal information. One of the questions concerned the political sympathies of the applicants. The question was open, so the applicants had the opportunity to respond in an individual way. As the answers are reviewed on a statistical basis, it appears that of the volunteers around 60% were right-wingers of various persuasions, among them around ten percent National Socialist adherents. The largest group, roughly a third, were sympathisers of the nationalist and anti-Communist *Isänmaallinen Kansanliike* (IKL, "The Patriotic League", "Patriotic People's Movement", 1932–44). The shares of other parties were small. Compared with the composition of the Finnish Parliament at this time, there was a striking discrepancy among the volunteers. The parties that were represented by around 90% of the sitting MPs, i.e. the Social Democratic Party, the Agrarian League (*Maalaisliitto*), the National Coalition (*Kansallinen Kokoomus*), the National Progress Party (*Kansallinen Edistyspuolue*), and the Swedish People's Party of Finland (*Svenska Folkpartiet*) were supported by only 10% of the volunteers. However, around 40% of the volunteers expressed no articulated party preference.[34]

In April 1943, the Finnish Army HQ decided not to continue the service contracts of the SS-volunteers. The Germans had been defeated in Stalingrad and the Finnish troops were needed back in Finland. In May 1943, the long, slow journey towards Finland got under way. Finnish SS-volunteers in a train passing through the Baltic States towards the Gulf of Finland. *OW Coll.*

It is not entirely clear to what extent the political views declared in the application form are valid or meaningful. Around 40% of the volunteers belonged to the age-group of 17–19 olds and may have been politically rather inexperienced, as they had not yet had any opportunity to vote in elections. As a matter of fact, most of the volunteers had never voted, as the age limit was set at 21 years and the previous elections were held in March 1939. This means that all those younger than 23 years at the time of recruitment in the spring of 1941 had not had the opportunity to express their political views in parliamentary elections. Some are known to have actively participated in party politics, so it is almost impossible to get a reliable picture of their political engagement.

A common factor among the volunteers was that around 80% had participated in the voluntary Civil Defence Forces (*Suojeluskunta*, also known as the White Guard or Civil Guard), which were also supported by the Social Democrats. Without more detailed research it is not possible to draw very reliable conclusions of the political sympathies of most of the volunteers. Nevertheless, the statistical information on the political views among the volunteers appears generally to reflect the political views – or the absence of any particular sympathies – in a predominantly genuine way. Among the history researchers there is no consensus on the character of the *Isänmaallinen Kansanliike*. Some historians regard the IKL as a fascistic organisation, whereas others consider it an ultra-right-wing movement. However, it is clear that only a rather small segment, i.e. a tenth of the volunteers, were National Socialist sympathisers. Fascistic political views do not seem to have been a common denominator among the Finnish volunteers. Here the concept or label of fascism cannot be directly applied to the Finnish right-wing nationalist organisations, such as *Akateeminen Karjala-Seura* (the "Academic Karelia Society", AKS), whose policies were expansionist, but not totalitarian.[35]

It is also unclear to what extent the recruiters utilised the information on the political views of the applicants. There is no reliable information on this issue, but the general impression is that the political views of the applicants were of no great significance. Generally, the difference between approved and rejected applicants was very small. However, there are two exceptions to this general pattern. First, the number of the approved among the applicants sympathising with the IKL clearly exceeded the average rate. Secondly, applicants with sympathies for the Swedish-speaking National Socialist organisation *Samfundet Folkgemenskap* were clearly rejected to a greater extent than the norm.[36] Thus a tendency existed to favour applicants supporting the IKL and to discriminate against those supporting *Samfundet Folkgemenskap*. Nevertheless, it is not entirely clear whether this tendency was the result of a considered policy or an effect of other factors, such as the policy to favour applicants with strong Finnish nationalist feelings and to restrict the number of Swedish-speaking applicants. As it appears, the impact of the various recruitment organisations and networks were of greater significance for approval than the individual sympathies among the applicants. However, to a greater or lesser extent, the recruitment organisations and networks had their own particular partisan affiliations.

A few former SS-volunteers have commented on the question of political views in the application form. Thus Konstanin Cande mentions that he did not belong to any political organisation, but nevertheless the interviewer in the Ratas Bureau had made a note that he belonged to the National Socialist Party.[37] Also Arvo Kokko reported that he didn´t belong to any party, but that his fellow Matti Lähtimäki asked him to mark "IKL" on the form.[38] However, these recollections were written long after the war and the common tendency in them appears to be to say that somebody else had actually influenced their registration of political views, i.e. the informants did not have much individual responsibility for it. Olavi Liesinen states in his recollections that he did not know what to mark on his political views in the application form, because he did not belong to any political organisation. As he left the question empty, the Ratas Bureau office manager responded that as far as she knew, the information on the political views was of no significance whatsoever for the approval decision.[39]

Also the SS-volunteers from the other Nordic countries favoured the radical right: around two-thirds in Denmark[40] and Sweden[41]. In Norway, the numbers were extraordinarily large, as around 90% of the Norwegian volunteers may have been members of the far-right Nasjonal Samling party under Vidkun Quisling, whereas the rest had right-wing sympathies of some description.[42] Rhetorical anti-Jewish opinions certainly existed among the Nordic SS-volunteers, but it is not established whether sentiments of this sort were as strong or as common as they were among the native German SS-men. When it came to anti-Soviet and anti-Communist views, there was probably little difference between the opinions of the *Reichsdeutsche* SS-men and those of the Nordic volunteers.

The Finnish SS-Volunteers' Recruiting Office started in secrecy at the Ratas Engineering Bureau. Lieutenant Aarne Kauhanen (sitting backwards) from the State Police acted as Head of Office. He was known for his anti-Semitic attitudes and his close contacts to the Gestapo in Germany. The man at the phone may be Bruno Aaltonen, Deputy Chief of the Finnish State Police. *Jokipii 1996.*

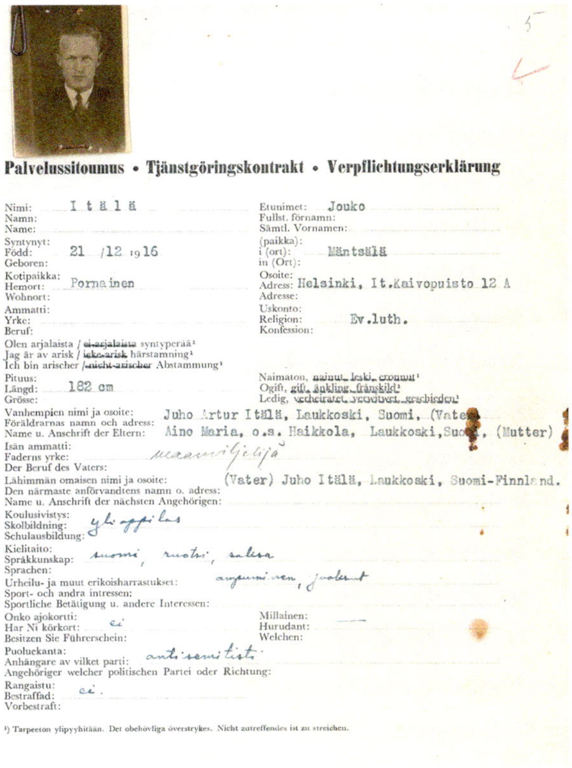

5

Palvelussitoumus • Tjänstgöringskontrakt • Verpflichtungserklärung

Nimi: / Namn: / Name: I t ä l ä
Etunimet: / Fullst. förnamn: / Sämtl. Vornamen: Jouko
Syntynyt: / Född: / Geboren: 21 /12 19 16
(paikka): / i (ort): / in (Ort): Mäntsälä
Kotipaikka: / Hemort: / Wohnort: Pornainen
Osoite: / Adress: / Adresse: Helsinki, It.Kaivopuisto 12 A
Ammatti: / Yrke: / Beruf:
Uskonto: / Religion: / Konfession: Ev.luth.
Olen arjalaista / ~~ei-arjalaista~~ syntyperää[1]
Jag är av arisk / ~~icke-arisk~~ härstamning[1]
Ich bin arischer / ~~nicht-arischer~~ Abstammung[1]
Pituus: / Längd: / Grösse: 182 cm
Naimaton, ~~naimut, leski, eronnut~~[1] / Ogift, ~~gift, änkling, frånskild~~[1] / Ledig, ~~verheiratet, verwitwet, geschieden~~[1]
Vanhempien nimi ja osoite: / Föräldrarnas namn och adress: / Name u. Anschrift der Eltern: Juho Artur Itälä, Laukkoski, Suomi, (Vater) / Aino Maria, o.s. Haikkola, Laukkoski,Suomi, (Mutter)
Isän ammatti: / Faderns yrke: / Der Beruf des Vaters: maanviljelijä
Lähimmän omaisen nimi ja osoite: / Den närmaste anförvantens namn o. adress: / Name u. Anschrift der nächsten Angehörigen: (Vater) Juho Itälä, Laukkoski, Suomi-Finnland.
Koulusivistys: / Skolbildning: / Schulausbildung: ylioppilas
Kielitaito: / Språkkunskap: / Sprachen: suomi, ruotsi, saksa
Urheilu- ja muut erikoisharrastukset: / Sport- och andra intressen: / Sportliche Betätigung u. andere Interessen: ampuminen, jalkapallo
Onko ajokortti: / Har Ni körkort: / Besitzen Sie Führerschein: ei
Millainen: / Hurudant: / Welchen: —
Puoluekanta: / Anhängare av vilket parti: / Angehöriger welcher politischen Partei oder Richtung: antisemitisti.
Rangaistu: / Bestraffad: / Vorbestraft: ei.

[1]) Tarpeeton ylipyyhitään. Det obehövliga överstrykes. Nicht zutreffendes ist zu streichen.

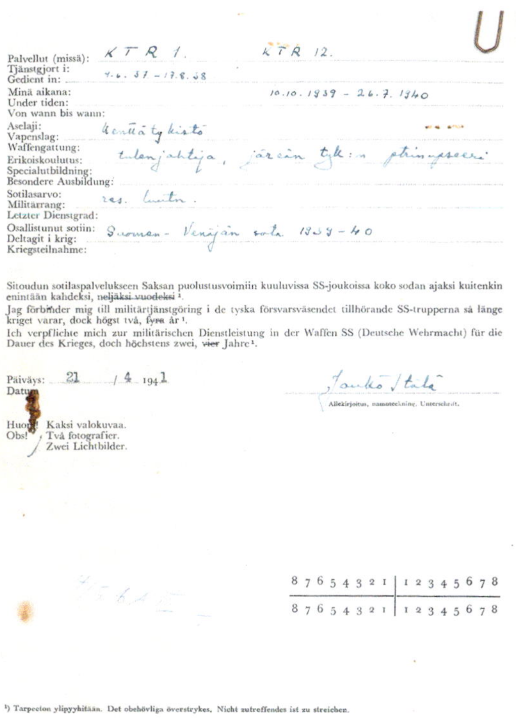

Palvellut (missä): / Tjänstgjort i: / Gedient in: KTR 1. 4.6.37 – 17.8.38 KTR 12.
Minä aikana: / Under tiden: / Von wann bis wann: 10.10.1939 – 26.7.1940
Aselaji: / Vapenslag: / Waffengattung: kenttätykistö
Erikoiskoulutus: / Specialutbildning: / Besondere Ausbildung: tulenjohtaja, järeän tykistön upseeri
Sotilasarvo: / Militärrang: / Letzter Dienstgrad: res. luutn.
Osallistunut sotiin: / Deltagit i krig: / Kriegsteilnahme: Suomen-Venäjän sota 1939 – 40

Sitoudun sotilaspalvelukseen Saksan puolustusvoimiin kuuluvissa SS-joukoissa koko sodan ajaksi kuitenkin enintään kahdeksi, ~~neljäksi vuodeksi~~[1].
Jag förbinder mig till militärtjänstgöring i de tyska försvarsväsendet tillhörande SS-trupperna så länge kriget varar, dock högst två, ~~fyra~~ år[1].
Ich verpflichte mich zur militärischen Dienstleistung in der Waffen SS (Deutsche Wehrmacht) für die Dauer des Krieges, doch höchstens zwei, ~~vier~~ Jahre[1].

Päiväys: / Datum: 21 / 4 1941
Jouko Itälä
Allekirjoitus, namnteckning, Unterschrift.

Huom! Kaksi valokuvaa.
Obs! Två fotografier.
Zwei Lichtbilder.

8 7 6 5 4 3 2 1	1 2 3 4 5 6 7 8
8 7 6 5 4 3 2 1	1 2 3 4 5 6 7 8

[1]) Tarpeeton ylipyyhitään. Det obehövliga överstrykes. Nicht zutreffendes ist zu streichen.

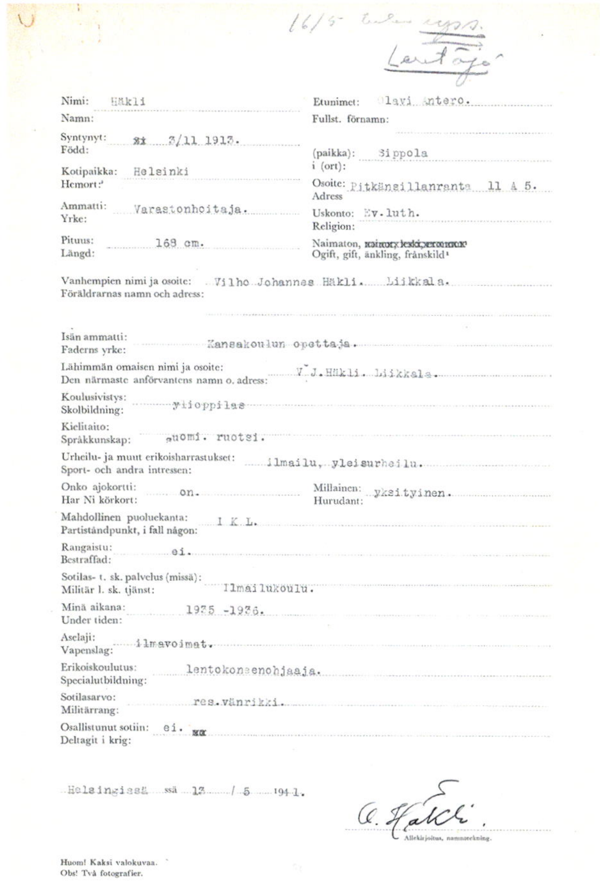

16/5 tulee ulos. Lentäjä

Nimi: / Namn: Häkli
Etunimet: / Fullst. förnamn: Olavi Antero.
Syntynyt: / Född: 31 3/11 1913.
(paikka): / i (ort): Sippola
Kotipaikka: / Hemort: Helsinki
Osoite: / Adress: Pitkänsillanranta 11 A 5.
Ammatti: / Yrke: Varastonhoitaja.
Uskonto: / Religion: Ev.luth.
Pituus: / Längd: 168 cm.
Naimaton, ~~naimut, leski, eronnut~~ / Ogift, gift, änkling, frånskild[1]
Vanhempien nimi ja osoite: / Föräldrarnas namn och adress: Vilho Johannes Häkli. Liikkala.
Isän ammatti: / Faderns yrke: Kansakoulun opettaja.
Lähimmän omaisen nimi ja osoite: / Den närmaste anförvantens namn o. adress: V. J. Häkli. Liikkala.
Koulusivistys: / Skolbildning: ylioppilas
Kielitaito: / Språkkunskap: suomi. ruotsi.
Urheilu- ja muut erikoisharrastukset: / Sport- och andra intressen: ilmailu, yleisurheilu.
Onko ajokortti: / Har Ni körkort: on.
Millainen: / Hurudant: yksityinen.
Mahdollinen puoluekanta: / Partiståndpunkt, i fall någon: I. K. L.
Rangaistu: / Bestraffad: ei.
Sotilas- t. sk. palvelus (missä): / Militär l. sk. tjänst: Ilmailukoulu.
Minä aikana: / Under tiden: 1935 -1936.
Aselaji: / Vapenslag: ilmavoimat.
Erikoiskoulutus: / Specialutbildning: lentokonesenohjaaja.
Sotilasarvo: / Militärrang: res.vänrikki.
Osallistunut sotiin: / Deltagit i krig: ei.

Helsingissä ssä 13 / 5 1941.
O. Häkli.
Allekirjoitus, namnteckning.

Huom! Kaksi valokuvaa.
Obs! Två fotografier.

Recruiting documents of Finnish Waffen-SS volunteers Jouko Itälä and Olavi Häkli. On Itälä's application reads "anti-Semitic" – one of the very few ones with this notice – and Häkli has marked I.K.L. as his party. Itälä's application was approved while Häkli was rejected. Many right wing candidates were rejected by Esko Riekki to keep better "political balance". *Jokipii Coll., NAF.*

Efforts by the Finnish National Socialist organisations to enforce the recruitment of Finnish volunteers

Shortly before the outbreak of the Winter War, representatives of the openly National Socialist organisations and the Swedish-speaking *Samfundet Folkgemenskap* went to Berlin in order to gather support against the Soviet Union. Among others, the former Chief of the Security Police Esko Riekki, the Bank Manager Pehr H. Norrmén, and the Engineer John Rosberg met Reichsführer-SS Heinrich Himmler. However, no tangible results were achieved. Also in the period after the Winter War, Norrmén made further efforts to establish close relations with Germany. Above all, he tried to induce the Swedish People's Party to implement a more pro-German policy. In the spring of 1941, Norrmén actively participated in the recruitment of SS-volunteers and performed in an influential role in the Swedish-speakers' National Socialist organisation *Samfundet Folkgemenskap* (1940–44).[43]

In the final phase of the Continuation War (1941–44), Norrmén focused on hindering the efforts to conclude a separate peace between Finland and the Soviet Union. He participated in the preparations for a pro-German government, which would have been established at the same time as the German forces occupied the country. As these plans failed and the armistice was settled in September 1944, Norrmén started to fear that he could be pursued along with the other recruiters, in particular in the case that the Soviet forces would invade and occupy Finland. Another Swedish-speaking representative of the National Socialist ideology was Gunnar Lindqvist, who like Norrmén had earlier participated in the Jäger movement. Jägers (*jääkärit* in Finnish) were volunteers from Finland who trained – clandestinely – in Germany as Jägers (elite light infantry) during World War I, fighting in the ranks of the German Army from 1916 before taking a pivotal role on the White side in the Finnish Civil War. From the early 1930s, Lindqvist enjoyed an influential position in the National Socialist circles in Finland, and he also maintained working relations to the German intelligence bodies. He acted from the fall of 1940 as Secretary of the *Samfundet Folkgemenskap* and was in practice the real leader of the organisation. Lindqvist had actively recruited SS-volunteers and in 1942 he became the Deputy President of the National Socialist organisation *Siniristi* (Blue Cross). As Finland severed her relations with Germany on 2.9.1944, he was one of the eight persons the Security Police judged most dangerous, and he was taken into custody.[44]

Another representative of the Swedish-speaking National Socialists was Rear-Admiral Hjalmar von Bonsdorff. He had an influential position in the armed forces and was known as public supporter of National Socialism and of anti-Semitic views. In 1932, von Bonsdorff was one of the founders of the *Isänmaallinen Kansanliike* (IKL) and was a member of the National Socialist *Suomen Kansan Järjestö* (SKJ, The Organisation of the Finnish People, active 1933–36). For a short while, von Bonsdorff was the editor-in-chief of the National Socialist periodical *För Frihet och Rätt* (For Freedom and Law). However, von Bonsdorff did not directly participate in the recruitment of the SS-volunteers. In 1940–42, he was the President of *Samfundet Folkgemenskap*. After the end of the Continuation War, von Bonsdorff fled to Sweden, where he died in the

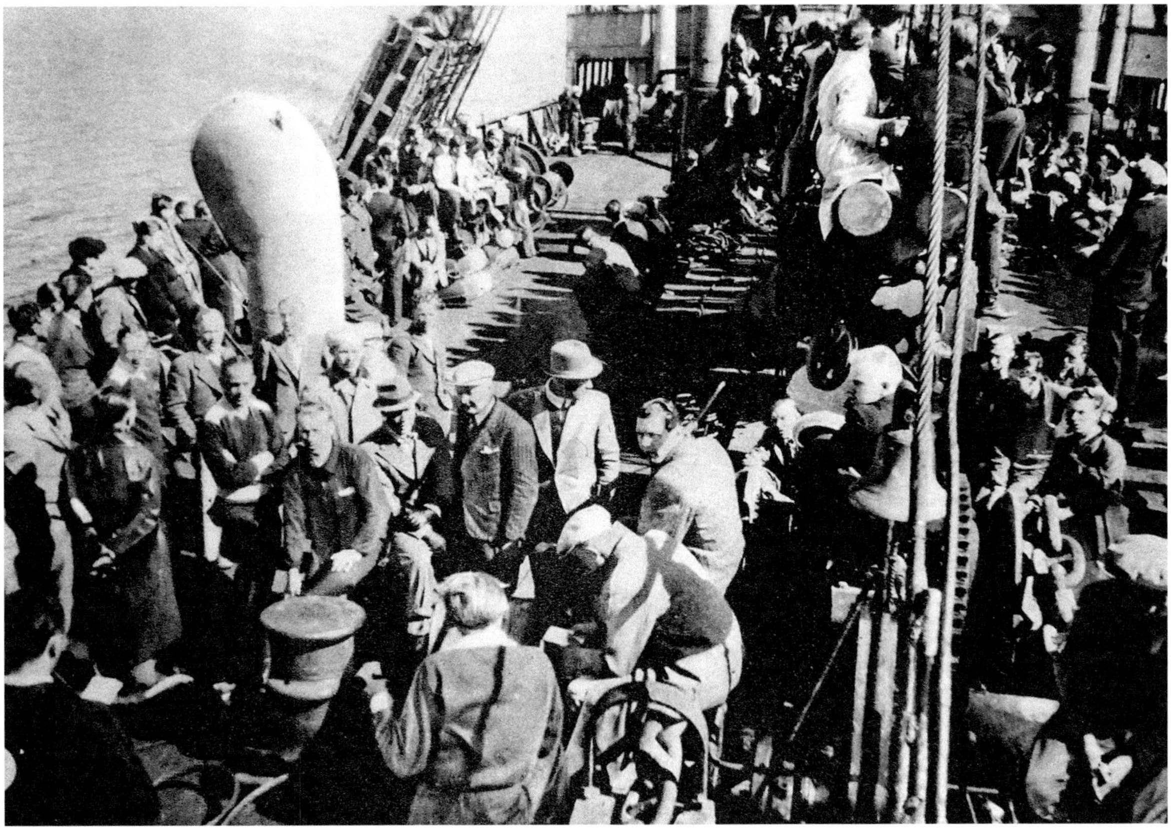

Finnish SS-volunteers onboard the *S/S Adler* in May 1941 on the way across the Baltic Sea to Germany. *Parvilahti 1958.*

spring of 1945.[45] One of the most notable participants of the founding assembly of the *Samfundet Folkgemenskap* in October 1940 was Unto Boman (from 1944 Unto Parvilahti), who volunteered for the SS in the spring of 1941.[46] Boman mentions in his memoirs that Finnish volunteer and SS-Obersturmführer Lennart Wallén was another member of the *Samfundet Folkgemenskap* – which he describes as an association of "economic politics".[47]

Among the Finnish-speaking adherents of National Socialist ideology, one of the leading individuals was the Ingrian-born Erkki Räikkönen. He had been a founding member of the *Akateeminen Karjala-Seura* (AKS), but left the organisation in 1924 and established together with his followers a new organisation called *Itsenäisyyden Liitto* (the Union of Freedom). He acted as the Secretary of the organisation in 1926–28 and President in 1930–33. The reason for leaving AKS was

Only some 400 Finns were accepted immediately to armed service within the Waffen SS-Division Wiking. The majority of the recruits were sent for military training first. *OW Coll.*

that Räikkönen did not approve the new national reunification programme of the organisation. This programme aimed at the strengthening of the position of the Finnish language and the unification of the Finnish-speaking part of the population. In 1939, Räikkönen started to issue and edit the National Socialist periodical *Kustaa Vaasa* (1939–1943).[48]

The *Siniristi* (Blue Cross) organisation emerged around the periodical in 1942. The main figures aside from Räikkönen were Gunnar von Hertzen and Martti Mustakallio. As the mouthpiece of Siniristi, the periodical *Uusi Eurooppa* (New Europe) was introduced and published from 1942–44. The organisation also published the membership periodical *Siniristi*, which reported on current political events. Siniristi also issued some books, of which the most well-known was a reprint of the anti-Semitic smear volume *Siionin viisaiden pöytäkirjat* (The Protocols of the Elders of Zion). The aforementioned Lindqvist was one of the members of the editorial board of the periodical *Siniristi*. The Siniristi organisation reported in 1944 that it had 12,000 members.[49]

The representatives of the National Socialist orientation did not, for all their efforts, get as many members as they would have wanted among the SS-volunteers. The orientation was supported by a small core group, which made efforts to promote National Socialist views, racial doctrines, and a totalitarian ruling concept in the volunteer circles. However, the influence of the core group remained generally insignificant. In the spring of 1941, the former leader of *Suomen Kansan Järjestö* (SKJ), Jäger Captain Arvi Kalsta, having made a return to political life at the head of the *Kansallissosialistinen Järjestö* (National Socialist Organisation, KSJ - basically a rebirth of the defunct SKJ, whose political platforms it adopted), took part in the planning of the recruitment of SS-volunteers. The representative of the KSJ in these activities was Väinö Kari, who was a member of the board of the organisation.[50]

The reason why many Jäger officers supported the recruitment of SS-volunteers is likely to have been the efforts to create an image of "the new Jägers". However, the reality of the SS-volunteers' service did not live up to the idealistic views. In a message that the U.S. Minister (Ambassador) H. F. Arthur Schoenfeld sent to the British Embassy in Washington on 16.12.1942, he wrote of attempts by the IKL. Member of Parliament Rauno Kallia to use the SS-volunteers in political work within Finland: "The IKL was said to be interested in bringing back Finnish SS-troops from Germany to do political work in Finland, but according to the informant, this procedure would not work, since these Finnish troops were disillusioned by their treatment in Germany." After the German defeat in Stalingrad, attempts of this direction would have been practically impossible.[51]

The illusion of an SS elite unit

From early 1941, the SS-Division Wiking and the whole Waffen-SS of the early war years enjoyed a particular reputation. According to this, the Division was not only one of the crack forces of the Waffen-SS, but was also given elite status among the entire German military.[52] The U.S. historian Gerald L. Weinberg has characterised the Waffen-SS of the early years of the war as "fanatical in spirit, favoured over the regular army in delivery of weapons, and not always particularly obedient; these contingents were in the process of becoming a kind of a fire brigade from critical points on the front".[53] The German historian Bernd Wegner has also highlighted the reputation of the Waffen-SS for fanatical loyalty and bravery, but also for brutality, the mistreatment and killing of POWs and civilians, and for massive involvement in atrocities.[54]

Major Leo Wikman was entrusted in 1942–43 with the task of dealing with matters relating to the Finnish SS-volunteers as an assistant to the Finnish Military Attaché in Berlin.[55] Wikman wrote:

> The Waffen-SS were the forces of the Party (...) They showed the utmost violence and tenacity of purpose, were indoctrinated and loyal towards the Party, and were feared for their lack of restraint and their cruelty (...) One characteristic trait among the Waffen-SS was the thesis that the German soldier had to be ruthless – twice as ruthless as the enemy, because the enemy was superior in numbers.[56]

However, although there were certainly some objective grounds for this widespread view of the Waffen-SS and particularly the SS-Division Wiking as elite units, the overall picture is rather different. Firstly, when set against an ordinary Wehrmacht division, the SS-Division Wiking was 50% larger, and as a result needed a greater share of the resources. The training targeted men who were capable of sustaining demanding physical effort, at the same time as the number of infantrymen exceeded that of ordinary infantry divisions.

Secondly, the SS-Division Wiking was exceptionally well-equipped with vehicles and materiel, enabling not only full and very rapid movement, but also backed up with an effective supply of explosives and field equipment. In the summer of 1941, the Division was akin to a "ghost division" (*Geisterdivision*, so named for agility, speed of movement, and the element of surprise), with 1,742 lorries, 108 half-track cars, 294 motorcycles, and 647 other vehicles at its disposal.[57] By contrast, ordinary infantry divisions had to rely to a considerable extent on horse transports. In one such division there were, for instance, 3,632 draft horses and 1,133 wagons, 1,743 saddle horses, around 1,000 motor vehicles and about 500 motorcycles. Of the 230 divisions committed in the Soviet Union by Germany and her allies, just 35 were armoured or motorised, i.e. only around 15%. On average, 1.1 million horses were permanently deployed in the East.[58] Moreover, of the 38 Waffen-SS divisions, seven were armoured tank units (*Panzerdivision*) and likewise seven armoured/mechanised infantry units (*Panzergrenadierdivision*). Whereas the manpower of the Waffen-SS corresponded to one-tenth of the Army as a whole, the share of tank units within the Waffen-SS exceeded one third. Furthermore, some of the SS Panzer Divisions were about 1/5 stronger than the equivalent army units.[59]

Thirdly, the SS-Division Wiking had been provided with the materiel to develop an extraordinarily strong firepower: the number of rifle squads totalled 324, the number of light machine guns 521, and heavy machine guns 124, with an additional 294 motorcycle squads, 156 mortars, and 72 anti-tank guns. In SS-Artillerie-Regiment 5, there were 74 pieces of light and heavy howitzers distributed between four battalion-sized units, whereas there were only three such units in the ordinary army divisions.[60] The sum of these qualities explain the field ability of the SS-Division Wiking, which – owing to its greater share of resources and degree of mobility – could be utilised as a highly agile and well-equipped task force.

In particular, loyalist authors have characterised the SS-Division Wiking as an elite unit. As the volunteers, at least initially, were selected and the Division was furnished with extra resources, this view leaves some room for doubt. However, it is not unusual that various military forces are presented as "crack formations" on apparently capricious and more or less subjective grounds like combat performance, endurance, and the number of awarded decorations at this or that level. Some of the arbiters in these cases may themselves have served in the units being celebrated, or they may have been in close contact with leading personalities from the unit. Quite commonly, the self-esteem of the soldiers is reinforced by boasting of the special identity and excellent composition of the unit to which they belong. In particular, continuous propaganda efforts were made on behalf of the Waffen-SS, by churning out periodicals, posters, and movies. On the other hand, there are no equivalent methods allowing a proper, comparative judgement of this degree of elite qualities. Hence the descriptions claiming the superiority of the SS-Division Wiking have reasonably been questioned in a convincing way.[61]

U.S. historian Kenneth Estes has remarked that the SS-volunteers "did not fight consistently well". He also notes:

> ...it seems hard to determine what volunteer units matched the performance of the elite SS divisions other than [in] the mixed SS-Division Wiking, in which the volunteers filled

mostly infantry companies and the majority of German troops manned the tank, artillery, and specialist units. By the end of the war, the volunteers hardly constituted 'formidable and reliable' fighting units. Some formed pockets of resistance in hopeless positions, but most were swept aside by the numerous and well-supplied Soviet forces.[62]

The U.S. historian Yaron Pasher has also concluded that the seemingly amazing exploits of some Waffen-SS divisions in 1944 are likely to have resulted more from the numerical weakness of the Red Army units than from the strength of the German troops. As the Soviet forces faced a manpower crisis, many divisions could by that stage no longer present an effective field strength, with some being down to 2,000 men or fewer.[63]

However, at the latest in early 1942 a modernisation process of the German Army (*Heer*) and the Waffen-SS was launched, as the forces had suffered increasingly from a lack of effective weapons and a shortage of manpower. Consequently, the men born in 1923 were drafted prematurely, whereas the general size of the infantry divisions was reduced from nine to six battalions. Historian Omer Bartov has concluded that

> ...the supply system reached a breaking point. The men at the front had to make do with inadequate clothing, insufficient food provisions, and extremely wretched accommodation facilities for long periods of time in the height of the Russian winter. All these factors combined to create an acute sense of crisis. Both physical and mental attrition were highly prevalent, and the incidence of illness and nervous breakdowns greatly increased.[64]

It has frequently been claimed that the Waffen-SS forces suffered unnecessarily high casualties in battle, owing to excessive zeal, aggressiveness, and poor leadership.[65] Nevertheless, the view of the SS-Division Wiking and particularly the Finnish volunteers as an extraordinarily gallant force has been commonly upheld. At the same time, contradictory information has been rejected and stifled. However, such information would have been available, as the Finnish career officer Yrjö Kaila, who in 1941-42 served as an SS-Hauptsturmführer, described in his recollections the tactical performance of the SS-Division Wiking as being mediocre at best. Kaila observed that the use of terrain in battle was poor, while there was short-sighted daring and straightforward sheep-like mania. The firing discipline was non-existent and the conduct of the various companies took the form of acting as champions. During the vehicle marches, Kaila witnessed poor driving discipline, and billeting was insufficient and dirty: "In every aspect, I got the impression of amateurism and either a lack of acquaintance with professional skills or an arrogant belittling [of their importance]".[66] In a nutshell, the elite image appears to have been a myth that did not correspond to the true divisional conduct.

In a 1959 review by Yrjö Kaila of the book *Die Freiwilligen der Waffen-SS* (1958), by the former Commander of the SS-Division Wiking Felix Steiner, Kaila continued to press home his criticism. He claimed that Steiner's praise of the voluntary nature of the SS forces was monotonous, dull, and inaccurate because only a small fraction of the men were genuinely volunteers, like the Danes, Finns, Norwegians, and other non-German nationals. Kaila took Steiner to task for giving the impression that foreign volunteers were a dominant element in the corps. According to Kaila, the bulk of the Germans in the Waffen-SS were men who either joined the corps voluntarily or were escaping from service in the Wehrmacht. A considerable number may have been compulsory drafted and during the last years of the war "volunteers" were even sent from prisons to the Waffen-SS ranks. Further, numerous *Volksdeutsche* soldiers, as well as foreign nationals, were actually conscripted from POW camps or joined for more or less involuntary reasons. Kaila even expressed surprise "...that a career General such as Steiner so greatly accentuates the significance of volunteering, which in this case was not even genuine".[67] However, the number of genuine volunteers was nevertheless probably considerably greater in 1941 than it was later.

Moreover, Kaila scrutinises Steiner's claim that the Waffen-SS "fought for Europe". Kaila bluntly states that the SS forces waged war for Germany, and not only against the East, but also against the Western powers: "Those hundreds of thousands of men who ended up in the SS forces hardly gave a thought to lofty ideas of this kind". As a matter of fact, Steiner's view is undisguisedly partisan in tone, with an emotional style. No attention whatsoever is paid to the SS spirit: "National pride, intolerance, arrogance, conceit, impudence, and disorderliness. The key strain of Steiner's book is melancholic and sometimes one of bitter memories". In Kaila's opinion, the foreign volunteers were nothing but "cannon fodder" to the Waffen-SS. This was reflected in the awarding of the Knight's Cross of the Iron Cross (*Ritterkreuz des eisernen Kreuzes*). Of a total of 426 awards, only 5% were given to foreign SS-men, a fact which illustrates the ethnocentric disproportion.[68] Kenneth Estes has reached a similar conclusion:

> The multinational Euro-Army never existed. On the contrary, German racial policy and crude handling techniques almost lost them the small national contingents they had, until the recruiting reforms and relaxed racial standards of Himmler and Berger temporarily restored the intake of recruits.[69]

Involvement of Waffen-SS in atrocities

This section will deal with the involvement of Waffen-SS troops in atrocities during the march eastwards from the summer 1941 onwards. A starting point will be the conclusions reached by the International Military Tribunal in Nuremberg in 1945–46. The Tribunal found that "(...) the units of the Waffen-SS were directly involved in the killings of POWs and the atrocities in the occupied countries. As a consequence, the whole SS was judged to be a criminal organisation".[70] This assessment was questioned with great indignation by the HIAG (*Hilfsgemeinschaft auf Gegenseitigkeit der Angehörigen der ehemaligen Waffen-SS*), whose main purpose in particular in the early 1950s was to claim the equal military footing of the Waffen-SS with the Wehrmacht, which in those days enjoyed a more "decent" military reputation than the commonly disparaged Waffen-SS. HIAG for its part claimed that the Waffen-SS on the whole was an equivalent to the Wehrmacht, and that the so-called Allgemeine SS was to blame for those atrocities, a claim it said could not be objectively denied.

The Australian criminologist Terry Goldsworthy has concluded that the Waffen-SS was integrated into the overall system of violence that was the SS organisation, and which cannot be regarded as a pure military force. Rather, the Waffen-SS had all the hallmarks of being a political tool of the German National Socialist regime. Thus "the role of the Waffen-SS was something akin to a holy crusade; its purpose was to destroy those groups who were abhorrent to the ideals of the Nazi Party. These included Slavs, Jews, and Bolsheviks". Indeed, during the march through Soviet territory, the shooting of POWs, massacres of civilians, and razing of villages became "signature behaviour" of the Waffen-SS.[71]

The U.S. historian George H. Stein concluded in 1966:

> The greatest number of Waffen-SS atrocities, however, seem to have occurred in the East. Taught that they were engaged in an ideological and racial war against a "subhuman" enemy, the SS-troops often applied a standard to warfare that differed sharply from accepted practices. The shooting of prisoners, the massacre of civilians, and the wanton destruction of villages, while not universal, seem to have occurred frequently enough to become a hallmark of Waffen SS operations along the Eastern Front.[72]

The SS-Division Wiking marched from Lemberg (*Lviv, Lwów*) to Złoczów (*Zolochiv, Zlotchov, Zlotshev, Zolotsjiv, Solotschiw, Zoltsjiv, Zlochiv*) on 1.–3.7.1941, following in the wake of several other divisions. The German historian Bernd Boll stated the division seems "to have considered the first days of the war in the East a sort of hunting expedition, with people as prey".[73]

Certainly, the Commander of the 4th Army Corps Generalfeldmarschall Günther von Kluge reported on 3.7.1941 to the Oberkommando des Heeres (OKH): "The SS-Division Wiking has since yesterday halted on the road from Lemberg-Złoczów [Note: now Zolochiv, in Ukraine]. All the traffic is blocked by trucks placed across the road, and everyone who approaches is turned away".[74] According to Boll, on July 2nd and 3rd the Division blocked the route of advance, apparently intentionally, while several members went "hunting for Jews".[75] The Corps Staff also received indignant reports from Wehrmacht units on the savage conduct of the Waffen-SS forces. The 295th Division reported on 2.7.1941 on "...the SS blindly shooting Russian soldiers and also civilians who appear suspicious". The 125th Division reported on 3.7.1941 on "...the unbelievable treatment by the SS towards the local population. The SS shoots all who appear even slightly suspicious, for instance civilians with bare-shaven heads" [as alleged Red Army soldiers].[76]

Boll also notes that civilians and in particular persons with shaved heads were shot, as they were considered Soviet soldiers.[77] The German historian Andrej Angrick has emphasised that SS-Division Wiking differed from other units in the Waffen-SS in that they took few POWs and they crushed civilians under their armoured vehicles as the Division headed east on the roads. He also concluded that members of the Division were as brutal as the crews of the mobile Einsatzkommandos.[78] The Swedish historian Lars T. Larsson concludes that the Wiking Division's battle exploits were accompanied "by war crimes on a large scale" such as implementing the so-called Commissar Order (*Kommissarbefehl*, 6.6.1941) and taking part in the "final solution" programme against the Jews.[79]

The personnel of the Einsatzgruppen was partly manned by the Waffen-SS.[80] According to historian George H. Stein: "On the basis of the evidence at hand it may be concluded that perhaps as many as 1,500 members of the Waffen-SS served with the Einsatzgruppen", and that at least some of the senior SS combat officers "were aware of the manner in which they were employed".[81] Criminologist Terry Goldsworthy notes that around 34% of the Einsatzgruppe appears to have been made up of Waffen-SS personnel. Other significant categories were various police forces (39%) and drivers (17%).[82]

However, Waffen-SS units were also sent as support units to help the Einsatzgruppen in achieving their aim of securing and pacifying the rear areas.[83] Several units of the Waffen-SS, the 1st and 2nd SS-Brigade, the SS-Kavallerie Brigade, the SS-Division Prinz Eugen and the SS-Brigade Dirlewanger were utilised in the so-called "cleansing operations" (*Säuberungsaktionen*) or for the so-called "special treatment" (*Sonderbehandlungen*, the standard euphemism for extra-judicial killing).[84] In the Waffen-SS drives against the partisans and other resistance forces (*Bandenbekämpfung*), numerous atrocities were recorded against civilian populations. Moreover, there was a continuous exchange of personnel between the guard parties in the concentration camps and the frontline troops; there was no exchange between the Einsatzgruppen and the concentration camps. A small percentage of Einsatzgruppen personnel were recruited from Waffen-SS reservists prior to the attack on the Soviet Union.[85]

Along with the planning of the military campaign against the Soviet Union, a secret understanding to form four separate units – the so-called SS-Einsatzgruppen – was reached in the spring of 1941 between the SS-Reichssicherheitshauptamt (RHSA) and the Oberkommando der Wehrmacht (OKW). If military action was to begin, the four German main armies were each to be joined by one of these SS-Einsatzgruppen. Their task was to carry out the mass killings of unwanted elements, particularly Jews.[86] Directives on the operations of the Einsatzgruppen were included in the complex of guidelines for the plan for the attack on the Soviet Union. The intention of these guidelines was to prevent friction between Wehrmacht and the SS during the advance. The Führer Adolf Hitler also specified that criminal acts against civilians perpetrated by the soldiers should not be prosecuted through the military courts, and they would hence go unpunished. On 13.5.1941, Hitler issued the so-called 'Barbarossa Decree': "Erlaß über die Ausübung der Kriegsgerichtsbarkeit im Gebiet 'Barbarossa' und über besondere Maßnahmen der Truppe" [*Kriegsgerichtsbarkeitserlaß*], concerning the implementation of military jurisdiction in the 'Barbarossa' Zone and special measures taken by the troops. Normal forms of military justice were rescinded for crimes committed by enemy civilians in Russia (*Straftaten feindlicher Zivilpersonen*), meaning that field courts (effectively a serving officer in the field) were authorised to determine whether suspects should be summarily shot, while the forces were expected to liquidate Soviet partisans or irregular forces (*Freischärler*) either in combat, or – if they sought to escape – by shooting them down without mercy. Moreover, battalion commanders or more senior officers were permitted to invoke principles of collective responsibility and authorise "collective enforcement measures" (*kollektive Gewaltmassnahmen*) against communities or villages in situations when it was not possible to swiftly determine the identity of any perpetrators.[87]

The spring of 1941 also saw the Generalquartiermeister of the Oberkommande des Heeres Generalmajor Eduard Wagner outlining the regulations that ensured that the German Army and the Einsatzgruppen would cooperate in the killing of Soviet Jews. Wagner did this together with the Chief of the RSHA, SS-Obergruppenführer und General der Polizei Reinhard Heydrich, and they agreed on cooperation between the Einsatzgruppen and the Army units concerning the so-called "special tasks" (*Sonderaufgabe*).[88]

On 28.4.1941, Generalfeldmarschall Walther von Brauchitsch ordered that when Operation Barbarossa started, all the Wehrmacht Commanders were to immediately identify Jewish locations in the occupied areas of the Soviet Union and to cooperate with the Einsatzgruppen. In May 1941, the Sicherheitsdienst, apparently Department VI (Ausland-SD) of the Reichssicherheitshauptamt (RSHA, the Reich Main Security Office) and Major-General Wagner agreed that the Einsatzgruppen in the immediate rear areas of the front were to operate under formal Army command. The Einsatzgruppen, however, used their own discretion, although the Army commanders could object, at least to some extent. The German Army provided logistical support to the Einsatzgruppen, including supplies, transports, housing, and occasionally also guards for the transport of prisoners. Beyond assistance from local collaborators and SS units, the members of the Einsatzgruppen were drawn from the so-called Allgemeine-SS, including the Sicherheitsdienst (SD), the Sicherheitspolizei (SiPo), the Ordnungspolizei, (Order Police, OrPo) and other police units, but also from the Waffen-SS.[89]

Einsatzgruppe C was deployed in the operational area of Heeresgruppe Süd in cooperation with the Höhere SS und Polizeiführer as the Ordnungspolizei Battalions. In the summer and early fall of 1941, Einsatzgruppe C set off from Kraków and fanned out across Western Ukraine in the general direction of Kharkiv and Rostov. The unit directed massacres in Lemberg (*Lviv*), Tarnopol (*Ternopil*), Kremenets, Kharkiv, and Zhytomyr (Žytomyr, Żytomierz, Žitomir, Schitomir, Zhytomir). In September 1941, in the vicinity of Kiev, the Sonderkommando 4a of Einsatzgruppe C carried out the massive and infamous massacre at Babi Yar.[90]

Finnish historian Mauno Jokipii has claimed that in the literature concerning atrocities the SS-Division Wiking "has not been accused over its behaviour". However, Jokipii did not rule out the possibility of involvement by the Division in atrocities. He remarked:

> Wiking would hardly, any more than other SS-Divisions, get a clean bill of health after rigorous investigative scrutiny. Among other reasons, the fact that most of the guilty ones have later been killed in action, as in the cases reported by Sakari Lappi-Seppälä, may explain why Wiking did not appear to any extent on the list of defendants. In this respect, Wiking is similar to the entire Waffen-SS organisation: men and units who fought fully within the bounds of international law are there in large numbers and are likely to be in a sizeable majority, but no universal absolution can be given.[91]

Commenting on these statements, the former SS-Hauptsturmführer Yrjö Kaila referenced a violent event that took place in Lemberg (*Lviv*) on 1.7.1941:

> During the short stay when we had to stop at a field covered with bodies, an SS-man was in the process of clubbing to death an old Jewish man with his rifle butt. The column with all its officers noticed the event with indifference, thus tacitly approving of it from a short distance. This was the racial doctrines of Steiner's division put into practice.

Kaila notes that the Liaison Officer (and military chaplain) SS-Obersturmführer Ensio Pihkala was also present on this occasion and expressed sorrow over the incident.[92]

At the International Military Tribunal in Nuremberg, the Soviet soldier Mojzez Goldberg gave evidence as a witness to Waffen-SS atrocities in early July 1941 in Pidvolochysk (Pol. *Podwołoczyska*; Rus. *Podwoloczysk*; Yiddish *Podvolitchisk*), about 180 km east of Lemberg (*Lviv*). He was taken prisoner by the Germans on 1.7.1941 and made the following statement after the war:

> At a locality some five kilometres from Podwoloczysk (*Pidvolochysk*), the SS companies sought the Jews out of the whole mass of prisoners and shot them on the spot. I remained alive as they did not recognize me as a Jew. I stress the fact that it was the Waffen-SS who did this.[93]

There were around 7,000 people living in the town of Pidvolochysk. Of these, approximately 60% were Jews, 20% Poles, and 20% Ukrainians. The Germans, including SS units, occupied the town on 5.7.1941 and a systematic killing of Jews started at the latest on 7.7.1941.[94]

In early July 1941, units belonging to the Leibstandarte SS Adolf Hitler executed about 200 civilians near the town of Slucz, when the locals were herded into a petrol-soaked cottage. "The windows and doors were then barricaded and a hand grenade dropped down the chimney. The explosion and holocaust were spectacular", noted the British historian Alan Wykes.[95] However, there was no town in Ukraine named Slucz, but there is a River Slucz. Consequently the town in question may have been either Novohrad-Volynskyi (Pol. *Zwiahel*, Rus. *Novograd-Volynsky*, Yiddish *Zvil*)[96] or Ostropol (*Staryy Ostropil, Stary Ostropol*)[97], on the banks of that river.

The Dutch volunteer Pieter Willems of 1st Company, SS-Regiment Westland, wrote in his diary, apparently in October 1941: "Mariupol fell into our hands and the most beautiful loot that we could have dreamed of were 13,000 Jews, who fell into our hands alive. But of course, they did not survive".[98] The city of Mariupol is situated on the north coast of the Sea of Azov, at the mouth of the River Kalmius. In 1941 it had around 241,000 residents. Mariupol was occupied by the German forces on 8.10.1941.[99] The entire Jewish population, around 10,000 people, were killed shortly after the German occupation on 8.10.1941.[100] Although Willems is not very reliable as an original source, as he made up some of the stories, his diary notes appear to be adequate in this case.

An officer in the Soviet 8th Guards Cavalry Division, Nikolai Dupak, told of his war experiences in the Kharkiv area in March 1943:

Already at Merefa [we] encountered the Wiking Division that they had transferred there. They were fierce fighters, both in size and fanaticism. They did not retreat. I was wounded there, and I was sent from the Medical Battalion to a hospital in Taranovka (*Taranivka*). My papers were forwarded there, but my comrades kidnapped me and brought me back to our unit. They were taking care of their commander. That saved me. The Germans broke through in Taranovka and killed everybody – nurses, wounded, and sick.[101]

SS-Division Wiking and atrocities witnessed by Finnish volunteers

There cannot be any reasonable doubt that numerous soldiers of the SS-Division Wiking participated in the mass killings of Soviet POWs, Jews, and civilians in Ukraine and the Caucasus between 1941 and 1943. Reliable research confirms such atrocities during the advance eastwards, in the town of Zolochiv (*Złoczów*) in July 1941.[102] U.S. historian Wendy Lower records members of the Einsatzgruppen on 9.7.1941 in Zhytomyr who collaborated "along with a Waffen-SS Platoon" in the shooting of 400 Jews.[103]

Dutch volunteer Broer Wiersma of SS-Regiment Nordland testified in a post-war trial on repressive actions in the area east of Lemberg (*Lviv*) in the summer of 1941. He had heard discussion on these in the Regimental Office and reported:

It was known to me as a clerk that there occurred excesses by the 1st, 2nd, and 11th Companies of the Westland Regiment. Citizens of two villages were killed by members of those Companies as well as by Ukrainians. I cannot tell you the names of those villages. I do know that in one of them a few dozen people were killed and in the other village a few hundred. I heard this from my Regimental Commander, Fritz von Scholz. Later this man was to become Division Commander. In those incidents, members of the Regiment together with Ukrainian nationalists shot dead and beat civilians (…)".[104]

Wiersma then went on:

A Finnish volunteer from the Westland Regiment, named Kuronen, told me about the events. When we were east of Lemberg [Lviv], he had seen Ukrainians arriving on German orders to point out suspect people (members of the Komsomol) and other Communist supporters, and also mostly Jews. Captain von Schalburg, a Danish volunteer, told me that a certain Neumann was killed at an execution in one of those villages, where hundreds of people were killed. That man was the People's Commissar there. The German name intrigued us.[105]

The Finnish volunteer must have been SS-Unterscharführer Eero Kuronen from 10th Company, SS-Regiment Nordland. 'Neumann' may have been a Volga German or similar, while the Dane was SS-Hauptsturmführer Christian Frederik von Schalburg, at that time on the Staff of SS-Division Wiking. von Schalburg was in Finland during 1940 as a Winter War volunteer, although not serving at the front.[106]

In a police interrogation in 1946, the volunteer Erik Liukkonen, who had been a member of the Finnish Volunteer Battalion in 1941–43, informed the officials:

The SS-volunteers were encouraged to keep diaries and to document their war-path. Diary of Finnish SS-volunteer Herkko Kosonen. *Private collection.*

The interrogated recalls that a man called Johansson had behaved as brutally as the Germans. In the same platoon as the interrogated, one Sulo (?) Kosonen had raped a Ukrainian girl by threatening her with a pistol. During the battles in Stalingrad, no prisoners were taken. Prisoners were shot on the order of the Commanding Officer. Finns were also among the shooters. The interrogated states that he served only in the forces at the front line and that he did not know of the behaviour of the Finns in the rear, for instance at the prison camps. After [the troops had spent] long times in the open air in Ukraine, the residents of the houses had been forced out for the purpose of getting quarters. The inhabitants had been forced to move into more compact civil facilities.[107]

The first man mentioned was apparently either the volunteer Per-Olof "Pärre" Johansson of 10th Company, SS-Regiment Westland, or Sulo Johansson of 3rd Company, Panzer-Jäger-Abteilung 5. However, there was no volunteer listed with the name "Sulo Kosonen". A couple of volunteers with that surname did nevertheless serve in the SS-Regiment Westland and the Finnish SS-Volunteer Battalion.

There were no Finnish volunteers precisely in Stalingrad, but actually Liukkonen does not claim this, as he mentioned that the atrocities occurred during the battles in Stalingrad, i.e. in the period from 23.8.1942–2.2.1943. The Finnish SS-Volunteer Battalion arrived in Rasvilnoye on 10.1.1943 and in the town of Salsk, some 400 km southwest of Stalingrad, on 11.1.1943.[108]

The town of Gigant, "between Zelina and Salsk", some 400 kilometres south west of Stalingrad. Gigant was home to one of the Soviet Union's largest sovkhoz state farms. It was eventually decided that the SS-Division Wiking would not take part in the Battle of Stalingrad. The drawing of the sovkhoz and the rail line by SS-volunteer Kaj Duncker dates from 22.1.1943. *KD Coll., SLS.*

There are no other sources that would confirm the information given by Liukkonen, but as he served for the Intelligence Department of the Finnish Headquarters in 1940–44 and in the Intelligence Department of the Finnish General Staff, he is most likely to have been aware of the events in which the Finnish volunteers became involved. As he was posted among the volunteers by the General Staff as an intelligence agent, it can be anticipated that he accurately followed the developments and reported his observations. Liukkonen appears to have been one of the National Socialist-oriented members of the so-called inner circle, with close contacts to Unto Boman, Kalervo Kurkiala, and Karl-Erik Ladau. As the Deputy President of the Court of Honour of the SS-Aseveljet in 1943–44, he is likely to have dealt with cases of disgraceful behaviour among the

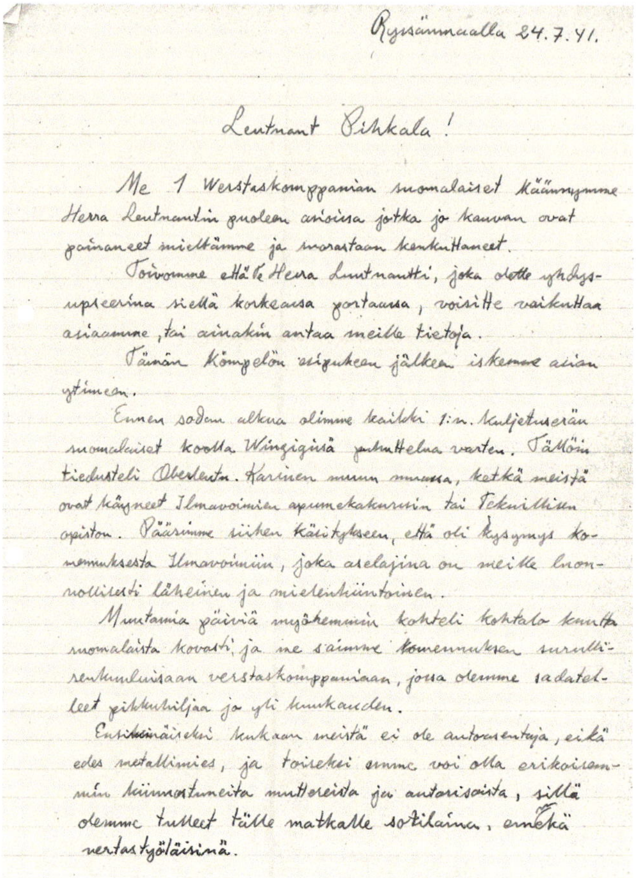

Ryssänmaalla 24.7.41.

Leutnant Pihkala!

Me 1 Werstaskomppanian suomalaiset käännymme Herra Leutnantin puoleen asioissa jotka jo kauvan ovat painaneet mieltämme ja suorastaan kenkuttaneet.

Toivomme että Te Herra Luutnantti, joka olette yhdysupseerina siellä korkeassa portaassa, voisitte vaikuttaa asiaamme, tai ainakin antaa meille tietoja.

Tämän kömpelön esipuheen jälkeen iskemme asian ytimeen.

Ennen sodan alkua olimme kaikki 1:n. Kuljetuserän suomalaiset koolla Wingiginsä pututtelua varten. Tällöin tiedusteli Oberleutn. Karinen muun muassa, ketkä meistä ovat käyneet Ilmavoimien apumekaanikurssin tai Teknillisen opiston. Pääsimme siihen käsitykseen, että oli kysymys komennuksesta Ilmavoimiin, joka aselajina on meille luonnollisesti läheinen ja mielenkiintoinen.

Muutamia päiviä myöhemmin kohteli kohtalo kuitenkin suomalaista kovasti, ja me saimme komennuksen surullisenkuuluisaan verstaskomppaniaan, jossa olemme sadatelleet pikkuhiljaa jo yli kuukauden.

Ensikinnäiseksi kukaan meistä ei ole autoasentaja, eikä edes metallimies, ja toiseksi emme voi olla erikoisemmin kiinnostuneita muttereista ja autorisoista, sillä olemme tulleet tälle matkalle sotilaina, emmekä verstastyöläisinä.

On 24.7.1941, SS-volunteer Olavi Karpalo and five of his Finnish companions wrote to the Finnish Military Chaplain and Liaison Officer Ensio Pihkala, asking him to facilitate their transfer to the front from the Repair-Shop unit: "...poorer shooting-skills than ours are enough for executing Jews." The Finnish volunteers wanted to fight against the Russians, not to participate in something that they had not come to Germany for. Olavi Karpalo had previously served in the Falangist troops as a volunteer in the Spanish Civil War. *Karpalo 1940 and Jokipii Coll., NAF.*

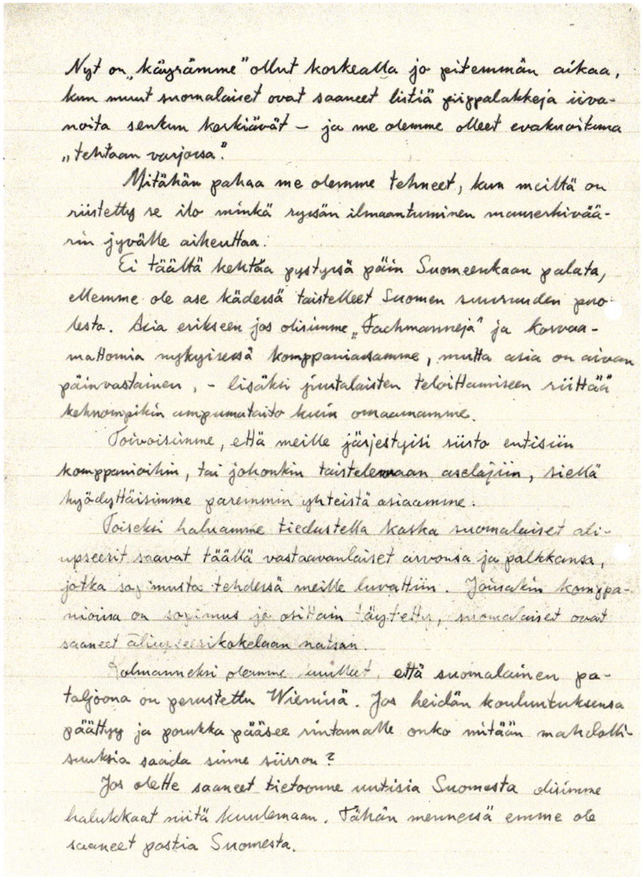

Nyt on „käyrämme" ollut korkealla jo pitemmän aikaa,
kun muut suomalaiset ovat saaneet listiä piippalakkeja iiva-
noita senkun korkiävät – ja me olemme olleet evakuoitunna
„tehtaan varjossa."
Mitähän pahaa me olemme tehneet, kun meiltä on
riistetty se ilo minkä ryssän ilmaantuminen mauserkivää-
rin jyvälle aiheuttaa.
Ei täältä kehtaa pystyssä päin Suomeenkaan palata,
ellemme ole ase kädessä taistelleet Suomen suuruuden puo-
lesta. Asia eikseen jos olisimme „Fachmanneja" ja korvaa-
mattomia nykyisessä komppaniassamme, mutta asia on aivan
päinvastainen, – lisäksi juutalaisten teloittamiseen riittää"
kehnompikin ampumataito kuin omaamamme.
Toivoisimme, että meille järjestyisi siirto entisiin
komppanioihin, tai johonkin taistelemaan aselajiin, siellä
hyödyttäisimme paremmin yhteistä asiaamme.
Toiseksi haluamme tiedustella kaska suomalaiset ali-
upseerit saavat täällä vastaavanlaiset arvonsa ja palkkansa,
jotka sa[illegible] muuta tehdessä meille luvattiin. Jonsakin komppa-
nioissa on sa[illegible] ja osittain täytetty, suomalaiset ovat
saaneet aliupseerikokelaan natsan.
Kolmanneksi olemme kuulleet, että suomalainen pa-
taljoona on perustettu Wienissä. Jos heidän koulutuksensa
päättyy ja porukka pääsee rintamalle onko mitään mahdolli-
suuksia saada sinne siirron?
Jos olette saaneet tietoonne uutisia Suomesta olisimme
halukkaat niitä kuulemaan. Tähän mennessä emme ole
saaneet postia Suomesta.

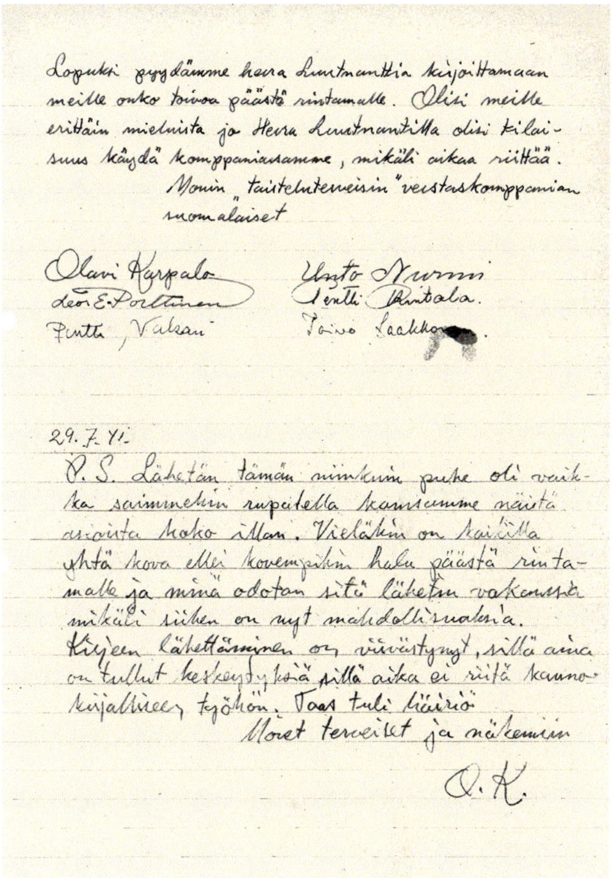

Lopuksi pyydämme herra luutnanttia kirjoittamaan
meille onko toivoa päästä rintamalle. Olisi meille
erittäin mieluista ja Herra Luutnantilla olisi tilai-
suus käydä komppaniassamme, mikäli aikaa riittää.
Monin „taistelutervehdyksin" vestaskomppanian
suomalaiset

Olavi Karpalo Unto Nurmi
Leo E. Porttinen Pentti Rintala.
Pentti Valkari Toivo Laakko[illegible].

29.7.41.
P.S. Lähetän tämän niinkuin puhe oli vaik-
ka saimmekin rupatella kanssamme näitä
asioita koko illan. Vieläkin on kaikilla
yhtä kova ellei kovempikin halu päästä rinta-
malle ja minä odotan sitä lähetin vakanssia
mikäli siihen on nyt mahdollisuuksia.
Kirjeen lähettäminen on viivästynyt, sillä aina
on tullut keskeytyksiä sillä aika ei riitä kauno-
kirjalliseen työhön. Taas tuli häiriö
Monet terveiset ja näkemiin
O.K.

volunteers.[109] Hence Liukkonen was not a person who could be expected to tell loose and unfounded stories.

In early October 1941, the volunteer Jaakko Lakeala of 5th Company, SS-Regiment Nordland was somewhere in the area of Dnipropetrovsk (now *Dnipro*). He noted in his diary: "We have heard that there are many Jews here. One of them was working here a little in the kitchen, and when the job was complete, he was sent to the happy hunting-grounds ('*toimittivat ukon autuaammille metsästysmaille*')".[110]

Dr. André Swanström has drawn attention to a letter dated 24.7.1941 from volunteer SS-Unterscharführer Olavi Karpalo [and five co-signatories] to the Finnish Liaison Officer and military chaplain SS-Obersturmführer Ensio Pihkala. In the letter, which was probably written near the town of Tarashcha (*Tarascha*, Ger. *Taraschtscha*), about 100 km south of Kiev, Karpalo claims among other things that for the execution of Jews poorer shooting skills than those maintained by the Finnish volunteers would be adequate. Owing to the vague wording, it is difficult to conclude precisely what Karpalo means. Dr. Swanström considers Karpalo's words to be clear evidence that Karpalo himself "really had shot Jews".[111] However, this claim stretches the information which can reasonably be gleaned from this single document alone. As it stands, his letter provides no information at all on the crucial issues: whom he would have shot, and when and where this would have happened. Nonetheless, as the rear troops of the Waffen-SS often had to support the Einzatzgruppen who took care of the systematic killings, it seems possible that also Karpalo and the other Finnish co-signatories may have been ordered to take part in such shooting.

From Karpalo's letter it can definitely be concluded that he regarded the shooting of Jews as a trivial matter. It is also obvious that Karpalo was aware of the killings of the local Jews, and that he is also likely at least to have witnessed atrocities of this kind. Moreover, he seems to approve of the executions, although he was greatly more enthusiastic about getting Soviet soldiers in the sights of his Mauser rifle. In Karpalo's eyes, fighting the Soviets was the prime issue, whereas the killing of Jews was nothing but a second-rate task, akin to the dull repair-shop chores in the rear that the frustrated, battle-ready Finnish SS-volunteers found themselves having to perform. The desire to get a transfer out of the workshop and to the front was the main thrust of the plea to Ensio Pihkala.[112] By that time also the volunteer Martti Leppälä of the SS-Panzerjäger-Abteilung 5 was with the unit in the neighbourhood of Tarashcha. He noted on 17.7.1941 that the Germans shot two prisoners, and that on 20.7.1941 a Cossack was found in a meadow "and was immediately shot".[113]

Swanström considers the letter from Karpalo as a piece of evidence that some of the Finnish SS-volunteers participated in the implementation of the Holocaust and were engaged in atrocities. Karpalo and his co-signatories to the letter, the Finnish SS-volunteers Unto Nurmi, Leo E. Porttinen, Pentti Rintala, Pentti Nakari, and Toivo Laakkonen in the Werkstatt-Kompanie of SS-Regiment Westland, were frustrated, as they "ended up using their shooting skills in executing Jews" instead of in fighting Soviet troops. Swanström has also considered the fact that Karpalo settled in Venezuela in the late 1940s to be an indication of his guilt. He suggests that Karpalo left Finland in order to avoid possible accusations of involvement in atrocities during his duty in the ranks of the 11th Company, SS-Regiment Westland.[114]

Some one thousand Jews lived in Tarashcha, in which the population totalled around 9,000 people. The town was occupied by the Germans on 23.7.1941. Shortly after the occupation, the Jews were forced to wear armbands bearing the Star of David. They were driven into forced labour and were not allowed to buy food. A ghetto was set up on Tarashcha Street. The executions started the same day as the occupation. One recollection mentions that a mass grave was dug outside the town and the Jews were brought there:

> They were forced to go and stand in line at the edge of the pit, facing the grave. Then they were shot in the nape of the neck with a gun, so they would fall down directly into the pit. There was only one shooter at a time, who walked up and down firing at the victims standing at the edge of the pit.

The number of the persons killed was 200–300 and the massacre was carried out by units of the German security forces, SS-Division Wiking, Einsatzkommando 5, and the local police force. In August 1941, a further action occurred and around 400 Jews were killed, and an additional few hundred more on 10.9.1941. One member of the 16th Company of the SS-Regiment Germania, Hans Wilhelm Isenmann, recounted in a partly dubious Soviet trial testimony that 400 persons were shot, and of those he personally had killed 60. The ghetto was finally liquidated on 9.11.1941: "Altogether up to 1,000 Jews were exterminated in Tarashcha between August and November 1941", i.e. almost the entire local Jewish community perished.[115]

In his memoirs, Professor Heikki A. Reenpää tells of a nameless Finnish SS-volunteer, an officer, who in early 1942 returned to Finland. The volunteer reported that he had witnessed mass executions of Jews and the burning of villages with living civilians trapped inside the buildings. From an interview, it can be concluded that the officer in question was SS-Obersturmführer Teuvo Hatara from the 15th Company, SS-Regiment Germania. He told Reenpää that he had observed how Waffen-SS forces were used as the Einsatzgruppen to kill Jews during a journey from the front to Rostov in order to fetch the post: "A synagogue full of people was burned, and none of those in it were allowed out". As the officer experienced the atrocities, his distaste grew so deep that he decided to leave the SS troops as soon as possible.[116]

Reenpää informed his father, Major Heikki Reenpää, the Director of Finland's wartime State Information Bureau (*Valtion Tiedoituslaitos,* VTL), who initially doubted the stories. However, he was interviewed on his observations at the headquarters of the Intelligence Division, which had already received similar reports on German-led massacres and offences against civilians in Ukraine and the Caucasus. The Germans explained that these actions were necessary as the only possible way of fighting Soviet partisans. Through indirect means it transpired that neither the Intelligence Division nor the State Information Bureau showed concern about this information, or at best they entertained an indifferent attitude to the atrocities. Among the persons informed on the issue were the Prime Minister J.W. Rangell, the Chief of Military Intelligence Aladár Paasonen, and the Finnish Military Attaché in Germany and Hungary, Colonel Walter Horn.[117]

From imprecise information documented by the Finnish writer on Waffen-SS topics Mark Parland, the SS-Volunteer Kaj Laurell of 3rd Company, Finnish SS-Volunteer Battalion, is reported to have participated, together with six other Finnish volunteers, in the shooting of around 600 Jews (in some renditions of the story it is 300).[118] SS-Untersturmführer Laurell is alleged to have told some comrades (no names are given) of this while at the front in 1943. However, no further information on either the location or the date of the event is known. If such an atrocity were to have been carried out, it is likely to have occurred somewhere in the Rostov region in August 1942, because the Finnish SS-Volunteer Battalion was by that time deployed in that area. German forces reoccupied Rostov-on-Don on 24.7.1942. At least 13,000 Jews were shot between 11th and 14th August 1942 by Sonderkommando 10a in the city, and more especially at the Zmievskaya Balka ravine in the vicinity of the Botanical Gardens. Gas vans were also used.[119]

Volunteer Heikki Lemettinen of 1st Company, Finnish SS-Volunteer Battalion, wrote from the Caucasus in a letter in late August 1942:

> We were waiting for a reconnaissance patrol of the Gebirgsjäger to return. However, as nothing was heard until the evening, a Finnish patrol was despatched next morning to clarify the matter (I and my brother were happy to get the opportunity to participate). We headed for the same target as the previous patrol, a village some 15 km ahead. The march was exhausting, because it ran through the middle of a barren region and we had to detour around the security positions of the enemy. After marching a long time, we eventually reached the outskirts of the village. Half of the village was occupied by the Russians and therefore we had to move carefully. We advanced from house to house towards the village centre, but we came to a sudden halt and witnessed a disgusting scene on a cross-street: the Gebirgsjäger patrol had been slaughtered in the most brutal way. The Russians had tortured the prisoners in the cruellest manner. One who saw this started to think about exacting a dreadful revenge on the Russians. We returned depressed. But the following day, our Battalion made a revenge attack on the village. Those Russians who survived will never forget the international law on the treatment of prisoners.[120]

Lemettinen avoids mentioning any details on the consequences of the attack nor does he mention the name of the village. However, according to Lemettinen at least some of the Russians may have survived. The reference to international law appears to suggest that Lemettinen had been aware of the 1920 Geneva Convention on the treatment of POWs. However, he is talking about "Russians" and not Soviet soldiers, wherein a more relevant instrument of international law would have been the application of the 1907 Hague Convention on Land Warfare, which included international rules on separation between civilians proper and so-called legal combatants. In any case, Lemettinen´s reference to the international rules on the treatment of prisoners indicates confusion on the proper application of these rules, which on the whole were strikingly poorly or not at all observed by the German forces on the Eastern Front. As it appears, Lemettinen would not have had any obvious reason to refer to international rules - unless he would have had some doubts on their significance in this case.

SS-Obersturmführer Kaj Duncker of the SS-Artillerie-Regiment 5 reports in his diary on another occasion when Soviet POWs were shot in revenge. The 3rd Battalion, SS-Regiment Germania and the 6th Company, SS-Regiment Westland engaged in a fierce firefight on 27.2.1943 along a road towards the village of Arkhangel'livka (*Arkhanhelivka*) in the vicinity of modern-day Barvinkove, south of Kharkiv. A force of 32 men met two Soviet T-34 tanks, which crushed several SS-soldiers by driving over them one after another, leaving only seven survivors. The 3rd Battalion, SS-Regiment Nordland, and the SS-Artillerie-Regiment later counterattacked against five Soviet tanks, which were destroyed with "huge piles of Russian bodies" (*stora högar av ryslik*) laid around: "Revenge was just as dreadful, only tenfold", Duncker noted starkly.[121] Generally Duncker avoids any mention of atrocities against Soviet POWs in his diary, and his notes on this event are exceptionally one of the few that may suggest that unlawful violent acts were carried out by his unit. Although he does not directly mention that survivors were mown down, this is likely to be what happened. In his diary, Duncker included photos of atrocities in Husiatyn and a Jew chase, but did not comment on them in any way and did not provide any further information on these events. It can be anticipated that he knew some details, although he avoided telling them. His brief remarks on the events in Arkhangel'livka are actually exceptional, but nevertheless selective, whilst the full picture remains vague and unclear. This was probably precisely Duncker's intention.

The Finnish war historian Helge Seppälä has concluded that the Germans' inhuman activities during the advance eastwards did not target merely the rear, but also the battle forces and civilians near the front:

> (…) in this respect the SS forces were the wildest. The soldiers of the Wiking Division began shooting Jews two weeks after the fighting started in Galicia, as revenge for atrocities committed by Soviet soldiers. In Ukraine, the soldiers of the Waffen-SS raged so wildly that the Ukrainians fled their villages and joined the Red Army. The Wehrmacht noted: "Thefts of cattle, whipping of the inhabitants, and rapes of women and girls stirred the population".

Moreover, Seppälä has concluded that the German police and security forces, and partly also the Waffen-SS units, treated the civilian population according to the harsh instructions issued, with a lack of consideration for international conventions and human respect. These actions cannot be defended on the grounds that the civilians started the guerilla war or by reference to the foul deeds of the Soviet soldiers. The German steps were considered in advance and ordered to expressly target Jews and Communists, regardless of the attitude of the population towards the occupier.[122]

As far as is known, the Finnish volunteers were at no time used as guards in the concentration camps and the numerous other custody facilities set up for civilians. In the summer of 1942, three Finns were deployed for brief periods at the Oranienburg concentration camp for supply work in modest and subordinate positions.[123] However, brief diary entries and recollection notes show that the Finnish volunteers were aware of at least the Dachau concentration camp and the penal camps, in which a few Finns also served out their own punishments for offences such as disobeying orders, petty theft, and other service violations. One of them attempted burglary in one of the kitchens in the training camp at Gross Born in October 1941 and another had assaulted two civilians and a police officer in a restaurant in Graz in September 1942. Both of the men were heavily intoxicated at the time of the incidents.[124] A third volunteer was convicted at the SS and Police Court in Wien in January 1942 for a service violation in Gross Born.[125] A sub-camp of the Dachau concentration camp carried out supply tasks for the SS-Junkerschule Bad Tölz, but although 53 Finnish volunteers attended the school and they must have known about this, there are no notes on the issue in either the diaries or the personal recollections. As it appears, an excursion to the Dachau camp was included in the training programme of the SS-Junkerschule.[126]

As the topic of the camps does not appear to be particularly crucial here, no further attention will be paid to it this report.

Atrocities by Danish, Norwegian, and Swedish volunteers

In this section, light will be shone on the information on atrocities committed by Danish, Dutch, Norwegian, and Swedish SS-volunteers. The purpose is to get a rough picture of the occurrence of the phenomenon among the volunteers of foreign descent in the Waffen-SS. As SS-volunteers of Finland's Nordic neighbour countries were involved in atrocities, the expectation is that the Finnish volunteers were not the sole exception from this pattern of violence.

Danes

Danish volunteers of the Waffen-SS participated in the more or less indiscriminate mass killings of various opponent groups in areas behind the front. In early July, 1941, volunteer Heinrich Husen of the 1st Battalion of the SS-Regiment Nordland met some Russian refugees near the town of Proskurov (Ukr. *Proskuriw*; Pol. *Płoskirów*; now known as *Khmelnytskyi*). As the refugees asked for bread, Husen put a hand-grenade in the pocket of one of them and said that the thing was bread. Shortly after, the grenade exploded.[127]

A Danish SS-volunteer who served as a motorcycle orderly of the SS-Division Wiking watched in 1941 as a German machine-gunner cut down half a dozen Soviet POWs. The original order was to bring the POWs to a prison camp. However, no precise date nor place is known for the incident.[128]

By the turn of the year 1941–42, an artillery soldier of the 327th Infantry Division, one Johan Schmidt, witnessed how units of the SS-Division Wiking and Leibstandarte SS Adolf Hitler committed systematic atrocities against civilians in Taganrog on the shores of the Sea of Azov:

> I could observe how hundreds of Jewish civilians were driven together with kicks and blows from the rifle butts. Dreadful scenes took place. Women carrying children in their arms asked for the lives of their little innocents to be spared, but they were again mercilessly kicked into the mass of the doomed. Other civilians had already dug a large grave, to the edge of which the poor victims were driven. The machine gun opened fire, and I watched how the victims crumpled.[129]

On 9.6.1942, in Staraya Russa, a Danish motorcycle orderly of Freikorps Danmark noted in his diary:

> A Jew in a grease-stained kaftan arrives, begging for bread. A couple of comrades catch him and bring him behind the building. In a while, his life is ended. There is no place for Jews in the New Europe. For that they have brought about too much distress and misery to the European peoples.[130]

In the spring of 1942, some Danish guards are alleged to have participated in the maltreating and killing of Jews belonging to Arbeits-Kommandos in the vicinity of Bobruisk in White Russia. In 1941, between 300 and 400 locals had been killed, although these civilians had no connections to the Soviet partisans.[131]

The Commander of Freikorps Danmark, SS-Hauptsturmführer Christian Frederik von Schalburg, was killed in action in the so-called Demjansk Pocket on 2.6.1942, and as a consequence an unknown number of Soviet POWs were shot in retaliation.[132] At least in single other cases Soviet POWs and Jews were shot in the Demjansk area.[133] The Danish SS-officer and Company Commander Oluf Krabbe recalls in his memoirs that a part of the SS-Regiment Westland and a unit of SS-Regiment Germania were deployed on 12.1.1943 near Orlovskaya. As the Soviet forces attacked, the Commander of the SS Regiment Westland was killed in action, and a revenge assault was planned. Whilst the forces of SS-Regiment Germania blocked off the entrances to a village shortly before occupied by the Soviet forces, SS-Regiment Westland prepared a surprise attack during the night. As a consequence, the Soviets in the village were completely surprised:

> There was no time for taking prisoners. The table was cleaned. Many thousands of Russians had to perish, and the few who were able to flee from the village were met by fire from the machine guns of Germania.[134]

In 1943, a Danish SS-volunteer shot a total of 25 civilians in the vicinity of Kiev as he was participating in an execution of 135 civilians. Another Dane forced a Soviet POW to dig his own grave. The prisoner had stolen three packages of tobacco and was shot. The volunteer was later tried in a Danish court and convicted.[135]

The mass arrests of Jews in Denmark in August 1943, and their subsequent deportation, were actively supported by Danish SS-volunteers and the so-called Schalburg Corps [Danish-Germanic SS]. A volunteer told how his group arrested two old Jewish women and a poor tailor.[136] A considerable number of these SS volunteers and Schalburg men were later cleared of murders of Danish citizens in the occupation years.[137]

Around 100 Danish SS-men are reported to have served as guards and supervisors in the concentration camps. At least a few of these are known to have maltreated the prisoners. A Danish SS-volunteer from the German-speaking Sønder-Jylland region who served in an Aussenkommando (or "subcamp") of the Alter Banter Weg concentration camp in Wilhelmshaven ordered in the spring of 1945 the execution of 52 internees, after a march to the Bergen-Belsen concentration camp. He personally shot six of them and was subsequently sentenced to death in 1947 by a British Military Court.[138]

Norwegians

According to his post-war memoirs, in early July 1941 the Norwegian volunteer Olav Ingemar Tuff from SS-Regiment Nordland observed how an alleged Soviet partisan was executed in a brutal manner west of Lemberg (*Lviv*). Jews were killed, and Soviet POWs who desperately crossed the road to drink water were crushed by a speeding lorry as the driver had no intention of stopping.[139] As a guard in Ukraine in the fall of 1941, Tuff also witnessed how 200 to 300 civilians were driven like cattle into a church and the soldiers of his unit poured gasoline on the church, set it on fire, and the people inside were incinerated: "There were many cries and much screaming, and we could hardly believe that we were a part of that criminal act. But there was not much we could do. We had to do what we were ordered". However, this incident was just one of many similar events as whole villages were burnt and defenceless civilians were driven from their homes or shot: "We walked from house to house because everyone had to come out. Those who did not were shot. They were told that they would be shot unless they assembled outside".[140]

On July 19th, 1941, war correspondent Egil Hartmann published an interview with an anonymous Norwegian SS-volunteer who had participated in the taking of a three-storey Soviet bunker somewhere in Western Ukraine. The volunteer reported that the captured prisoner had been shot.[141]

The Norwegian SS-volunteer Olaf Wahlman, from SS-Artillerie-Regiment 5, published an article in the militantly National Socialist (Quislingist) propaganda broadsheet *Hirdmannen* on 16.8.1941, containing a recollection of how a Jew found in a house-by-house search was shot:

> By the railroad line, in a little house we came across a frightful scene. Outside the house lay three Ukrainian women maltreated in the most terrible way with stabbed eyes, etc. In the building we found six other women, likewise abused. From a hiding place under a blanket emerged a Jew, still alive. As he found himself discovered, he bleated to us: "I have done nothing. Me wounded. Me live nearby". Short work. He was shot from a distance of three metres in front of the house. His head split open and his rotten brain oozed out from it.[142]

Further reasonably reliable stories with sometimes vague details speak about Norwegian SS-volunteers who killed women and Jews.[143]

Swedes

No precise information on the involvement of Swedish SS-volunteers is known. However, the journalist Bosse Schön claims that in the summer and fall of 1941 Swedes were deployed in places where tens of thousands of Jews were shot: Odessa, Kamianets-Podilskyi, Kerch, Lemberg (*Lviv*), Berdychiv (Pol. *Berdyczów*, Rus. *Berdichev*, Yiddish *Bardichev*) and Mariupol. He concludes that the SS-volunteer Ragnar Linnér of 1st Company, SS-Regiment Westland is likely to have witnessed several mass atrocities. In September 1941, Linnér's units were present on the frontlines near Dnipropetrovsk as hundreds of surrendered Soviet soldiers were shot on the spot. For the most part, the treatment of POWs was ruthless and they were driven forward with kicks and blows from the rifle butts.[144] Schön presumes that as guards they would have witnessed how Polizeibataillon 314 of the Ordnungspolizei (OrPo) shot 7,000–8,000 Jews in Dnipropetrovsk between 10. and 14.10.1941. Linnér may also have known of some repressive acts by Einsatzkommando 6. At around this time, the unit shot Jews in Zaporizhia (*Zaporižžja, Zaporizhzhya, Zaporozhye, Zaporozie*) and in Borodaievka.[145] Regarding Soviet POWs, a Swedish SS volunteer from the Eastern front revealed shortly after the war: "Captured *Politruks* and NKVD soldiers didn't usually live long".[146]

The SS-volunteer Kurt Lundin told the Swedish police authorities he was a member of the Reserve Battalion of SS-Regiment Westland in 1941–43. His unit was, as it appears, present in Husiatyn (*Husyatin, Husiatin, Husictyn, Hysuatin Gusjatin, Gusiatin, Gusyatin, Gusatin, Usiatyn*) on 6.–7.7.1941, when his Company was ordered to cleanse the town of Soviet partisans. However, another Company had already started gathering people who were to be shot. The bulk of these were Jews. All of them [the Jewish captives] were ordered to carry away the bodies of victims shot by Soviet forces before their withdrawal from the town. The bodies were in the cellar of the City Hall:

> Here Lundin had observed an elderly Jew, who could not stand carrying bodies any further. An SS-man then forced him to lay down among the bodies, and he shot him in the neck. After burying the bodies, the persons taken as hostage were forced to dig their own graves. Some of them were shot in the neck by the graveside, while others were killed with blows from the rifle butts. Moreover, some others had been "permitted" to beat each other to death, under the promise that the survivors would be pardoned and spared. However, also these were shot.[147]

During the march, Lundin

> had experienced that the SS-Division Wiking, of which he was a member, for a long time took no prisoners, but killed all who crossed the Division's path. The origin of this practice came from an event in which officers and men carrying out their reconnaissance patrols had been caught by surprise by the Russians and were found dead and mutilated (...) These acts had stirred feelings to the effect that for some months no prisoners were taken.

On one occasion, Lundin had witnessed how an SS-officer had grabbed a baby from its mother and – keeping the infant in his hands – had slit the baby open and thrown it back to the mother. A common way of killing babies was to grab the children by the legs and smash their head against a wall. On one occasion, women sneaked into the barracks. They were, however, driven out and all of them were shot with machine guns. On several occasions, Lundin witnessed the killing of Jews – men, women and children – involving about 800 victims. A member of a special SS-Company, named the Jew Company, had told him that he was commissioned to hunt down Jews and kill them. In five months, the Company had killed about 300,000 Jews in the area south of Kiev. They had been shot with machine guns or asphyxiated in gassing vans.[148] However, the reliability of Lundin's information is in some doubt, as at least the number 300,000 appears much exaggerated.

The SS-volunteer Elis Höglund told a Swedish radio programme in 1963 that he had witnessed the killing of Jews in Rostov-on-Don, where a considerable number of Jews were summarily shot. According to journalist Bosse Schön, this event occurred on 24.–28.7.1942 as the Sonderkommando 10a executed Jews in the Rostov area. [149] SS-Obersturmführer Curt Birger Norberg of the Leibstandarte SS Adolf Hitler deserted from his unit after serving in the vicinity of Kharkiv, and in March 1943 he was interrogated by the Swedish security services. He then reported: "In Russia, all Jews are shot behind the front".[150] In August 1944, a Swedish Company Commander of the SS-Panzer-Aufklärungs-Abteilung of 11. SS-Freiwilligen-Panzargrenadier-Division "Nordland" shot three Soviet POWs of Ingrian descent at the south-eastern front in Estonia.[151]

Surviving archives of the Waffen-SS

The field archives of the SS-Division-Wiking were destroyed on orders in May 1945. However, in the Bundesarchiv-Militärarchiv (BA-MA) in Freiburg, there is a collection of documents on 34 Waffen-SS Divisions out of a total of 38, in Record Group RS 3 (*Divisionen der Waffen-SS*). Among these, documents relating to the SS-Division Wiking are included in the sub-collection RS 3-4, 5. SS-Panzer-Division "Wiking". However, only primarily minor reports of the divisional and regimental archives have survived. There is also the large collection of Wolfgang Vopersal. Vopersal served during WWII in the 3. SS-Panzer-Division "Totenkopf", and was later the archivist of the HIAG, the former members' lobby group seeking to "rehabilitate" the Waffen-SS in the post-war period. A considerable part of the archive consists of documents gathered from the collections of various archives, but the significance of the Vopersal collection for the current SS-Investigation is modest.

In the BA-MA in Freiburg there is also an extensive document collection, B 438, the archive of the veterans' association of SS-Division Wiking, *Truppenkameradschaft 5. SS-Panzer-Division "Wiking"*. The documents are from the period 1939–92. This archive was released in 2018 and only some of the documents have been utilised; the usefulness of the archive is not particular significant.

In the Berlin-Lichterfelde branch of the *Bundesarchiv* there is an SS card index as well as the archive of the Personnel Staff of the Reichsführer-SS, i.e. Heinrich Himmler. Some 50 documents on the Finnish SS-volunteers are also included in this archive. These documents concern only organisational issues and German-Finnish SS-relations, and not the events on the battlefield.[152] Actually, the archive of the Reichsführer SS survived quite by chance, as did the member register of the NSDAP (Mitgliederkartei) and the SS personnel archive.[153] Among the *Bundesarchiv-Militärarchiv* collections in Freiburg is also the war history of the Finnische Freiwilligen-Bataillon der Waffen-SS as a part of the III. (finn.) SS-Pz. Gr. Rgt "Nordland" for the period 1.11.1941–3.12.1942.[154]

There are also various personal service records and documents in the *Deutsche Dienststelle für die Benachrichtigung der nächsten Angehörigen vor Gefallener ehemaligen deutschen Wehrmacht* (formerly WASt). This archive has been based in Berlin since 1951.[155] The significance of these documents is nevertheless not particularly remarkable, as there is scant information on the SS-volunteers in the Finnish service cards and the published member list.[156]

Since 1958, the Central Office of the State Justice Administrations for the Investigation of National Socialist Crimes (*Die Zentrale Stelle der Landesjustizverwaltungen zur Aufklärung nationalsozialistischer Verbrechen*) has been situated in Ludwigsburg. This bureau, the so-called *Ludwigsburger Zentrale Stelle*, has gathered numerous copies of original documents, police interrogation records, and witness testimonies also on the atrocities committed by the German forces during their service in the East.[157] This investigation has made use of a set of their documentation.[158]

In the Czech War Archive (*Vojenský ústredmi archive*), in Prague, there is a collection of documents on 16 Waffen-SS divisions. They have two volumes on the SS-Division Wiking. It appears these documents are of merely minor significance for this SS-Investigation, and none of them have been used for this report.

Other Archives

Other archives contain extensive documentary collections on or related to the Waffen-SS and SS-Division Wiking. Such institutions include the National Archives and Records Administration (NARA) in the USA, the National Archives in Great Britain, the Institute for War, Holocaust and Genocide Studies (*Instituut vor Oorlogs-, Holocaust- en Genocidestudies*, NIOD) in Amsterdam, Netherlands, the *Rigsarkivet* in Copenhagen, Denmark, *Riksarkivet* in Oslo, Norway, and *Riksarkivet* in Stockholm, Sweden.

In the *Kansallisarkisto/Riksarkivet* (The National Archives of Finland) in Helsinki, there are three extensive collections on the SS-Division Wiking: Professor Mauno Jokipii's collection, the archive of the association *SS-Aseveljet r.y.* (SS-Brothers-in-Arms) from 1942–44, and the archive of the SS-Investigation of 2018. Smaller useful, personal archives are those of Jukka Tyrkkö and Kaj Duncker.

The 76 diaries by the Finnish SS-volunteers

For this investigation a total of 76 diaries kept by the Finnish SS-volunteers have been examined. The greater part of these diaries, 44 in all, are included in the collection of Professor Mauno Jokipii, and seven in the collection of the former volunteer Jukka Tyrkkö in the National Archives. One diary is in the War Museum and another in the Helsinki University Library. A total of 23 diaries have been made available for the project either by the representatives of the veterans' association *Veljesapu r.y.* or by private individuals.

The physical form of the diaries varies from small calendars to notebooks of varying quality. As a rule, the volunteers favoured handy notebooks, which could easily be kept in uniform pockets, backpacks, and satchels. As the units were often on the move, conditions allowed for only short entries in the field. The size of the notes depended on the size of the notebooks. If a calendar was small, the writing was cramped and compact. Because the notebooks and notes differ, it is difficult to get a picture of the total mass of written material. However, the length of 63 diaries are known. The total number of pages in these comes out at 3,891, which are again of varying size. A few of the diaries are brief and a few are extensive, one for instance is 578 pages long. However, the average length is estimated at some 60 pages. A few of the diaries are simultaneously scrap-books and of varying page-sizes which makes an estimation of the length impossible. However, as it appears, the 76 diaries can be judged to form a text mass of around 5,500 pages.

Of the diaries used, 34 are hand-written. Fair copies are made of 42 diaries, either typewritten or written out by hand. This is a crucial issue, because it is not always possible to determine whether the diaries in these cases truly reproduce the original text or not. It is thus quite conceivable that a part of the fair copy diaries were partly re-written sometime during the post-war period. This means that original entries can have been changed, amended, or removed for the purpose of providing a sanitised picture of the atrocities described, events, or troubled personal relations, etc. However, it appears that fair copies have at least in part in some cases been produced by typists, research assistants, or by persons other than the original authors. The SS-Investigation has carefully studied the diaries and made systematic analysis on the authenticity of them by paying attention to the paper quality, ink and pencil traces, the provenance, and their general appearance. As far as can be observed, no case is known where a diary has been "improved" afterwards. It has been possible to examine many of the diaries only as fair copies so it is not yet entirely possible to exclude the possibility of faked diary notations.

When examining the diaries, attention has predominantly been paid to information on atrocities, reactions to them, and attitudes towards Jews, Russians, and other ethnic groups. Many volunteers noted these incidents and their observations are included in every diary kept by those serving in the Division during the summer and fall of 1941. Concerning the diaries of the men in the Volunteer Battalion, the situation is different because these volunteers did not arrive at the front until the winter of 1942. Nevertheless, notes of the aforementioned sort were found only in around half of the diaries.

The diaries of the volunteers used in the SS-Investigations are distributed among the various sub-units of the SS-Division Wiking in the following way:

TABLE 1.
The distribution of diaries of the Finnish SS-volunteers among the sub-units of the SS-Division Wiking and SS-Junker-Schule Bad Tölz

UNIT	NUMBER (NO.)
SS-Regiment Nordland[159]	5
SS-Regiment Westland[160]	7
SS-Regiment Germania	-
SS-Aufklärungs-Abteilung 5	-
SS-Artillerie-Regiment 5[161]	2
SS-Panzerjäger-Abteilung 5[162]	3
SS-Flak-Abteilung 5[163]	2
SS-Divisions-Nachschubführer 5[164]	1
The Division Staff[165]	3
Finnisches SS-Freiwilligen-Bataillon[166]	57
SS-Junker-Schule Bad Tölz[167]	3
TOTAL	**83 (76)**

As the information in Table 1 shows, there are diaries from 76 volunteers who were either members of the Division or of the Battalion. Some of them served in more than one sub-unit of the SS-Division Wiking. Therefore the total number of descriptions about the sub-units is 83. Two thirds of the diaries were kept by members of the Finnish SS-Volunteer Battalion and only a third by the volunteers serving in the Division in the summer of 1941. As the bulk of the atrocities known occurred in that earlier period, some 20 diaries can shed light on these events.

However, the main purpose of the diaries has not been an aspiration to document atrocities, but to follow the daily events of the unit and operational conditions, including movements and positions of longer duration. In his instructions to the Finnish SS-Volunteer Battalion, the Finnish Liaison Officer, Lieutenant-Colonel Kustaa Eemil Levälahti urged the volunteers to make notes on the events of the battalion and the companies, including precise dates and descriptions.

Furthermore, also photos and newspaper clippings were to be gathered.[168]

Although notes on atrocities certainly were made, the diary writers observed an unwritten practice of caution. Some did write at length, while others made only brief entries. The atrocities described tended to be written using vague wordings, euphemisms, and messages "to be read between the lines". There seem to have been two reasons for this. First, there was a risk that their superiors could have inspected the diaries, and to temper that risk, the diarists favoured vague wordings. Secondly, the atrocities were for many so shocking that they needed time to sort and work them out. The consequence of this seems to have been an avoidance of final conclusions. Some key words rather than categorical statements were included in single sentences, lines, and pages. From the viewpoint of the SS-Investigation, this means in particular two things: generally the diaries do not provide a full picture of the described atrocities, and the wording must be interpreted with this in mind. Notwithstanding these reservations, the mass of the diaries nevertheless provide a most useful documentation for the Investigation. The diaries of volunteer Keijo Kääriäinen are illustrative in this respect. In his original diary, Kääriäinen made only short and general notes on atrocities. Later, as a patient in a military hospital, he added more detail and information. The reasons for this seem to be twofold: in the first place, at the front there was not always time or opportunity to make copious notes, and, secondly, over time he acquired a broader perspective when dealing with the events.

Some diaries have either been destroyed or disappeared. In 1958, Paavo Alkio reported that his notes had all disappeared, while Juha Veikkola's notes had been destroyed in an accidental fire. Additionally, the former volunteer Haikala (either Kauko or Sakari Haikala) reported that his diary had gone up in flames in an accidental fire.[169] In 1952, the Finnish Security Police (*Suojelupoliisi, Supo,* now *Supo,* the Finnish Security Intelligence Service) returned five diary notebooks to the former volunteer Jukka Tyrkkö. Tyrkkö is reported to have later destroyed them. When the former volunteer Aarne Nyberg asked for his confiscated diaries in 1954, the Finnish Security Police informed him his diaries were not to be found. In 1946, the former volunteers Mika Hellemaa and Erkki Anttonen are supposed to have burned parts of the archive of the SS-Aseveljet r.y. association.[170] Actually a considerable number of diaries have not been available to the SS-Investigation. The investigation has utilized 76 diaries, but the actual number of produced diaries may well be greater. In 1958, the SS-Aseveljet r.y. asked the members for information on existing notes from the advance of 1941–43. A total of 166 volunteers responded, and of these 51 reported that they had notes. A total of 37 known diaries are still either genuinely missing or the owner does not grant access to them.[171]

Ten diaries by Dutch and Norwegian SS-volunteers

The SS-Investigation has also examined ten diaries kept by Dutch and Norwegian SS-volunteers. In the *Instituut vor Oorlogs-, Holocaust- en Genocidestudies* (NIOD), there are six diaries kept by Dutch members of the SS-Regiment Westland, which cover the advance eastwards during the summer of 1941.[172] Extracts from these diaries have been received with the assistance of the journalist Stijn Reurs and the historian Cees Kleijn in the Netherlands.[173]

Three diaries of Norwegian SS-volunteers are known from the campaigns of the SS-Division Wiking in 1941: two from the SS-Regiment Nordland[174] and another from the SS-Artillerie-Regiment 5.[175] There are also some other Norwegian diaries[176] and recollections[177] from the Division. However, these are of no particular use to the SS-Investigation. There are no known diaries by Danish or Swedish SS-volunteers that would cover the events in Ukraine in the summer of 1941.

An obvious question of interest is why there are 76 surviving diaries from the Finnish SS-volunteers, but only a handful from the other Nordic countries? It appears at least a few per cent of the Finnish volunteers kept diaries. The real rate may be higher, as some probably have remained unknown to the SS-Investigation. If we imagine that 5% of the 12,000 or more SS-volunteers from Denmark and Norway kept diaries, this would mean something of the order of 600 diarists. As it is, only approximately 20 diaries seem to have survived. The likely explanation is that the great bulk of the Danish and Norwegian diaries were destroyed by their writer-owners. In the early post-war period, these men were tried and convicted. In this way the volunteers avoided the seizure of their diaries, personal documents and correspondence, which could have been used against them as evidence in court. By comparison, the Finnish SS-volunteers were – with only a few exceptions – not accused of anything, and they could continue their lives in Finland after their repatriation in the summer of 1943, and equally after the armistice with the Soviet Union in September 1944, meaning they had no pressing need to destroy or hide their diaries. This seems to be the main reason for the relatively large volume of surviving diaries in Finland. However, senior officers and persons like K.E. Levälahti, Kalervo Kurkiala, Jukka Tyrkkö, and Unto Boman did also ask the volunteers to keep diaries.

Recollections by and biographies on Finnish volunteers

A considerable volume of material in the form of memoirs and biographies on the Finnish volunteers has been produced. In the realm of printed books, a total of 16 such presentations have appeared.[178] Moreover, there are some 100 shorter recollections, interviews, and biographies. Of these the bulk are published as articles in various journals, and particularly in the mouthpiece of the *Veljesapu r.y.* veterans' association, the quarterly *Achtung*, from 1993 onwards. Another 20 or so remain unpublished.

Compared with the diaries, the published recollections and biographies generally provide an embellished picture of how the SS-Division Wiking, the volunteers, and various personalities conducted themselves. There is, however, one exception to this pattern, the book of recollections *Haudat Djneprin varrella* (Graves Along the Dnieper) by SS-volunteer and SS-Rottenführer Sakari Lappi-Seppälä, which appeared in 1945. Also the recollections contained in *Farligt spel* (Dangerous Game) by the former SS official Erik Nupnau (1946) can be mentioned as an example of a critical presentation, although Nupnau was not a member of either the Division or the Battalion.[179]

Although the published presentations include much essential information about the volunteers, the unpublished diaries are generally more candid and a notable part of them pay attention to atrocities and describe them in some detail. For this reason, efforts have been made to use the diaries, and to raise awareness of previously undocumented information.

Photo documentation

The German campaigns in 1939–45 were documented in a great number of photos, sketches, films, etc. In the period from September 1939 to April 1942, German war correspondents took more than one million photos, including around 40,000 colour photos, made 4,000 drawings, and produced some two million metres of movie film. There were 23 Propaganda Companies with 10,000 war correspondents and personnel, with an additional 5,000 personnel at the Main Office in Berlin.[180] Apart from the war reporters, many officers and soldiers in the field had their own cameras and are likely to have taken hundreds of thousands of photos. As the sheer volume of photos is so huge, it can be presumed that among other scenes, atrocities and killings were documented in photos. However, all the negatives of the photos taken by the war reporters of the Waffen-SS were completely destroyed on highest order in the spring of 1945 shortly before the end of the war. By chance almost 100,000 contact prints of the size 24 x 36 mm survived, although without captions and mostly undated.[181]

Among the Finnish volunteers there was at least one war correspondent authorised by the Staff of the SS-Division Wiking, SS-Oberscharführer Jukka Tyrkkö, who filed stories for the illustrated weekly *Suomen Kuvalehti* among others. He had a camera, and he also obtained photos from the German war correspondents. SS-Sturmmann Tauno Aarni has been characterised as a "war photographer" (*sotakuvaaja*), and Aarni took a series of photos at the front.[182] Also some Finnish SS-officers and men such as Kaj Duncker and Unto Boman (later Unto Parvilahti) had their own cameras as several others. From Boman's own information, he was the owner of a cine-film camera during the campaign in the summer of 1941. In a libel case tried in Helsinki in the fall of 1958, former SS-volunteer Matti Tamminen was a witness and explained how he had seen when Boman took a few photos of an incident as the Germans executed Jews. Tamminen could not name the place, which appears likely to have been the town of Ozerna, north-west of Ternopil, on 3.–4.7.1941. Ex-volunteer Sakari Lappi-Seppälä actually handed over one of these photos to the court. Tamminen had years earlier given him this photo, which, however, cannot be found among the court records.[183]

There is no information on the number of photos produced by the Finnish SS-volunteers. However, the photo collection of Jukka Tyrkkö in the Finnish War Museum includes thousands of photos. However, all of these are not related to Waffen-SS topics. As the veterans' association Veljesapu r.y. in 1958 asked the members for information on diaries and notes, attention was also paid to photos. Hence of the 166 respondents, 32 or roughly a fifth reported that they had photos, among them Alvar Lantto with between 150 and 200 of them. Others reported "a few" photos, "7 or 8", "some dozens", "a fine photo album", etc.[184] Although it is not really possible to estimate the

Finnish volunteer Herkko Kosonen also kept a photo album, but unfortunately it is mostly lacking dates, locations, and descriptions for the photos. This is the case for many of the other photo-albums used for the survey. *Private collection.*

precise number of photos, the total is likely to have been impressive because practically everyone of the former volunteers probably had at least a minor collection, while others may have gathered hundreds of images.

Photo documentarist and history enthusiast Olli Wikberg has an estimated at least several thousand photographs from the Finnish volunteers of 1941–43. There are probably numerous photos among photo collectors as well as in the hands of relatives of the former Finnish volunteers. Some photos may have been destroyed or simply disappeared. As a whole, there may be tens of thousands of wartime photos that pictorially document the war events and daily conditions of the Finnish volunteers.[185] Many photos are included in this presentation in order to illustrate the conduct of SS-Division Wiking and the Finnish volunteers in Ukraine, Caucasus, Germany, and Finland in 1941–43.

THE UNITS OF WAFFEN SS-DIVISION WIKING AND THEIR COMMANDERS

In this section, light will be shed on the units of the SS-Division Wiking and the Regiment and Battalion Commanders. Initially the Finnish contingent of the Waffen-SS is briefly presented. Also a section on the Division Commander Felix Steiner is included.

THE SS-REGIMENT NORDLAND

The SS-Regiment Nordland was formed in 1940, trained in Germany, crossed the Soviet border on 29.6.1941, and it engaged in battle for the first time at the River Zbruch in early July 1941. Later it advanced as far as the vicinity of Dnipropetrovsk. In November 1941, the Regiment reached Rostov-on-Don.[186] The number of Finnish volunteers in the Nordland Regiment was 203, comprising seven officers and 196 men. A few Swedish volunteers also served in the unit.[187] By 13.5.1942, the subunit I/G (presumably a *Gefechtgruppe*) of the Regiment included 92 Danes, 91 Norwegians, two Swedes, and around 40 Dutch volunteers.[188]

From 1940 to January 1943 the Commander of the SS-Regiment Nordland was SS-Standartenführer Fritz von Scholz.[189] He was an Austrian nobleman and was nicknamed "Alte Fritz", like the former Kaiser Friedrich der Grosse. Fritz von Scholz was most popular among his subordinates. In the recollections of the SS-Standartenführer Poul Rantzow Engelhardt there are several notes illustrating the conduct of von Scholz and his unit. As the Regiment lodged in Mokroyelanchyk (*Mokrij Jalantschinskij*, *Mokryi Jelanschiki*) south of Amvrosiivka (*Amvrosijevka, Ambrojewka*), in what is now the Donetsk Oblast, two Russian girls were assaulted and raped during the night. The Russian-speaking SS-Hauptsturmführer Christian Frederik von Schalburg listened to the victims in his capacity as officer on the staff of the SS-Division Wiking, but Engelhardt reported that nothing was done: "The perpetrators were not prosecuted". Also a few days later civilians were assaulted again, and two more girls were raped. In Amvrosiivka on 19.5.1942, two drunken SS-officers let off hand-grenades under the window of the Regimental Adjutant and Ordnance Officer. Consumption of alcohol continued, and on 23.5.1942 the Danish volunteer Madsen was given a good beating by his comrades for theft. Madsen had also been absent without leave for two days. As a guard, he intended to kill five Communists who were threatening to shoot him. The punishment was, however, not this time carried out.[190]

SS-Standartenführer von Scholz was particularly attached to the "Finnenbataillon" and was also popular among the Finnish SS-volunteers.[191] He was even characterised by them as "a Finnish Officer". On 8.9.1942, von Scholz was awarded the Finnish Order of the Cross of Liberty (*Vapaudenristi*), 2nd Class.[192] In the war years, the Finnish and German co-belligerents made extensive use of military decorations in order to strengthen the common relations. The crosses were, however, awarded with discretion.

At the front, von Scholz was somewhat indifferent as regards food, but was keen on having something to drink. Engelhardt noted on 16.11.1942 in Amvrosiivka: "His nerves are shot, like a good deal of other officers. He would daily consume an entire bottle of cognac to keep him going. Alcoholism seems to be worse here than in the Wehrmacht". When von Scholz was ordered to attack Sagopshi (in modern-day Ingushetia) on 27.9.1942, he marked this piece of "sheer madness" by getting drunk. A month later, on 30.10.1942, in the vicinity of Pavlodol'skaya (*Pavlodolskij*), on the Terek River, von Scholz was drunk and agitated, and he assaulted Officer Scheffer.[193] Much later, von Scholz was in killed in action west of Narva, on 28.7.1944.[194]

The Commander of the 1st Battalion in 1941–42 was SS-Sturmbannführer Harry Polewacz. He was an early member of the NSDAP and was Commander of SS-Panzer-Grenadier-Regiment Westland when killed in action, 12.1.1943, at Orlowski (*Orlovskiy, Orlowsky*) near Rostov.[195] On 8.9.1942 he was awarded the Finnish Order of the Cross of Liberty, 3rd Class.[196]

After the war, Felix Steiner told a story of how SS-Sturmbannführer Walter Plöw, Commander of the 3rd Battalion, played a kind of a theatrical trick at the front in the Rostov-by-Don area in October 1941. The Battalion fought Soviet tanks with 'Molotov Cocktails'. Steiner recalled how:

> Plöw, who had gained a taste for liquor, allowed himself to play, shall we say, a simpleton trick (*Schildbürgerstück*) on the enemy. At the next attack he encountered a Soviet tank, which came upon him from behind sand dunes as he was sitting in his staff car with the Finns. As he had nothing but a bottle of cognac to hand, Plöw raised the cognac bottle as if he was about to sling it like a Molotov cocktail. At this gesture, the tank turned around and departed.[197]

In Sagopshi in September 1942, Plöw was very nervous and drinking heavily together with the Commander of SS-Regiment Nordland, Fritz von Scholz.[198]

THE SS-REGIMENT WESTLAND

SS-Infanterie-Regiment Westland was formed in the summer of 1940 after the German campaign in the West.[199] A report on the personnel strength dated 29.6.1941 lists the regimental strength as 3,756: 2,875 Germans, 85 Danes, 661 Dutch, 69 Finns, 52 Flemish, two Norwegians, and two Swiss volunteers.[200] A few Swedish volunteers also served in the Regiment.[201] Despite the above figures, the actual number of Finnish volunteers serving was 82: five officers and 77 men.[202] At least ten Norwegian volunteers served in Westland in the course of the summer of 1941, the total number being rather insignificant.[203] Barely a quarter of the total complement were foreigners.

The Commander of the 1st Battalion was SS-Sturmbannführer Hans-Joachim "Hajo" Freiherr von Hadeln. He joined the NSDAP in 1931 and characterised himself as driven by "fanatical National Socialism". He presented his doctoral thesis in 1935 on the essence of National Socialist world history as expressed in the movement's leaders. A part of SS-Regiment Westland on 27.2.1942 was seriously ambushed at Sagopshi near of Malgobek, with many casualties. It was a dark and ghastly day in this "valley of death", as the place became known. Von Hadeln was said to have experienced a nervous breakdown. "He sat all night crying as the bodies of those men killed in action were retrieved by the Battalion medics", noted SS-Obersturmführer Kaj Duncker of the SS-Artillerie-Regiment 5. Among those who perished were five Finnish volunteers.[204] Later, von Hadeln was himself 12.1.1943 killed in action (shot by a Soviet sniper, along with SS-Sturmbannführer Harry Polewacz) at Orlowski near Rostov.

In June 1941, the Commander of the Regiment was SS-Standartenführer Hilmar Wäckerle. He joined the NSDAP in 1922 and he participated in the so-called Beer Hall Putsch (*Bürgerbräu-Putsch*) in Munich on 8.–9.11.1923, and in the assassination of Franz Josef Heinz, the Prime Minister of the French-administered "Autonomous Palatinate" in the Rhineland, in January 1924. In 1933, Wäckerle functioned as the Commander of the newly-established Dachau concentration camp for a few months. As a Camp Commander he installed terror as a way of life at the camp.[205] The Reichsführer-SS Heinrich Himmler removed Wäckerle in June 1933 owing to the furore caused by arbitrary killings in the Dachau camp.[206] Wäckerle was killed in action in the village of Novosilky, in the Lviv Oblast, on 2.7.1941.

The new Regimental Commander after Wäckerle was Karl Diebitsch, although he served only a few days. Diebitsch joined the NSDAP in 1920 and appears to have been a party member up to 1925, when he went to complete his art training. He worked as a designer and drew up much of the SS regalia, such as the distinctive chained SS-officer's dagger scabbard, and in 1932 he drafted together with graphic designer Walter Heck the all-black SS uniform. Diebitsch also was the Head of SS porcelain manufacturer Allach and Reichsführer-SS Heinrich Himmler's adviser on art matters. He rejoined the NSDAP in 1937 and became a Professor in 1939. From that year he also received staff assignments to the SS-Totenkopfstandarte 11 and the SS-Regiment Germania. Diebitsch had sympathies for the Finnish volunteers, and the son of the Recruitment Chief Esko Riekki, SS-Untersturmführer Tero Riekki, appears for a while to have served as an Adjutant of Diebitsch.[207]

SS-Oberführer Artur Gustav Martin Phleps (he also used his mother's maiden name of Stolz) was the Regiment's Commander from 5.7.1941–30.11.1942. He originated from Siebenbürgen (Transsylvania), a German Volksdeutscher area in Romania, and was a former Romanian General. Phleps enlisted in the Waffen-SS under his mother's maiden name Stolz, but started after some time to use the name Phleps once again.[208] In the fall of 1942 he took command of the new SS-Freiwilligen-Division "Prinz Eugen", which engaged in actions against the Yugoslav partisans in Croatia. Under his command, reprisals against the partisans were widespread and his units destroyed numerous villages.[209] Phleps was captured by advancing Soviet forces in Romania in September 1944. He was shot dead on 21.9.1944 by the guards as the prisoners tried to escape during an air attack.[210] At the Nuremberg Military Tribunals, he would have faced prosecution by the Yugoslav authorities for war crimes in Montenegro dating from the end of May 1943, and the court record states:

> The officers and men of the SS-Division Prinz Eugen committed crimes of such outrageous cruelty on this occasion. The victims were shot, slaughtered and tortured, or burnt to death in

burning houses (...) It has been established from the investigations entered upon that 121 persons, mostly women, and including 30 persons aged 60–92 years and 29 children of ages ranging from 6 months to 14 years, were executed on this occasion in the horrible manner narrated above. The villages (...) were burnt down and razed to the ground.

Among the officers responsible, Phleps was mentioned first.[211]

THE SS-REGIMENT GERMANIA

The regiment was formed in 1934 and in 1936 given the name SS-Infanterie-Regiment Germania. In the fall of 1939, the regiment participated in the march into Poland, and in late 1940 became a part of SS-Division Wiking. Nine Finnish officers served in the SS-Regiment Germania. In the summer of 1941, a total of 34 Norwegians served in the 2nd Company and 31 in the 3rd Company.[212] A few Swedish volunteers also belonged to the unit.[213] The regiment was almost completely composed of Reich Germans and ethnic Germans (*Volksdeutsche*).

The Commander of 1st Battalion was SS-Sturmbannführer August Dieckmann.[214] He joined the NSDAP in 1937 and in 1943 was Commander of SS-Standarte Westland. He was killed in action in Ukraine, on an island of the River Dnieper, on 10.10.1943. The Commander of the 2nd Battalion was SS-Sturmbannführer Wolfgang Joerchel. In 1934, he became the military sports leader (*Wehrsportführer*) of the Hitler Jugend organisation and participated in the march into Poland in the fall of 1939 as an officer of SS-Regiment Germania. He later joined the Regiment again and served in other SS-Regiments and Divisions. He died in Prague in obscure circumstances on 12.5.1945.[215] On 15.3.1943, Joerchel was awarded the Finnish Order of the Cross of Liberty, 3rd Class.[216]

The Commander of the Regiment from December 1940 to June 1942 was SS-Standartenführer (and later SS-Oberführer) Karl Ferdinand Joseph Ritter von Oberkamp. After the war, the Yugoslav authorities named von Oberkamp as the second responsible officer for the atrocities taking place at the end of May 1943 in Montenegro. The first was Phleps.[217]

SS-ARTILLERIE-REGIMENT 5

The founding of the SS-Artillerie-Regiment 5 took place during the fall of 1940, formed by the Staff of the Command Department (*Kommandoamt*) of the Waffen-SS. It was trained and equipped in Übungslager Dachau.[218] The Regiment was almost entirely composed of Reich Germans and ethnic Germans. However, seven Finnish officers belonged to the unit. Around 50 Norwegian SS-volunteers also served in the unit.[219]

SS-Standartenführer Herbert Gille was Commander of this unit, serving from 1940–43.[220] Gille was regarded as a dedicated and professional soldier by his fellow Waffen-SS and Wehrmacht generals. Throughout his service in the Waffen-SS, he was keen to give the impression of being a committed soldier with no particular interest in either politics or the ideology of National Socialism. Consequently, he was not a member of the NSDAP and even maintained a certain distance to the *Bonze* (party hacks).

Gille's subordinate, SS-Sturmbannführer Ernst Fick, visited him in January 1942 in his capacity as SS-Division Wiking "ideological observer" or political indoctrination officer (*Weltanschauungsoffizier*), and Gille made it plain that he was not welcome. Moreover, during a conversation with Gille in front of several persons, Fick criticised his colleague for the lack of any ideological instruction for the SS-Artillerie-Regiment and insufficient National Socialist attitude displayed by Gille and his staff officers. Gille had then demonstratively announced to the assembled officers that "Wearing a brown shirt is not permitted in the aristocratic Artillery Regiment. I'll put a clean-out squad in your room". This was a response to Fick, who was wearing a brown SA-shirt, whereupon Fick departed in a huff. After the incident he reported Gille's poor attitude to SS-Obergruppenführer Karl Wolff on the Staff of Reichsführer-SS Heinrich Himmler. Nothing came of it, however, possibly owing to Steiner's intervention on Gille's behalf.[221]

Gille's career did not suffer, as later he was appointed Commander of the SS-Division Wiking and then of IV SS-Panzer Corps. Eventually he become one of the most highly decorated members of the German armed forces.[222] On 15.3.1943, Gille was awarded the Finnish Order of the Cross of Liberty, 1st Class.[223] The Norwegian newspaper *Aftenposten* ran a piece on Gille in April 1944, after he had received an exclusive decoration. The article stated:

> Every time when it mattered, he suddenly popped up and calmly handled the most difficult situations in a cool manner. He was never agitated, always exemplarily calm. He had no nerves at all (...) He is a man of firm duty, a soldier without fear or faults, an uncompromising National Socialist personality. SS-Gruppenführer Herbert Gille is one of the Führer's best soldiers.[224]

The outstanding qualities attributed here to Gille are likely to have been exaggerated. Interestingly, despite his not formally being a Party member, Gille was nevertheless characterised as a committed National Socialist and one of the most loyal supporters of Hitler. Gille survived the war, was released from captivity in 1948, and in 1951 became one of the leaders of HIAG (*Hilfsgemeinschaft auf Gegenseitigkeit der Angehörigen der ehemaligen Waffen-SS*), the veterans' main lobby group and revisionist organisation.[225]

The 1st Abteilung of the SS-Artillerie-Regiment 5 was under command of SS-Sturmbannführer Ernst Fick. Fick joined the NSDAP in 1929 and in 1931 became Local Group Leader (*Ortsgruppenleiter*) of the Party in Spiegelau, Gau Niederbayern. Later he held positions in various Luftwaffe and SS-units with an emphasis on National Socialist education of the personnel. In the spring of 1941, he joined SS-Artillerie-Regiment 5 to acquaint himself with how the Division worked (*zur informatorischen Dienstleistung*). Despite his quarrel with the Regimental Commander Gille, Fick's career was rising and in January 1944 he was promoted SS-Brigadeführer und Generalmajor der Waffen-SS. Fick died (shot in his car by U.S. troops) on 29.4.1945 in Murnau am Staffelsee.[226]

Fick was replaced at the head of SS-Artillerie-Regiment 5 by SS-Sturmbannführer Paul-Albert "Peter" Kausch, who in 1941–43 had served as the Adjutant to the Division Commander Felix Steiner during the advance to Rostov, Krasnodar, Maikop (*Majkop, Maykop*), and the Terek River area. Kausch joined the NSDP in 1933, served in the SS-Division Totenkopf, and in the spring of 1941 transferred to SS-Artillerie-Regiment 5 of SS-Division Wiking. On 21.10.1942, he was awarded the Finnish Order of the Cross of Liberty, 3rd Class.[227] Later he served in other SS units and became a POW in Soviet custody, 1945–56.[228]

SS-Sturmbannführer Constantin Heldmann, the Commander of the 4th Abteilung, joined the NSDAP in 1931 and served as an Officer in SS-Division Totenkopf 1939–41, SS-Division Wiking in 1941, SS-Division Nord at Kiestinki (Karelia) 1941, and the SS-Ersatz-Regiment in 1942. In 1942–43, he was in charge of acquisition of complementary personnel for the Finnish SS-Volunteer-Battalion and was then Chief of the SS-Verbindungsstab Finnland in Helsinki.[229]

SS-AUFKLÄRUNGS-ABTEILUNG 5

The SS-Aufklärungs-Abteilung 5 included four Companies. A total of 43 Finnish SS-volunteers served in the unit: four officers and 39 men.[230] Also Norwegian SS-volunteers served in the unit.[231] Among the Finnish volunteers, the unit was jokingly called the "Fifth Column" (*Viides kolonna*) as an allusion to the Number 5.[232] The Commander during 1940–42 was SS-Hauptsturmführer Hans-Albin Freiherr von Reitzenstein.[233] He committed suicide on 30.11.1943 after involvement in the rape and death of a Russian volunteer (*Hilfswilliger*, Hiwi) of the Waffen-SS.[234]

SS-PANZERJÄGER-ABTEILUNG 5

The Panzer-Jägerabteilung 5 was composed of three Companies. The number of Finns in the unit was 44, four officers and 40 men.[235] Around 30 volunteers from Norway also served in the unit.[236] The Commander was SS-Brigadeführer Berthold Maack.[237] He joined the NSDAP in 1930. In the summer of 1934, Maack participated in the arrests and executions carried out in suppressing the Ernst Röhm wing of the SA and in the fall of 1934, he worked as an officer at the Dachau concentration camp. Maack has been characterised as an excellent combat commander, who took great care in looking after the men under his command.[238]

Finnish SS-volunteer Rolf Labbart throwing a hand grenade. *Jukka Tyrkkö Coll. FWM.*

THE FINNISH SS-VOLUNTEER BATTALION

The Finnish SS-volunteers – numbering around 1,200 men recruited in the spring of 1941 – were transported from Finland to Stettin by ship during May and early June 1941. The *SS-Freiwilligen-Bataillon Nordost* was formed on 15.6.1941. However, as the bulk of the Finnish SS-volunteers were inexperienced and undrilled, they were sent to basic training during the following months. The Battalion was renamed on 13.9.1941 as *Finnisches-Freiwilligen Bataillon der Waffen-SS,* with a strength of 1,180 members. – However, of these a minor part were Germans. The Battalion was drilled in several training centres, initially in June 1941 in the Schönbrunn Barracks area at Vienna. In July it transferred to Stralsund and in August 1941 to the large training ground in Gross Born, situated between Stettin and Danzig. On 3.12.1941, the Battalion moved from Gross Born to the Soviet Union and in the winter attached to SS-Division Wiking, who were in holding positions along the River Mius (Mius-Front). The Finnish newcomers were included in the SS-Regiment Nordland, initially from 16.2.1942 as an extra 4th Battalion (IV (finn.)/Nordland) and from 20.5.1942 as the 3rd Battalion (III (finn.)/Nordland). After that a popular name for the Battalion became "Dritte Nordland".[239]

SS-Hauptsturmführer Hans Collani had been appointed Battalion Commander in the spring of 1941, and he held this position to July 1943 when the unit was dissolved. Collani joined the NSDAP in 1932 and was assigned to the Leibstandarte SS Adolf Hitler in 1933. He served as the Adjutant to the notorious Leibstandarte Commander, SS-Gruppenführer Josef "Sepp" Dietrich in 1935–39. On 8.9.1942, Collani received the Finnish Order of the Cross of Liberty, 3rd Class.[240] Division Commander Felix Steiner admitted that Collani "was perhaps not so successful from the psychological viewpoint". However, Steiner knew him well, as he had served under him in his Regiment. In his opinion, the Finnish Volunteer Battalion was "in good hands". Steiner would have preferred a Staff Officer from the Division rather than Collani, but as Battalion Com-

SS-Obersturmbannführer Hans Collani was appointed Commander of the Finnish Volunteer Battalion of the SS-Division Wiking during training in Vienna on 15.6.1941, and was in this position until the disbanding of the Battalion in July 1943. *OW Coll.*

mander, Collani had coped well, and as Steiner believed, had gradually acquired "the full trust" of the Finnish volunteers. Among the Finnish volunteers themselves, the dominant view was that Collani remained distant, and poorly understood "the Finnish mind".[241] At the front in 1942, he was known for loving good food and spirits.[242] Collani served for ten years as a SS-Hauptsturmführer before he was promoted SS-Sturmbannführer in 1942, and in 1943 he became SS-Obersturmbannführer. He committed suicide on 29.7.1944, as he was about to be overrun by Soviet forces in the battles in Eastern Estonia near Narva. Collani was posthumously appointed SS-Standartenführer and was also awarded the Iron Cross (*Ritterkreuz des eisernen Kreuzes*) after his death.[243]

THE FINNISH CONTINGENT OF THE WAFFEN-SS

The Finnish volunteers made up only a small fraction of the Waffen-SS forces. Of around 900,000 SS men in arms, the share of 1,400 Finnish volunteers represented less than 0.2%, and in the summer and fall of 1941 the share of the Finnish volunteers in SS-Division Wiking corresponded to around 2%. In the winter of 1942, the share rose for a while to perhaps around 5%, as the Finnish SS-Volunteer Battalion was then incorporated into the Division in the East. Finnish volunteers served in the ranks as enlisted men and although some 30 Finnish officers belonged to the volunteers, these did not carry out troop commands and were simply observers. The first Finnish Company Commander was not put in place until March 1942.[244]

Only a minority of Finnish volunteers were deployed at the front. Hypothetically, the Finnish volunteers in 1941–43 represented a service effort of around 33,600 soldiering months, of which a fifth were carried out in frontline service.[245] By noting these circumstances, it is quite clear that the general role of the Finnish volunteers in the advance into the Soviet Union was not, broadly speaking, of any great significance.

THE DIVISION COMMANDER FELIX STEINER

The Commander of SS-Division Wiking from late 1940 was Felix Steiner[246], who had on 9.11.1940 been promoted SS-Brigadeführer und Generalmajor der Waffen-SS. Being a member of the SA[247], his career developed well after the *Machtübernahme* in 1933. He left the Reichswehr and joined the SS in 1935, becoming a SS-Standartennführer and Commander of the SS-Regiment Deutschland in 1936. Later, he was appointed SS-Gruppenführer and Generalleutnant des Waffen-SS (1.1.1942) and finally SS-Obergruppenführer und General des Waffen-SS (1.7.1943).[248]

Steiner has been characterised as "a conservative idealist and an eminent army leader".[249] However, Steiner's reputation and personal image do not quite match the common type of Waffen-SS Commander. Steiner has been reckoned as corresponding to a Wehrmacht general.[250] It is not quite clear when he joined the NSDAP. This appears to have happened in 1937 and he received Nazi Party number 4,264,295.[251] Thus he was not a so-called *Altkämpfer* ("Old Warrior") – one of those who had been members of the Party already before January 1933.

As a Waffen-SS Commander, Steiner introduced a creative training and operations concept, which combined emphasis on the athletic quality of the volunteers, enabling 'shock troop' (*Stosstruppe*) tactics, convenient motor transport facilities, and weighty firepower. He is credited with developing successful assault tactics and with reliance on heavy infantry firepower in small unit engagements, which formed a sort of Waffen-SS power-action signature style. Steiner's physical approach rather combined recruits' training in athletics and sports with traditional parade-ground drills.[252] Steiner did not reject the traditional Prussian "*Kadaverdisciplin*", meaning an extremely strict and unquestioned discipline,[253] although the training was geared towards operations carried out by force, speed, and individual and unit commitment.

In the view of Kenneth Estes, Steiner proved to be "a progressive, intuitive and enthusiastic officer who stressed leadership by example and the maintenance of high morale among the troops. His persuasive enthusiasm and sensitivity to the disparate national characteristics of his foreign troops and the new volunteers made him an ideal choice as the Commander of the first multi-national unit in the German armed forces". To Steiner, "the Western volunteer phenomenon had deeper psychological foundations" that reflected "the spiritual crisis of European youth". "Disenchanted with the nationalism of their fathers, they would prove responsive to Steiner's characterisation of a common European culture and heritage as a binding force in the Wiking Division". Estes continues: "Steiner's innovative grasp of military leadership principles probably led him to accentuate a pan-Germanic or European bond among his men in order to establish unit integrity and cohesion". However, there was also considerable rhetoric and no little hot air in the European and pan-Germanic vision. The numbers of Western volunteers remained quite modest in comparison to the home population of the Waffen-SS units, to the deep disappointment of the prime visionaries of the SS-volunteer program like Gottlob Berger, Felix Steiner, Franz Riedweg, and Heinrich Himmler.[254]

However, systematic efforts were also made to reinforce the mental spirit of the soldiers: building soldierly character, promoting self-confidence by belonging to an elite unit, fearlessness, prestige, and comradeship steeled by common hardships. The experiences of the efforts of the Division Leibstandarte SS Adolf Hitler, the SS-Division Das Reich, and the SS-Division Totenkopf during the march into Poland in 1939 were applied. In analysing the cohesive and creative factors of the Waffen-SS units, Steiner concluded:

> An extensive interest in the welfare of the troops and the cultivation of the feeling of comradeship increased the already close feeling of unity among the ranks. It strengthened the spiritual unity of the troops and the confidence between the officers and men.[255]

As Steiner's so-called "dynamic" troop concept appeared successful, it soon influenced other SS divisions. Nevertheless, the concept did not become a dominant model in training the Waffen-SS units.[256] Although Steiner's training concept highlighted physical fitness and individual initiative to produce the "hunter-poacher", athlete type of soldier, British historian Adrian Weale has remarked that this was nothing new. In fact, the *Jäger* (hunter) warrior, i.e. a handy and fast-moving light infantry soldier, was as such firmly entrenched within the long German military tradition. Whereas the Jäger detachments usually operated as specialists in relatively small units, Steiner's innovation was to apply this concept to the conduct of regular and heavier infantry units:

> Even so, the Special Purpose "Troops" training was not revolutionary; it simply focused on producing the kind of adaptable soldiers demanded by Steiner. All of its elements would have been entirely familiar to most professional soldiers of the period.[257]

The essence of Steiner's philosophy on military training and education is expressed in his brief monologue on military leadership and training, "*Menschenführung und Erziehung im Kriege*", written on 22.1.1942: "The basic presupposition of a reasonable, human leadership is the indefatigable and continuous care by the superiors of their subordinates". The task of the officer was to achieve the complete trust of their dependents and be recognised as a true comrade. As a consequence, this required a decent, human, and benevolent treatment of the men in the ranks: "The crew shall love him. Every Chief must beyond this be firmly attached to his troops. In particular, the platoon and company commanders must be present among the crew, appear as an example and a confidant concerning all issues, and never distance himself as a human from his men".[258] Steiner thus completely rejected the strong arrogant tradition of the German officers' corps, but not the traditional practice of firm discipline.

There is a set of connections between Steiner and Finland, as all of the Finnish SS-volunteers in the spring of 1941 were included in his Division. Steiner also showed much considerable personal interest in the Finnish volunteers and in maintaining Finnish contacts. In 1941–43, he was in close contact with the Finnish Liaison Officer, SS-Obersturmbannführer Kalervo Kurkiala. Steiner invited Kurkiala for supper on 10.12.1941, where the mass shooting of Jews was discussed and at another supper on 29.5.1942 the typical conversation topics were race, reciprocal actions between nationalities, and National Socialism.[259] Also faith and church issues were topics of common interest.[260] The representative of the Finnish Headquarters, Lieutenant-General Paavo Talvela twice visited Steiner at the Mius-Front, on 16.–22.5 and 20.–22.10.1942. The visit included inspections, excursions, concerts, social parties with caviar, shellfish, Crimean champagne, and Finnish sauna baths. Several of the subordinate commanders also took part: Herbert Gille, Karl Diebitsch, Harry Polewacz, Fritz von Scholz, Paul-Albert Kausch, and Hans Collani.[261] Also Lieutenant-General Harald Öhquist inspected the Finnish volunteers in late August 1941 and visited Steiner and his commanders at the Mius-Front on 27.–28.8.1942.[262]

Steiner was awarded the Finnish Order of the Cross of Liberty, 1st Class on 8.9.1942.[263] He visited Finland in early June 1943 and met prominent decision-makers, including the President Risto Ryti, the Minister of Defence Karl Rudolf Walden, the Foreign Minister Henrik Ramsay, Major-General Aaro Pajari, and the Finnish C-in-C, Field Marshal Gustaf Mannerheim.[264] Before the Finnish SS-Volunteer Battalion was dissolved in July 1943, Steiner had made continuous efforts not only to prolong the service of the Battalion, but also to expand it. He is reported to have been saddened that his plans were not realised.[265] As late as August 1944, the Foundation of the III. (Germ.) SS-Panzer-Korps under Steiner decided to support the relief of injured volunteers operated by the Finnish association *SS-Aseveljet r.y.* (SS-Brothers-in-Arms) with one million Finnish Markka.[266] However, as the Finnish-German relations were severed in early September 1944, the money support never arrived.

Steiner reported extensively in 1941–43 to the SS-Hauptamt (SS-HA) and the Reichsführer-SS Heinrich Himmler about his Finnish experiences. He included a travel report of ten typewritten pages and an evaluation of four pages on the leading military and political personalities in Finland: the C-in-C Carl Gustaf Emil Mannerheim, the Lieutenant-Generals Lauri Malmberg, Hugo Österman, and Harald Öhquist, President Risto Ryti, Minister Henrik Ramsay, and the President of the so-called official SS-Committee, the Rector of Helsinki University Rolf Nevanlinna. On Mannerheim he wrote:

> The Marshal represents without doubt the archetype of the old Czarist Guard General in his total intolerance and subtle scheming. He has also taken over certain control of reporting practices at this time (...) Occasionally from political and military parties this suggests that his operative skills are not judged very highly. Of a dominating nature, leaning towards rigidity with "despotic" personal whims.

In contrast to his views on Mannerheim, the other six evaluated personalities received positive reviews.[267]

In October 1952, around 5,000 former members of the SS gathered in the City of Verden an der Aller at a mass rally, for the first time since the end of WWII. The conference was summoned with the permission of the Ministry of Interior of the Niedersachsen government. In advance, Steiner negotiated with the British City Commandant, who approved the arrangements. The first national "Traditionsverband" of the Waffen-SS was introduced in 1951 when the regular mouthpiece *Der Wiking-Ruf* journal was first published. In Verden, the members organised themselves according to their old units. One of the main issues of the conference of the former

Evangelical-Lutheran pastor and SS-Sturmbannführer Kalervo Kurkiala (left) with SS-Sturmbannführer Erwin Reichel in the summer 1942. Kurkiala was one of the few supporters of National Socialist ideology among the Finnish SS-volunteers. However, he did not share the atheistic views commonly held among the Nazis. *OW Coll.*

8 — N:o 36 — 1944 RINTAMAMIES Perjantaina syyskuun 8. p:nä

ϟϟ-ASEVELJET

An association for the Finnish SS-volunteers, SS-Aseveljet r.y., was established on 1.11.1942 as a link between the volunteers. The Chairman was SS-Obersturmbannführer Kalervo Kurkiala and war correspondent Jukka Tyrkkö (far right) also a SS-volunteer, was appointed as Secretary. The association was banned, along with other "pro-Hitler organisations (of a Fascist type)" in the Moscow Armistice between Finland and the Soviet Union in September 1944. *JT Coll., FWM.*

members of Waffen-SS was establishing an Army of 12 Divisions in the Bundesrepublik Deutschland. The Western Allies approved all this, and in 1951 Steiner became one of the leaders of the *Hilfsgemeinschaft auf Gegenseitigkeit der Angehörigen der ehemaligen Waffen-SS* (HIAG, a revisionist lobby group and mutual aid association of former Waffen-SS members).[268]

In 1952 Steiner participated in the establishment of the *Gesellschaft für Wehrkunde* (Association for Military Science) and was appointed Vice President of the association. The enterprise was supported by the U.S. Military Academy West Point. The society became crucial in preparing the eventual establishment of the Bundeswehr in 1955. However, the leading politicians of the Bundesrepublik Deutschland were not overly eager to have any former SS-General as the figurehead of these military efforts, and Steiner withdrew, embittered at the slight.[269]

Steiner visited Finland in August 1956 as a guest of *Veljesapu r.y.* (Brothers' Aid, a veterans' association). This charitable organisation was established in 1955 as a successor to the *SS-Aseveljet r.y* (SS-Brothers-in-Arms), which existed from 1942–44. There are several photos documenting the visit: one photo of Steiner in the company of Unto Parvilahti on the airfield and others from a party at the Finnish Officer's Casino at Katajanokka in Helsinki, Steiner meeting Ruth Munck at the Leponiemi Manor[270], and Steiner visiting the military cemetery in Seinäjoki.[271] There was also a meeting between Steiner and a former SS-volunteer living in the region of Southern Ostrobothnia, in Hotel Kino in Seinäjoki.[272] A *Kameradschaft-Abend* with Steiner was held in the *Teatteriravintola* restaurant in the City of Tampere on 6.8.1956, and he visited the local groups of former Finnish SS-volunteers in Jyväskylä and Lahti.[273]

THE REGIMENT AND BATTALION COMMANDERS

In the overview, a total of 26 Regiment, Battalion, and similar Commanders of the SS-Division Wiking in the summer of 1941 (including the Division Commander) have been briefly examined. As a whole, these present a very tough image: at least eleven were members of the NSDAP,[274] but the number was probably greater because information is missing on a few commanding officers. Research indicates that three-quarters of the SS Generals joined the NSDAP prior to 1933, and a further fifth after the Party took power. No precise figures are available on the Waffen-SS officers commanding the regiments and battalions in the field, but as these officers were relatively young, the Party membership may have exceeded that of the Generals.[275] German historian Martin Cüppers has analysed a sample of 101 officers of the Kommandostab Reichsführer-SS and the 1. SS-Brigade. It is not clear how representative these were for the SS complex as a whole, but of the officers belonging to these units, 94% were party members. Of these, almost 2/3 were so called "Old Warriors", i.e. they had joined the party before 1933.[276] In comparison with these, the rate of NSDAP membership among the leading Commanders of the SS-Division Wiking was hence considerably lower.

Of the 26 Commanders examined in this presentation, no fewer than eleven were killed in action[277], and a further two committed suicide while in uniform.[278] Thus as many as a half of the commanding officers perished in the field. As a comparison, 253,000 members of the Waffen-SS were killed in action or disappeared at the front. Of a total of 0.9–1.0 million SS-men, this would correspond to 25–28%.[279] Around 40% of them were killed in action, whereas the suicide rate appears to correspond to the common pattern. In his study of 105 Waffen-SS army corps and division commanders, historian Mark Yerger has observed that some 11% of them committed suicide by the end of the war.[280]

At least seven of the Commanders had prior to their service in the Waffen-SS been engaged in the Sturmabteilung (SA) movement.[281] However, the actual number of former SA-officers was probably greater. It should be noted nevertheless that some of them may have just been members, rather than active in the SA and commissioned as SA-Führern.

Two of the Commanders, Hilmar Wäckerle and Berthold Maack, were leading officials at the Dachau concentration camp in 1933–34. Also Artur Phleps may have had some connection to the camp, as he lived in Dachau in 1933–34. According to his personal Lebenslauf he held a position as "HW-Dachau",[282] which may be an abbreviation for Heimwehr, i.e. Home Guard. Historian French L. MacLean has carried out a study on some 900 German officers who served in the National Socialist camp system. A total of 45 concentration camp officers served in SS-Division Wiking.[283] As the officers of the division numbered 528 in June 1941, this means that some 8% had served in a concentration camp.[284]

In particular, representatives of the post-war Waffen-SS rehabilitation movement have claimed a fundamental qualitative difference between on the one hand the Allgemeine SS and the SS-Totenkopfverbände, and on the other hand the SS-Verfüngstruppen and combat units of the Waffen-SS combat units, such as the SS-Division Wiking. However, current studies do not weigh the differences as being very decisive. In Finland, Mauno Jokipii certainly underlined the distinction[285], whereas André Swanström has tended to understand them as a more or less coherent entity.[286] According to his results, 43% of these concentration camp officers served in the Waffen-SS combat units either before or after their service in the camps.[287]

At least Felix Steiner, Alfred Schade, and Artur Phleps (Stolz) have, according to documentary sources, ordered or participated in atrocities. Two of the surviving commanders, Felix Steiner and Herbert Gille, rose to leading roles in the HIAG in the post-war period. At least three were heavy drinkers.[288] The picture, however, is not complete, as further details on a few commanding officers are missing. It can be noted that whereas a total of 167 German Generals were executed by the Allies,[289] none of these served in SS-Division Wiking.

It can be said that Steiner exerted considerable influence in selecting the Regimental and Battalion Commanders to his Division. This influence is likely to have been crucial, although not exclusive. In late 1940 it was Steiner who decided on the choice of Herbert Gille as Commander of the SS-Artillerie-Regiment 5. There were two other candidates for the post, but Steiner persuaded Reichsführer SS Himmler to appoint Gille.[290] In Ukraine in late August 1941, Steiner ordered SS-Obersturmbannführer Paul-Albert "Peter" Kausch to take command of SS-Artillerie-Regiment 5.[291] However, it can reasonably be presumed that a similar pattern occurred with the appointment of the other Regimental Commanders and also the Battalion Commanders. The Kommandoamt der Waffen-SS certainly played a role in the appointments, partly as a tool of the SS-Reichsführer Heinrich Himmler, who personally interfered in individual appointments. Nevertheless, Steiner's role is likely to have been pivotal and his continuous influence on appointments to leading command posts in his Division remained strong.

The general profile of Regimental and Battalion Commanders of SS-Division Wiking not only reflects the personal qualities of these commanders, but also Steiner's preferences and choices. Steiner certainly wanted a superior, decent and cultivated role for his Division leadership, obviously in company with his most loyal associate Herbert Gille. However, he did not extend this system to his independent sub-unit commanders. On the contrary, he must here have preferred the rough-and-tumble commanders (*Durchdränger*), i.e. tough-skinned, hard-boiled, and battle-hardened men: career officers, former SA- and concentration camp commanders, NSDAP members, and generally individuals who were not inclined to handle matters with kid gloves on.

The active use of these commanders made it possible for Steiner to deploy his Division in subduing the resistant elements among the local civilians and getting rid of Jews, Soviet officials, Communists and POWs, while at the same time keeping a personal distance to these repressive actions. To a considerable degree, it can be assumed that Steiner directed the various steps of persecution in an informal and veiled way. The various violent acts occurred without any visible participation from the Division Commander. Further light on Steiner's role in this respect will be shone more extensively later in this report.

THE HARSH GERMAN OCCUPATION POLICY IN POLAND, 1939–40

The German onslaught on Poland in the fall of 1939 and the consequent occupation of western districts of the country were of a very severe and brutal character. There is a parallel with the German offensive into the Soviet Union in the summer of 1941, as a similar policy was carried out when areas were occupied. U.S. historian Alexander B. Rossino concluded that the German invasion of Poland in 1939 was a catastrophe of unparalleled proportions for all inhabitants of the country, Gentile as well as Jewish.[292] During the first 56 days of the occupation, a total of 16,376 civilians perished in 714 separate executions, while 531 towns and villages were razed to the ground. Of these executions, approximately 60% were carried out by ordinary Wehrmacht forces, and the rest by various German Police (e.g. Ordnungspolizei) and SS-units.[293] The Germans captured some 694,000 Polish POWs.[294] A Polish military estimate claims that approximately 100,000 civilians were murdered or otherwise lost their lives during the hostilities in the fall of 1939.[295]

During the war years, an average of approximately 400,000 ordinary German troops were stationed in the Polish areas, and an additional 50,000 police and SS-men. The ordinary forces were involved in a merciless and systematical campaign of persecution and destruction.[296] The German historian Peter Longerich reports Waffen-SS and Army units shot thousands of civilians during the 1939 campaign, often in the course of retaliation measures against supposed or actual attacks on German forces. In September 1939, more than 16,000 people fell victim to such executions, but also German Self-Defence Corps (*Volkdeutscher Selbstschutz*) – integrated later into the Order Police (*Ordnungspolizei*) and Einsatzgruppen – actively participated in such measures.[297] It can be noted that Felix Steiner participated in the Polish campaign in the fall of 1939 as the Commander of the SS-Regiment Deutschland.

The Polish population under German rule was about 21.8 million people, of which 16 million were gathered in the General Government (Ger. *Generalgouvernement*) in the centre and south. As a consequence of the harsh German occupation policy, Poland as a nation was systematically destroyed. Between 1939 and 1944, Poland lost 6,028,000 of its citizens, of whom the bulk were Jews. Of this six million, around 644,000 Poles and others are estimated to have perished through direct military action, in individual or mass executions, or through other atrocities.[298] The remaining 5.4 million died in camps, in other forms of custody, or in other places than the areas of direct military action. A total of 2,841,500 Poles were deported to slave labour in the German Reich.[299] As the German forces occupied the Western part of Poland in the fall of 1939, some 3.3 million Jews came under German rule.[300] Approximately 550,000 Jews from the Polish areas incorporated into Greater Germany were deported to the *Generalgouvernement*.[301]

MASS KILLINGS IN UKRAINE IN 1941

In this section a review of the mass killings by German forces in Ukraine is included. The presentation covers 1) civilians, 2) Soviet partisans, 3) Red Army POWs, and 4) Soviet political commissars (*Politruks*).

CIVILIANS

From the summer of 1941 to the summer of 1942, the German forces occupied the greater part of the European Soviet Union. The population living in these occupied areas in the East under German, Romanian, Hungarian, and Italian rule has been estimated at around 90 million people. However, in those areas formerly under Soviet control, men fit for military service, i.e. several million men, were drafted into the Red Army. There was enough time for the Soviet authorities to evacuate some 16 million civilians before the arrival of the advancing German forces. The evacuation conditions were chaotic, and many Soviet citizens and others fled eastwards on their own initiative. Nevertheless, it is presumed that 55–65 million Soviet citizens came under German rule.[302] However, of these, around 20 million are likely to have been resident of those areas incorporated into the Soviet Union in 1939–40, i.e. Poles, Estonians, Latvians, and Lithuanians, as well as the local populations in Bessarabia and North Bukovina.[303]

Hence the population in the German-occupied parts of the Soviet Union can be estimated at 32–42 million – when the populations in the areas incorporated in 1939–40 are excluded. Of these 32–42 million, as many as a half may have been children, a fifth in particular elderly men and a third [adult] females. However, the German occupation caused a successive and considerable reduction of the Soviet population. Around 13.7 million Soviet civilians are estimated to have perished in the war years 1941–45. Of these, 7.4 million are believed to have been willfully killed by the Germans or their allies. In the areas occupied by the Germans, estimates put famine deaths at 4.1 million, including one million civilian losses in the siege of Leningrad and 100,000 prisoners of war included as civilians.[304] Estimates of the number of Ostarbeiter commonly brought to other places range between 3 and 5.7 million, of which as many as 2.5 million are likely to have been Ukrainians. The figure of 5.7 million clearly also include those Poles, Moldovans, and Balts who became Soviet citizens after annexation in 1939–40.[305]

In spite of the trying war operations, arriving German forces in the summer of 1941 were largely welcomed by the Ukrainian population in the western part of Ukraine. Nevertheless, the German occupation proved to be a very devastating turn, with numerous atrocities and great hardship.

The bulk of the mass killings occurred in Ukraine beyond battlefield casualties, and it is estimated that around four million Ukrainian civilians lost their lives during the German occupation of 1941–44 and that 2.3 million people were transferred to Germany as manpower and forced labour.[306] It can be noted that a Soviet estimate from the early 1960s claims 4.5 million "resistants and civilians" were killed in Ukraine during the German occupation.[307]

In Ukraine in the summer of 1941, The Wehrmacht 11th Army (*Armeeoberkommando 11, AOK 11*) was a part of the Heeresgruppe Süd. The Commander of AOK 11 was Generaloberst Eugen Ritter von Schobert. On 23.7.1941, von Schobert suggested to the Oberkommando des Heeres (OKH) that the units of the Wehrmacht and Waffen-SS should be reminded of the importance of treating loyal civilians in a good and fair manner. In an Army Order of the Day it was stated that cases of sabotage were relatively few, and those that were occurring were committed by individual Communist elements, in particular Jews. It was, the Order stressed, unwise to target the civilian population as a whole in carrying out repressive actions. Such repressive measures should target merely snipers (*Heckenschütze*). The Order explained that such perpetrators were mainly soldiers in civilian clothing. Hence the local population should not be held responsible for the deeds of the snipers.[308]

Rather earlier, on 11.6.1941, the Commander of the SS-Division Wiking, SS-Brigadeführer und Generalmajor Felix Steiner, issued his own Divisional Order on the struggle against enemy deceit and cunning. In this extensive order, Steiner declared: "The best means in every suspicious case is the discharge of one's own weapons (light fire directed into suspicious buildings), swift measures against suspicious civilians (some shots are mostly enough) and careful security steps (...) Watchfulness, sharp observation, and a reflex, early use of weapons and continuous mistrust". The order included twenty-two typical cases of suspicious acts with instructions on counter-measures, and it ended in a call to systematically observe the most intense mistrust towards opponents of foreign race.[309]

The guidelines given to the Finnish SS-Volunteer Battalion in the training centre at Gross Born in 22.9.1941 (by the non-commissioned officer Wegman), concerning the troops' behaviour towards civilians, are illustrative. In his diary, the SS-volunteer Uuno Ström noted how Wegman drilled that

> guns are to be used ruthlessly on the battlefield also against civilians, because the enemy is sly. The international laws on war are of no significance to us. It has been a great pity that the German military leaders have acted too softly (...) The enemy makes use also of women and children for giving sound signals. One may not feel any mercy towards them (...) The civilian population must with the threat of death be sworn not to report what it has witnessed. If then some resistance action occurs in some village, this will be cordoned off and shot to pieces together with the inhabitants (...) Every suspicious or dangerous building will be mercilessly destroyed along with the inhabitants (...) It is good to take hostages of value as a pledge against deception. If, however, some trickery occurs, shooting should be carried out and the village destroyed. Vigilance must be maintained that nobody from there will manage to escape.[310]

JEWS

A common accusation given by the German commanders during their advance into Soviet territory in the summer of 1941 was that Jews carried out roadside attacks against German transport columns. However, there is not much evidence that would support this claim. On the contrary, a member of the German Military Economics Department in Ukraine produced a report on the Jews. It concluded that there was "no evidence that they were widely engaged in sabotage and similar acts, nor that they could be considered to represent a threat to the German Wehrmacht".[311] Many of the small-scale roadside raids actually appear to have been organised by Soviet soldiers belonging to scattered units.

In the summer of 1941, the number of Jews living in Ukraine was c. 2.5 million, of whom 85% lived in large cities like Vinnitsa (*Vinnytsia, Winnica, Vinnica, Winniza, Vinitse*), Zhytomyr, and Kamenets-Podolsky (*Kamianets-Podilskyi, Kamieniec Podolski*).[312] By the end of 1941, a total of approximately 300,000 Jews had been killed in Ukraine.[313] Of these, altogether 38,000–39,000 Jews are believed to have been killed in Galicia and Western Ukraine in July 1941 alone.[314] It has also been estimated that Ukrainian nationalists had killed around 24,000 Jews by the end of July 1941 in the western districts of Ukraine annexed by the Soviet Union in September 1939, i.e. in Eastern Galicia and Volhynia.[315] This figure may, however, be exaggerated. In the course of all the war years, some 530,000 Jews from Galicia are estimated to have been either killed or deported to the Belzec death camp.[316]

German actions against the Jews on occupied Soviet territory included three phases. From late June 1941 to the winter of 1942, the bulk of the Jews in Belorussia, the Baltic States, and Ukraine were liquidated. In March 1942, three-quarters of all the victims of the Holocaust were still living, while a quarter had already perished. From early 1942 to the winter of 1943, the Jews of Western Belorussia and the rest of Ukraine were annihilated, along with the Polish Jews and Jews from Western and Central Europe. Finally, from early 1943 to the summer of 1944, those Jews still living in German-occupied Soviet territory were killed in the places where they lived or were transferred to the concentration camps.[317]

Shortly after the assault on the Soviet Union, the apparatus of Reichsführer-SS Heinrich Himmler stepped up its actions: Einsatzgruppen, OrPo police battalions, and the Waffen-SS units started their murderous programmes. It has been estimated that a total of approximately 600,000 Jews were killed in the first nine months of the war, from the launch of Operation Barbarossa (22.6.1941) onwards. Of the Jews in Ukraine, 1.6 million perished in the course of the war, whereas 0.9 million escaped eastwards and 0.1 million survived, either in detention or in hiding.[318] Eventually about 2.4 million Jews perished as a result of German activities in the occupied Soviet territory.[319] Of these, 450,000 to 500,000 Jews perished between 1941 and 1945 in areas controlled by the Wehrmacht.[320]

In a few days from late June to early July 1941, large-scale massacres of Jews occurred in thirty-five towns in the former Polish part of Ukraine. The largest mass slaughter was carried out over 29.–30.9.1941 in the Babi Yar ravine in Kiev, when Sonderkommando 4a and two SD and SS police battalions killed 33,771 Jews.[321] In 1941–44, SS-Einsatzgruppe C, including the Sonderkommandos 4a, 4b, 5, and 6, partly operating along the marching route of the SS-Division Wiking, killed at least 118,000 civilians and probably considerably more.[322] As early as 16.7.1941, Einsatzgruppe C,

Soldiers of the Waffen SS-Division Wiking in an Ukrainian village 1941. *Narodowe Archiwum Cyfrowe, Warsaw.*

operating in the Lemberg (*Lviv*) and Tarnopol (*Ternopil*) areas, reported back to Berlin:

> The Security Police has rounded up and shot around 7,000 Jews in reprisal for inhuman and malicious deeds committed (*Greueltäten*). A total of 73 functionaries and officials of the NKVD were investigated and shot. Forty men were released on the basis of reliable information given by the population. All Jews between 20 and 40 years were imprisoned, although craftsmen and specialists were released. Aside from these executions in Lemberg, reprisal actions have been carried out also in other places (...).[323]

This report appears, however, somewhat dubious. The actual source of the figure is not known, and 7,000 seems exaggerated.

On 2.10.1941, the staff of the Wehrmacht III. Armeekorps forwarded the directives of the Oberkommando der Wehrmacht (OKW) on the treatment of Jews (*Behandlung von Juden*) to a number of units, including the SS-Division Wiking. In these directives, OKW ordered: "Single events give reason to refer to the directives on the stance of the forces in the Soviet Union. The battle against Bolshevism demands a unreserved (*rückhaltlos*) and energetic intervention above all against the Jews, the main agent of Bolshevism".[324]

Several Norwegian volunteers have reported on the German atrocities against Jews. The Norwegian volunteer Ørnulf Bjørnstad of 12th Company, SS-Regiment Germania, recalled an entire sequence of atrocities he had witnessed. On one occasion in the summer of 1941 at an unknown place in the vicinity of Lemberg (*Lviv*), the Germans ordered 15 Jews to lie down in the bottom of a bomb crater:

> There they lay and sat on each other while the Germans shot at them with a Russian machine gun! After firing several salvoes with the machine gun, the Germans left the piles of bodies in the crater. They did not bother whether some of them were still alive down there. When the Germans had left, two wounded Jews crawled up from the crater, and started off towards the forest. They were shot, of course.

The executioners were volunteers from the 10th Company.[325]

On another occasion, volunteer Jan Taarneby of 9th Company, SS-Regiment Nordland witnessed at the end of June 1941 how Germans from his unit shot Jews, of whom there were a great many, in the village. Taarneby watched

> how the Germans ordered the Jews to dig their own graves and after that to lie down in the bottom of the grave, face downwards. A German stood astride the grave and shot a bullet through the head of the Jew. After that the next Jew was ordered to lay on the body of his recently-executed fellow – whereafter he, too, was shot. Then a third Jew was ordered to close the grave holding the two dead Jews, and after that he had to dig his own grave and lay down at the bottom of the pit – and was shot in his neck. The next Jew laid down on the previous one and was shot. The fifth Jew had to close the grave, and to dig his own grave. In this way the event continued as long as it appeared to be amusing.

Taarneby states the executioners were ordinary privates in the presence of officers, who permitted the shootings.

Bjørnstad recounted that many Jews (...) were actually buried alive. The were beaten to the ground and summarily buried. However, it turned out that they did not perish, and small grave heaps could be seen moving. These were 'living' graves of the Jews. It was terrible". He also mentioned a young Jew in early July 1941, who was forced by Ukrainian deserters to gnaw at a half-rotten horse's head, which he had to pick up from the side of the road. It stank and was in such a bad state that observers had to vomit. The Jew begged the Germans for help, but they just smiled. After gnawing at the horse's head for a while, the Jew was stabbed with a sharp spade and other things the executioners had to hand. Bjørnstad noted that a Norwegian non-commissioned officer "(...) went to the Jew and put a bullet through his head".[326] This NCO was Hans Otten, a member of 11th Company, SS-Regiment Germania. He was killed in action at Mykulyntsi (*Mikulińce, Mykulynce, Mikolintza, Mikulincie, Mikulinie, Mikulinste, Mikulintza, Mykulinski, Mykulintsi, Mykulintse, Mykulinksi, Mykylinski*) in Western Ukraine (later, *Distrikt Galizien*) on 5.7.1941.[327]

An unidentified Norwegian volunteer in a Panzer-Grenadier unit spent a few months from December 1941 in the guard detail of a camp for Soviet POWs in Kraków. There were around 20,000 prisoners in the camp. Small working parties were sent out on a daily basis away from the camp to carry out heavy and dangerous work, such as demolishing damaged buildings and removing unexploded bombs and mines. These POWs were not given any rations and were shot at least by the thousands two days later, after they had dug their own graves. There were around 2,000 Jews among the POWs, and these were ordered to clear mines. As these blew up, the Jews were torn into pieces. In the summer of 1942, the unit of this volunteer was deployed in the area south of Rostov-on-Don. Many Jews were taken into custody and some of these were employed in moving tanks on the roads: "As the tank commander eventually got tired of watching the efforts of the Jews to move these colossuses, he shouted to the driver: 'Go ahead'. The driver carried out the order and 'stepped on the gas' and the Jews were crushed beyond recognition."[328]

PARTISANS

At the beginning of the war on 22.6.1941, small detachments of Soviet partisans operated in German-occupied areas. Following the initial German assault, scattered Soviet units and large detachments of Red Army soldiers were outflanked and cut off from their units. Parts of these turned to disorganised resistance, and to some extent these troops were successful in carrying out small-scale surprise attacks. Harrassed by frequent incursions of this kind, one regimental commander from the SS-Totenkopf-Division ordered that the straggler Soviet soldiers were to be regarded as partisans, and so merited ruthless treatment. As a consequence, the SS-units "shot the majority of the Russian stragglers they encountered", regardless of whether they offered resistance or not.[329]

An organised partisan movement did not emerge in Ukraine until 1942. However, the then First Secretary of the Central Committee of the Communist Party of Ukraine Nikita Khrushchev addressed this issue as early as 6.7.1941, asking Ukrainians to begin a resistance struggle against the occupying German forces. This was taken up and 133 partisan groups were claimed to have been formed by mid-July 1941. Including the areas that had not yet been occupied, 122 partisan units (*Partisanenabteilungen*) were established in Ukraine with 5,809 members, and 69 "diversionist groups" with 743 members. During 1941, around 800 Communists infiltrated Ukraine and 23 illegal regional committees were reported to have been founded. An additional 63 city committees and 564 district (*raion*) committees were organised. The Ukrainian Komsomol set up eleven partisan units with 1,500 members, and around 7,000 Komsomol members were reported to have joined other partisan units.[330] U.S. historian Kenneth Slepyan gives the number of partisans in the sector of Heeresgruppe Süd in the summer and fall of 1941 as around 35,000.[331]

Soviet sources have claimed that more than 700 paramilitary "destruction battalions" (Russ. *istrebki*; Ukr. *strybki*) were deployed by the NKVD in Ukraine by the end of July 1941. The bulk of these remained in the occupied territory or moved into that area.[332] The partisan units in Ukraine eventually derailed and destroyed around 5,000 trains, more than 60 Panzer trains, 2,200 bridges, 1,500 tanks and armoured cars, 200 aircraft, 700 howitzers, and around 15,000 field cars. During the Soviet counter-offensive in the fall of 1943, the partisans also controlled 25 bridges over the Rivers Desna, Dnieper, and Pripyat and held them until the arrival of the Soviet forces. A total of 16 provincial capitals were occupied and some 460,000 German soldiers killed.[333] On the face of it, these and other similar figures are probably considerably exaggerated.[334] However, British historian Richard Overy gives the total number of 12,000 destroyed bridges and 65,000 vehicles for the entire Eastern Front.[335] Furthermore, it has been estimated that around 8% of the German personnel casualties in WWII were caused by partisan and guerilla raids.[336]

The partisans numbered around 90,000 at the end of 1941, grew to at least some 100,000 in 1942, and to perhaps 150,000 in 1943.[337] In the course of the war, some 150,000–200,000 partisans operated in Ukraine. A small number were Jews, in Ukraine perhaps 2,000–3,000 and in the occupied Soviet territories as a whole perhaps 25,000.[338] Consequently, the initial share of Jews among the partisans in appears to have corresponded to some 10% in 1941–42.

In any case, it is quite clear that these subversive actions started shortly after the German invasion. SS-Einsatzgruppe C in Lemberg reported to Berlin on 6.7.1941 that twelve Soviet agents had stayed behind with the task of committing sabotage against bridges and other installations. Telephone wires in the countryside were cut, and on 16.7.1941 it was reported that escaped *Politruks* had attacked villages in the vicinity of Zolochiv (*Złoczów*) by night in order to get food. In the Tarnopol (*Ternopil*) area, 54 Poles and Jews were identified as Soviet agents. The Germans were successful in arresting only eight of these, among them two female Jews. All of them were executed. In the city of Zhytomyr, a 12-year-old Jewish boy was seized on 10.7.1941 after firing on a vehicle of Einsatzkommando 4b. However, most attempts to catch the organisers of resistance were in vain. Hence the only response that could be used was the common practice: "As a reprisal measure, a renewed action against the Jews was carried out".[339] It cannot be determined how adequate these reports were as it is quite possible that they exaggerate enemy actions. Simultaneously, the report also "legitimises" the German counter-measures, which may partly have been directed against occasional passers-by.

On 25.7.1941, Oberkommando des Heeres (OKH) issued a decree on the treatment of civilians and Soviet POWs, "*Behandlung feindlicher Zivilpersonen und russischer Kriegsgefangener*". In this key directive it was stated that:

> The guiding principle in all actions and for all measures (...) is the unconditional security of the German soldier (...) The Russians have always been used to hard and unforgiving action by the authorities. The necessary rapid pacification of the country can be attained only if every threat on the part of the hostile civil population is met with ruthless action. Any pity and softness are [evidence of] weakness and constitute danger.[340]

Also the Oberkommando der Wehrmacht (OKW) on 16.9.1941 issued a directive pertaining to the suppression of the insurgent movement in occupied territories. "Erlass des OKW" included a drastic rule:

> One must bear in mind that a human life frequently counts for naught in the affected countries and a deterrent effect can only be achieved by unusual severity. In such a case [exercising] the death penalty for 50 to 100 Communists must in general be deemed appropriate as retaliation for the life of one German soldier. The manner of execution must increase the deterrent effect still further (...).[341]

During the fall of 1941, the Norwegian volunteer Eivind Reichelt served in an Ersatzkompanie of SS-Regiment Nordland and later in SS-Aufklärungs-Abteilung 5. In September 1941, the unit was deployed in the area between Lemberg (*Lviv*) and Bila Tserkva (*Biała Cerkiew, Belaya Tserkov, Belaja Tserkov, Bila Tserkva, Bila Zerkwa, Biala Cerkiew, Belaja Zerkow, Bjelala Zerkow, Belaja Tserka*). He reported on his experiences in a police interrogation in 1946:

> A Russian civilian tried to blow up our ammunition car, but he was caught in the act. The German Wehrmacht and SS-soldiers abused the Russian most dreadfully by kicking him in the face and on his body so that his blood gushed. I could not watch this and stay silent, and I shouted that treatment like this was unworthy of German soldiers, and that only pigs could come up with something like that. I got completely sick by watching this and hid myself in a train carriage. I heard that the man had to hang himself using a rope that was too thin and weak. Hence he had to hang himself twice without losing his life. Finally, he was shot by a Scharführer.[342]

In the winter of 1943, Norwegian volunteers were in Stalino (nowadays *Donetsk*) and participated in hunting partisans. As a rule, Soviet men and boys spotted in the villages were condemned to death by a Waffen-SS officer and were hanged regardless of whether they were armed or unarmed. German patrols combed the area and promptly hanged 40–50 captured local males from the nearest tree, although the men were unarmed: The simple fact that there were males in the village was sufficient for the hangings". German officers frequently gathered in wild drinking parties in Stalino, in which young women from the town were ordered to participate and offer sexual services to the officers: "As time went by, the party ran wild and everything was smashed into pieces – and the following day the party house was usually burned to the ground. An excellent way of covering the orgies of that night". For no reason, German officers randomly shot non-violent citizens walking in the streets. The Norwegian mentions three women and two young male Russians who perished in this way.[343]

Several Finnish SS volunteers also made remarks on their experiences of the partisans. Volunteer Olavi (Veikko) Liesinen of the 16th Company of the SS-Regiment Nordland recalls in his memoirs:

> The beginning of the assault gave the impression of human hunting. Over wide areas we observed Russian stragglers. It felt like the army of Great Russia did not even exist. We waged small skirmishes against badly-armed enemies. Usually the clashes occurred in villages and population centres. The motorised army advanced, destroying anything in its path. Sometimes during our march crowds of surrendering Russians arrived, wearing the most miserable gear (...). Our column marched as if in an ecstasy of victory (...) The civilians did not greatly scare us. The conquered villages were looted, the invaders satisfied their cravings. Along the sides of the roads, the stink of dead people and destroyed machines. The Stukas thundered in the air above, destroying the results of human endeavour. The German army marched on, taking revenge for all alleged wrongs.[344]

Liesinen's continues his story:

> In the villages where the locals participated in the defence, severe punishment was meted out. The resistance of one or two men could cause the death of 20–30 villagers, owing to the state of mind of the Germans in command. And all this because the orders of Hitler were stressed and followed. We Finns did not accept this sort of treatment, although we were not able to prevent it. Certainly, it was natural that everyone defended his own. This was my view and I did not feel any common feeling whatever among my brothers-in-arms or any other Finns towards the Germans. All that we saw horrified us. The Germans viewed us with indifference and let it be understood that we were granted an equal status only as a consequence of Hitler's permission.[345]

As Eino Koskimies of the Finnish SS-Volunteer Battalion was killed by a shot to the head at Bachmutskij (*Bachmutskij; Bahmutski* now known as *Novobakhmutskiy, Novobachmutskiy*) (close to the Mius River line in Rostov Oblast) in early March 1942, the war diary noted:

> In spite of all exhortations and bans concerning going to Skelyanskiy [*Skeljanskij, Skeljanski*], the man had run in the vicinity of the place. He was struck by a bullet when he was returning. Not until nightfall was it possible to bring him away from there, with great difficulties".[346]

A group of some twenty partisans in Lineinaya (*Lineinaja*) (close to the strategically important oilfields of Maikop in the Northern Caucasus, during the German "Case Blue" Offensive) attacked a platoon of the 2nd Company, Finnish SS-Volunteer Battalion on 8.9.1942. The volunteer Elias Matti was wounded and died the following day.[347]

Volunteer Simo Heliste of the 4th Company of SS-Aufklärungs-Abteilung 5 has reported on the shooting of a civilian near Tarashcha (about 100 km south of Kiev) in mid-July 1941. On the road, a young man in civilian clothing and with raised hands approached the cars from the forest. As he was examined, it appeared that he had a hand-grenade in his pocket. The Platoon Commander, called "Engemann" by Heliste, ordered him to shoot the youngster. However, Heliste steadfastly refused, whereupon "Engemann" shot the man in the back.[348] However, as it appears, Heliste is likely to have mistaken the name, as the Platoon Commander may actually have been SS-Oberscharführer Josef Engelmann.[349]

SS-Obersturmführer Kaj Duncker noted sniper or partisan activities on a few occasions. On 4.8.1942, he wrote in his diary at the Novo Michailowka (*Novomikhaylovskiy*) bridgehead in Kuban: "A day of casualties, snipers everywhere. A nasty business". Some time later, on 1.9.1942, he mentioned a partisan assault on the SS-Regiment Westland in Temnoselskaya. A sawmill was set on fire as a counter-attack was carried out.[350] Volunteer Sakari Haikala of the Finnish SS-Volunteer Battalion has spoken of his experiences against partisans in the vicinity of Lineinaya, where the Finnish volunteers stayed for eight days in August 1942: "The conditions during the nights were worse than in the daytime because the partisans shot at the guards and tried to torch our vehicles. The Germans responded by hanging seized partisans on high poles. The hanged men had a sign around their neck with the text: Partizan".[351]

Volunteer Åke Kelin returned on 3.9.1942 from a field hospital to the Finnish SS-Volunteer Battalion in the village of Kabardinskaya (*Karabinskaja, Kabardinskaja*), around 50 km west of Maikop in the North Caucasus. In the middle of the village, between two trees, four men were hanged from a cross-beam.[352] SS-Oberscharführer Leo Heikurainen of 1st Company, Finnish SS-Battalion, reported an incident in September 1942 when some Finnish volunteers, among them the amateur boxer Pauli Asikainen of the same Company, refused to shoot women and children after a surprise attack by partisans. This may have been near the village of Lineinaya in the Northern Caucasus. However, superior officers turned a blind eye to the issue.[353] The volunteer Jaakko Hintikka of the 12th Company noted during 25.–26.11.1942 in Tšikola (*Tschikola, Chikola*), in the upper reaches of the Terek River:

> By the way there are many partisans in this village, one does not know which day will be one's last. The same day as we arrived the partisans had killed four Germans. They had stabbed them with a bayonet and torn their eyes out of their heads. Such grim deeds they commit.[354]

SS-Kriegsberichter Jukka Tyrkkö of 3rd Company, Finnish SS-Volunteer Battalion, tells in his memoirs of an incident from 22.2.1942 in the village of Skelyanskiy, on the River Mius. A crowd of Russians were approaching the battalion's positions, where volunteer Erkki Voutilainen was on guard:

In answer to his question, I shouted 'Feuer frei!' Our light machine guns rattled, some of the Russians fell, and the crowd scattered. Only then did a telephone message arrive, telling us that they were civilians. Then the Russians raised a white rag and were allowed to enter the positions of our 3rd Platoon in peace. They were around 40 persons, predominantly women and children. Their wounds were dressed behind our hospital hut. The first of them in the front of the crowd was an old man with heavy steps. In one hand he had a bundle and in the other one a long cane.[355]

Also this recollection illustrates the jumbling of combatants with civilians and the unease of the volunteers.

Fallen Red Army soldiers at the Mius River battlefields in Eastern Ukraine, in 1942. *JT Coll., FWM.*

SOVIET PRISONERS OF WAR

During the German march from Lemberg (*Lviv*), eastwards, numerous Soviet soldiers fell into German hands and became Prisoners of War (POWs). The number captured from late June to the end of July 1941 is estimated to be about 250,000. In the Uman area, over 103,000 prisoners were taken in August 1941, and 665,000 in the Kiev area in September 1941. However, of these some 445,000 were brought to ten so-called permanent camps, while the rest were penned in extremely harsh and open field conditions.[356] Of the 3.8 million Red Army soldiers captured in 1941 by the German forces, 1.3 million were Ukrainians.[357]

The death rate among the Soviet POWs soon soared. The Wehrmacht Commander in Ukraine, Generalleutnant Karl Kitzinger reported in December 1941 that the monthly death toll was around 75,000, i.e. some 2,500 perished daily.[358] Of the Soviet POWs of Jewish descent, around 50,000 perished. SS-Division Wiking captured numerous Soviet POWs in July 1941, some 6,000, in August at least 2,000, and in September a further 11,000.[359] This would make a total of around 19,000. However, as a part of the Soviet POWs were either summarily shot or escaped, the real number is surely larger.

Considerable numbers of the Soviet POWs were certainly also released in the first months of the war. Following a German order dated 8.9.1941, Ukrainian and Belorussian prisoners were eligible for immediate release, as were prisoners from Estonia, Latvia, and Lithuania. In the period between September and November 1941, a total of 270,000 Soviet Ukrainian POWs were released, i.e. some 96% of the Soviet POWs discharged in this period. However, the release of Ukrainian prisoners was soon halted and confusion took hold in the fall of 1941.[360] A newspaper article from January 1942 by the Finnish war correspondent Mauno P. Sjöstedt, who had obviously interviewed a few SS-volunteers on leave in Finland, reproduced a statement from one of them:

> When we arrived in the villages, arches with leafy decorations were often erected to the liberators, and the locals welcomed us with various hospitalities. Among the Ukrainians, there had already dawned a longing for independence and they had never approved of Soviet rule. The soldiers surrendered themselves in great numbers as prisoners to the Germans, in particular when the front lines started to pass their homes. The prisoners were immediately released, and they turned their weapons against the Russians. Furthermore, the civilians in the cities had stayed where they were, in spite of their fears. The exceptions were Jews and (Soviet) leaders.[361]

The Finnish SS-volunteer Vilho Kellokumpu from 2nd Company, SS-Aufklärungs-Abteilung 5, has spoken of an incident that supposedly occurred in Ukraine during the summer of 1941. Events kicked off when a Panzer Company returned after an attack. There were Soviet POWs on a field, and – together with the volunteer Jorma Vesenne from the same Company – Kellokumpu watched as a German officer threw spades to the prisoners. They dug a large grave and were then shot with submachine guns. The last man was ordered to cover the grave containing the bodies of his compatriots: "When he finished, he was told to leave, and was then shot in the back.

The event deeply touched Vilho and Jorma, who chatted with each other about the incident".[362]

The volunteer Arvo Vidberg from the 11th Company of the Finnish SS-Volunteer Battalion remembered for his part:

> There were no (front) lines after the retreat from the Caucasus. Sometimes the Russians were ahead of us, although later they were encircled. The villages were full of them. No prisoners were taken (...) We lived as if the last day is coming. The prisoners were shot, regardless of how they raised their hands. I did not do it. Those doing it were others. In battle situations on the steppe, shooting occurred. They were so many that I started to feel ill. There were rows of dead at the outskirts of the villages (...).[363]

The volunteer Markus Käenmäki of SS-Nachschub-Abteilung 5 noted similar experiences:

> Particularly at the beginning (in the summer of 1941), the attitude of the Germans to POWs was very hostile. Those (prisoners) who were brought to the rear were shot for very insignificant reasons. The number of prisoners was enormous.[364]

As the Finnish SS-Volunteer Battalion was in training in Gross Born (now Pol. *Borne Sulinowo*, in West Pomerania) on one occasion, Martti Sinervo was guarding Soviet POWs at the camp. On 13.9.1941, he noted:

> Rumours on the treatment of the prisoners of war have surely reached the Battalion (...) sometimes there were discussions on mass executions as POWs had been shot in graves they dug for themselves. Sometimes stories were told about mass murders connected to German test firings with machine guns.

However, Sinervo regarded the truthfulness of the stories as very debatable, since nobody had witnessed events like this and there was no certifiable evidence. During his own guard turn of more than four hours, he did not observe any offence against the prisoners.[365]

One volunteer from 4th Company, Finnish SS-Volunteers Battalion, named Tauno Pajunen how three Soviet POWs had been shot in the fall of 1941, somewhere east of Dnipropetrovsk. However, the event may have occurred either in late 1941 or early 1942. Three Soviet soldiers arrived in a village building, whereupon the Finnish SS-Oberscharführer "K" had taken them prisoner: "The programme was then very clear", he wrote: "Three shots and peace prevailed again", indicating that the unarmed and defenceless prisoners were shot dead. The identity of the SS-Oberscharführer is unknown.[366] The SS-Kriegsberichter and SS-Oberscharführer Jukka Tyrkkö also mentions the event, although he uses slightly less direct terms to describe it.[367] The shooting of POWs is also mentioned in the biography of Yrjö Pyyhtiä of the 10th company of the Finnish SS-Volunteers Battalion, written on the basis of his own stories, at the battle in Tšikola, Caucasus, on 26.11.–7.12.1942. A total of 246 Soviet POWs were captured, including 13 officers. As Pyyhtiä later asked volunteer Kalevi Könönen about the fate of the prisoners, he was told: "You must certainly know the German attitude to prisoners". Pyyhtiä had a good grasp of the situation: "I felt sorry for the men. They had been drafted by force into the Red Army and had been executed after surrendering".[368]

In 1981, the author Jaakko Korjus published the historical work *Otsassa kuoleman kuva* ("Death's Head on the Forehead"), based partly on genuine narratives from the Finnish SS-volunteers Pentti Koivisto, Heikki Lapinjoki, and Paavo Maunula. In a section on events from the Dnipropetrovsk area in September 1941, Maunula captured a young Soviet soldier as a POW and made him an ammunition carrier and helper. However, a few days later he was ordered to give up his contented, loyal, and grateful prisoner. At this, Korjus wrote:

> The Germans treat their prisoners badly. Often they do not take prisoners at all. The Finns are appalled by the brutality of the Germans. There are only two kinds of Germans, the good and the disgusting. The latter are unfortunately many in number! Among the foreigner volunteers there are also killers. The Finns are almost without exception different: We certainly kill, but only when necessary. The unarmed are not killed, that's for sure.[369]

Korjus's story no doubt almost unequivocally idealises the Finnish volunteers, but nevertheless as it appears it adequately brings out a certain nuance between the German and Finnish attitudes to the Soviet POWs.

POLITICAL COMMISSARS

Among the Wehrmacht and Waffen-SS, the Political Commissars or *Politruks* were targeted Soviet officials. The guidelines on the treatment of Political Commissars, "*Richtlinien für die Behandlung politische Kommisare*", the so-called 'Commissar Order' (*Kommissarbefehl*) were issued by the OKW on 6.6.1941, prior to the launch of Operation Barbarossa. The essence of the directive was that Soviet POWs who could be identified as "thoroughly Bolshevised or as active representatives of the Bolshevist ideology" should be liquidated without delay.[370] Consequently, at the front 5,000 Soviet Commissars were shot, and another 5,000 were sent to prison camps.[371]

However, generally the documents on Political Commissars are missing in the archive collections of the Waffen-SS Divisions. Only a few documents have survived, and the reported figures of executions are low. Concerning the SS-Division Wiking, no information at all is available in this respect. Nevertheless, it is only to be supposed that the SS Divisions also carried out the Commissar Order as requested.[372]

In 1948, the former Commander of Heeresgruppe Süd, Feldmarschall Erich von Manstein, was convicted by a British Military Court and sentenced to 18 years imprisonment for war crimes. During the trial, von Manstein claimed that the Commissars did not belong to the Soviet ordinary forces, although they were armed. Consequently, the German forces had not granted them status as POWs.[373]

In the report of the 9th Panzerdivision, it is noted that the unit moved on from Pluhiv to Ozerna (Pol. *Jezierna*) and Zboriv (*Zborów, Zborob; Zbvorow*) in Galicia on 2.7.1941. A rearguard unit brought in a Soviet Political Commissar, who informed them that he was a Czech. The man was fluent in German, but he refused to make any further statements: "He was shot". In nearby Tarnopol (*Ternopil*), two suspects were brought in on 4.7.1941: "In the course of the interrogation it became clear that it was a question of Political Commissars. They were shot."[374]

Cooperating Wehrmacht forces and Ukrainian nationalists shot 34 Political Commissars in the city of Zhytomyr on 30.7.1941.[375] It appears that Finnish SS-volunteers participated in the liquidation of Commissars. A document testifies to this, a letter by SS-Schütze Ilmari Autonen from Bensberg near Köln, 25.11.1941, to the SS-official Unto Boman (from 1944, Unto Parvilahti) in Berlin. Autonen wrote: "By the way, a Commissar on the banks of River Dnieper gave this writing paper to me. For reasons that don't matter, he did not need it anymore. The only thing he needed was 60 cm of earth over his snout"[376]. On the day of the liquidation of this Russian, Autonen was a member of 2nd Company, SS-Regiment Westland. Later, SS-Kriegsberichter Jukka Tyrkkö mailed a photo to Boman in March 1942. This photo "shows the Comrade Commissar, holding the rank of Major, who our boys captured and shot during the taking of Dnipropetrovsk".[377] As SS-Regiment Westland only reached Dnipropetrovsk on 22.8.1941, the event probably occurred in late August 1941. The Finnish Liaison Officer, SS-Obersturmbannführer Kalervo Kurkiala, mentioned on 11.8.1942 the interrogations of Soviet POWs in the Maikop area in the North Caucasus, writing: "... a Commissar tried to escape and was shot".[378] This may be the same occasion about which the war correspondent Jukka Tyrkkö reported in September 1942. A platoon of Finnish volunteers had occupied a building used as a bunker. In the course of this action, a Bolshevik Commissar was killed.[379]

NO PRISONERS WILL BE TAKEN

As the German onslaught against the Soviet Union was launched on 22.6.1941, the German commanders in the field faced the question of treatment of the anticipated Red Army POWs. It was therefore necessary to issue some guidelines. The units of the SS-Division Wiking received their instructions on POWs promptly, on the first day of the march, although the Division did not engage in any significant battle until two weeks later. The Commander of 3rd Battalion, SS-Regiment Nordland, SS-Hauptsturmführer Manfred Schönfelder said in 1964 that the unit was involved in some small firefights in Lemberg (*Lviv*) on 1.7.1941. Actually the first real fighting SS-Division Wiking faced was 5–6 kilometres north of the village of Mykulyntsi, though this did not take place until 5.7.1941.[380] The Commander of SS-Division Wiking, Felix Steiner, stated for his part that the first "heavy struggles" (*die ersten schweren Kämpfe*) of the Division occurred at Tarnopol (*Ternopil*), i.e. around 4.7.1941, and this was also a kind of baptism of fire for the Finnish volunteers.[381]

SS-Hauptsturmführer Yrjö Kaila, serving as an observer officer in the Aufklärungs-Abteilung 5 of SS-Division Wiking, noted that on 22.6.1941 the Division remained in position for a few days. Initially, the force moved south-east as a second-level unit and crossed the 1939 Soviet border along the front of Sokal – Rawa-Ruska. From here it marched from Lemberg (*Lviv*) through to Tarnopol towards the old (pre-1939) Soviet-Polish border:

> At least in this period the Division experienced no larger battles, but on the contrary participated in the taking of several empty villages after softening up through artillery barrages (...) In general there occurred some skirmishes against presumed snipers and open firefights, etc. As I understand, the bulk of these were launched by careless handling of weapons, the shooting of prisoners and Jews, etc.

According to Kaila, the first serious military engagement did not occur until 7.7.1941, in the area of Satanovka-Kuzmyn, east of Tarnopol (*Ternopil*).[382]

Kaila's view may well be seen as adequate, and also that of volunteer and SS-Rottenführer Sakari Lappi-Seppälä, who noted in his diary for 3.7.1941 that no fighting occurred in Lemberg (*Lviv*) and that the city was largely left undamaged. In the evening the transport column of 1st Company, SS-Regiment Westland left Lemberg and headed east. Lappi-Seppälä reported:

> Our lorries sped through burning villages. From these, single shots rang out, sometimes a volley from machine guns, and the sharp crack of hand-grenades as the German troops in the rear carried out their cleansing operations (*Säuberungsaktionen*). We did not, however, stop in any of these villages, although fighting was were still going on, because we had to dash forward. Eventually the Company was ordered to prepare for action and a platoon at-

tacked an already heavily-shelled village while others remained securing the rear and chasing the remnants of a scattered Soviet unit. The only losses of the Company so far were two Dutch volunteers convicted for stealing butter, a Danish volunteer shot in the stomach, and a lightly wounded German.[383]

Volunteer Ahti Paikkala, SS-Untersturmführer of 6th Company of SS-Regiment Westland, was informed by the Commander on the first day of the assault (22.6.1941), that "the SS takes no prisoners".[384] The volunteer Martti Uusi-Jaakkola of 9th Company of SS-Regiment Westland noted on 22.6.1941 that the crew received the order not to take any prisoners (and equally that surrendering to the enemy and being taken prisoner was expressly forbidden).[385] Further, volunteer Keijo Kääriäinen of 2nd Company of the SS-Regiment Westland mentions on 23.6.1941 that the unit received instructions for the forthcoming engagements: all prisoners should be shot.[386] Likewise volunteer Olavi Liesinen of 16th Company, SS-Regiment Westland noted that his unit was summoned on this day shortly before the general assault. The volunteers were told that they had been given the honourable task of forcing the Barbarians of the East across to the far side of the River

Finnish Waffen-SS troops ready to start the march to the East in May or early June 1941. *OW Coll.*

Finnish SS-volunteers passed through Lemberg (Lwów, Lviv) on 1.–2.7.1941. From here are the first entries in the diaries of the atrocities they witnessed during the march eastwards. SS-Artillerie-Regiment 5 convoy in Lemberg. *KD Coll., SLS.*

Volga. The instructions were that "the Russians must be destroyed, even to infant babies (...)". Moreover, for an SS-man, it was his duty not to take prisoners.[387] However, the recollections of Penna Konttinen of 6th Company of the SS-Regiment Westland note that the Finnish volunteers were not forced to shoot POWs: "Shooting their prisoners in the back was something the Germans took care of themselves".[388]

The Norwegian volunteer Jan Taarneby of 9th Company, SS-Regiment Germania remembered that in late June 1941, during the first days of the campaign in Ukraine, he was told that no prisoners should be taken:

> When the Germans crossed the border, the order was to shoot everyone – and to take no prisoners at all. The justification for this was that the Russians did not take prisoners, and for that reason none of the Germans would do so (...) A proclamation on the issue was distributed among the men, to the effect that the prisoners should be ruthlessly mown down. This was also in the case where Russians arrived with their hands over their head or wearing a white flag: they were to be shot. 'No prisoners!' was the watchword.

Taarneby's compatriot from 12th Company, Ørnulf Bjørnstad, reported:

> At the first onslaught (in late June 1941) he was present when the order to take no prisoners was issued. This was a kind of retaliation for some Germans the Russians had captured in Lemberg (*Lviv*) and then killed. The Russians who surrendered were shot in the middle of the battlefield.[389]

All units of the SS-Division Wiking were given the same instructions for the treatment of POWs. However, as the Germans included not only Soviet partisans, but also male and female civilian combatants and possible enemy supporters in their list of those to be executed, there was no fixed penalty which would have clearly separated prisoners of war from ordinary locals. As a consequence, practically anyone could be arrested and as everyone arrested was de facto a prisoner, there were no obstacles to shooting such persons.

In spite of these instructions, it is obvious that a great number of Soviet POWs were captured in the summer of 1941. Many recollections and photos show long columns of POWs marching along the roads or gathered in rest places. However, the explanation may be that the Wehrmacht units had seized these POWs and were marching them to the rear. Furthermore, the SS-Division Wiking also captured a considerable number of Soviet POWs without killing them.

1.

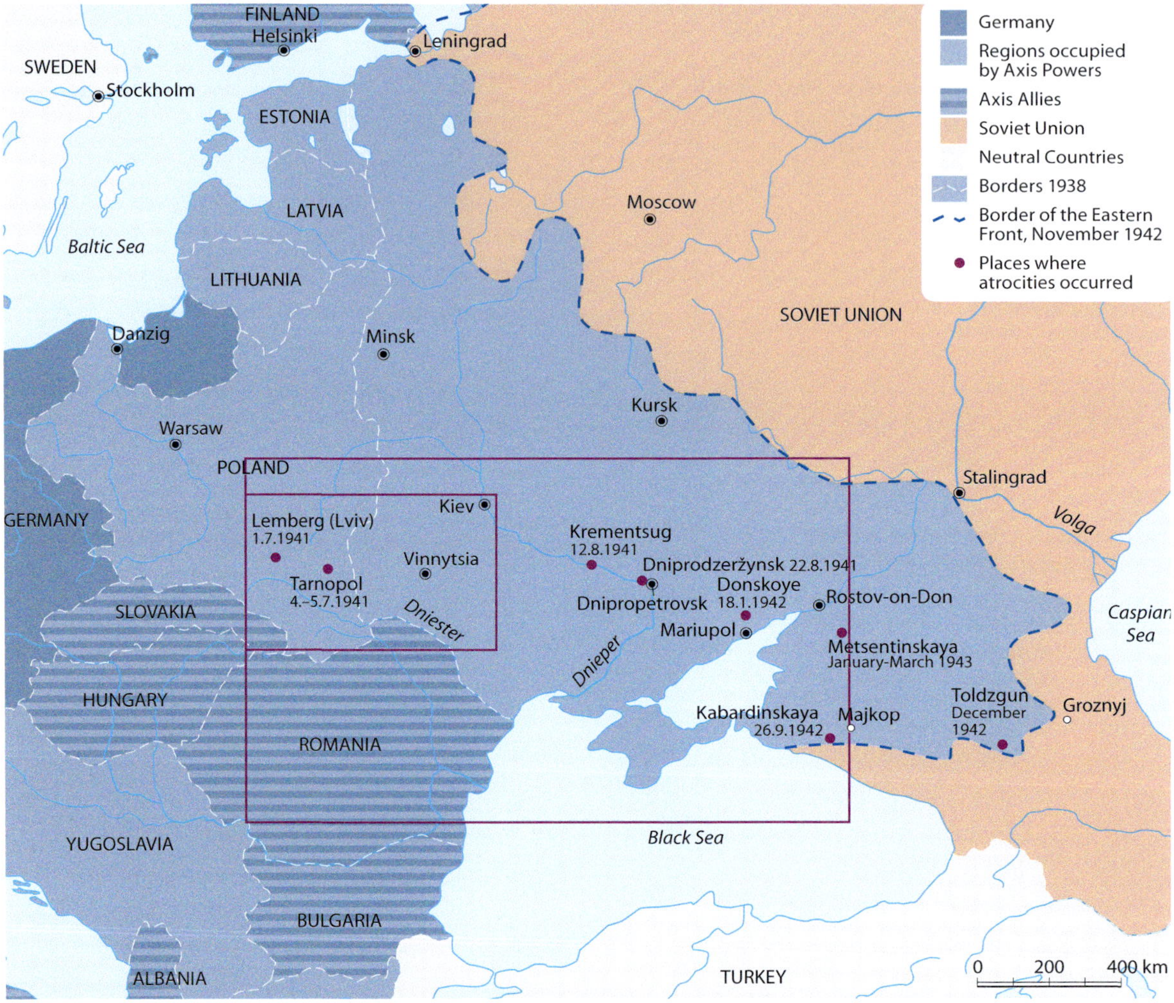

Germany
Regions occupied by Axis Powers
Axis Allies
Soviet Union
Neutral Countries
Borders 1938
Border of the Eastern Front, November 1942
Places where atrocities occurred
FINLAND
Helsinki
Leningrad
SWEDEN
Stockholm
ESTONIA
LATVIA
Baltic Sea
LITHUANIA
Moscow
SOVIET UNION
Danzig
Minsk
Kursk
Warsaw
POLAND
Stalingrad
Volga
GERMANY
Kiev
Lemberg (Lviv) 1.7.1941
Krementsug 12.8.1941
Vinnytsia
Dniprodzeržynsk 22.8.1941
Tarnopol 4.–5.7.1941
Donskoye 18.1.1942
Dnipropetrovsk
Rostov-on-Don
SLOVAKIA
Dniester
Mariupol
Caspian Sea
Metsentinskaya January-March 1943
Dnieper
HUNGARY
Toldzgun December 1942
Groznyj
Kabardinskaya 26.9.1942
Majkop
ROMANIA
Black Sea
YUGOSLAVIA
BULGARIA
ALBANIA
TURKEY
0 200 400 km

2.

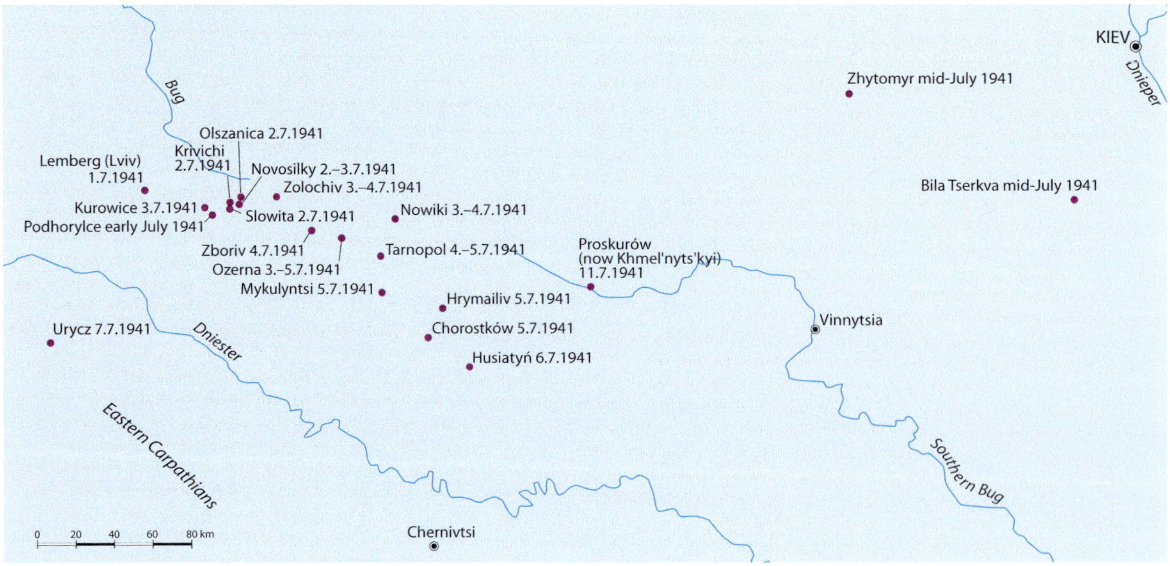

KIEV
Dnieper
Bug
Zhytomyr mid-July 1941
Olszanica 2.7.1941
Krivichi 2.7.1941
Lemberg (Lviv) 1.7.1941
Novosilky 2.–3.7.1941
Zolochiv 3.–4.7.1941
Bila Tserkva mid-July 1941
Kurowice 3.7.1941
Slowita 2.7.1941
Nowiki 3.–4.7.1941
Podhorylce early July 1941
Zboriv 4.7.1941
Tarnopol 4.–5.7.1941
Proskurów (now Khmel'nyts'kyi) 11.7.1941
Ozerna 3.–5.7.1941
Mykulyntsi 5.7.1941
Hrymailiv 5.7.1941
Urycz 7.7.1941
Chorostków 5.7.1941
Vinnytsia
Dniester
Husiatyń 6.7.1941
Eastern Carpathians
Southern Bug
0 20 40 60 80 km
Chernivtsi

3.

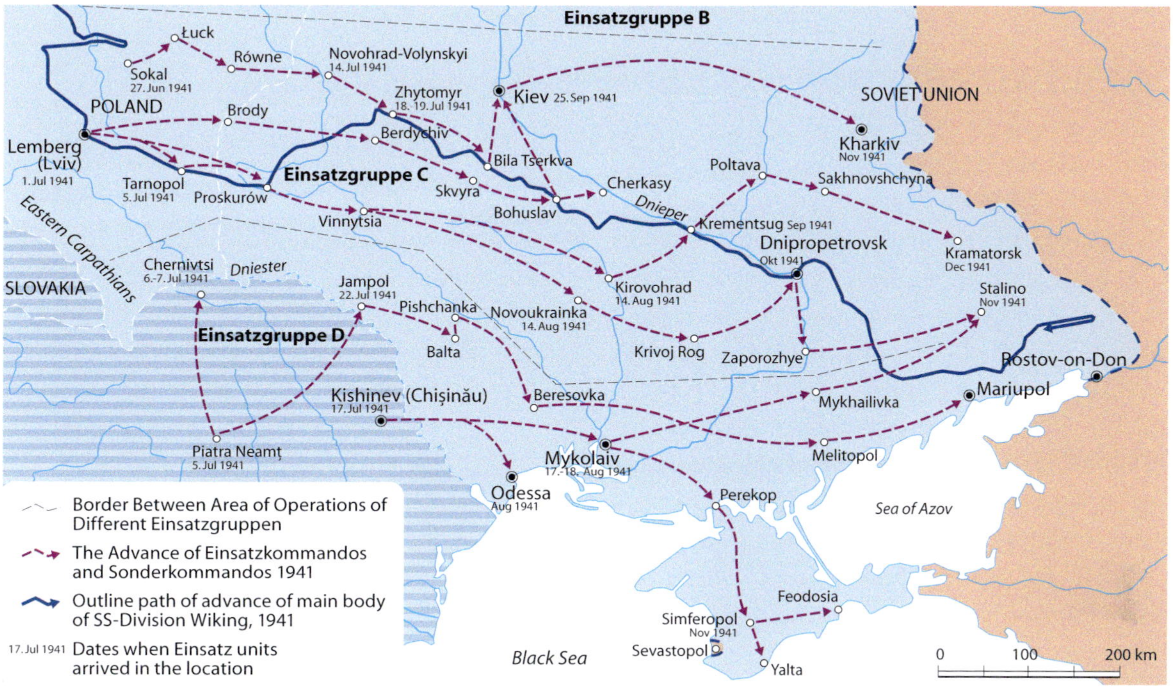

1. Areas in Ukraine and the Caucasus where the Finnish Waffen-SS Volunteers Witnessed Atrocities, 1941–1943
The Finnish SS-volunteers belonging to SS-Division Wiking took part in Operation Barbarossa, the invasion of the Soviet Union, advancing through Ukraine and into the Caucasus from late June 1941 to April 1943. As the division pushed around 2,500 kilometres eastwards, the Finnish volunteers moved over large areas and would have witnessed numerous atrocities. As it appears, the Finnish volunteers may in some places merely have been witnesses to the atrocities, whereas a certain number of the men became involved in them.

2. Locations of Atrocities in Western Ukraine in the Summer of 1941
At the launch of Operation Barbarossa on 22.6.1941, some 400 Finnish volunteers were included in the various regiments and other sub-units of SS-Division Wiking. Over a period of three months, the division pushed eastwards from Lviv/Lemberg to the River Dnieper. Since these sub-units took different marching routes, the Finns passed through some twenty places where atrocities against Jews, civilians, and POWs took place. As is shown in this research, most of the atrocities along the route of SS-Division Wiking were carried out in Western Ukraine in the summer of 1941.

3. The 1941 Advance of SS-Division Wiking, Einsatzgruppe C, and Einsatzgruppe D
The Einsatzgruppen consisted of Einsatzkommando and Sonderkommando units (purple dotted lines), which were tasked with carrying out the mass killings against Jews and other "unwanted" elements. Einsatzgruppe C operated within the same area as the SS-Division Wiking and the two also worked together. The map shows a rough estimate of how the main part of SS-Division Wiking advanced during 1941 (blue line). Since the Division consisted of nearly 20,000 men, the actual area of operations was much broader. At this stage, the Finnish volunteers (some 400 men) were dispersed among different sub-units within the formation. During the summer and autumn of 1941, Wiking also loaned its various regiments to other corps for specific missions, and these movements are not shown on the map. *Source: Jokipii 1996; Memnon335bc: Karte - Einsatzgruppen in der Sowjetunion 1941.png (Wikimedia Commons, CC BY SA).*

MASSACRES IN THE LEMBERG AREA, 1.–7.7.1941

This part of the report deals with the massacres that took place in the Lemberg (*Lviv*) area between 1.–7.7.1941. In the region of Galicia, there were an estimated 540,000 to 650,000 Jews, representing about 10% of the population. Of these, 40,000–50,000 are believed to have fled eastwards before the arrival of German forces.[390] There were Jewish settlements in several hundred individual municipalities and locations.

In terms of the incidence of place-names, some impression of the numbers of local atrocity events can be gathered from the 16-volume *Die Verfolgung und Ermordung der europäischen Juden durch das nationalsozialistische Deutschland 1933–1945* (The Persecution and Murder of European Jewry by Nazi Germany, 1933–1945). In the registers of the occupied Soviet Union, the Baltic States, and Transnistria, there are listed over 1,100 place names, cities, towns, municipalities, villages, etc. Of these around one thousand were situated in areas through which SS-Division Wiking advanced. Although the list is not likely to be totally comprehensive, it nevertheless gives an inkling of the size of the region covered.[391]

However, as has been seen previously in this document, the names of villages, towns, and entire regions in Eastern Europe were frequently subject to change in the period from 1850 to 1950. These name-changes reflected the nationality of the various rulers or occupiers and also changing topographical concepts. Moreover, during the advance of 1941–43, the German forces introduced old Germanic names of places, in particular towns and regions, using German transliterations.[392] In this Report, the names occurring in the diaries and recollections of the Finnish volunteers are used and their other names are mentioned in parentheses where necessary and where possible.

LEMBERG 1.7.1941: THE BAPTISM OF SHOCKING SCENES

The bulk of SS-Division Wiking passed through Lemberg (*Lviv*), in broad daylight on 1.7.1941. The staff of SS-Regiment Westland arrived in the city at 1 p.m.[393] It is a significant place in the history of the Division, as a great number of SS-volunteers experienced for the first time, during a few hours in the city, the first uncontrolled repressive acts and witnessed German-supported mob rule at close hand. The relatively short stay for most of the volunteers was a baptism of shocking scenes of atrocities – incidents that shortly afterwards were to be repeated in numerous other municipalities in varying combinations. SS-Division Wiking spent only a few hours in the city and its advance continued eastward towards Tarnopol (*Ternopil*). In October 1941, the number of Jews in Lemberg (*Lviv*) had decreased to 119,000[394] and some 37,000 are reported to have left the city or perished.

Lemberg (*Lviv*) was situated in the buffer area of Galicia and was incorporated in three states: up to 1918 it was a part of Austria-Hungary, between 1919 and 1939 a part of Poland, and from the fall of 1939 a part of the Soviet Union. In 1941, the city had an estimated population of 361,000 people, of which about 160,000 were Jews, approximately 140,000 Poles, and around 70,000 Ukrainians.[395] Several separate mass killings occurred in the period from 30.6. to 2.7.1941 in Lemberg and its surroundings. Considerably large numbers of Jews murdered have been presented in the literature, ranging upwards from 4,000.[396] However, these figures are commonly exaggerated and the German historian Kai Struve has estimated that a total of no more than some 700 locals would have perished in the first two days (1.–2.7.1941). Only by including the victims of the mass shootings in Lemberg (*Lviv*) on 5.7. and 25.–26.7.1941 can the number of 4,000 or more executed be reached.[397]

The Ukrainian nationalists

In late June 1941, Luftwaffe bombed Sknilów Airfield in the Lemberg (*Lviv*) area, but bombs were also dropped over the city and some buildings were destroyed and the streets filled with rubble. As Soviet forces hastily prepared to leave, they torched the great Brygidki Prison, killing countless political prisoners (mainly Poles and Ukrainians), and shops on the outskirts of town were looted.[398] Posters put up by the Ukrainian nationalists early in the morning of 30.6.1941 appeared on bulletin boards and the walls of buildings. The posters greeted the German forces and Stepan Bandera, who would liberate the Ukrainians from the rule of Jews and the NKVD. The headlines had slogans such as: "Smash the Jews and the Communists" and "Long Live Stepan Bandera, Long Live Adolf Hitler". The influential Bandera (1909–1959) was head of a militant wing of the Organisation of Ukrainian Nationalists (OUN). A local described the triumphal arrival of the invaders: "When the Germans entered Lemberg (*Lviv*), Kopernik Street and Marjacki Square were paved with flowers. The German vehicles moved around in a sea of flowers. The cars were open, and officers stood erect in them, clutching maps of the town (...).[399]

The Wehrmacht 1. Gebirgs-Division occupied Lemberg (*Lviv*) on 30.6.1941. Two days earlier, SS-Division Wiking received orders to march south from Lublin, passed the Soviet border on 30.6.1941, and entered Lemberg (*Lviv*) the following day. Simultaneously numerous repressive acts took place in the city, as Ukrainian collaborators with background support from the German forces killed several hundred Jewish residents. A Ukrainian nationalist militia had been organised and the German commanders allowed this ad hoc police force to attack Jews and Bolsheviks, together with local Ukrainians and Poles.[400]

In his study on the history of the Jews in Lemberg (*Lviv*), Eliyahu Yones personally witnessed the arrest of 80 Jews who were later released, and he depicts the dreadful scenes of early July 1941: "Young men, sporting blue and yellow armbands, roamed the streets from early morning, stopping any Jew they encountered. They broke into Jewish homes, attacking the occupants savagely. They used all available weapons: metal poles, sticks, axes, and knives".[401] Severe political friction occurred between the ethnic groups in Lemberg (*Lviv*). Among the German forces occupying the city was the Nightingale Battalion (*Bataillon Ukrainische Gruppe Nachtigall*), composed of volunteer Ukrainian nationalist soldiers (adherents of Bandera) under German officers.[402] The Polish historian Halik Kohanski mentions that the

Ukrainians "flocked to help the Germans, providing much of the manpower needed to shoot the Jews, joined German military formations, and wore German uniforms".[403] The Polish underground reported the persecution had been ordered by the Germans and carried out by "Ukrainian and Polish scum".[404]

The local Jew Jacob Gerstenfeld-Maltiel remembered German forces entering Lemberg (*Lviv*) on 1.7.1941:

> At the head of the Army marched two Tyrolean Regiments. On the streets, crowds gathered to greet the new liberators. Of course, the Jews did not participate in their reception, which I can only describe as enthusiastic. The population greeted the marching soldiers with cheers and applause and even threw flowers to them. Most of the people on the streets were Poles; the Ukrainians, a minority in Lvov (*Lemberg*) were lost in the crowds (...) The Jews, summing up the situation and realising that hard times were drawing upon them, remained in their homes and kept out of sight. It was clear that this would not protect us from the Germans, and that hard times could not be evaded.

However, it was not possible to imagine the colossal scale of the upcoming massacre and the participation of Poles and Ukrainians in the bloody repression against the Jews.[405]

Gerstenfeld-Maltiel stresses that the mass murder of the Jews in Lemberg (*Lviv*) began without that proper organisation later so favoured by the Germans, as the Jews remained in their homes, not daring to leave them. It was necessary to lure them from their homes and on 1.7.1941

> (...) placards were posted on all the streets calling everyone to go immediately to their work-places during a three-hour period, under penalty of death (...) People accustomed to discipline and obedience hastened to factories and offices. No one believed that it was a trap. On the streets, Ukrainian militiamen, mobilised during the night, sought out the Jews. Now the population could run wild: the victims were there. The mob in the streets soon forgot about work; it was more fun to set about the Jews. Not far from where I was living, on Sapieha Street, there was a bomb crater, a place especially created for fun with Jews. The neighbourhood Jews were brought to fill in the crater. From the window of my flat, I could observe in this one place the mirror of a thousand other places – the actions of the brutal mob. Old people, children and women, were forced under hails and blows to wrench out the paving stones with their bare hands, and to move the dirt of the street from one place to another. One woman was tied to a man working nearby and they were forced by blows to run in the opposite direction. A teenage boy fainted under blows and others were called to bury the apparent corpse alive. In this one place, I saw four or five persons murdered. About 60 persons were involved.

Despite the barbarity of the mob in the street, life continued as if nothing was happening. The streets appeared quite normal, interrupted only by brief halts from passers-by, who glanced away and calmly walked on: "Indignation was not expressed by one single word. If someone disapproved, he passed by quickly, playing short-sighted, pretending not to understand what was going on."[406]

Similar scenes were played out in and around the prisons of Lemberg (*Lviv*), the Brygudhi (Brygidki) prison in Kazimierzowska Street[407], and others on Lontskogo Street,[408] Zamastrynovskaya Street[409], and Yakhovica Street[410], as several thousands of Jews were rounded up and brought to these prisons and other places. Some 2,000 Jews were dragged to the courthouse at No. 59, Pelchinski Street, where the Gestapo had set up its headquarters. They were, however, released already in the course of the same evening. Most acts of violence took place at three of the four prisons, to which the Jews were brought on German orders by the militia and local civilians in order to retrieve the bodies of the thousands of prison inmates who had been killed, en masse, by the retreating NKVD forces. The Jews, who were deemed responsible for these newly-revealed Soviet atrocities, in accordance with the Nazi theory of Judeo-Bolshevism, were attacked when arrested, during the march through the streets, and at the prisons, as alleged supporters of Soviet rule.

As it appears, Einsatzgruppe C contributed to the escalation of violence since far more Jews were brought to the prisons than could have been practically employed in the cleaning-up work.[411] After the atrocities on the first day of occupation, the German masters nevertheless brought the mob violence to a halt and began to put local conditions in order. To the great disappointment of the Ukrainian nationalists, the Germans established a new order under their own control. All important posts in the city administration were taken over by the Germans and the Ukrainians, who had already seized many offices, were summarily removed from their posts.[412]

The actions of Einsatzgruppe C

The German occupiers certainly initially allowed the Ukrainian nationalists free rein on 1.7.1941. However, some mob acts of violence occurred also during the two following days, although they are not always clearly distinguishable from the mass arrests that started on 3.7.1941. These were carried out by the Ukrainian militia and the German police and ended eventually up in mass executions on 5.7.1941. On that day Einsatzgruppe C transported around 1,400 persons in trucks into the deep forest of Bilogortscha and shot them. Throughout July, representatives of the Jewish activists, the local political leaders, and the liberal youth were also taken to Lisinichi Forest and executed.[413]

The German forces sought to incite the Ukrainian nationalists to participate in the repressive acts against the Jews, encouraging for a while a quasi civil war situation by creating the preconditions. The Commander of Einsatzkommando 5, SS-Sturmbannführer Erwin Schulz, reported in a post-war trial that "the Military Command had already (i.e. by 1.7.1941) organised a local Ukrainian militia in the town and ordered Sonderkommando 4 and thereafter Einsatzkommando 6 to help the militia".[414] Schulz testified that in the course of the rounding-up action in Lemberg on 3.–5.7.1941 "his Kommando arrested some 2,500–3,000 people, who were gathered in a stadium. Over the next four days they were all shot".[415] However, such a large figure does not correspond to known facts.

A member of 16th Company of SS-Regiment Germania, SS-Rottenführer (Corporal) Hans Wilhelm Isenmann, told a post-war Soviet trial in Kharkiv about his experiences in Lemberg (*Lviv*).

In early July 1941, he may have been a member of Einsatzkommando C. In any case his testimony touches on the mass executions in the Lemberg area on 5.7.1941:

> Our Platoon Commander Renner had explained that it was necessary to assemble the Jewish population and shoot them. He told me that I should take part in searches, and also in executions (...) We found Jews with the help of informants who pointed out the houses for us. We came into Jewish homes, took away the entire family, and ordered them to stand in the street. We took everything of value, gold, silver, etc. All the Jews, with no exception, were brought out, old men, women, and children. At the first round-up 150–200 persons were taken and sent away eastwards to a place around four kilometres from Lvov (*Lemberg*). Our group accompanied them. The escort stood at a distance of 70 metres from the pits, and a Platoon Commander made the following arrangements: six persons made an escort for six persons to be shot at one time. I got the order to shoot and the executions proceeded as follows: 45–60 persons were brought to the pits, they were ordered to line up, and we shot them. We had submachine guns, two automatic devices, and others used carbines. I have personally shot 120 persons in Lvov, and our group shot a total of 800 persons. The victims begged for mercy and asked us not to shoot, but given the orders from Renner, they were to be killed.[416]

Isenmann's testimony, however, appears exaggerated and somewhat dubious. The Platoon Commander mentioned may have been SS-Unterscharführer Fritz Renner from 7th Company of the Regiment, or alternatively Hermann Renner of the Einsatzkommando 5.[417] In the trial, Isenmann was found guilty and given a capital sentence. He was hanged in Kiev on 29.1.1946.

The German Einsatzgruppe C was deeply involved, and they reported around 1,000 Jews were roughly herded together and delivered to the prison, which was by this time occupied by the Wehrmacht. These Jews were employed to remove the numerous victims killed by the NKVD in various prisons before the Ukrainian militia in turn killed some of them. The bulk of the Jews were, however, also released in the evening of 1.7.1941. Notably, the German repression targeted also Poles, who belonged to the local elite in Lemberg (*Lviv*).[418]

The Wehrmacht City Commandant and German recollections

There are a few German recollections and documents on the events in Lemberg (*Lviv*) during early July 1941. The first German forces to enter the city were battalions of the 98. & 99. Gebirgs-Jäger-Regiments and a battalion from Lehrregiment Brandenburg z.b.V 800.[419] The Staff of 44. Gebirgskorps instructed the Commander of the Gebirgs-Artillerie-Kommando of 1. Gebirgsdivision, Oberst Karl Wintergerst, to prevent with all urgency any kind of excesses "by the Army members". Nevertheless, the violent acts continued for three days without any preventative action from Wintergerst, who is mentioned as the German City Commandant as early as 1.7.1941.[420] He was unable to avert continuing smaller repressive acts anymore than his successor, Generalleutnant Maximilian Rentz, who was appointed City Commandant just three days later. When a Ukrainian nationalist newspaper was handed out in Lemberg (*Lviv*) on 5.7.1941 it ran a greeting and leading article by Rentz.[421] One member of an Einsatzkommando, SS-Hauptscharführer Felix Landau, reported after the war of his experiences in Lemberg: "(...) there were hundreds of Jews walking along the street with blood pouring down their faces, holes in their heads, their hands broken and their eyes hanging out of their sockets. They were covered in blood."[422] According to Landau's diary the Einsatzkommando arrived in Lemberg (*Lviv*) on 2.7.1941 in the afternoon and shortly after their arrival the first Jews were shot, and on 3.7.1941 he noted: "800 people were murdered here in Lemberg". In early July 1941, an entire set of Einsatzkommando units arrived in Lemberg (*Lviv*): Sonderkommando 4a under Paul Blobel, Sonderkommando 4b under Günther Herrmann, Einsatzkommando 5 under Erwin Schulz, Einsatzkommando 6 under Erhard Kroeger and Einsatzkommando z.b. Verfügung under Eberhard Schöngarth. The Einsatzkommando 6 alone shot 133 Jews on 2.7.1941.[423]

Mob rule in Lemberg in early July 1941. A crowd of Ukrainians confronts a seized man with the statue head of Lenin, obviously in order to humiliate him. Local Ukrainians and German forces killed and maltreated Jews and Soviet officials. Acts of mass extermination had already started when the Finnish volunteers passed though Lemberg 1.7.1941 towards the front. *WC.*

Eyewitness Philip Friedman, then a young Jewish historian living in the city, has spoken of his Lemberg (*Lviv*) experiences during the first days of July 1941:

> (...) the city became a witness to a spectacle of severe occupation and bloody pogroms. The German soldiers were quickly joined by the dregs of society, among them Ukrainian nationalists as well as a so-called Ukrainian auxiliary police [force], which was hurriedly organised by Germans. It started in the streets with chasing Jewish men. Lvov (*Lemberg*) Jews, stricken by panic and fear, predominantly stayed indoors. The majority of them hid in their apartments, in various shelters, or in basements and attics. The Ukrainian police and Germans, dissatisfied with a meagre catch in the streets, started to comb Jewish apartments in search of their victims. They took away men and sometimes entire families under the pretext of needing to clear Lvov (*Lemberg*) prisons of corpses (...) The mobs were on the rampage, the howls of the killers mingled with the screams of the victims, and the slaughter in the streets continued.[424]

Wehrmacht soldiers were observed being continuously curious bystanders to these massacres, and some of them participated, not only in Lemberg (*Lviv*), but a few days later also in Niemirow (Ukr. *Nemyriv*), Sokal, and Tarnopol (*Ternopil*). On one occasion, a Wehrmacht sergeant in Lemberg (*Lviv*) was spotted stabbing a Jew with his bayonet.[425] Individual German soldiers and SS representatives were observed participating directly in the cruelty. The retired law Professor Maurycy Allerhand later witnessed the active participation of Germans assisting in rounding up Jews in some streets. German soldiers and officers watched the atrocities, some taking photos, and a film crew made a film on the arrival of the German forces.[426]

A Dutch report

The Dutch volunteer of 1st Company, SS-Regiment Westland, Edmond Henri le Roux, described his experiences of Lemberg (*Lviv*) in early July 1941:

> While we were fighting, we arrived at Lemberg, [which had already been taken] by the Wehrmacht. The cells of the prisons were opened (…); there were lots of dead. Even we could hardly bear the stench that came from those cells (…) [It was] terrible to see. Then we got possessed by the will to win. This is how the fight against Russia developed. We saw it in Lemberg, we were all filled with horror of all that was Bolshevist, as you saw what came out of those cells. They said they were Jews who are being shot. I saw them digging there, they had to dig their own pit, and they were shot, disgusting, what you do that to people. It's disgusting. I will consider this one of the blackest pages of 'wartime National Socialism'.[427]

Observations by Norwegian volunteers

During the summer and fall of 1941, several Norwegian SS-volunteers published newspaper articles in which they told of their involvement in the "reprisal action" against the Jews in Lemberg (*Lviv*). Norwegian volunteer and Nazi activist Per Pedersen from the Staff of SS-Artillerie-Regiment 5 recalled:

> There were fights around and inside Lemberg and the Russians evacuated the city. Here and there lay dead persons in the streets and the prisoners were gathered in the big open square of the NKVD-building. The population was excited and joyful. Shortly afterwards, the inhabitants put up flags and banners around the city. But these were no longer Communist flags – swastikas were painted on the bright-red flags. Across the streets, big white cloths were put up with the inscriptions: 'Long live the German soldiers', 'Long live Hitler', etc. Everywhere along the main streets people gathered, waving handkerchiefs and enthusiastically shouting this or that (…) Typically this was before the city was even cleaned from enemies: young Ukrainian girls seized the rifles from the dead Russian soldiers and fetched the Jews from their hiding lairs (…) So the young Polish-Ukrainian girls arrived with rifles on their shoulders and with the Jews herded before them. The volunteers quickly understood why

A boy surveys his family, killed by the Einsatzgruppe C, in Ukraine in July 1941. The boy was also shot soon afterwards. *Bundesarchiv. WC.*

the population reacted in this way, as a part of them got a glimpse into the NKVD cellars. It was impossible to go on. After this day, there was no one who felt any pity for the Jews, on the contrary. But one recollection remains from this city, a trace of the delicate, longing, and trembling melody of a big city. This was the recollection of bare-boned, ragged, poor boys of the street begging for food, for bread: *Pan – Cjjeb – Bester Herr, gib mir Brot.*[428]

The Norwegian volunteer Olof Brenna of 3rd Battery, SS-Artillerie-Regiment 5, has spoken of his participation in killing Jews in the City with his bayonet.[429] The Norwegian volunteer Olav Ingemar Tuff from SS-Regiment Nordland travelled by railway from Germany to the Eastern front, and on 23.8.1941 he was in Lemberg (*Lviv*) and noticed some Jews hanging from the lamp-posts, just like he had seen earlier in Kraków. He recalled: "The bodies hung like rag dolls."[430]

Norwegian volunteer Bernhard Johansen served as a driver of 1st Battalion, SS-Regiment Germania. In October 1941, in the area north of Lake Azov, he belonged to the battle group (*Kampfgruppe*) Dieckmann, named after the Commander of the 1st Battalion, SS-Sturmbannführer August Dieckmann. When SS-Division Wiking was forced to retire, this battle group was deployed to examine Soviet POWs. Among the numerous POWs, a group was picked for execution. Johansen refused to join the firing squad, but he observed how the prisoners were brought up to the grave. Shortly afterwards he heard the rattle of machine guns, though he did not witness the execution itself.[431] However, Johansen's account does not appear to be beyond dispute. He did not mention this until after the war, and in another interview he claimed that he had never heard any guns being fired.[432]

Norwegian volunteer Erik Østenby was a member of a Transport Company subordinated to SS-Flak-Abteilung 5. According to his post-war recollections, Østenby drove his truck through Lemberg (*Lviv*) at some unknown date. Along the road east of the city, the column of vehicles met long rows of civilians: men, women, and children. These people were guarded by German soldiers carrying their sidearms. Østenby notes:

> "Why?" he asked the soldier sitting beside him in the truck, a Dane (...), who answered that they were Jews being taken to be shot". The confused Østenby asked his Chief, SS-Sturmbannführer Alois Braun, what was going on. However, Braun coloured, becoming red in the face, scolding all the Jews of the world. They had no right to exist, he declared. But Østenby had to promise to remain silent about what he had seen. It was an issue he simply should not show any interest in.[433]

Volunteer Helge Laerum, serving in the SS-Artillerie-Regiment 5, arrived in Lemberg (*Lviv*) on 1.7.1941 at 0900 hours. In his diary he noted: "

> In Lemberg our column remained stationary for hours because fighting was going on east of the city. The stay did not become dull, because the Ukrainian auxiliary were hunting down Jews, who fled panic-stricken over roofs and fences. While running, they were shot like sparrows by the auxiliaries.[434]

However, as far as is known, it was only the Germans who carried guns in Lemberg on 1.7.1941.

Another Norwegian SS-volunteer, probably Olaf Wahlman of 5th Company, SS-Artillerie-Regiment 5, spoke many years after the war on his experiences when entering Lemberg (*Lviv*) on 1.7.1941:

> Suddenly the crowd of people opened up. There were old men, women, and children with canes and iron bars on both sides. Between them people were being driven with foul language and beatings up to the Citadel, which was burning. These were Jews being made to atone, for what I do not know. Houses were looted, and people thrown from windows. An old man with a flapping beard hit the top of the lorry in front of ours, went through the tarpaulin roof and supposedly got blown up by the ammunition load. A little girl hit the street by the side of our car.[435]

Also the aforementioned Hans Isenmann of either the Einsatzgruppe or SS-Regiment Germania spoke of the same kind of atrocities in Lemberg (*Lviv*) in early July 1941: "Apartments belonging to Jews were looted of anything of value". His closest superior, SS-Untersturmführer Eberhardt Heder of 16th Company "personally threw Jews out through the windows."[436]

In early 1942, Norwegian SS-volunteer Josef Hansen published a newspaper article on the execution of 12 Jews at an unknown place near Lemberg (*Lviv*) in early July 1941. The brief paragraph concerning the incident reads: "At one place we took 12 Jews, who were put to work for us. I have never before seen such poor workers. A field court was summoned, and short work was made of them".[437] It is believed that Hansen may have been a member of 9th Company, SS-Artillerie-Regiment 5.[438]

Experiences of Finnish volunteers

As far as is known, no Finnish SS-volunteers were involved in any atrocity in the city of Lemberg (*Lviv*). However, large purges and pogroms certainly did occur there, and a considerable number of the Finns are likely to have got a grim first impression of the bloody reprisals carried out by SS-forces. As the Finnish SS-volunteers may have been influenced by German behaviour, attention is paid here to the impressions of the volunteers. The historian of the Finnish SS-volunteers, Mauno Jokipii, has presented a somewhat incoherent picture of the conquest of Lemberg (*Lviv*). On the one hand he stresses that SS-Division Wiking just passed through the city, staying only a few hours. The locals handed over their tokens of favour like flowers, food, and other small presents. On the other hand, he claims that officers of SS-Division Wiking acted in a state of emergency as there was gunfire being exchanged in the side streets and ongoing fights in surrounding hills. Hence it was not possible for the Division to involve itself in any police actions in Lemberg (*Lviv*) among those inhabitants who resisted the Germans. This is, nevertheless, an apologist view, since the purpose is obviously to give an explanation of why the Germans allowed the illegal shootings that were carried out by the Ukrainian auxiliary forces. Nothing indicates that SS-Division Wiking would have been in any danger whatsoever during their short stay in Lemberg (*Lviv*).[439] The Division was not needed for any ongoing reprisals in the city. The situation in the Lemberg (*Lviv*) area was, however, admittedly still unsettled. Soviet units moved on 1.7.1941 around to the east of the city, and over and above the regular German forces even parts of the Einsatzgruppen were called in for defensive actions, although without engaging in any significant fighting.

A Finnish volunteer of 9th Company, SS-Regiment Westland Martti Uusi-Jaakkola, arrived in Lemberg (*Lviv*) on 1.7.1941 at 11 a.m. and put down his observations in writing:

> The population showed its favours with enthusiasm, and threw flowers to us. Young girls dressed in folk costumes brought flower-garlands. The hatred against Jews is strong, but [it is] no wonder when one thinks about what they have done here. A comrade spoke about his visit to a cellar containing hundreds of bodies, killed by the Jews and the Russians before they fled from the city. The people are in a frenzy and are drawing out the remaining Jews into the streets and beating them mercilessly. Not even the children nor the elderly receive any pardon. The end of the "gauntlet" for many Jews is to be shot. As far as I had the opportunity to observe the Jews [were made to] run between two rows of men, where they were beaten with sticks. The soldiers do not make much resistance [to the Ukrainians] and neither do they beat [the Jews] much. Rather they just shoot them. The shops belonging to the Jews are looted, and in particular alcohol and cigarettes disappear in a moment. Too much is too much, and I am not really ready to take this all in. I feel pity for them, especially the elderly and the women, although there must be weighty reasons for everything. Liquor, tobacco, etc. are thrown into our trucks (...)[440]

Finnish volunteer Reino Suonio, also of 9th Company, SS-Regiment Westland, noted in his diary that the unit had been woken at 4 a.m on 1.7.1941, and had set off for Lemberg (*Lviv*). During the march he witnessed scenes of destruction and desolation like those the day before, on entering Soviet territory:

> We arrived in the city of Lemberg at 11.20 a.m. It had been bombed a little, but the streets were crammed with people forming queues for bread and the like. We spent a few hours here and observed the treatment of Jews. The trash of the city's population raided the apartments of the Jews, drove them out half-naked, and threw stones at them and hit them, also the children and the elderly. One could not expect to witness such things in a cultivated century (...).[441]

The volunteer Markus Käenmäki wrote in his recollections that beyond the local known Communists and those formerly in power, the Jews became the primary victims. He reported that the Jews were "brought into the parks in families". They were executed by 'free troopers' hastily formed of the locals equipped with booty weapons."[442]

SS-Obersturmführer Kaj Duncker, as it appears holding the position of an observing officer in SS-Artillerie-Regiment 5, drove slowly through Lemberg (*Lviv*) before noon on 1.7.1941. He registered the sounds of sporadic shooting and noted: "Massacres of Russians and Jews in the city; lots of Polish prisoners shot by the [departing] Russians before the arrival of the Germans. The first Russian bodies are visible in the ditches."[443] Volunteer Pentti Nikkola of 9th Company, SS-Regiment Nordland, arrived at noon and saw some houses were still burning.[444] Also the Liaison Officer SS-Obersturmführer Ensio Pihkala noted on 1.7.1941:

> Ruins to be seen. People look like they have been liberated. In Lemberg, Poles searched for Jews in their homes. They bring them to the cellars, women are screaming. The poor Jews are beaten and trampled until they are dead. The stomachs of the women have been 'opened', they have lost their hair, and their heads have been crushed. All this occurred in front of the still living Jews. In a cellar there are around 200 bodies! German soldiers, for their part, force their way into the shops, targeting Jews and vodka, juice, cookies, etc. Poles decorate Germans with flowers and some already shout 'Heil Hitler!' (...) Jews were brought to the prison by the Poles for cleaning-up work. They must know that they will be soon shot. A terrible place, indeed, a terrible place. I hurried away.[445]

The events he personally experienced are likely to be accurately recorded.

SS-volunteer Unto Boman reproduces his impressions of the pogroms against the Jews in his recollections. He reports that the Germans did not actively participate in these, but were equally incapable of preventing them:

> The inhabitants of Lemberg, the majority of them being Poles, Ukrainians, Rutens and Slovaks, immediately started to bring in their revenges against inhabitants they knew were Communists and Jews (...) The crowds went crazy in the streets and pushed Jews before them like herds of cattle. Among the Jews there were people of both sexes and all ages.

Running alongside, they drove these unhappy people to the outskirts of the city to kill them. If one of them did not have the strength to run that person was beaten to death in the street. Everywhere echoed calls of alarm and shots, and the bodies of Jews were laid out in the parks and the yards. Living people were thrown down into the streets from the windows of the buildings, and the Jewish homes were looted thoroughly. All the inhabitants of the city appeared to participate in the massacre. They were caught up in some sort of a bloodthirsty mass frenzy that nothing could curb or control.[446]

Units belonging to SS-Regiment Nordland arrived in Lemberg (*Lviv*) at noon on 1.7.1941. SS-volunteer Keijo Kääriäinen of 2nd Company observed burned-out tanks, smashed weapons, and perhaps hundreds of bodies of dead Soviet soldiers, whereas the Germans had already buried their soldiers killed in action "under beautiful crosses". Kääriäinen observed that the damage to the city was not particularly severe. However, the locals experienced many hardships. He reported:

> From somewhere, a large party of men bring a man, who was to be shot. He is shoved and pushed. Somewhere else, a woman leads her wounded husband home, and over there a mother is supporting her 14-year-old daughter, who has lost her sight. Crying children, looking for their parents. Lemberg provides a view of much misery the day after the conquest.[447]

SS-volunteer Martti Leppälä of Panzer-Jäger-Abteilung 5 arrived the same evening, spotting a burning factory and other traces of destruction: "The windows were shattered in all the buildings. In the streets there was all sort of stuff, Russian money, egg boxes, and whatever."[448]

SS-volunteer Sakari Lappi-Seppälä of the 1st Company of SS-Regiment Westland arrived in Lemberg (*Lviv*) on 3.7.1941 in the early afternoon. He observed how armed guards brought entire Jewish families to be shot in a park. These people had been fetched directly from their home, as they wore light clothing. Lappi-Seppälä depicted the disgusting street scene:

> An old father walked with his daughter, the mother being so old and shocked that the relatives often had to support her during the march to the summer park. From there gunshots echoed. A young mother arrived with a begging glance in her eyes and her only child at her breast. Hysterical women shrieked desperately with tears in their eyes and other women were forced down by their hair, trembling elderly people, and young schoolboys.[449]

The Company was ordered to search a residential area, and Lappi-Seppälä's story on the behaviour of the Germans continues:

> We parked our trucks in the centre of Lemberg under thick elms. We jumped from the trucks and headed for the buildings to be inspected. A young Russian soldier had hidden himself in the basement, where my Swedish comrade found him. He was immediately brought out for interrogation. In one of the rooms, pictures of Stalin and Lenin were torn from the walls and kicked about the floor. Some windows were smashed with rifle butts as it was necessary to get fresh air in.[450]

An SS-Division Wiking motorised column moving east from Lemberg 2.7.1941. *KD Coll., SLS.*

SS-volunteer Ahti Paikkala from the 6th Company of SS-Regiment Westland marched through Lemberg (*Lviv*) on 1.7.1941 and noted: "Little damage. Friendly people. Flowers".[451] SS-volunteer Boman, although adequately describing the atrocities committed by the street mobs in Lemberg (*Lviv*), also gave them credit:

> We experience a genuine intoxication of joy in Lemberg after the occupation. The public brought us everything that they imagined we would appreciate: candies, musical instruments, cakes, flowers, and so on. The crowds looted the shops owned by the authorities and brought colossal amounts of alcohol. We had to down these drinks immediately while the crowds screamed their hurrahs. There was no time to look for any corkscrews; the bottlenecks were cut with the pistol butt and the strong cherry liquor consumed with the help of sparkling wine from the Crimea. Litre-sized bottles of vodka were brought from the Russian stores in numbers so great that owing to lack of space we had to throw them from our cars. We were grateful when we were ordered

to continue and to leave this blood-stained city behind us.[452]

However, the volunteer Jaakko Lakeala of 5th Company, SS-Regiment Nordland, noted in his diary on 3.7.1941 that other Finnish volunteers arrived in the same quarters:

> They told us that they had been celebrating in Lemberg with alcohol taken from the Jewish shops". For his part, Lakeala did not mention that any of the alcohol would have been thrown away; rather the diary entry intimates that also the Finnish volunteers may have participated in the looting spree.[453]

The volunteer Martti Koivula of SS-Flak-Abteilung 5 approached Lemberg (*Lviv*) on 1.7.1941 with his unit. He noted that:

> (...) traces of fighting were everywhere, three horse carcasses, two dead dogs, and two Russian corpses. Wreckage and articles strewn on both sides of the road, ruins, ashes, potholes. We had a break for four hours. Arrival in Lemberg. Corpses, tanks, rags and shreds of cloth. Advance beyond Lemberg, where we camped. Fair-quality thunder in the evening. Softening-up of the Jews.[454]

According to volunteer Jaakko Lakeala of 5th Company, SS-Regiment Nordland, the unit made camp on 1.–2.7.1941 in "Nienveeki", probably the village of Winniki (*Vynnyky, Wynnyky*), just a few kilometres east of Lemberg (*Lviv*). He reported his observations on 3.7.1941: "On both sides of the road there were many tanks and cars and ammunition, artillery guns, and other items. Along the road was the body of a civilian, presumably a Jew (...)."[455] The volunteer Sakari Pöyhönen of 6th Company, SS-Regiment Westland, was in a village 25 km north-east of Lemberg (*Lviv*) on 1.7.1941. The soldiers advanced over open fields towards a village occupied by the Russians, and Pöyhönen wrote: "In the outskirts of the village a Russian made attempts to surrender, and he was shot (...)".[456]

OLSZANICA, 2.7.1941: THE FIRST SHOOTINGS OF SOVIET POWS AND CIVILIANS

The village of Olszanica (Ukr. *Velyka Vil'shanytsya or Vilshanytsya,* Pol. *Olszanica Wielka* or *Olszanica,* Rus. *Olshanitsa,* Other spellings *Olszancia, Velyka Vilsanycja, Velika Vilyshanicya, Olszancica, Olszancia; Olszenica*) is situated about 50 km south-east of Lemberg (*Lviv*), and it was the location of one of the first atrocities committed by members of SS-Division Wiking, on 2.7.1941. The villagers, with the exception of the local Jewish population, were obviously welcoming the Germans, as a triumphal arch had been erected.[457] The precise number of perished villagers is not known, but there may well have been over 30 victims.

On 2.7.1941, SS-Obersturmführer Kaj Duncker of SS-Artillerie-Regiment 5 entered the village of Olszanica and noted: "Throughout the entire day searches for Russian snipers (partisans). Firing squads at work, I saw some twenty being shot." Later in the evening, as Soviet POWs and civilians were shot in the nearby village of Novosilky (*Nowosielki, Nowosielce*), Duncker observed that "round-ups occurred also in our village", i.e. in Olszanica.[458]

The Dutch volunteer Jan Olij, a member of 1st Company, SS-Regiment Westland, wrote an entry on 2.7.1941 to the effect that the volunteers had captured 30–40 looters, all of them Jews. He noted: "All are shot, five by five, after having dug their own graves. I am sickened by this shooting. It is not an everyday job to shoot people."[459] Olij does not mention the name of the village, but Olszanica would fit with the date and the unit information. Hence it is not surprising that a grave was found in Olszanica in 2006 with the remains of nine Soviet soldiers who had been shot in early July 1941. Among them was found the military identification dog-tag of Senior Sergeant S. Hetiyev.[460] It can also be noted that volunteer Martti Uusi-Jaakkola of 9th Company, SS-Regiment Westland, noted in his diary, 2.7.1941: "One of our field couriers got lost and was shot. The consequence was that ten prisoners were shot under the direction of a platoon commander (who was later killed in action)."[461]

The village that – in the words of the war diary of 2nd Company, SS-Panzerjäger-Abteilung 5 – "went up in flames" on 2.7.1941, was Olszanica. Many of the villagers perished. However, it was obviously not the SS-Artillerie-Regiment that shelled the village, as Duncker did not report anything about grenades being discharged, although he commonly made daily notes on the number of launches. The Artillery of 295th Infantry Division, which passed through the village, may have been the unit that launched the grenades. "The entire village levelled to the ground", noted Duncker the same day.[462] Volunteer Uusi-Jaakkola for his part noted on 2.7.1941: "At 1300 hours we watched how German artillery set fire to a village in Russian hands with precision firing from a distance of 1.5 to 2 kilometres".[463]

NOVOSILKY, 2.–3.7.1941: BLOODY REVENGE FOR THE REGIMENT COMMANDER WÄCKERLE

The village of Novosilky (*Nowosielki,* Pol. *Nowosielce*) was situated in the same area as the villages of Vilshanitsa (Pol. *Olszanica*), Slovita (*Slowita, Slowida*), and Kryvychi (*Krivici, Krzwice, Krivitisji, Krywcza, Krziewice, Krzywicze, Krywice*), between Lemberg (*Lviv*) and Zolochiv (*Złoczów*). In the evening of 1.7.1941, at least the 1st, 5th, 6th, and 7th Companies of SS-Regiment Westland occupied the area around the village of Novosilky. This village is exceptional in two respects. Two separate massacres occurred, one on 2.7.1941 as the village was burned down, and the second on 3.7.1941 as Jews who arrived on the road were arrested and shot. A dozen SS-volunteers made notes on these events and examining the documentation as a whole gives us relatively extensive information on what happened in the village area.

Actually, there are seven separate Finnish recollections of the atrocities in Novosilky. The main sources are a Security Police (then known as *ValPo*, for *Valtiollinen Poliisi*) interrogation record from 1947 provided by SS-volunteer Thor-Björn Weckström and a recollection by SS-volunteer Sakari Lappi-Seppälä. Pretty much identical information, although somewhat more extensive, was given by Lappi-Seppälä also in the Security Police interrogation in 1947. Later, in 1958, he mentioned that only a fraction of the ghastly events he had experienced were included in his book.[464] In addition, the diaries of Finnish Liaison Officer and military chaplain SS-Obersturmführer Ensio Pihkala, SS-Untersturmführer Ahti Paikkala, SS-Obersturmführer Kaj Duncker, and SS-Unterscharführer Martti Uusi-Jaakkola

SS-Standartenführer Hilmar Wäckerle was Commander of the Westland Regiment of SS-Division Wiking. He was an early member of the Nazi Party (NSDAP) and the first commandant of the Dachau concentration camp in 1933. Wäckerle was killed in action east of Lemberg on 2.7.1941. His death was ferociously revenged by the SS-troops, destroying the village and killing civilians and POWs. Also Finnish troops served in the SS-Infantry-Regiment Westland. *Private collection.*

contain further details. There is also a recollection by volunteer Juhani Sarasalo.

In the interrogation by the Finnish Security Police (ValPo) in 1947, Weckström mentioned the unexpected incident when the Commander of the Westland SS-Regiment, SS-Standartenführer Hilmar Wäckerle, was fatally wounded by enemy sniper fire on 2.7.1941 at 1100 hours. His death stirred resentment among the SS-volunteers.[465] The order was then given to shoot all the inhabitants of the village in revenge, to burn the buildings down, and to slaughter the cattle.[466] However, Weckström did not mention the name of the village, which may have been either Novosilky or nearby Slowita.

The incident caused Finnish Liaison Officer and SS-Obersturmführer Ensio Pihkala to write about the event in his diary:

> (...) Wäckerle had just been shot. Yesterday in the evening he rode in his car to the occupied village. Russians hiding in the grain fields picked him off. In order to bring in their revenge, some tens of Russian prisoners were shot (and this continues over there) as punishment. The Finns (II/Westland, 5th and 6th Companies) took part in the battle yesterday. The boys have done well and were among those who entered the village first. They considered this (in some respect) a 'war game' whereas 'a real war' occurred in Finland.[467]

At 1400 hours, the 7th Company was ordered to "take revenge on the village, where the snipers operated" as the war diary of SS-Regiment Westland bluntly puts it (*7 Kp wird 14.00 Uhr zur Vergeltung auf das Dorf, in den sich die Heckenschützen aufhielten angesetzt*).[468]

The Dutch volunteer Pieter Willems of 1st Company, SS-Regiment Westland, noted on 2.7.1941: "This day is recorded in the annals of the Regiment 'Westland' as one of the darkest during its existence. It was on that day our Regimental Commander, SS-Sturmbannführer [sic] and founder of the Regiment was shot from behind by a sniper. A headshot, so he almost immediately died. It is to be understood that the sadness and indignation in the Regiment was great, because he was the first one who made soldiers out of us Dutch volunteers."[469] Also his compatriot Martinus Weers from the 4th Company reported:

> Today is a hard moment for us. Our Regiment Commander Wäckerle has fallen from a shot by a franc-tireur. The loss is heavy. We shared our love and sorrow with Wäckerle for a year. When he finally could lead his Regiment into battle, he was one of the first to be killed in action. No mercy will be allowed the Russians who fall into our hands until an order brings us to order again. Reluctantly we will agree to take Russian soldiers as prisoners anew.[470]

The Germans soon got the village Novosilky into their possession, burned it to the ground, and "seized a considerable number of civilians".[471] The SS-Volunteer Ahti Paikkala noted in his diary:

> The 7th Company went on a 'vengeance excursion' and after that the village was nothing but ash. As a revenge for the death of the Commander, a few Russians and Jews stopped growing older. A Russian was found hiding in a cooking pot. From there it was a short distance to the place of execution.[472]

Also SS-Obersturmführer Kaj Duncker reported that Wäckerle was shot by a partisan in the village of Novosilky and that "the whole village was razed to the ground".[473]

The German SS-Untersturmführer Carlheinz Behnke of SS-Artillerie-Regiment 5 claims in his memoirs that Wäckerle was actually shot by Polish partisans in an ambush (*durch polnische Partisanen aus dem Hinterhalt erschossen wurde*).[474] In a recollection, the Finnish volunteer Juhani Sarasalo of the 3rd Company of SS-Aufklärungs-Abteilung 5 mentions the soldiers of the SS-Regiment Westland combing corn fields near the place where the Regiment Commander was killed. He was told that partisans had shot him and that the soldiers were chasing the perpetrators. He wrote:

> Later we heard that they had directed revenge acts against the inhabitants of a village in order to make them informers on the partisans. As far as I know this was the only event when some soldiers from the units of the Division became involved in reprisal acts against the local population.[475]

The German literature commonly describes Wäckerle's death as a mean act, and it is claimed that he was shot by a Soviet sniper lying in ambush. The circumstances of the incident are certainly conflicting, and according to SS-Hauptsturmführer Yrjö Kaila of the SS-Aufklärungs-Abteilung 5, Wäckerle may have been killed accidentally.[476] The Dutch SS-Schütze Martinus Rademaker of 2nd Company, SS-Regiment Westland noted that "the deadly bullet struck him in the neck".[477] Moreover, volunteer Martti Uusi-Jaakkola of the 9th Company of the same regiment wrote in his diary on 2.7.1941: "We got a message that our Regimental Commander has been killed in action, the victim of an ambush. That is to say that the marksman was wearing a German helmet and uniform, despite being a Russian".[478]

In 1995, the former German SS-volunteer Ludwig Ergert reported his impressions of the death of Wäckerle. In his story, the Gefechtsgruppe Wäckerle formed the vanguard of SS-Regiment Westland while Ergert together with some motorcyclists (*Kradschütze*) headed a column of 15 trucks. When this was targeted by enemy fire, Wäckerle ordered a counter attack on the northern flank of a village. After driving 500–600 metres along the road, Wäckerle suddenly stopped the car and left it as an apparently wounded Soviet soldier cried for help in German. Ergert noted:

> Wäckerle approached him and stood over him, turned him over, and shouted to his driver that he should bring the First Aid Box. As Wäckerle again stood over the wounded man, he picked up his rifle and shot the Commander in the chin, to the effect that the whole of his head flew off. The driver said the same thing, that this happened a short while before. As we arrived at the site of the incident both Wäckerle and the Soviet were dead.[479]

The historian Jonathan Trigg writes that on 2.7.1941, Wäckerle had stopped his staff car on the road in order to check an abandoned Soviet tank. A surviving crew member in the wrecked tank fired at Wäckerle.[480] If so, it was a Soviet soldier, who was continuing the fight. This was not an act of deceit, because firing from ambush or a concealed place is a completely legitimate way of waging war. Furthermore, the event was strictly military, with no obvious connection to the villagers in the vicinity. In a battle zone, surprise is a method commonly used. On the German side, practically every major assault started with surprise attacks: Poland on 1.9.1939, Denmark and Norway on 9.4.1940, the Western Offensive on 10.6.1941, and Operation Barbarossa on 22.6.1941. However, Soviet snipers specifically targeted German officers. Initially these tactics surprised the Germans and consequently the insignias of the officers were changed in order to make them less conspicuous or distinguishable at distance.[481] The absence of officer's insignias can be observed on photographs.

There is no doubt that the German forces in the field carried out numerous tactical surprise attacks. Nevertheless, the SS documentation brings out the impression that the attack on Wäckerle was somehow improper and devious, although he endangered himself through his own oversight and carelessness. However, the Hague Convention on land warfare from 1907 does not protect German or any other forces from so-called legal war feints. Neither does the Convention outlaw ambushes nor unexpected fire. It seems the main reason for the Westlanders' repressive actions was annoyance at the unexpected and cheap loss of the Regiment's commanding officer, and not at any unjustifiable Soviet way of waging war. However, in German eyes, the soldier who shot Wäckerle dead was a sneaky sniper (*Heckenschütze*) using underhanded methods. Hence the snipers could be characterised as cheats and the repressive steps justified.[482]

Actually, it was not merely Hilmar Wäckerle who was killed in the Novosilky incident on 2.7.1941, but also a part of his command staff team (*Führungsstaffel*).[483] Steiner issued the same day a Division Order on the death of Wäckerle: this indicates that the developments were closely followed. Wäckerle was buried shortly afterwards in the village of Slowita. The Dutch volunteer Martinus Rademacker from 2nd Company, SS-Regiment Westland, noted in his diary: "We had to clean ourselves up and polish our boots, as we had to stand as Ehrenkompanie. Our weapons were cleaned and presentable (*Appellfähig*)".[484]

The bodies of slain civilians, probably Jews, at the pond in Husiatin in early July 1941. *LW Coll. In private ownership.*

Danish Historians Claus Bundgård Christensen, Niels Bo Poulsen, and Peter Scharff Smith have paid attention to the same events, as SS-Division Wiking marched along the road from Lemberg (*Lviv*) to Zolochiv (*Złoczów*) on the evening of 2.7.1941. In the course of this march, soldiers of SS-Regiment Westland started to shoot a large number of Soviet civilians and POWs. It appears that remarks made on the basis of the war diary of the AOK 17 refer to the events in the area of Olszanica-Novosilky-Slowita.[485] The volunteer Martti Koivula of SS-Flak-Abteilung 5 noted in his diary for 2.7.1941, supposedly in the same vicinity: "At 5.30 p.m. I left with Raun (a German) to the Westland Staff. The head of our column just fired at escaping Russian prisoners; around 25 of them were killed."[486]

Professor Mauno Jokipii, who prepared the basic study *Panttipataljoona* ("The Pledge Battalion", 1968) was financially supported to produce the work by the Finnish SS-tradition organisation Veljesapu r.y.,[487] and he has included a section on the executions triggered by the Wäckerle incident in his study. In the text, he briefly mentions that "some Russians and Jews" suspected of cooperation with snipers were executed. However, he continues the presentation in an extensive footnote. Here he seems to conclude that the only unequivocal matter is that it was a real event, although the different sources are so much at odds with one another that the question of what exactly happened cannot be answered.[488] Although not formally belittling the event, Jokipii avoids providing any detailed involvement of the Finnish SS-volunteers and the responsibility of the German officers. His solution is to remove the issue by referring to the various and conflicting sources.

Finnish historian Antero Holmila has paid considerable attention to interpreting Jokipii's uncomfortable footnote. He regards it as an "apogee" and one of "concomitant concealment of awkward questions" like the atrocities against Jews and civilians in Lemberg (*Lviv*) and Zolochiv. Jokipii avoids giving any explanation and although presenting the cachet of objective scholarship, Jokipii "could not avoid, willingly or unwillingly, abrogating the past to his own aims", i.e. committing himself as an agent of the organisation of the Finnish SS-veterans. Moreover, Jokipii also tends to ignore the ideological framework within which the Finnish SS-volunteers operated.[489]

Jokipii pays no attention to the huge scale of the repressive actions. The village, misunderstood as Slowita by Jokipii where Wäckerle was buried, was burnt down, was burnt down, the villagers were shot, and the Jewish men arriving along the road were summarily executed. The precise number of victims is unknown, but no doubt a considerable number of defenceless people were shot, and not just "some" Russians and Jews. A set of events occurred where the spectators observed different moments of the actions and registered them in their diaries. Thus, there was a group of snipers,[490] not just one of them, and hangings and shootings may well have occurred. Jokipii deals with the issue as if it was a limited incident, properly recorded by nine persons.

There is no further information about the slaughtered people the Finnish troops saw alongside the road while passing by. *LW Coll. In private ownership.*

KRIVICHI, 2.7.1941: THE ANNIHILATION OF A LOCAL COMMUNITY

The neighbouring villages of Krivichi (*Krivici, Krzwice, Krivitisji, Krywcza, Krziewice, Krzywice, Krywice*) and Slowita are situated in the same broad area as Olszanica and Novosilky. At least some twenty civilian villagers and roughly 40 Soviet POWs are likely to have been killed in Krivichi and Slowita on 2.7.1941.

SS-Regiment Westland occupied the village of Krivichi on 1.7.1941 and drove out the Soviet forces.[491] In the diary of the 2nd Battalion, SS-Regiment Westland, ineffective enemy movements near Kurowice (Ukr. *Kurovychi,* other spelling *Kurowich*, a village near *Krivichi*) were observed in the afternoon of 1.7.1941. These are described as scattered, and a skirmish of short duration allowed the Battalion staff to take Slowita village. A short time later the vanguard reported: "Krzywicze [Krivichi] is occupied by the Russians. It is the enemy rearguard". As a consequence, Battalions 1–3 of SS-Regiment Westland were grouped for an attack at 4 p.m. and by 6 p.m. the village was in German hands and the enemy had withdrawn north-eastwards.[492] Three SS-soldiers had been killed in action on 1.7.1941 in the village of Krivichi: the Germans Ulrich Herold and Walter Ressler as well as the Dutch volunteer Wilhelm Preng. All these were buried near Slowita village the same day, and Steiner personally attended the ceremony.[493]

An article in the local newspaper *Gazeta Vilna Oekraina* in 1986 claimed a total of 22 people were killed in Krivichi on 2.7.1941 by Dutch SS-volunteers, members of the 5th Company of the SS-Regiment Westland, who set fire to the houses and church.[494] Subsequent Dutch newspaper articles from that time included some additional information:

> On the first day of the occupation of Krivichi, on July 2nd 1941, Dutch SS-men surrounded the village and set fire to it. Later they started hunting for women, the elderly and children, who could not escape, according to eyewitnesses. Survivors later found the bodies of 22 villagers in burnt-out houses and the surrounding wheat fields.[495]

A detachment of 5th Company, SS-Regiment Westland, marched into the village of Krivichi and the Dutch volunteer Ferdinand Frehé noted in his diary:

> On our way in, we spotted nine Russians laying higgledy-piggledy on the road. We halted to check what was going on. 'These are already dead', the others said. We shot two of them in the head, but none of them moved. As we continued to the last man, Hans Rijksen moved on, but looked around and cast a glance at the nine Russians. Then he observed how one of them raised his head to check whether we were all gone. Rijksen shouted to warn us that the Russians were alive. Then we riddled them all with bullets, as one bullet is not sufficient to kill a Russian. Also those two recently shot in the head were seen moving.[496]

As the village of Krivichi was occupied, the volunteers of the same 5th Company participated by strafing the buildings with machine guns, rifles, and grenades, and the 5th Company suffered losses as the aforementioned Herold, Preng, and

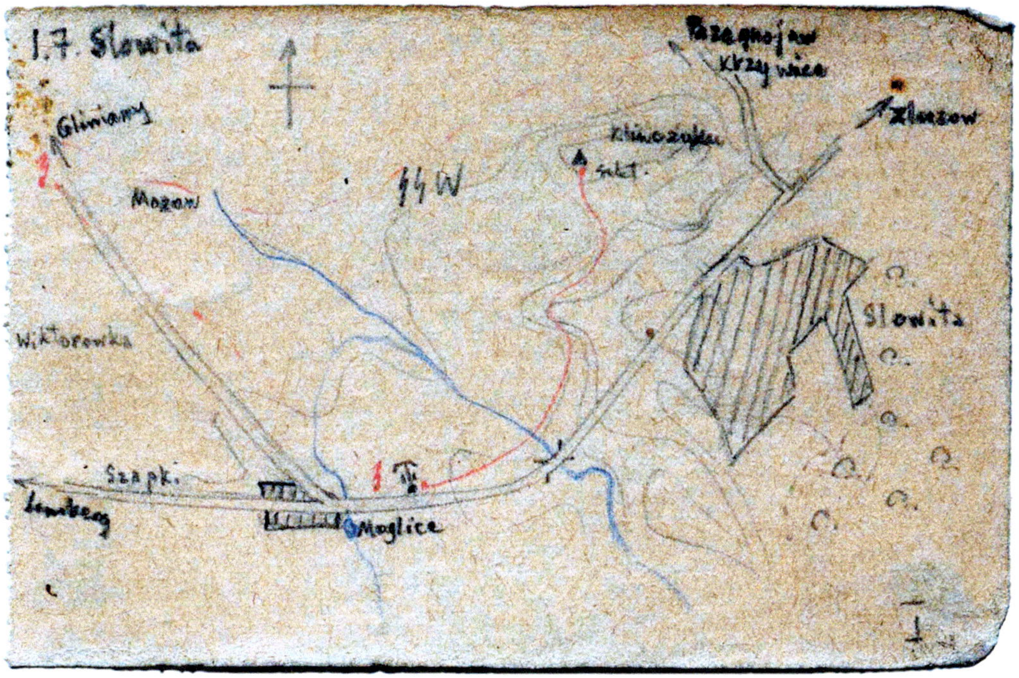

Map drawn by Finnish SS-volunteer Kaj Duncker of the area around the village of Slowita, where SS-Standartenführer Hilmar Wäckerle was buried on 2.7.1941. Slowita and the nearby village of Noviki were taken and destroyed by the SS-troops after this. *KD Collection, SLS.*

Ressler were killed in action, with several others wounded. Some crying and yelling female villagers said there were wounded villagers in their houses, to which the Dutch volunteers replied: "They can perish, we are thirsty, that matters more to us [than wounded villagers]." The women then returned with milk and water. The volunteers had been forbidden to drink anything provided by the locals. However, wrote Frehé: "We could not endure the thirst any longer and let them drink first, and then we drank".[497]

Finnish members of the 5th Company numbered nine SS-volunteers: Mauno Olavi Alhainen (later Olavi Alsta), Lars Fagerholm, Pekka Kujala, Gösta Lundqvist, Antti Mäkinen, Kalevi Porttinen, Jussi Pääkkönen, Paavo Sahari, and Paavo Vuolento.[498] The 6th Company may also have participated in the assault. Volunteer Sakari Pöyhönen, a member of the Company, wrote of his knowledge of the death of Wäckerle:

> All day Russians hiding themselves in the wheat fields have been unearthed. In the village we occupied yesterday there were 30 of them. All of them were put in the Bolshevik prison, which is situated close to our camp-

ing place (...) Now the Bolsheviks have the opportunity to die in the same place. As they went to their deaths many of them were quite afraid, mad with fear, whereas other died like men.[499]

SLOWITA, 2.7.1941: FIRE-RAISING, WILD SHOOTINGS, AND EXECUTIONS

The village of Slowita (Ukr. *Slovita*) was situated a little to the south of Krivichi.[500] It appears 40–50 civilians were killed there in early July 1941. The Swedish historian Lars T. Larsson has estimated that the act of vengeance for Wäckerle cost the lives of around 150 Jews,[501] i.e. embracing the civilian losses in the villages of Olszanica, Novosilky, Krivichi, and Slowita. However, also Soviet POWs were shot, but these are not included in Larsson's figures.

Events started as 7th Company, SS-Regiment Westland, was ordered to attack the village. A Dutch newspaper article described

> Russian eyewitnesses who survived the reprisal action later stated that the furious SS-men shot wildly like savages and threw hand-grenades into wooden houses with thatched roofs. In a short time, soldiers of the 7th Company turned the farming village into ashes (...) Many residents of Krivichi and Slowita were shot or burned alive. A few managed to escape and fled into the wheat fields, but they were tracked down and shot.[502]

The German SS-Hauptsturmführer Landoald Stücker recalled that around two-thirds of the 7th Company were Dutchmen, and there were also some Danish members and a Swede.[503] Among the soldiers of the Company were a further nine Finnish SS-volunteers: Aarne Hakkarainen, Niilo Kaila, Antti Kärki, Pentti Launonen, Torkel Noisniemi, Heikki Rahola, Ahti Setälä, Veijo Vauhkonen, and Esko Tiainen.[504] The officers who ordered the reprisals were the new Regimental Commander, SS-Standartenführer Karl Diebitsch, and the officer commanding the *Versehrten-Bataillon* (Supply Reserve Battalion) of SS-Division Wiking, SS-Standartenführer Heinz Fanslau. Diebitsch sent the 7th Company to the village. It has been supposed that Fanslau told his men that killing the Jews would not be a punishable offence.[505]

On 3.7.1941, 20–30 Jewish refugees and male civilians arrived near the village of Slowita along the road from the direction of the front, but German officers stopped the group. The Commander of 1st Company, SS-Hauptsturmführer Alfred Schade, ordered the SS-volunteers to search the men, finding only money and valuables that were collected in a small pile. At the same time, the Jews had been asked to take off their coats and put them in a pit. Subsequently, Schade ordered seven or eight of the volunteers to carry out the execution of the Jews. Among them was also the Finnish volunteer Thor-Björn Weckström. Rifles were used for the execution. However, before the execution took place, a German non-commissioned officer had started to drill the captured men, giving commands of up-down, squat jumping, etc. When Schade returned he ordered the NCO to discontinue the exercise. Schade did not regard that as in keeping with the usual military behaviour, which expected swift and expedient handling of matters.[506]

The Jews were brought one by one to the edge

of a pit, which they already had been ordered to dig. The firing squad had then executed the Jews with a rifle salvo. The first firing squad had shot five Jews, and after that another squad continued. Thor-Bjorn Weckström walked away from the site of the execution, joined the other Finns, and told them that he thought the action unpleasant, but that it was necessary to follow a given order. To his interrogators, Weckström claimed that "as he fired against the refugees, he [deliberately] aimed away, because of his feelings of disgust against the action". Weckström admitted that he certainly "had never had any sympathies for the Jews, but with regards to humanity he could not approve of actions like this". Weckström informed his compatriots of the incident so they would know about it.[507]

The purpose of Weckström's last remark was probably to explain why the event was known among his Finnish compatriots. Some of the Finnish SS-volunteers had probably informed Valpo, the Finnish Security Police, of Weckström's involvement in the incident. Consequently, it was not wise for Weckström to remain silent on the matter, rather it was a rational step to admit his involvement and to put forward his own version of events. It appears that Weckström had been a member of the firing squad and had fired his rifle as the command was given. However, as he claimed to have respected human values he avoided aiming at the victims, shot wide, and told his Finnish comrades of his distaste and reluctance. Weckström wanted to give the impression that he disapproved of the execution order, but that he had no other choice than to join the firing squad.[508] Thus, he presented his story on the execution as a case of so-called "necessity to obey orders" (*Befehlsnotstand*). Nevertheless, after the war some SS-men targeted by the courts claimed that they had been forced to participate in executions, as refusing orders would have exposed them to the risk of being executed themselves. However, not a single case of that kind in 1939–45 has been confirmed by any German court in the post-war period.[509]

SS-volunteer Sakari Lappi-Seppälä describes in his recollections the same event in Slowita, although with differing details. In the version by Lappi-Seppälä, Wäckerle was carrying out an inspection of his units when he was shot by a Soviet Jewish sniper sitting in a tree. The soldier was captured and hanged, but the men were still fired up and keen to take revenge. As a small group of 20 men – appearing to be Jews – were approaching the Company, along the road from the direction of the front, they were stopped. The Jews were ordered to line up in three rows, and as further Jews joined the group the number of men finally grew to 36. The Jews were ordered to hand over their money, personal documents, and photos to the Germans. On being questioned, the men said they were workers, and the Germans punched each of them in the face. The reason given was that the Germans claimed the Jews were telling lies. All their money was gathered in a pile at the roadside, a sum of about 10,000 Polish złoty in banknotes. The villagers present at the scene were ordered to the other side of the road, and when a sign was given they were allowed to grab the money.[510]

After these developments, the Jews were ordered to bury a foul-smelling carcass of a horse. They were, however, only given three spades. As a result, the other Jews had to dig with their bare hands. During the digging, the Germans beat them with stout sticks in order to urge on the finishing of the pit. As the grave was finished, the Jews dragged the horse carcass into the grave and covered it with soil. However, the commanding officer stopped the activities at this point, and the Jews were again ordered to line up and undress down to their underwear. Then the Jews were ordered to undergo a military exercise, punctuated and encouraged by beatings. An SS-Hauptscharführer made them use work tools and stones as weapons, ordering them to throw one another to the ground and target each other. The Jews had to keep their arms over their heads when ordered to jump up and down. Those who tired or fell to the ground were forced to continue at the end of a bayonet. As this continued for three hours, the Jews became exhausted and desperate.[511]

At the end, the Jews were given spades and ordered to dig a grave on the other side of the road behind a Soviet barbed-wire fence. The Jews dug a pit a metre deep and finally had to hand over their rings and watches, which Lappi-Seppälä and his compatriot Keijo Aalto collected. Then five Finnish SS-volunteers were ordered to carry out the execution. Lappi-Seppälä has commented on his reaction:

> We did not know from where our Company Commander got the idea to order us Finns to carry out the executions. We were quite stunned when this happened. Then, for the first time, we responded by saying that we strongly opposed the order. We told him frankly that we would not shoot Jews for any reward, because they had never done us any harm. SS-Hauptsturmführer Schade, our Company Commander, was furious. He could not believe that we were such cowards. His intention was to demonstrate how his soldiers earned the name of men. His impression of the Finns now completely changed, as we were good for nothing.[512]

Schade then ordered German SS-soldiers, together with the Finnish volunteer Weckström, to carry out the execution and the first five Jews lined up at the sand embankment at the edge of the grave with their faces towards the firing squad, 5 metres away. Schade gave the order to aim at the faces of the Jews because Wäckerle had been murdered at close range in the same manner. At the order "Ready to Fire", the submachine guns of the *Schiesskommando* rose and on command of the Platoon Chief, SS-Untersturmführer Ludwig Lieb of the 1st Company of SS-Regiment Westland, everyone in the squad launched a volley of five shots. "Fragments of brains and skulls blew off from the two first victims as they collapsed into the grave", Lappi-Seppälä noted. The next five Jews stepped over the naked and bloody bodies of their comrades and lost their lives in the same way. This scene was repeated five times as a new group of victims stepped on the earlier bodies. Lappi-Seppälä observed: "Before us appeared a big heap of bodies, and the last victims were busy trying to maintain their balance as they climbed over the dead bodies".[513]

The executions were still going on when two more Jews arrived along the road and were arrested and stripped naked, whereupon German soldiers hounded them into a barbed wire fence using bayonets. With bleeding wounds, both Jews were kicked into the execution pit and shot. Soviet POWs were then given the task of filling in the grave. After the execution, Schade ordered that cognac and cigarettes would be brought from the canteen truck as a reward for members of the firing squads: "Their names were noted and they were hailed for their work, which they had carried out on behalf of their fathers and ancestors. The New Europe needed more such men, who were of genuine German character", noted Lappi-Seppälä.[514]

In his interrogation in 1947, Lappi-Seppälä added:

> The Finnish SS-men gathered together to watch this 'performance'. The Finns present were Keijo Aalto, Hukari, Hemmo, Gröndahl the younger, Laaksonen, and myself. All of the Finns in this group regretted the German measures and had loudly expressed as much. When the Jews were still digging, Company Commander Schade said: 'Now, let's give our Finnish men an honorary task to perform the execution of these Jews', at which SS-man Aalto told Schade (...) that the Finns do not carry out such things. Schade got annoyed and replied: 'Oh you are such womenfolk, but my boys are soldiers'". Schade then ordered Aalto and Lappi-Seppälä to guard the Jews as they dug the grave.[515]

According to Lappi-Seppälä's recollections, all the Finnish volunteers refused the order from Schade to join the firing squads and shoot the Jews. However, Lappi-Seppälä's information does not appear entirely to be entirely truthful. Weckström himself reported that he was a member of the firing squad. Members of the 1st Company, aside from Lappi-Seppälä, were Keijo Aalto, Veijo Hukari, and Unto Hemmo. Lappi-Seppälä does not mention Matti Lehto, Helge Rosenqvist, and Timo Räihä, who also belonged to the 1st Company. The volunteer Aulis Gröndahl was a member of the 3rd Company, and there was no volunteer listed by the name Laaksonen.[516] For whatever reason, Lappi-Seppälä is likely to have protected at least Weckström, and possibly some other volunteers, or he did not properly remember the details.

Volunteer Christian Rosenbröijer of 6th Company, SS-Regiment Nordland, gives a different version in two respects. First, he associates the killing of Wäckerle with the Jews. Second, he presents Ukrainians as the perpetrators. Rosenbröijer stated:

> When the Commander of Westland was shot, some stalker in the bushes got him. We arrived with one of the columns. Westland had driven ahead of us, and from the car I observed on the left side around ten Jews digging graves for themselves. As I had the time to watch, I saw how the scamp (*vekkuli*) was shot in the grave after digging it.

However, the executioners were in this case not Germans, but locals who forced the victims to dig. After finishing this work, they [the Jews] were shot in the back. It is quite possible that Rosenbröijer is here describing a different execution, in which local people were involved. However, it is also possible – and more likely – that his intention was to downplay the role of the Germans and to blame the Ukrainians. He claimed that this was the only time he witnessed the killing of Jews. As he passed Lemberg (*Lviv*) two days earlier, he had not noticed any massacres. The only change he mentioned was that the Germans had reserved some of the cafés and restaurants for the Germans and some for the Poles.[517]

A party of captured Comsomol members in Kamenka in September 1941. *KD Coll., SLS.*

Soviet POWs in Ukraine, summer 1941. *KD Coll., SLS.*

KUROWICE, 3.7.1941: 180 SOVIET POWS WERE SHOT AND SOME JEWS

The anti-tank SS-Panzerjäger-Abteilung 5 passed through Kurowice (*Kurovychi, Kurowich*) - Zolochiv (*Złoczów*) on 3.7.1941, possibly near the Kurowice airfield, which was one of 21 Soviet airfields in the Lemberg (*Lviv*) area. Finnish volunteer, SS-Untersturmführer Veikko Hallavo commented upon the march a few days later in his diary:

> A little skirmish occurred this morning. We defeated a Russian column; all the 180 prisoners were shot. We spotted the column and we accurately fired at it, quite easy sport, but we just had to shoot all of them! At one point a civilian reported that there were still Russians at the sides of the road. Four or five men went to look for them! When we were 15–25 metres from them the Russians put up their hands, but the men shot them, children as well.[518]

A few days later, on 8.7.1941, Hallavo noted:

> Now we leave (...) We spent the night in a house where all Jews were shot! These (German) recruits can certainly be cruel. First they ordered [the Jews] to dig a grave for a horse, all the diggers were more than 60 years old. As half of the horse was covered, one of the Jews had to lay down beside the horse and one of the men shot him. The others covered this over and the exercise continued![519]

ZOLOCHIV, 3.–4.7.1941: LIEUTENANT-COLONEL GROSCURTH RESTRAINS THE BRUTALITY OF SS-DIVISION WIKING

The small town of Zolochiv (*Złoczów*) is situated approximately 60 km east of Lemberg (*Lviv*) along the highway leading to Tarnopol (*Ternopil*). The area belonged to Poland between 1923 and 1939, and in the fall of 1939, it was incorporated into the Soviet Union. In 1939 Zolochiv had about 20,000 inhabitants, of whom around 10,000 were Jews, 5,000 Poles, and 5,000 Ukrainians.[520] By the summer of 1941, the population may have been around 16,000, of whom 8,000–9,000 were Jews, i.e. roughly a half. It has been estimated that 600 to 1,000 of the local Jews were killed in the town in early July, mainly on 3.–4.7.1941.[521]

Town Zolochiv fell to the Germans 3.7.1941. *KD Coll., SLS.*

The atrocities in the recollections of the locals

In late June, Zolochiv was bombed daily, first the railway station and the road junctions and later the buildings and streets.[522] German forces occupied the town on 2.7.1941, when the 9th Panzer Division rolled in. The very first German motorcycle squads entered Zolochiv early in the morning of 1.7.1941. In the market place stood a damaged truck with wounded Soviet soldiers. In a report by surviving locals the initial events are described: "The Germans poured benzene over the truck and burned it along with the wounded." The local Jewish population were hiding in cellars and makeshift air-raid shelters when Luftwaffe bombed the town on 30.6.1941, killing around 40 Jews. This Luftwaffe action may have been a result of the collaboration with Ukrainian nationalist elements, who were equipped with secret radio transmitters and directed the German bombers to the places where Soviet forces had concentrated.[523]

The 1st Company of either Nordland or Germania Regiment of SS-Division Wiking arrived in Zolochiv in the afternoon or evening of 2.7.1941. A surviving Jew reported that the invaders: "in unison, young members of the SS started to go wildly through the houses; they raped Jewish girls, murdered pregnant women, robbed and plundered Jewish possessions". Among the first local victims were 'the town simpletons', two feeble-minded brothers nicknamed Jopaks. They fell to the first German bullets, not understanding that one could be killed for no reason at all, and that it was necessary to hide. A woman holding her child in her arms stood behind a closed door at Lemberger Street. When the child cried a passing German noticed this and murdered the mother with two shots.

> A neighbour, a pregnant woman, started to scream, not understanding the gravity of the situation and trying to appeal to the conscience of the offender. His response took the form of wild laughter and a bullet into her stomach.[524]

The proprietor of a printing shop, Samuel Lipa Tennenbaum (note: the family name in those days was spelled *Tenenbaum*), witnessed the street events from a window:

> I saw a motley mob, perhaps a hundred people, rushing out of the government stores across the street. They were looters. There was a bearded Jew in the crowd, and a young, pretty peasant girl (...) A German military vehicle drove up, two non-commissioned officers jumped out, and without a word of warning one of them pulled out a revolver and started shooting into the crowd. Several people, among them the Jew and the girl, fell to the pavement.

Then Tennenbaum observed youngsters pointing out the apartments of Jews to the German soldiers. Around noon, several soldiers forced their way into Tennenbaum's home, rummaged through the closets seizing suits, a silk coat, and two expensive cameras. In the early afternoon the first signs of a pogrom started to appear as German soldiers and Ukrainian nationalists began rounding up Jewish men in the streets and buildings. Some of the victims were battered or shot dead and others were dragged to the Citadel.[525]

However, worse was shortly to follow, according to Jewish eyewitnesses:

> Many Jews paid with their lives for their naivety that same day. No one could yet conceive of what the Germans were capable of. One looked out through a window, another stood at the door, and a third dared to fetch water. Immediately, on the first day, the local Ukrainians appeared as loyal collaborators of the "victors" [the Germans]. Rich and poor, the members of the intelligentsia, the workers and the peasants, all of them with no distinction, presented themselves for service with the Germans (...).

Under German protection

> the Ukrainian peasants from the surrounding villages, incited by the intelligentsia, armed with weapons, clubs, and provided with sticks, raided Jewish houses. They stole whatever there was: jewellery, clothing, shoes, food – everything of any value. The out-of-towners, who did not know exactly where the Jews lived, were assisted by the local Ukrainian neighbours. These knew about everything and in the majority of cases they played a leading role. The more sensible and decent among them tried to maintain 'neutrality' (...) The rampaging in the [Jewish] quarter was boundless, and the Jews did not even try to defend their possessions, but they were ready to give everything away in order to spare their lives. The murder-

ers moved in groups, one raiding group left and another arrived.[526]

The Ukrainian nationalists

The very same day as Zolochiv (*Złoczów*) was occupied, i.e. 2.7.1941, local Ukrainians and farmers from the surrounding area flooded in and greeted the arriving Germans. Groups of members of the Ukrainian nationalist organisation OUN's underground militia (led by Ivan Klymiv) joined the Germans. Tennenbaum reported that the leaders of the nationalist-leaning Ukrainian intelligentsia gathered in the Casino Hall and a Committee of thirty representatives was elected. The Committee promptly issued a proclamation, which claimed – quite falsely – that the Jews had been responsible for the mass arrests and summary executions of some Ukrainian nationalists in the Citadel in Zolochiv in the first days of the conflict. As in Lemberg (*Lviv*), the killings were in fact carried out by the departing Russians, quite possibly by the NKVD in reprisals for sabotage by the anti-Soviet Ukrainian nationalists. The blood libel of blaming the 'Jewish Bolshevists' was a handy tool to 'justify' and 'legitimise' the anti-Jewish pogrom that was planned. The non-Jewish locals were called upon to take revenge against the Jews for the spilled 'innocent' blood. The Germans received the initiative of the Ukrainians with satisfaction, approved their plans, and promised far-reaching assistance for their actions.[527]

In the afternoon of 2.7.1941, the German Town Commandant ordered that all Jews from the age of six years should wear white armbands with a blue Jewish star and the inscription "Jew". Any Jew without such an armband would be shot. The Ukrainian militia put up posters ordering all Jews to gather at the Town Hall Square the following day. Those refusing to attend would be shot. Consequently, many captured Jews were not brought to the Citadel, but they were simply butchered in various locations: at the marketplace, on the old ramparts, on Lemberger Street, at the sports ground, in the courtyards of the Linsk Hasidim and Lippa-Mehr, and in numerous other places.[528]

Instead of arriving in the square as ordered, a considerable number of Jews preferred to stay in hiding. Nevertheless, Ukrainian militia searched their homes and rounded up Jews and brought them to the Citadel. Jews forming a long line were waiting outside for admission, where SS-men at the gate beat the new arrivals with truncheons. In the prison courtyard there was a pit with the bodies of the NKVD victims, and the Jews were ordered to remove the corpses, to wash them, and to lay them out for inspection and identification. A guard of Ukrainian militia and ten German soldiers beat, kicked, and killed some of the Jews. Other Jews were ordered to jump into the now-empty graves, where, according to one account: "...they were machine-gunned by the SS men. Without bothering [to check] whether the victims were alive or dead, they were covered with new people and the procedure repeated. The screams of the wounded and those buried alive rose to heaven, but none heeded them". Also the Ukrainians participated in the shooting and by throwing hand grenades acquired from the subunits of the SS-Division Wiking. As a result of these actions, considerable numbers of the local Jewish population were killed.[529]

One of the Jewish survivors, Solomon Altman, spoke about the events of 3.7.1941:

Crowds armed with axes, hatchets, shovels, iron bars, hammers, and firearms simultaneously stormed all the Jewish streets and houses, dragging their occupants into the streets. The pogrom began from pre-selected places like Targowica, the old market square, the Lwowska Street, and the courtyard of Lippa Mehr at Klonowicza Street, with the main centre of operations nevertheless being the Citadel. Hordes of Ukrainians and SS-men swooped down upon their defenceless victims with whatever they had in their hands. The Jews could not even hide. Those who tried to escape were forced back by new waves of offenders. Ukrainian neighbours with whom only the day before there had been friendly or business relations now turned relentless enemies. They lured Jews into their homes, only to hand over the city inhabitants to the savage mob. When the wave of terror eventually died down, people were found drowned in latrines and sewage holes, some with their heads chopped off. A number of scoundrels had caught Rabbi Ellenberg, tied him to a motorcycle with a rope, and dragged him up the street. The Rabbi, with his tongue hanging out, had to keep up with the motorcycle to the delight and the wild laughter of the street urchins. As the motorcycle gathered speed, the venerable old man fell from exhaustion, and his body was dragged along, mutilated and unrecognisable.

The Rabbi had been tied by his beard to the motorcycle.[530]

Among those driven to the Citadel were Joseph Zimmer and Dr. Moses Eisen. A Ukrainian acquaintance of theirs pulled them out of the mob and sent them home to bring ropes. He asked them to fetch strong ropes as he badly needed them. Zimmer and Eisen returned with the requested tools: "They were politely thanked in the presence of the spectators and hanged with the ropes they had brought." In the late afternoon, piles of bodies laid everywhere in the yard and by the mass grave. Many German officers "watched the pogrom with calm cynicism, clicking their cameras all the time". A few months later a German illustrated weekly published a few of these photos from the Zolochiv Citadel courtyard. One depicted women weeping over a pile of corpses, among them the Jew Luisa Freimann. The photo text read: 'Ukrainian women mourning their husbands who were murdered by Jews'. Then, as Altman describes it, "...something like a miracle happened". As dark and heavy clouds suddenly appeared, followed by a strong wind and heavy rain, the offenders were forced to disperse, and further actions were interrupted."[531]

However, the reason for the exceptional great number of Jewish victims in Zolochiv 3.–5.7.1941 in comparison with other municipalities situated on the marching route of the SS-Division Wiking was the mass shootings in the Zamek Citadel. The SS soldiers of the sub-units of the the division combed the town streets and living quarters for Russians and Jews and engaged local OUN-led Ukrainian militias as auxiliaries. To some extent this locally enlarged the role of the militia in Zolochiv. The SS units committed numerous acts of violence against the local civilians and encouraged by their example to participate in the atrocities.[532]

Oberstleutnant Helmuth Groscurth

The German forces in Zolochiv (*Złoczów*) did not act on the basis of a common conception. Oberstleutnant Helmuth Groscurth, the General Staff Officer of 295th Infantry Division arrived in Zolochiv. Altman continues:

> At the sight of the bodies, the General [sic, Groscurth was a Lt. Col] ordered the slaughter to be stopped. SS-Hauptsturmführer [Heinz] Schultze, Head of the 'Death Platoon' initially objected, but eventually had to obey. The Ukrainians (...) did not like this turn of events and sent a delegation to the General [sic] to persuade him to change his order. They were so sure they would get the command withdrawn that they did not allow the fresh graves in the Citadel to be covered or the scattered corpses in the yard to be collected. But their hopes of liquidating the entire Jewish population at one stroke were disappointed, for neither the General [sic] nor the District Commander acceded to their demands."

Actually, it was an order promulgated by the District Commander that finally put an end to "the wild orgy of the Ukrainian hoodlums and

Destruction after battle in Ukraine, summer 1941. *JT Coll., FWM.*

the SS hangmen", as it included a ban on any violence towards civilians, irrespective of their creed or nationality.[533]

However, in the publication "Der Untergang fun Złoczów", written by the survivors of the Złoczów [Zolochiv] Jewry and edited by Szlojme Mayer, the General [sic, Lt. Col. Groscurth] arrived at the execution site in the Citadel on 3.7.1941 at 3 p.m. to ascertain the number of victims. He considered the number sufficient and ordered the persecution to end at 4 p.m. A survivor described the event:

> Those carrying out the pogrom still had authority for not quite another hour. They tried to make as much use of the time as they could. The General stood with his watch in his hand and counted the minutes. When four o'clock arrived, he ended the slaughter. At this time, he told the surviving Jews to run home, 'schnell'. The murderers shot after the fleeing Jews, who ran over each other in fear and panic. There was a stampede. The bulk of them were exhausted and could not run fast enough, and they paid with their lives. Only a small number successfully saved themselves from the hell of this day.[534]

On 2.7.1941, Groscurth reported to the 4th Army Corps that "the SS are randomly shooting great numbers of Russian soldiers and civilians who look suspicious to them". He now urged the Town Commandant and the Commander of 518th Infantry Regiment, Oberst Otto Korfes, to stop the shootings and to establish proper order, using force of arms if necessary. Korfes was informed by a dispatch rider that "the SS together with civilian bandits were plundering, dragging people out of their homes, and had already killed a lot" of them. However, the steps undertaken by Korfes were half-hearted, as only the women and the children were allowed to be released from the Citadel. Shortly after, the shootings started again and continued in the following days. It has been estimated that during 4.–6.7.1941 also other Jews were shot. However, information about the events in the Citadel courtyard is hard to come by, as only a few of the Jews succeeded in escaping there with slight wounds, saved by the downpour and by the increasing darkness.[535]

The SS-Division Wiking

SS-Regiments Nordland and Germania of SS-Division Wiking remained in Zolochiv (*Złoczów*) over 2.–3.7.1941, and Westland passed through Zolochiv on 3.7.1941 at 1 p.m.[536] Several sources report that the SS-soldiers got involved in the atrocities. The German historian Bernd Boll emphasises the supporting background role of SS-Division Wiking:

> Certainly the OUN is responsible for many cases of mistreatment and murder. But the exhumation of the [Ukrainian] corpses in the Citadel turned into mass killing only because of the participation of the soldiers of SS 'Wiking'. This Division (...) had been marching from Lemberg (*Lviv*) to Zolochiv, following directly behind several other divisions, and it seems to have considered the first days of the war in the east as a sort of hunting expedition, with people as prey. On July 2nd and 3rd, it blocked the route of advance, apparently intentionally, while several mem-

bers went 'hunting for Jews' and in the process shot everything and anybody that looked even the slightest bit suspicious, e.g. civilians with shaved heads (Russian soldiers).[537]

The German historian Kai Struve has for his part characterised the killings in Zolochiv as the first large-scale massacre of SS-Division Wiking.[538]

A German SS-officer picked up the student Shlomo Wolkowicz from his home on 3.7.1941. The SS-men stood waiting at the gate to the Zolochiv Castle (Citadel) where the killings later occurred. In the prison-yard, ten SS-men watched as the prisoners dug a grave. Wolkowicz reported that SS-men "tortured" Orthodox Jews in the prison-yard. Other SS-men set up the machine guns, turned them on the pit, and shot long uninterrupted volleys, which killed a considerable number of the Jews. On 5th of July 1941, the 4th Army Corps reported "that soldiers of the Waffen SS Division Wiking were also participating in these murders".[539] A German SS-soldier fired three times at the local Jew Dovid Lwow, who, nevertheless still remained standing on his feet. Shortly after this, a local Ukrainian hit him and split his head in half with a spade. Under SS leadership, a band of Ukrainians raided the Jewish Houses of Prayer. They broke down the doors, looted whatever had a practical value, and destroyed everything else. They gathered all the sacred books and set fire to them.[540]

Thereafter Oberst Otto Korfes of 518th Infantry Regiment was successful for a while in stopping the executions, but on 4.7.1941 the murders began again, with the participation of the Waffen-SS. A report from the 4th Army Corps stated: "From Złoczów [Zolochiv] there are again reports of the most gruesome shootings by the retreating Russians as well as by Ukrainians and the SS. At least 300 Ukrainians and 300 Jews have allegedly been shot." Korfes drove to the Castle and encountered a dozen Ukrainian nationalists with spades, axes, pickaxes, and hand grenades, led by an SS-officer. Around 60–80 men, women, and children were standing in the grave where many others had already been killed or maimed by hand grenades. Korfes observed two SS-volunteers in the Citadel and suspected that the hand grenades the OUN supporters used originated from supplies of SS-Division Wiking. The German historian Bernd Boll, who has extensively studied the Zolochiv events of early July 1941, concludes that "the Ukrainians found welcome help from the SS-Division Wiking (…)."[541] Actually, it was rather the other way around, for the SS-soldiers of the division engaged the Ukrainians.[542] SS-Einsatzgruppe C reported to Berlin on 16.7.1941 that the Ukrainian militia of Zolochiv had arrested several hundred Jews as revenge for earlier NKVD killings. The report stated: "These were shot. The number of liquidated Jews is between 300 and 500".[543]

In 1960, Korfes reported to the authorities on the grave containing Jewish bodies:

> It had apparently once been a parade ground, an open square within the Citadel which these gangs (i.e. the Ukrainian nationalists) had used to pile up the dead. Evidently, in order to be better able to count them, they had heaped them up in piles five or six. As far as I can remember, there were about 500 to 600 lying there. I walked past the dead with a Doctor to ascertain whether any of them were still alive. But most had either received an additional pistol shot to finish them off, or, as in the case of

children, were immediately torn to pieces by hand grenades, while the rest had their heads split open. The civilians carried pickaxes, axes, and spades. They had used these to smash the skulls of the seriously wounded in the pit, and they had then taken them out and piled them up for counting.[544]

In mid-July 1941, a Judenrat was established in Zolochiv at the request of the Germans. It was ordered to list the perished locals and carry out a census of those still living. The Judenrat was also expected to supply forced labour and to pay four million rubles in fines or ransom to the Germans, levied for being "primarily responsible for the outbreak of World War II". The German forces introduced traffic restrictions, prohibitions on buying food, and confiscations of apartments and valuables. The common effects of the contributions and the paralysis of economic activities led to a general worsening of the living conditions for local Jews.[545] The Germans were not satisfied with the local supply, as they intended exploiting the town and this could be only done with the participation of the locals, of which the majority were Jews. Hence the continuation of looting carried out by Ukrainians went against German interests, since they were intent on reserving the economic benefits for themselves. As a result, posters in German and Ukrainian went up all over the town, warning the locals against further anti-Jewish actions and looting. These proclamations cooled the temper of the Ukrainians to a certain degree. The Judenrat was ordered to make a large financial contribution to the Town Commandant.[546]

The minor role of Einsatzkommando 4b

A small party of Einsatzkommando 4b may have passed through Zolochiv on 4.7.1941. This is, however, not very clear and their passage may have taken place the previous day. The Einsatzkommando may have encouraged violent acts, but it is unlikely to have participated in any larger-scale encouragement.[547]

According to a report from Einsatzgruppe C, the Ukrainian militia in Zolochiv captured 300–500 Jews "on instructions of the Wehrmacht". The war diary of the 295th Infantry Division mentions that the shootings were carried out by Ukrainians and SS, whereas the units of the Einsatzgruppe are reported not to have participated in these killings. Korfes, for his part, identified the shooters as members of SS-Division Wiking. When the SS-Einsatzgruppen were organised in May-June 1941, they were given instructions on their forthcoming actions on Soviet territory. The Einsatzgruppen should wherever possible incite local anti-Semitic and anti-Communist militias and armed groups to attack the Jews and Soviet collaborators in their municipalities. These guidelines recommended measures "without leaving traces" and in a decentralised way, directly after Wehrmacht forces having occupied a town or village.[548]

The Einsatzgruppe marched closely behind the Wehrmacht units, following their orders to stay in the background for the time being while the Ukrainian militias were busy attacking Jews and any remaining Soviet officials and Communists. Only if the Ukrainians did not organise themselves as expected were the Einsatzkommandos to be ready to get involved. In this way, Einsatzkommando 4b under Günther Herrmann held back their forces in Zolochiv and watched developments of the events.[549] Einsatzgruppe C reported to Berlin on 11.7.1941: "EK 6 in Złoczów [Zolochiv] in the morning of 8.7.1941. At this time 16 Communist functionaries and informers executed, among them 3 Jewish females."[550]

Actions by the Dutch and Norwegian SS-volunteers

Dutch volunteer SS-Schütze Martinus Rademaker from the 2nd Company, SS-Regiment Westland, noted in his diary (2.7.1941) in 'Zlasczow' (probably Zolochiv):

> Some "Partisans" were killed (...) The sun was shining, and we all walked about in sports shorts. The 1st Company used the free time to shoot the Jews, who had fought partisan warfare. There is no other solution for these animals. The money [the Jews possessed] was divided among the Ukrainians. The sharpshooters joined in, and [the Jews] were shot dead two by two. They tumbled into the grave that they had dug themselves.

As some Russian prisoners had escaped from the Gebirgsjäger, a Westland Battery quickly tracked them down: "They got what they deserved. A Russian officer, going to be hanged, had to put the loop around his neck himself." Rademaker's notes continue:

> Our group had to be ready at 2 o'clock. We were to make a motorised reconnaissance force (*Spähtruppe*), but it was cancelled. The Finns of 1st Battalion had also undertaken a patrol early in the morning (...) At the last moment, Teschmann and Gerard de Swat brought in a Jew, carrying a sack of potatoes on his shoulders. Chop! (Allez hup) – the sack on the truck – it was welcome food.[551]

The volunteer Jan Olij of the 1st Company, SS-Regiment Westland, wrote for 3.–4.7.1941: "Hundreds of Jews are killed. They had to dig up the murdered victims with their hands, and they were immediately shot in these same graves. All blood, blood, rain and fire".[552] The place of these events is not mentioned, but the description and the dates and the unit information would fit with Zolochiv.

In an unknown place in Galicia, a Norwegian SS-volunteer shot a Jew, who the Ukrainians shortly before had badly beaten. However, it is likely that this incident occurred in Zolochiv, either on July 2nd or 3rd, 1941.[553]

Experiences of the Finnish volunteers

At least 25 Finnish SS-volunteers are likely to have been present in Zolochiv (*Złoczów*) in early July 1941 and to have observed the massacre of the local Jews. Liaison Officer Ensio Pihkala appears to have passed through Zolochiv, which he erroneously names 'Zokowice'. In any case, he writes of 3.7.1941: "Here the Russians acted against the civilians like in Lemberg (*Lviv*). SS-men caught Jews, made them dig graves and shot the diggers afterwards. Or made them swim in the river".[554] SS-Artillerie-Regiment 5 passed through Zolochiv in the early afternoon of 3.7.1941, where Kaj Duncker described the town as "rather desolated, outrages on Jews".[555] The volunteer Sakari Pöyhönen of 6th Company, SS-Regiment Westland, noted on 3.7.1941: "A significant number of Russians were executed (in) a Ukrainian town", probably Zolochiv. He also added: "In the very early morning we found a couple of Russians, who perished."[556]

ZBORIV, 4.7.1941: FURTHER MASSACRE OF JEWS

On 1.7.1941, units of the 9th Panzer Division occupied the town of Zboriv (Russ. *Zborov*, Pol. *Zborów*, other spellings *Zborov, Zborob, Zbvorow*), 85 km south-east of Lemberg (*Lviv*). The number of inhabitants is unknown, but it may have been around 5,000 people, of whom some 2,000 may have been Jews. The first mass shooting occurred on 4.7.1941. A report from Sonderkommando 4b belonging to Einsatzgruppe C mentions "(...) at Zborów [Zboriv], 600 Jews were liquidated by the Waffen-SS as a reprisal for Soviet atrocities" (*In Zborow von der Waffen-SS als Vergeltungsmassnahme für die Greuel der Sowjets 600 Juden liquidiert*).[557] On 5.7.1941, an additional 100–150 Jewish males were brought to the courthouse and shot. A total of 600 to 800 locals are estimated to have been killed.[558]

As German forces entered the town, the shootings began, and a recollection by a surviving local inhabitant describes the events:

> Germans and Ukrainians took Jewish men from their homes and concentrated them in an enclosure near the store owned by Meir Adler, with the excuse that they were needed for work (...) More than 1,000 men were executed in two mass pits: one near Meir Adler's store and the others in the municipality courtyard.[559]

However, German historian Kai Struve estimates the number of Jews and local civilians killed at between 600 and 850. A number of local Jews did not obey the order to assemble, but instead they hid themselves for a while. To counter this, in August the Germans and the Ukrainians organised a round-up of the surviving Jews who had worked in Soviet-run institutions during 1939–41. Dozens of these were then executed in the Prisovtza Forest.[560] In Zboriv, the role of the Ukrainian nationalists and the militia was a minor one, as units from SS-Division Wiking were involved in these actions and used the Ukrainians simply as assistants.[561]

On 4.7.1941, the Germans organised a kind of mock procession, which was described by the local inhabitant Salomon Berger. He reported that one of the leading men of the Jewish congregation was nailed to a board, put into a wagon and pulled through the village. Another prominent Jew, Namen Zephorah, was tied by his hand to the wagon and his beard was burned. Other Jews were forced to follow the procession, singing and dancing. The local Jew Lejd Kronisch concluded that the idea appeared to have been presented as a kind of parody of the Crucifixion of Jesus. All the victims were brought to the vicinity of the storehouse of businessman Meir Adler, abused, ordered into a bomb crater, and shot by volleys from a machine gun. After the shooting, the Jewish women of the male victims were ordered to close up the mass grave. [562]

SS-Regiment Westland passed through Zboriv on 3.7.1941 and Dutch volunteer Ferdinand Frehé of 5th Company noted in his diary the following day: "Still on the road. We stopped in a village and had a one-hour break. In that hour, a Mongolian and two Jews were executed after we made the Jews dig a pit for three persons. They lay down in the pit to check whether they would fit in, and as that was done, they were executed. When the pit was full it was covered over".[563] Frehé does not mention the name of the village, but it could have been Zboriv as this locality fits, as does the date for his unit.

Finnish volunteer Jaakko Lakeala of 5th Company, SS-Regiment Nordland, arrived in Zboriv on 4.7.1941 at 10.30 a.m., and observed ruined houses and wrecked tanks. He visited a local hospital, where he spotted seven dead and three living Ukrainians. He also noted: "A minor scene was the Jews (*julit*) digging a grave with their bare hands for the civilians they have killed. There were certainly many men watching them dig. In the evening some Jews were shot".[564]

OZERNA, 3.–5.7.1941: 180–200 JEWS KILLED, AND TWO SYNAGOGUES BURNED

The small town of Ozerna (Pol. *Jezierna*) is situated some ten kilometres south-east of Zboriv. Around 1,000 Jews are likely to have lived there in 1941. Of these, 180–200 are estimated to have been shot in early July 1941, probably mainly between 3.–5.7.1941.[565]

Forces of the SS-Division Wiking arrived in Ozerna on 2.7.1941 and started to take out Jewish males from their place of abode. Local Ukrainians pointed out the houses and hideaways of the Jews to the SS-men. The arrested Jews were then transported to a meadow around 200 metres north of the town and were ordered to dig a large grave. The bulk of the Jews on 4.–5.7.1941 were mowed down with bursts of fire from machine guns, but individual shootings of Jews did also occur in the streets. After the departure of the sub-units of the SS-Division Wiking, the German instances issued posters, which stressed the need for calm and good order. The locals were also urged to return to their work. On 7.7.1941, the relatives of the murdered Jews were permitted to open the grave on the meadow and to bury the corpses due to the Jewish rituals.[566]

Volunteer Martti Uusi-Jaakkola of 9th Company, SS-Regiment Westland, noted in his diary on 4.7.1941:

> All male Jews seized by the Germans were brutally shot in a meadow on the outskirts of the village. More than hundred Jews were gathered at the end of the day. The last group had to first dig a large mass grave, into which later all were buried. It was said that some of them were only half-dead. I could not have imagined that I would encounter brutality of this kind among 'a cultivated nation'. The local population certainly feel joy at getting rid of the Jews. The jubilant population is bringing and throwing flowers. It is certainly a pleasure to enjoy the support of the native population in the fight against the Bolshies.[567]

Uusi-Jaakkola does not mention the name of the village, but the event he describes would fit with the atrocities in Ozerna. Further, the volunteer Matti Tamminen of the 11th Company of the same Regiment reported in a trial in Helsinki in 1958 that Jews were shot in a field near a synagogue. Speaking of these reprisals, he stated that:

"The shooting had been carried out by the Germans because the Jews had shot their Regiment Commander" [568] (i.e. Hilmar Wäckerle, in Novosilky (*Nowosielce*), on 2.7.1941). However, Tamminen could not remember the name of the village. As it appears, that place may well have been Ozerna[569].

Not far from the field where the Jews were shot, a synagogue was also burned to the ground the very same morning. SS-Rottenführer and Finnish volunteer Sakari Lappi-Seppälä of the 1st Company of the SS-Regiment Westland described this event in his recollections. He wrote that SS-volunteer Unto Boman (later Unto Parvilahti) of 11th Company, SS-Regiment Westland, destroyed an ancient and beautiful "chapel" (*rukouskappeli*) in early July 1941. Initially Boman tried to start a blaze in the building with a few hand grenades, and as a consequence the altar caught fire. After smashing the painted windows, the draught increased the blaze and the chapel burst into flames.[570] There is no precise note on the place, but it may well have been Ozerna, where the Germans reportedly burned two synagogues (*Gebetshäuser*).[571] In 1958, the former volunteer Matti Tamminen of 11th Company appeared as a witness in a libel case in the Magistrates' Court in Helsinki, stating that he had been on night watch at the time and witnessed how the 'Synagogue' burned. The next morning after the fire, Boman had told Tamminen of his participation in the burning, with all the details. Papers had been piled up at the altar and the fire started by throwing a hand grenade. Boman had boosted the fire by breaking the windows. Tamminen, however, could not name the location of either the synagogue or the execution place.[572]

In his own recollections, Boman noted that he had participated in the battles of *Husiatyn*, *Tarashcha*, *Tarnopol (Ternopil)*, *Bila Tserkva*, and *Zhytomyr*, and "in some other small skirmishes together with my Company". Although he did not mention Ozerna, he is likely to have passed through it, because it is situated along the marching route to Tarnopol. It can also be noted that Boman told the physician Olli Somersalo of the Finnish SS-Volunteer Battalion on one occasion, after drinking alcohol: "... I've nevertheless killed, for the sake of my convictions".[573]

NOWIKI, 3.–4.7.1941: MINOR SCUFFLES AND THE KILLING OF STRAGGLERS

In the early morning of 4.7.1941, close to the village of Nowiki (*Novyky*), approximately 25 km north of Tarnopol (*Ternopil*), Soviet stragglers and snipers fired on the advancing SS-trucks carrying 2nd Company, Nordland Regiment. German SS-Sturmmann Wilhelm Heim was badly wounded by a stray bullet from a Danish SS-volunteer[574] when the 9th Company engaged in an insignificant exchange of fire near Nowiki in the evening of 2.7.1941, as the column of vehicles was surprised by the actions of a Soviet patrol. However, the following day the Germans countered vigorously, as documented on 3.7.1941 by volunteer Pentti Nikkola of 5th Company, Nordland:

> Today we saw how Germans destroyed a village. The Germans fired at the village from their vehicles on the road. A platoon of soldiers was shooting civilians in the village, brutal troops. In the evening we captured the village where the enemy first fired at us. A gre-

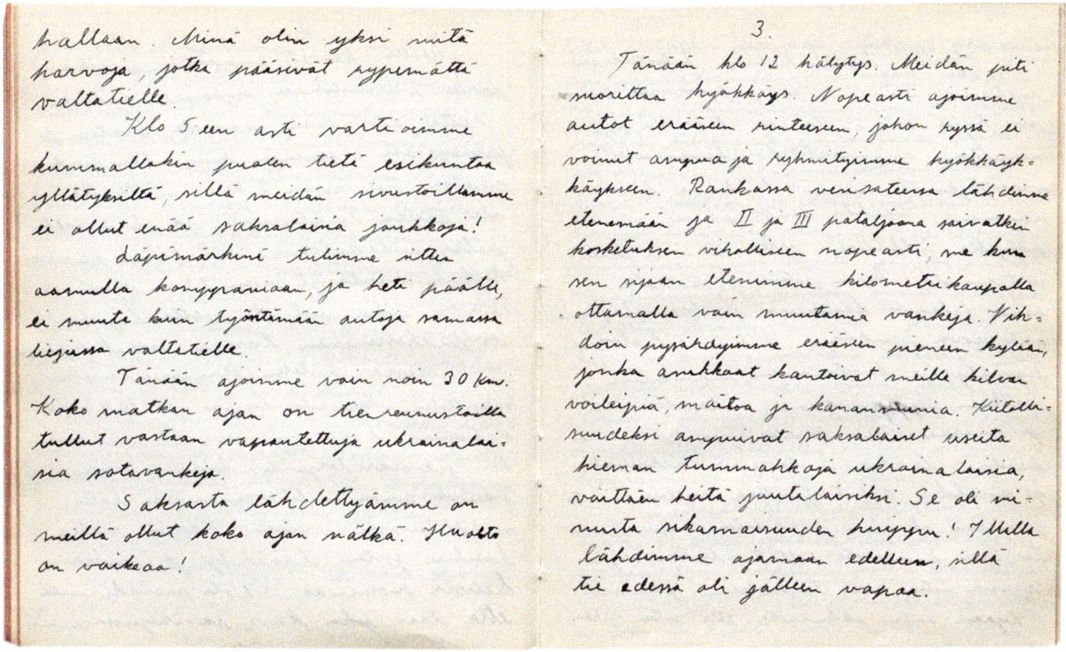

hallaan. Minä olin yksi niitä harvoja, jotka pääsivät rypemättä valtatielle.

Klo 5:een asti vartioimme kummallakin puolen tietä esikuntaa yllätyksiltä, sillä meidän sivustoillamme ei ollut enää saksalaisia joukkoja!

Läpimärkinä tulimme sitten aamulla komppaniaan, ja heti päälle, ei muuta kuin työntämään autoja samassa liejussa valtatielle.

Tänään ajoimme vain noin 30 km. Koko matkan ajan on tienreunustoilla tullut vastaan vapautettuja ukrainalaisia sotavankeja.

Saksasta lähdettyämme on meillä ollut koko ajan nälkä. Huolto on vaikeaa!

3.

Tänään klo 12 hälytys. Meidän piti suorittaa hyökkäys. Nopeasti ajoimme autot erääseen rinteeseen, johon ryssä ei voinut ampua ja ryhmityimme hyökkäyk-käykseen. Rankassa vesisateessa lähdimme etenemään ja II ja III pataljoona saivatkin kosketuksen viholliseen nopeasti; me kun sen sijaan etenimme kilometrikaupalla ottamalla vain muutamia vankeja. Vihdoin pysähdyimme erääseen pieneen kylään, jonka akkaat kantoivat meille kilvan voileipiä, maitoa ja kananmunia. Kiitollisuudeksi ampuivat saksalaiset useita hieman tummahkoja ukrainalaisia, väittäen heitä juutalaisiksi. Se oli minusta sikamaisuuden huippu! Illalla lähdimme ajamaan edelleen, sillä tie edessä oli jälleen vapaa.

Finnish SS-volunteer Keijo Kääriäinen tells in his diary 3.7.1941 about an incident, when after beating the Soviets the SS-men came to a Ukrainian village. The locals brought sandwiches, milk and eggs to them, but the Germans shot many of the more dark skinned villagers claiming that they were Jews. "I think it was the most disgusting thing to do!" wrote Kääriäinen. *Private collection.*

nade came close, but it did not harm me. We spent the night in our positions. I could sleep in a house, as I am an orderly (*Melder*) to our Lieutenant.[575]

The German officers sent a patrol to burn a nearby building and to shoot the inhabitants. The reason given was that they supposed the bullet that wounded Heim was fired from there. "I did not belong to that patrol, but this kind of warfare is abominable", Keijo Kääriäinen of the 11th Company of Nordland noted in his diary. Heim died from his wounds on 5.7.1941 in the German Military Hospital in Tarnopol. After a day's ride, Kääriäinen's unit reached an urban centre in the evening, most probably Tarnopol: "The Germans again killed Jews and set fire to the synagogues".[576]

Nikkola noted in his diary for 4.7.1941: "We started the march at 4 o'clock in the morning. After a couple of kilometres, we spread into a chain [formation]. There was heavy rainfall as we entered the first village. No enemy was found. A couple of civilians were shot there (…)".[577] Later, volunteer Yrjö Tenomaa of the 9th Company of the SS-Regiment Nordland summed up the whole incident concisely by describing "our first village scuffles, nothing but small noises".[578]

PODHORYLCE, EARLY JULY 1941: TWO FINNS SHOT TWO SLAUGHTER VICTIMS

The village of Podhorylce (*Pohoril'tsi, Pohorylce*) is likely to have been the site of an atrocity in early July 1941, in which two Finnish SS-volunteers were involved. Podhorylce is situated around 30 km east of Lemberg (*Lviv*) in the district of Vyzhnuany.[579] However, in this case the topographic situation is muddled. In the broad area of Lemberg (*Lviv*) there are quite a few villages with names that sound somewhat similar, and which consequently have been confused with one other over the years. The village of Podhorodce (Ukr. *Pidhorodtsi,* Other spellings *Podgorodcy, Podhajce, Pidhorodce, Podhoroce, Podhorode, Podhorodch*), on a tributary of the River Stryj, is situated around 100 km south of Lemberg (*Lviv*)[580], close to another village that features in this report, Urycz. In the same general area there is also Pidhaitsi (Pol. *Podhajce*)[581] some 100 km south-east of Lemberg (*Lviv*) and around 60 km south of Zolochiv (*Złoczów*), and the village and castle of Podhorce (Ukr. *Pidhirtsi*) around 50 km east of Lemberg and about 20 km north of Zolochiv.[582] Yad Vashem records that Jews were killed here in Podhorce, but that these atrocities occurred rather later, in November 1941.

Dutch volunteer Hendrikus Valks of 11th Company, SS-Regiment Westland, declared in a post-war (1977) trial testimony:

> One day in early July 1941, the Battalion to which I belonged was drawn to the south, towards the Carpathians. (…) I ended up with a troop in the village of Podhoroce [*sic*]. We bivouaced there for three days. On our first day, a mass execution was carried out after our Battalion Commander was killed.[583]

Valks mentions the village as 'Podhoroce', and actually also uses the form 'Podhorice'. However, the place is likely to have been Podhorylce,[584] although there are no records in the registers of the Yad Vashem Holocaust Remembrance Center in Jerusalem to indicate mass killings in this precise location. The 'Battalion Commander' Valks refers to was probably actually the Regiment Commander Hilmar Wäckerle, who was killed in Novosilky (*Nowosielce*) on 2.7.1941. A Battalion Commander, SS-Hauptsturmführer Alfred Miklos, was also a casualty, but he was killed in action some considerable distance away, in Husiatyn, on 6.7.1941, and it is probable in any case that the events described by Valks would have occurred some days *before* the 6th of July.

Valks continues his testimony:

> German soldiers took Jews and Poles from their homes on instructions from members of the Ukrainian militia. Those people were brought to an execution place and had to dig the pit in which they were going to be buried. I was not involved in that execution myself. I stood at a distance of 200 metres on a slightly higher position (…) The execution place was surrounded by a few houses. The pit was quite big. Most of the victims were killed with a revolver shot to the neck. Two Finns shot two victims with rifles, standing a greater distance from the pit. With S.M.G.H. ammunition (*Twee Finnen schoten met een geweer twee slachoffers dood, die op een grotere afstand van de kuil stonden. Met S.M.G.H.-munitie*).[585]

This last appears to refer to a submachine gun. Two of the Jews were shot when they ran, attempting to escape.[586]

There were ten Finnish volunteers serving in the 11th Company: Unto Boman (later Unto Parvilahti), Eino Hautala, Tapio Ilkama, Olavi Karpalo, Risto Kivi, Auvo Nieminen (later Auvo Mattelmäki), Reino Rantanen, Matti Tamminen, Eino Välimaa, and Martti Välimäki.[587] The two Finns who shot the civilians were probably drawn from these men.

Further information on the atrocities in what we assume to be Podhorylce on 6.7.1941 is included in an article in the Dutch newspaper *De Telegraaf.* An interviewed former volunteer from Haarlem reported that the 11th Company had sent scouts to the village. They returned quickly with three Ukrainian militiamen wearing yellow-blue armbands. The militiamen had taken over the local authority after the departure of the Soviet forces. These Ukrainians were all locals, who pointed out 30 Jews and Poles to the Germans. The execution was attended only by SS-men and not by the local population. However, after the shooting, the inhabitants were called to close the grave.[588]

The former volunteer mentioned that six or seven people were executed each time. The bodies were covered with sand, and subsequently another party of six or seven people were shot: "Several women were shot. If I am not mistaken, there were three of them. These women did not want to let go of their husbands. About six soldiers were ordered to carry out the execution, relieving each other (...) I estimate the number of people who were executed at 25–30".[589] The interviewee remembered the execution was carried out on 5.7.1941, but as Wäckerle was killed on 2.7.1941, this day or the following day is probably more likely. Historian Dieter Pohl has contrastingly concluded that the massacre occurred on 7.7.1941 and that 30 people were shot, most of them Jews.[590]

URYCZ, 7.7.1941: AT LEAST 300 CIVILIANS WERE SHOT

The village of Urycz (Ukr. *Urych*) was situated around 85 kilometres southwest of Lemberg (*Lviv*). The number of inhabitants can be estimated at some 2,000, of whom a few hundred at best were probably Jews. All of these individuals were killed between 1941 and 1943. On 27.8.1942, approximately 180 of these Jews were murdered. However, indications are that some were shot in the village in early July 1941.[591]

Dutch SS-volunteer Hendrikus Valks also was told of the events in Urycz by another volunteer, Meeuwis Reedijk. He appears to have served in SS-Artillerie-Regiment 5, because he mentioned the commander of this unit, SS-Standartenführer Herbert Gille. Reedjik was killed in action in 1943, but he had been present in a village near Podhorodce. In that village a mass execution had occurred, "several hundreds of people were killed, many of them Jews."[592] The name of that village may have been Urycz. Dutch volunteer Jan Henri Albert Keuter of 10th Company, SS-Regiment Westland, mentioned in a post-war trial testimony that troops of the Wehrmacht and SS had carried out revenge actions in the "villages of Podhorodce, Urycz, and the town of Drohobycz

(Ukr. *Drohobych*)". Keuter himself had observed the events in Lemberg (*Lviv*) in the period between 2. and 13.7.1941. The information on the retaliatory actions outside of the city may well have reached him, as there were numerous truck transports between Lemberg (*Lviv*) and the locations along the march route of SS-Division Wiking.[593]

An anonymous former Dutch volunteer also told the same story about the massacre where at least 300 innocent civilians had been killed in Urycz, close to Podhorodce:

> The massacres in Urycz and Podhorodce were acts of revenge for the assassination by partisans of one of our Battalion Commanders. That man was shot dead on July 4th, and we got the order to comb Podhorodce and Urycz because enemies were expected there. Early in the morning, we reached the outskirts of Podhorodce and another group went to Urycz.

After the war, 24 male and two female skeletons were found in a mass grave at Podhorodce.[594]

ACTS OF MASS VIOLENCE IN THE TARNOPOL AREA, 4.–6.7.1941

This part of the presentation focuses on the acts of mass violence in the Tarnopol (*Ternopil*) area between 4. and 6.7.1941. These atrocities occurred almost contemporaneously with those in the Lemberg (*Lviv*) area and were operationally linked together as events aside from the main German march eastwards.

TARNOPOL, 4.–5.7.1941: AN URBAN MASSACRE

The city of Tarnopol (*Ternopil*), some 130 km east of Lemberg (*Lviv*), was overrun by the German forces on 2.7.1941. There were approximately 40,000 people living in the city, including almost 18,000 Jews.[595] At least several hundreds of these fled, following on the heels of the retreating Soviet military units. The number of civilian victims in Tarnopol has been estimated at between 2,400 and 4,000, with the significant factor in this case being that almost all of them were males.[596] The Ukrainian Holocaust historian Alexander Kruglov has estimated the death toll of Jews in the entire Tarnopol Oblast at approximately 9,000 in July 1941 alone.[597]

The City Commandant Erwin Sander

Units of the 9th Panzer Division occupied Tarnopol on 2.7.1941 and units of SS-Division Wiking arrived early in the afternoon of the following day. However, the loyalist SS-Division Wiking history writers have been eager to mention that the Division Staff did not enter the city until 4.7.1941.[598]

Large-scale repressive actions against the Jews of Tarnopol started on 4.7.1941. Units of SS-Division Wiking were subordinated to the City Commandant and played a central role in the massacres. In particular, 3rd Company, SS-Regiment Nordland played a crucial role in carrying out the atrocities.[599] After the raids by German and Ukrainian units, the town was littered with bodies and the surviving Jews searched for their lost relatives. One of the survivors recalled: "People dug up bodies from the mass graves in the places of the mass murders". The Commander of 9th Panzer Division, General Gustav von Wietersheim, appointed a City Commandant in Tarnopol on 4.7.1941. This was the artillery officer Oberst Erwin Sander. He oversaw the production of posters, announcing severe punishments for violent acts. The Norwegian journalist Egil Ulateig presumes a platoon or another unit of the 3rd Company of SS-Regiment Nordland was used by Sander for maintaining the order. However, the sources for this presumption are somewhat vague.[600]

Several locals confirmed the participation of German Waffen-SS soldiers in the atrocities. The Pole Wladyslaw Kaniuk witnessed how soldiers in the company of Ukrainian nationalists armed with sticks drove Jews out of their homes in Mickiewicza, Tarnowskiego, and Ostrogskiego

Streets. The Jew Sara Frydman reported how Jewish men were forced out of their homes in Listopada Street and how elderly women were tied up and their daughters raped. The local girl Anna Terkel also noted on 4.7.1941 that Germans with "Totenkopf badges" raped numerous girls in the better-off Jewish quarters. Other locals mentioned several cases of individuals and families being shot dead.[601]

Later in July 1941, the Germans announced the confiscation of property, forbade retailing and production, lowered the rations, and limited freedom of movement and of changing one's place of residence. The Germans and the Ukrainians confiscated the best Jewish houses and entered and occupied apartments that could be seized. In the streets, there were hunts for Jews. Those captured were sent to various labour sites where the guards abused them. At the beginning of August, Jews were ordered to wear armbands with a Jewish star and to put Jewish signs on the houses where they lived. One day the municipality set new taxes at 400 rubles for the Jews. In August and September, the Jews had to pay a contribution of 1,500,000 rubles arising out of the trumped-up charge that the Jews had caused the destruction of the Ukrainian Club of Tarnopol.[602]

The Ukrainian nationalists

According to survivors' accounts, over 4.–5.7.1941 the sub-units of the SS-Division Wiking were assisted "by Ukrainian policemen taking Jewish men out of their apartments and shooting them in the courtyards of the houses. Jews were seized in the streets and taken to collection points, where they were shot". Homes were looted and destroyed, and the Polish Jews were immediately killed in various locations such as the local prison and the Gurfein School. Around one hundred Jews were killed in the synagogue Reb Yankel's Kloise on Staroshkolna Street. The synagogue was burned to the ground. As had been the case in Lemberg (*Lviv*), in Tarnopol the German forces found corpses of those prisoners killed by the retreating NKVD, this time in the jail on Mickiewicz Street. The conclusions drawn and the response – a savage pogrom – were much the same as in Lemberg (*Lviv*).[603]

As another local narrative relates:

> Although there were some Jews among the murdered prisoners, the Jews of Tarnopol were blamed for these Soviet atrocities. As a consequence, the prison itself became the place for special tortures of Jews. Hundreds of Jewish men were brought there and ordered to kiss the bodies, bathe them, and drink the bath water. Afterwards they were cruelly killed. The Germans ordered them to bury the piles of bodies in mass graves in the two Jewish cemeteries, bodies that were heaped in the city during the repression, or to bury them temporarily in the courtyards. Often those who buried the bodies were shot after finishing their work. The Ukrainian policemen and the urban mobs were very active in the persecution. Usually the Germans used to shoot only men, whereas the Ukrainians also shot women and children. They murdered them barbarically with iron clubs, knives, and in other ways. They also destroyed the apartments of the Jews, their places of prayer and looted their property. At the same time as the pogrom was running wild all over Tarnopol, farmers – and especially the

Ukrainian farmers – murdered Jews in the surrounding villages. A terrible mass execution happened in the village of Gayavillkaya, and the situation was so bad that the Germans announced that the 'acts of retaliation' against the Jews were concluded, and it was completely forbidden to kill and rob. Nevertheless, the pogrom continued for a few more days.[604]

The soldiers of the sub-units of the SS-Division Wiking enlisted local Ukrainians in order to find the Jews and they also encouraged them to kill. Nonetheless, the bulk of the violent actions were carried out by the SS-soldiers. There were piles of bodies in the streets after the rampaging of the SS-units, and Tarnopol became the major scene of atrocities of the division.[605]

The Sonderkommando 4b

Sonderkommando 4b, attached to Einsatzgruppe C under SS-Sturmbannführer Günther Herrmann, did not arrive in Tarnopol until 4.7.1941. However, it is possible that a Vorkommando may have arrived during the previous day. It is also possible that the unit carried out the shooting of about 1,000 Jews. Some 500 of the Jews were shot in the suburbs in the Christian Cemetery with small arms handed out by the German forces. However, soldiers of SS-Division Wiking and Wehrmacht troops participated in the atrocities in Tarnopol. In spite of relatively poor documentation to support the hypothesis, the Norwegian journalist Egil Ulateig has argued that among others Norwegian volunteers from the 3rd Company of SS-Regiment Nordland took part in the action.[606]

Einsatzkommando 4b reported on 6.7.1941 on the local situation in Tarnopol, noting that members of the Jewish intelligentsia had been imprisoned. The report states: "Around 70 Jews gathered up by the Ukrainians and finished off with hand grenades. Twenty other Jews were beaten in the street by the military and Ukrainians as a reaction to the murder of three (German) soldiers (...)." By 11.7.1941 the Einsatzkommando informed Berlin that the actions in Tarnopol were ended: "127 executions. Moreover, in following-up repressions Jews have been liquidated, inspired by the Einsatzkommando". A few days later, Einsatzkommando C reported that 180 Jews used in taking care of the bodies had been beaten, partly in the prison yard and partly in the street: "Further, members of the Waffen-SS have destroyed Jewish apartments with hand grenades and set them on fire".[607]

Actions by the Dutch volunteers

Dutch SS-Schütze Martinus Rademaker of 2nd Company, SS-Regiment Westland, noted in his diary, 2.7.1941:

> In the afternoon we entered Tarnopol. It was raining, and the water flowed in wide streams in the gutters. Burned-out Russian tanks were left at all corners of the streets. Bodies of Jews were scattered everywhere. These Jews had looted yesterday and were now suffering their well-deserved punishment (...) We swiftly rounded up some Jews, who swept and cleaned the quarters. They were constantly obsequiously polite and greeted us always

> by taking off their hats – these 'chosen' people (…) On the opposite side of the hotel there is a large mansion, which used to be owned by a now-evacuated Jewish family. With a few comrades I entered the building – and was met by an indescribable mess. This was a genuine Jewish household. We checked all the rooms, but a similar disorder prevailed everywhere.

The volunteers checked the cupboards, in which plates, glasses, saucers, and many other utensils were stored. Rademaker continued: "We took a stack of gramophone records to try on our own pick-up (gramophone)." At 9 o'clock the company left Tarnopol, heading southwards.[608]

Rademacher's compatriot Ferdinand Frehé of the 2nd Company had for his part seen enough by 3.7.1941 and stated: "We drove further and arrived in the town of Tarnopol. I do not have to write down what I saw there, because I'll never forget that for the rest of my life".[609] The Dutch volunteer of 4th Company, SS-Regiment Westland, Martinus Weers noted on 4.7.1941:

> We arrived in Tarnopol at 3.15 in the morning. Here, too, the Russians had been indulging like animals. As everywhere, the Jews have had everything in their hands and celebrated their lusts on the sacrifice of the people. It will become clear to everybody that we men of the SS act mercilessly against Jews. It was therefore very welcome that the civilian population drove the Jews into a prison, where they received their deserved punishment. Hundreds of Ukrainians were killed in that prison days before. Mainly Jews had played a major role here. They deserved their punishment in the same place. An eye for an eye and a tooth for a tooth.[610]

In a post-war testimony from 1947, a German soldier recorded that SS-Regiment Westland had handed over around 500 persons for shooting to Einsatzgruppe 4b in early July 1941. No mention of the location is provided, but the date and the circumstances point to Tarnopol.[611]

Dutch volunteer Pieter Willems of the 1st Company of SS-Regiment Westland told of his experiences of the chaotic situation in Tarnopol in those days:

> Russian soldiers tried to hide themselves after our breakthrough, and to wear civilian clothes in order to escape imprisonment. As we from the beginning hardly felt any pity for our prisoners, we had no sympathy for them. With the exception of the Ukrainians, many of them were shot, and naturally the same thing happened to any civilians looking suspicious (…) Ambushed by the Russians, including Russians dressed like civilians, we were fired upon from a basement window. We threw 20 litres of gasoline into the place and two hand grenades. There was a loud bang and huge flames flared up. Within a few minutes, 12 civilians fled from the basement. Of these, seven were Jews, and another eight had been killed by the hand grenades. The Jews had first to dig their own graves and were then executed. Among them were three women – if one can even call these animals that. A Jewish Commissar made the noose with which he was hanged.[612]

In the 1970s, as Willems was under investigation, the judicial instances regarded his story of the incident as open to doubt. If it had occurred, the connection to the fire fights was so strong that it was also doubtful whether the killing would have violated the laws of warfare.[613]

In a village in the vicinity of Tarnopol, Dutch SS-volunteers had a break during the advance. They arrested a Mongol and two Jews, who were forced to dig a pit for three persons. As the victims lay down in the pit they were killed before the volunteers continued their advance into Tarnopol.[614]

Experiences of the Finnish volunteers

Several sub-units of SS-Division Wiking passed through Tarnopol on 5.7.1941: at least the the 9th Company of SS-Regiment Nordland,[615] the 2nd Company of SS-Regiment Westland, SS-Aufklärungs-Abteilung 5, and SS-Flak-Abteilung 5. The Finnish volunteer Reino Suonio of 9th Company, SS-Regiment Westland arrived in Tarnopol on 5.7.1941 at 5 a.m. He noted: "Here is the same scene as in the other cities: repression of the Jews, looting of shops, etc.".[616] Also the volunteer of 5th Company, SS-Regiment Nordland, Jaakko Lakeala arrived in Tarnopol on 5.7.1941 at 8 p.m. During the march his comrades "had relieved a couple of boxes of eggs from the Jews (*juteilta*)". On arrival in the city, Lakeala noticed that "the Jews are here involved in the same business as in other places", i.e. in digging their own graves.[617]

It is doubtful whether SS-Regiment Westland entered Tarnopol. At least the 2nd Battalion was close to Tarnopol on 4.7.1941 at noon, with orders to march on to Borki, east of the town.[618] However, the Finnish Liaison Officer and military chaplain SS-Obersturmführer Ensio Pihkala had arrived in Tarnopol the day before, and he noted: "The plundering was in full swing. Tens of barrels of Vermouth were loaded into cars as well as a lot of clothes from the Russian stocks, swimming trunks, shoes, underwear, etc." On the next day, 4.7.1941 Pihkala reported in Tarnopol: "In the evening there was some shooting just about 40 metres from the Staff HQ. I ran to the place where five Jews had just been shot next to a grave. The soldiers who had done this had gone. One of the victims was still alive. I gave my pistol to the NCO, who relieved the victim from his misery."[619] Also the Finnish SS-volunteer Ahti Paikkala of the 6th Company of SS-Regiment Westland arrived in Tarnopol that day and saw "systematic looting" taking place, attacks on Jews, and the destruction of synagogues. Paikkala was himself among the looters. With some satisfaction, he mentions that he got a good piece of oilcloth, a storm-lantern, and some candles. However, his unit favoured spoils like butter, eggs, champagne, vodka, socks, shirts, and so on.[620]

The 6th Company of SS-Regiment Westland reached Tarnopol on 4.7.1941, SS volunteer Sakari Pöyhönen recorded: "By noon we were in Tarnopol. A thorough looting exercise had begun, and the subjugation of Jews. The Red Army's food store was emptied".[621] Volunteer Penna Konttinen from the same Company watched scenes unfold in the city: "Our truck column stopped in the street. There is a lot of noise. Shops are empty, the nearby church has been damaged. We noticed Jews being taken from their homes and from everywhere. As we see it, the situation appears threatening; abusive words and threats heard".[622]

SS-Obersturmführer Antti Karinen from the 13th Company decided to shepherd some elderly Jews to safety. Afterwards he said he had been afraid that German SS-men in the trucks would shoot at him and the Jews he was guiding. However, nothing happened. The action by Karinen was seen by the Finnish volunteers as a demonstration of their opinion about repressive acts against Jews.[623]

Finnish volunteer Martti Koivula of SS-Flak-Abteilung 5 recorded in his diary: "(...) at 11.30 a.m. we were at a prison camp, where we took up positions. In a nearby town, SS-men and Ukrainians shot 300 Jews. The synagogue is burning."[624] Volunteer Olavi Liesinen of 16th Company, SS-Regiment Nordland, has talked about his experiences from Tarnopol. After the breakthrough, German tanks and his unit were ordered to occupy the city. Of the events witnessed, he noted:

> This was no pleasant duty. We followed the tracks of the tanks, bodies lay along the road, people and horses here and there. We drove past them until we encountered firing. The blazing sun made all this the more unpleasant. Some of the local civilians participated in the defence of the city. Their sabotage caused the Germans considerable annoyance.

Nevertheless, the occupation was successfully carried out and Liesinen's unit were making preparations for leaving, when the order was given to gather all males aged 16–60 years from their homes and to assemble them in a town square. The formal reason was that the identity papers of these males would be checked.[625]

After duly assembling them, Liesinen and his Company comrades were waiting at the trucks in order to continue the road march. However, the sound of machine guns rang out from the square. Liesinen wrote:

> Initially we apprehended this as a surprise attack and went to check the situation. A dreadful scene was waiting for us. At the square, where we had ordered the men to go, a massacre happened. Around 500–600 youngsters and men formed heaps as five Germans fired on them with submachine guns. Animal shouts were heard, and others ran off at full speed to avoid death – in vain. The piles of bodies were transported to a grave, heaps of those recently-living people. Relatives of the victims, wives, mothers, and children watched this ghastly scene (...) The Germans defended their actions by referring to sabotage, but this was pointless. Those who had arrived in the square were innocent. The German command acted like lunatics".[626]

In a post-war interview, volunteer Christian Rosenbröijer of 6th Company, SS-Regiment Nordland, claimed that the local population of Tarnopol organised an unbelievable massacre, which "our men" (*meikäläiset*) made efforts to stop. Rosenbröijer reported:

> These Ukrainians just shot Jews in the streets, their own neighbours and friends and any others. There was an incredible hatred of Jews in Ukraine. I remember this hate disgusting me in some way. I went to a house and entered it. Some family owned that house and we tried to buy some eggs and something to eat and suchlike. There were two locals in the house, and they had grabbed two daughters of the age of

15–17 years by the throat. I took a firm grip on the neck of the man and said go to hell and quickly. It was neither the Germans nor the men from the Division who participated in this work. The perpetrators were just locals, who acted in a kind of frenzy (…).[627]

However, the information given by Rosenbröijer can reasonably be questioned, because another set of sources report involvement of the Germans as representatives of SS-Division Wiking.

The possible gauntlet of the Butchery Company

In a post-war testimony, Günther Otto, who was a butcher in the Bakery and Butchery Company (*Metzgerei- und Bäckerei-Kompanie*) of SS-Division Wiking, reported how officers of his Company organised a "running of the gauntlet" (past bayonet-wielding SS-men) and mass shooting of Jews as a reprisal for Hilmar Wäckerle's death. Neither the precise place nor the date of this massacre is clear, as Otto apparently confused essential details. However, it has been generally supposed that the atrocity took place in Zolochiv (*Złoczów*) on 4.7.1941, as the event is connected to retaliations directly caused by the killing of Wäckerle. Otto certainly named the place 'Zelozow'. However, a gauntlet incident is known to have occurred in a courtyard of the prison on Lackiego Street in Lemberg (*Lviv*) in early July,[628] and it is possible that Günther Otto mixed up the events. In this case the gauntlet massacre mentioned by Otto would have occurred in a location east of Lemberg (*Lviv*) in early July 1941, i.e. supposedly in Zolochiv.

The International Military Tribunal in Nuremberg concluded in 1946, on the basis of available evidence, that the atrocity committed by the Supply Units (*Verpflegungseinheiten*) did in fact occur in Tarnopol during the days around 4.7.1941.[629] The defence lawyer Curt von Stackelberg asked the Commander of SS-Division Wiking, Felix Steiner, as a witness, how close SS-Standartenführer Heinz Fanslau and SS-Standartenführer Erwin Tschentscher[630] had been to him during the march through Ukraine during the summer of 1941. Fanslau was Commander of the Supply Reserve Battalion (*Versehrten-Bataillon*) of the Division, and Tschentscher commanded the Logistics Battalion (*Versorgungsbataillon*). Steiner explained that Fanslau was 30–40 kilometres from his command and control centre (*Gefechtsstand*), whereas Tschentscher worked in nearby places, perhaps eight kilometres behind him. Steiner replied that "the supply troops could not have remained in Tarnopol any more than two or three days". On the basis of this answer, Stackelberg suggested that the atrocities by the Butchery Company occurred in Tarnopol during the two or three days around 5.7.1941.[631]

Otto said that in the village of Berosow, Tschentscher had read an order issued by Fanslau. In this it was said that the Westland Regimental Commander Wäckerle had been shot by a Jew. Hence from this point onwards no one would be prosecuted for killing any Jews. The following day, three Jews were shot.[632] According to Otto, the soldiers of his Supply Company systematically rounded up all Jews on the orders of SS-Obersturmführer Walter Braunagel and the veterinarian, SS-Untersturmführer, Dr. Helmut Kochalty, who was a Sudeten German from Prague and the Commander of 3rd Company, SS-Wirtschafts-Bataillon 5. Two rows of soldiers were formed, and according to Otto:

> (…) the Jews were then forced to run between them and while doing so the men on both sides beat them with their rifle butts and bayonets. At the end of this path was a bomb crater being used as a mass grave, where some SS and Wehrmacht officers stood with submachine guns, with which they shot the Jews dead as soon as they emerged from the gauntlet. Senior officers of the Regiment were part of the group that conducted the shootings. About fifty to sixty Jews were killed in this manner.

On the next day, Fanslau ordered the shooting of three Jews, among them an elderly man who had to dig a grave for himself and his eight-year-old son.[633] Otto also claimed that Tschentscher and Fanslau had been present at the gauntlet event in Lemberg on 1.7.1941.[634]

When the interrogator in 1947 asked Felix Steiner why he could not be held responsible for the atrocity committed by the Butchery Company, Steiner replied:

> I consider it out of the question that such a crime has occurred (…) I have not heard that any German troops whatsoever would have committed this evil deed. This is completely out of the question (…) It is very difficult for me to even imagine that officers like Tschentscher and Fanslau, who were in charge of these troops, would have been so disobedient. They were obedient and well-behaved soldiers, and it is hard to imagine that these must have been so insubordinate concerning this issue (*dass diese gerade in diesem Punkt ungehorsam gewesen sein müssen*).[635]

MYKULYNTSI, 5.7.1941: THE BERSERK RUN OF THE WIKINGERS

The small town of Mykulyntsi (Pol. *Mikulińce*, *Mikulincie*, Yiddish *Mikolintza,* Ger. *Mikolince*, Russ. *Mikilinits*, also known as *Mykulynce, Mikolintza, Mikulincie, Mikulinie, Mikulinste, Mikulintza, Mykulintsi, Mykulintse, Mykulinksi, Mykylinski*) is situated some 18 kilometres south of Tarnopol (*Ternopil*) on the Seret River. The area belonged to Poland until the fall of 1939, when it was incorporated into the Soviet Union. The number of inhabitants in 1941 is not known, but it can be estimated as a few thousand persons at the most. It was certainly a small place, as the locals knew everyone else. However, prior to the German occupation there were 1,891 Jews living in the town. Some of these moved east when the war started, and when rumours circulated about the harsh German attitude towards the Jews in the already-occupied territories. Among the local Jews, confusion and panic occurred, indecision about where to go and what to do.

Unidentified man with his scull smashed at River Don in 1943. *JT Coll., FWM.*

The peasants from the surrounding villages brought information about repressive measures. Heavy fighting took place near the town, and Soviet forces demolished the steel bridge over the Seret on 3.7.1941 as they withdrew eastwards.[636] Ukrainian nationalists are said to have shot around 60 Jews in a small forested area at Mykulyntsi on 5.7.1941, and to have buried them in a pit.[637]

The raids of the Ukrainian nationalists

The first Germans to arrive in the town on 4.7.1941 were greeted by the local Ukrainians with the traditional bread and salt welcome, whereas the Jews locked themselves in their homes. The Ukrainians were rejoicing and ecstatic, turning on the Jews in fury. They started to raid buildings with Jewish residents, and at least 20 Jews were summarily killed. The next day, the Mayor of Mykulyntsi ordered the Ukrainian militia to mop up the Jews. Later, the militia carried out executions outside of the town. The bodies are reported to have been dumped in the craters left from air-raids. Among others, Norwegian SS-volunteers participated in these atrocities.[638]

Holocaust survivor Nusia Schweizer Horowitz mentions that Jews who remained behind followed the events with great anxiety. During the short interval between the retreat of the Soviet units and the arrival of the German forces the local Ukrainians from the vicinity used the power vacuum to seize initial control of the town. They put posters on the walls of buildings with the message that the Germans would grant an independent Ukrainian state once the war was over. However, the local Mr. Schmulevic recounted that Ukrainians "broke into Jewish homes, robbing and murdering the inhabitants". It was not all Ukrainian violence: some Poles also participated in the malicious actions. When the Germans arrived, they demanded that the Ukrainian Mayor should bring them two Jews to be executed publicly. According to Horowitz, the repressions "continued with the participation of German soldiers, the Ukrainian police, and Ukrainian farmers from the surrounding area who flocked to the town for that very purpose. They all stormed Jewish homes, robbing and murdering".[639]

On 6.7.1941, the remaining Jews were summoned to the river bank to help in removing the remains of the bridge destroyed by the retreating Red Army. The attitude of the Ukrainians was aggressive, but the German Commanding Officer prevented further pogroms, ordering the Ukrainians to move on and to release the Jews. Some Ukrainians then chased Jews and drowned them in the river until the German officer suddenly arrived on the scene and declared that it was forbidden to torture the Jews. He "warned the Ukrainians that they would be held responsible if so much as a single Jew disappeared".[640]

The locals reported on the event:

> A town council was elected, headed by the Ukrainian Fedewich. The Ukrainians considered themselves rulers and did whatever they wanted. They harassed the Jews, beat them, looted their property, insulted them, and cut off their beards and *payot* (sidelocks, ringlets). One day the Ukrainians arrested a group of 12 to 15 Jews in the orchard beside the brewery. They ordered the Jews to dig a grave for

> a horse. The bloodthirsty Ukrainians then [shot and] buried the Jews in the same pit and threw the horse on top of them.

Shortly after this, some people were arrested as the Ukrainians claimed that they had been supporters of the Communists. The arrested persons were later beaten and killed by the Gestapo in the jail in Tarnopol.[641]

The actions of the SS units

Horowitz recalled that "...the town was full of German military. Soldiers came to Jewish homes and took what they could, particularly foodstuffs." She also casts light on German policy towards the Jews in Mykulyntsi:

> The authorities put the economic squeeze on the Jews. They were required to provide two grammes of gold per person as well as money, furs, pillows, sheets, and blankets for army hospitals. We were forced to wear a patch of white cloth with a blue Jewish star. Later they distributed armbands made of cardboard covered with plastic. Each had a Jewish star and an identity number. Anyone found on the street without this tag was liable to the death penalty.[642]

Rabbi Leon M. Kahane testified about his recollections of brutal behaviour and recalled:

> One night, trucks filled with SS- men arrived in Mikulince [*Mykulyntsi*]. We ran for cover in bunkers and heard the screams and shootings. Homes were entered forcibly, food and provisions were confiscated, people were rounded up. The Germans did their work with premeditated precision. Everything was laid out by a plan. Soldiers were trained in mass murder (...) I remember the convoys of SS trucks passing through Mikulince [*Mykulyntsi*], on the way to other towns to do the same brutal work.

Consequently, the town became "Free of Jews" (*Judenfrei*) as the remaining Jews were brought to the Tarnopol Ghetto. Nobody could escape and "those who ran away were hunted down like dogs".[643] However, there is no known documentary evidence of any large-scale killing of Jews in Mykulyntsi, although food and commodities are likely to have been looted.[644]

The 15th Company of SS-Regiment Nordland and the Commander of the 3rd Battalion Manfred Schönfelder reached Mykulyntsi on 4.7.1941. Schönfelder did not personally arrive in the village. Later he questioned whether any massacre had occurred:

> I do not know whether an armed Ukrainian auxiliary police unit was in Mykulyntsi and carried out a Jewish pogrom. In my opinion, this was hardly possible at that date, as Russian forces had been there up to that time and remained in the vicinity (...) At that time fierce fighting was taking place in the municipality, and Ukrainian civilians would hardly have appeared.[645]

Steiner is claimed to have ordered the execution of 200 Soviet POWs, 5.7.1941

In the battle around Mykulyntsi, German forces seized approximately 300 Soviet POWs, and these were ordered to line up. Norwegian SS-volunteer Jan Taarneby from 9th Company, SS-Regiment Germania, later said 200 Soviet POWs were shot on orders from the Commander of SS-Division Wiking, Felix Steiner. He personally

> ...walked along the rows and pointed at those who in his opinion appeared 'less Germanic'. These were ordered to line up to the right. Around two hundred individuals whose faces he did not like were selected in this way and condemned to die. After finishing the sorting, Steiner ordered several squads to each take a section of these 200 prisoners, lead them away and shoot them. And this was done.

Volunteer Ørnulf Bjørnstad of 12th Company in the same Regiment witnessed the event and adds that there were two women among those shot. He observed "...that those picked from the rows of prisoners sported an Asiatic look. What later happened to them he does not know. However, he believes that the Jews were promptly shot – without mercy".[646]

However, Norwegian journalist Egil Ulateig has found it hard to accept the story told by Taarneby and Bjørnstad after examining all the documents gathered by the International Military Tribunal in Nuremberg. Ulateig concludes:

A Red Army soldier taken as a POW by the Finnish Volunteer Battalion of the Waffen-SS in 1942. *JT Coll., FWM.*

> The U.S. officials and lawyers studied Steiner's case for more than two years before his release, without accusing him of even a single war crime. The dreadful accusation by the Norwegians contradicts all available information on Steiner. A man like Steiner would never, as a basic rule, have condescended to carry out a 'shitty' job like this. A Battalion Commander could, meanwhile, possibly have taken liberties of this kind. If so, he too would have had to have a confident understanding that such a cleansing of undesirable elements must have been approved by his superiors.[647]

Ulateig basically presents a character judgement of Steiner, concluding that a man of his qualities could certainly not have selected Soviet prisoners and given any killing orders.

Instead Ulateig suggests that one or another Battalion Commander could possibly have acted in that way, although only with the tacit or explicit consent of his superiors. As the closest superior of the Battalion Commander was Steiner, this approach would nevertheless point precisely towards Steiner. Ulateig concludes that if Steiner was not the Commander who picked the prisoners to be shot, this person must either have been the Germania Regimental Commander, SS-Standartenführer Karl Ritter von Oberkamp, or the Commander of the 3rd Battalion, SS-Sturmbannführer Alois Braun.[648]

Finnish SS-volunteer Keijo Kääriäinen noted in his diary for 22.8.1941: "We do not generally shoot all our prisoners anymore." At the beginning of the advance, all prisoners were shot, with the exception of Ukrainians. Kääriäinen mentioned such an event: "Once our Company drove 300 Russians into the river and shot all of them with machine guns. The life of the Jews was of no value, regardless of their civilian or military status." This kind of butchery left a disgusting and abhorrent impression on the Finns, and Kääriäinen wrote that he so far had avoided being forced to shoot prisoners. The place could, however, have been somewhere in the vicinity of Mykulintsi, where approximately 300 Soviet POWs were shot on Steiner's order dated 5.7.1941.

HRYMAILIV, 5.7.1941: SWIFT SETTLEMENT IN PASSING

There were around 2,200 Jews living in the town of Hrymailiv (Pol. *Grzymałów*, Yiddish *Rimalov*, Russ. *Grimaylov*), some 40 km south-east of Tarnopol (*Ternopil*). The municipality was occupied by Wehrmacht forces on 5.7.1941. However, the previous day, SS-Regiment Westland was in Hrymailiv at 5.30 a.m. on the morning.[649]

A Ukrainian National Committee had been established in the village on 4.7.1941 and after the arrival of German forces the pogroms against the Jews began. A Ukrainian militia also appeared and played a significant role in the atrocities. The militiamen dragged Jewish men into the street where they were beaten and a considerable number of them were shot. However, some were brought to a pond, where they were driven into the water and shot. Numerous bodies remained stretched out in the streets and other Jews were ordered to bring these, as well as the bodies from the pond, to the local graveyard, using horse-drawn carts. At the graveyard, more Jews were killed. After carrying out these transports as ordered, these Jews were shot at the edge of a pit and pushed into it. It has been estimated that

300 to 350 Jews were killed. However, a Soviet investigation concluded that approximately 450 Jews, among them women, children, and the elderly, were driven into a lake and shot in Hrymailiv between 5.–7.7.1941.[650] Members of SS-Regiment Westland participated in these actions. It is possible that this occurred under the eyes of Sonderkommando 4b from Einsatzgruppe C, although no proper documentation is known to exist.[651]

In his diary, Ferdinand Frehé, a Dutch volunteer from 2nd Company, SS-Regiment Westland, describes how his unit entered a village. There were many Jews, and persecution of them had already started. Frehé told:

> We grabbed a few Jews and made them clean our car until it was shining. First we shaved them, leaving one side of the beard untouched and the other cut with scissors. With others we burned them off with petrol. So it went. With a sabre and a wooden stick, we gave them hell and let them sweat. We delivered them to the (Einsatz)commando. There they were swept up through a gate alongside a pond. Then the MP rattled *ptrr ptrr* and a lot of Jews fell into the pond. The next morning, I checked the pond, which was chock-full with dead, half-dead, shouting, and stench. I put my handkerchief in front of my mouth because I had to vomit and leave. There I also spotted a Russian tank, in which there were a couple of dead *Flintenweiber* [Russian female soldiers].[652]

Liaison Officer Ensio Pihkala passed through Grzymałów (Hrymailiv) on 5.7.1941 and noted in his diary:

> Another terrible spectacle. Ukrainian 'revolutionaries' who had obtained side-arms were torturing Jews. Several hundreds of them were already murdered before we entered the place. Some of them were driven to a small lake or buried there. I saw dead women in Russian uniforms. Jews cleaned the yards with their bare hands. Some of them were beaten and occasionally taken to another place to be shot. One German tried unsuccessfully four times to shoot an old man age 62. He then ran up to the man and smashed his head with his rifle.[653]

Actions like these also raised disgust among the bystanders, as Pihkala notes: "Many German officers found this kind of brutality disgusting." On Pihkala's return journey to Okno, a Ukrainian waved his hand to show something in a rye field. Five men from the cars went with loaded weapons to the place to check it, crying "Sto ruki djert" (Hands Up!). Finally, three men rose and one of them had a rifle in his hand: "We shot immediately. Nearby lay a fourth one, whom we concluded was an officer, so we shot him". [654]

The SS-Regiment Westland and possibly also other units from the SS-Division Wiking are believed to have engaged in massacres in the village of Skalat, in the neighbourhood of Hrymaliv, on 5.–6.7.1941. Over those two days, between 250 and 400 local Jews were killed.[655] However, as there are no diary notes by the Finnish volunteers on Skalat, this report will pay no further attention to the atrocities in the town.

CHOROSTKÓW, 5.7.1941: OUTRAGES AGAINST THE JEWS

The town of Chorostków (Ukr. *Khorostkiv*) is situated on the banks of the River Taina near the town of Husiatyn. There were around 5,000 Jews living in Chorostków. As the first German forces entered the village on 5.7.1941, the local Ukrainians took control. German historian Kai Struve considers that a taunting incident happened in the village, but with no reported deaths. Around twenty Jews were forced to form a procession, to carry flags with portraits of Lenin and Stalin, and to sing Russian songs. The local Jew Zipora Kiperman said the parody march was ordered by the Ukrainian militia, which also intended to execute the participants. Nevertheless, none of those taking part in the procession appears to have been killed.[656]

However, according to the information given by the local resident Yitzchak Goldflies, 22 Jews, including women and children, were shot on 5.7.1941 by the Germans as a first act of violence. In his recollections, the local Abraham Witoff tells for his part that the Germans "shot 200 Jews" in Chorostków in early July. A few days later "Jews were snatched in the streets, taken in trucks, and deported. We never heard of them again". These violent acts may have been carried out by a sub-unit of the Sonderkommando 4b.[657]

SS-Obersturmführer Kaj Duncker of the SS-Artillerie-Regiment 5 arrived on 4.7.1941 in the village of Janowka, some 27 km from Tarnopol. There the Germans undertook a hunt for Russians near the village. The following day, Duncker's unit reached the village of Chorostków and Duncker noted: "Outrages by the Ukrainian population against the Jews (the Germans watching passively). I walked around in the village".[658] However, there is no documentary evidence for the involvement of soldiers from the SS-Division Wiking in the killings.[659]

HUSIATYN, 6.7.1941: THE MOWING DOWN OF CIVILIANS AND SOVIET POWS

On 6.7.1941, SS-Regiment Westland reached the small town of Husiatyn (Pol. *Husiatyń*, alternative spellings *Gusyatin*, *Husyatin*, and *Hsiatyn*), some 70 km south-east of Tarnopol (*Ternopil*). Of the 2,000 inhabitants there, approximately 400 were Jews.

Following its arrival, SS-Regiment Westland took up positions on the outskirts of the settlement. The 1st Battalion took over a few trains that had been loading at the railway station; the 3rd Battalion followed them into the town, and 2nd Battalion formed a defensive line 1.5 km south-east of the centre. This was the first occasion when the Regiment got involved in a serious battle involving many casualties. On the next day, the Regiment started to march towards Proskurov[660], (Pol. *Proskurów, Płoskirów*, now known as Khmelnytskyi).

Recollections by Dutch volunteers

Dutch volunteer Ferdinand Frehé from 2nd Company, SS-Regiment Westland, noted in his diary for 6.7.1941:

> Husiatin Railway Station. Terrible scenes here. In a shell-damaged house lay naked women,

men, and children sprawled over each other, dead and mutilated (...) There had been an enormous battle to defeat those six trains and people, who wanted to escape, along with tank wrecks, the Red Cross, and Soviet soldiers. Our Company Commander, SS-Hauptsturmführer Fred. *(Alfred)* Miklos, got shot in the mouth and died almost instantly. In the evening we experienced some shooting from the Russians. We were driving in a column of trucks when one of our vehicles (PKW) arrived from the opposite direction. From the middle of the column, someone spotted an MG coming out of the vehicle window and the gunner shot like a madman. Berghuis was injured in the arm and Jan Rijsdijk fatally wounded in the chest, and he died after half an hour. The vehicle was stopped and out of it came two Russian officers and two Russian soldiers, who were swiftly executed.[661]

As several of the corps were dead or wounded, the volunteers were furious. This was calmed down somewhat by shooting the Russian prisoners. The volunteer noted that: "(...) hidden Russians and francs-tireurs are not brought into captivity, and we'll be happy with that". He also mentions that the treatment was even more ruthless towards partisans and towards people who did not openly fight dressed in Russian uniforms. Frehé reported: "Russian soldiers tried to hide themselves and later on wore civilian clothes in order to avoid capture. Initially we showed prisoners almost no sympathy, and many were taken off – with the exception of Ukrainians".[662]

Dutch historian Evertjan van Roekel concluded that "...the volunteers became cold-blooded murderers under such circumstances, as they became acquainted with the awful face of death. The step to kill the Jewish, civilian population could be taken with ease". According to van Roekel, women were killed in cold blood as there was obviously no difference relative to men.[663] One of the volunteers, Pieter Willems, noted in his diary: "I would need to tell a great story about how I shot a Jew, but this would go too far. If the reader would like to hear the story, I'll tell it orally".[664] On 12.7.1941, a Dutch SS-volunteer served as a prison camp guard in the Husiatyn area and noted: "The conditions here are indescribable. At first, we fired our machine gun a couple of times, re-establishing order in the camp. Obviously, the Russians understood that the new guard did not allow itself to be mocked".[665]

Experiences of Finnish volunteers

Artillery Officer Kaj Duncker of SS-Artillerie-Regiment 5 noted in his diary for 6.7.1941: "Walking during the day; Husiatyn, just taken. I watched the infantry subdue various pockets of resistance. Hard struggles throughout the day, considerable casualties on our own side." Two days later, 8.7.1941, he reported on Husiatyn: "The town is completely burned and blown away. Russians in every house, lots of killed in action (at least a Regiment)." In his diary he included four photos. The first showed "Burning Husiatyn", the second the bridge over the River Zbrucz, the third a blown-up enemy nest, and the fourth "Murdered Women". In the last image, two dead young women lay in a bed covered in their own blood.[666]

Finnish volunteer Martti Koivula of SS-Flak-Abteilung 5 noted on 7.7.1941 in Husiatyn after observing fighting all day:

The Russians are resisting fiercely and in desperation. Our unit has already lost one man killed in action, the young [Aulis] Gröndahl [of 3rd Company, SS-Regiment Westland]. Owing to the situation it was no longer possible for us to fire. The infantry was busy. Two escaping Russians were shot. From a train on fire, I rescued a mandolin and some underclothes. I shot eight Russians without feeling any pity whatsoever.

The following day Koivula and the German Rau shot a Russian officer, whereupon Koivula took the dead officer's Nagan-pistol.[667]

In the summer of 1942, Finnish SS-volunteers took part in work on the fields, as there was a constant shortage of food both among the local people and among the troops. *OW Coll.*

Wehrmacht efforts to check the atrocities

The Commander of the rear area of Army Group South, General Karl von Roques, issued orders on 29.7.1941 on the use of harsh measures to prevent German forces participating in excesses instigated by certain groups in the civilian population.[668] SS-Division Wiking was subordinated to 16. Panzerkorps under General Gustav von Wietersheim. In Tarnopol on 4.7.1941, Wietersheim told Steiner that an order from OKW to prosecute members of the German forces would be restricted in the operational area of Operation Barbarossa. Punishable acts against civilians would not be prosecuted. Steiner's biographer Karl-Heinz Mathias presumes Steiner would have answered Wietersheim of his unwillingness to refrain from seeking prosecution in such cases. For his source, he refers to a statement Steiner made in July 1946 for the International Military Tribunal in Nuremberg.[669]

The local Jews were regularly ordered to dig graves and were then shot. Soviet POWs were also systematically executed, until Steiner gave the order to stop shooting them.[670] Swedish SS-volunteer Kurt Lundin said that ordinary officers in the Wehrmacht had disliked the SS's methods of treating Jews, civilians, and POWs, and that conflicts occurred. As a consequence, the Division Commander Felix Steiner was finally given the order to take people prisoner instead of killing them (*Schliesslich erhielt der Kommandeur der Division Wiking den Befehl, die Menschen, statt sie umzubringen, wieder gefangen zu nehmen*).[671] Also two Norwegian SS-volunteers reported in 1945 that Steiner was urged in early July 1941 to stop shooting Soviet POWs.[672]

VIOLENT EVENTS IN THE EASTERN AREAS, 11.7.1941 – JANUARY 1943

The rest of the atrocities dealt with in this presentation are included in this chapter as a series of violent events in "the Eastern areas". The events farther east are of various types and differ from the atrocities in the Lemberg (*Lviv*) and Tarnopol (*Ternopil*) areas primarily in two respects. First, the area in question was much larger than before, and secondly, where the initial atrocities of the Lemberg (*Lviv*) and Tarnopol areas occurred within an eleven-day period, 1.–11.7.1941, the time span of the violent events farther to the east embraces a period of 18 months, i.e. from 11.7.1941 through to January 1943. Furthermore, the pattern of atrocities is not as uniform as in the first days of July 1941. Although violent acts did occur over the entire period, there emerged a process of disenchantment with such things among those serving in SS-Division Wiking.

In spite of there being numerous local atrocities, the frequency of them decreased as the months passed. In the Lemberg (*Lviv*) and Tarnopol areas, the spate of local atrocities took place within a very short period. There were several reasons influencing this, but in the western parts of Ukraine the German offensive launched on 22.6.1941 set in motion a series of events strongly reminiscent of a civil war all along the advancing front. In contrast, the later operations in the Caucasus were "regular warfare", although German forces did carry out numerous shootings of Soviet POWs and civilians in these eastern areas. However, one reason for a lessening of the incidence of atrocities is simply that the number of Jews decreased the further east the advance went. In comparison with the Lemberg (*Lviv*) and Tarnopol areas, there were fewer Jews to be found farther to the east, and consequently there were fewer Jews to be shot. The violent events in eastern and south-eastern areas of Ukraine and Russia and in the Caucasus are dealt with in this chapter.

PROSKUROV, 11.7.1941: MOPPING-UP ACTIONS IN THE STREETS

On 8.7.1941 German forces occupied Proskurov (Pol. *Proskurów, Płoskirów*, now known as Khmelnytskyi), situated some 340 km south-east of Kiev. The number of inhabitants may have been around 40,000 and included approximately 10,000 Jews. From the outset a sequence of atrocities occurred: plunder, humiliation, abuse, and murder of Jews. During the first days of the occupation, a group of elderly Jewish men were shot at one of the wells in the city. Shortly afterwards, the registration of the Jewish population began, with instructions issued to wear yellow stars on their backs and chests. They were also forced to hand over their valuables to the Germans. In reprisal "for acts of sabotage", some Wehrmacht units gathered up "all civilians" and an unknown number of them were killed.[673]

The units that carried out the repressive measures belonged to Einsatzgruppe C, together with the self-organised Western Ukrainian Bukovina

Battalion, headed by Peter Voinovsky. A total of 12,000 Jewish civilians are estimated to have been killed in the Proskurov area, the greater part of these perishing during the period from late fall 1941 until the end of 1942.[674]In July 1941, the Jewish death toll in the Proskurov area was 1,800.[675]

Several Finnish volunteers passed through Proskurov in early July 1941, at least 10th Company, SS-Regiment Nordland on 8.7.1941. The 2nd Company, SS-Regiment Westland, arrived four days later. In the city of Proskurov, the Liaison Officer Ensio Pihkala received information about an atrocity committed by a few German soldiers the day before, and he reported the incident: "Yesterday evening three German soldiers entered a house, murdered a mother and a small child, and committed violence on a young woman. An investigation was immediately launched and as soon as the culprits are found they will be shot".[676]

On 11.7.1941, SS-volunteer Reino Suonio of the 9th Company of the SS-Regiment Westland watched while the civilians looted the city: "Everything was in a complete piggish condition, with no order at all. There are but a few civilians in the city, as the bulk of them have left. Soldiers participated in the lootings".[677] The volunteer Martti Uusi-Jaakkola of 9th Company of the same Regiment noted on 11.7.1941 in his diary: "[Goods] were taken from the apartments of Jews. However, I did not take anything but a flag from a military academy and a small streamer, which I intend to take back to Finland".[678] Uusi-Jaakkola did not mention the municipality by name, but Proskurov would fit his description. The volunteer of the 11th Company of the SS-Regiment Westland Martti Välimäki noted on 11.7.1941 in "Brusgururu" [= Proskurov] how he – together with other members of his unit – forced the remaining local Jews to clean their muddy uniforms and then deprived them of their "good clothes".[679] The volunteer of the 5th Company Jaakko Lakeala arrived in Proskurov on 12.7.1941 in the early afternoon: "I went to look inside the houses where there might be something good. Here are the most decorated buildings. We took some small things. One of the comrades put a man to death (*otti yhden äijän veivin*). At 5 p.m. we left the city and rejoined our unit".[680]

BILA TSERKVA, MID-JULY 1941: SHOOTING OF JEWS

The town of Bila Tserkva (Russ. *Belaja Tserkov*, Pol. *Biala Cerkiew*, Yiddish *Shvarts-Timeh*, Ger. *Bila Zerkwa*) is situated about 80 km south-west of Kiev. The population in 1941 can be estimated at between 20,000 and 30,000, of which a minority were Jews.[681] German forces occupied Bila Tserkva on 16.7.1941. Approximately 700 Jews were killed by the Einsatzkommando 4a between 19.–20.8.1941. Soldiers of 295th Infantry Regiment reported to four Wehrmacht chaplains that some 90 recently-orphaned Jewish children were left behind in a church. Before that the SS-Sergeant on guard at the church had turned away any soldiers wishing to intervene.[682] As a consequence, the General Staff Officer for the Regiment, Oberstleutnant Helmuth Groscurth, ordered the postponement of the planned massacre of the children.[683] However, the Commander of the 6th Army, General Walther von Reichenau thwarted efforts to save the children and on 22.8.1941 allowed the shootings to go ahead.[684] The children were shot the same day.

Shortly after the occupation of Bila Tserkva, the Commander of 3rd Company, Aufklärungs-Abteilung 5, SS-Hauptsturmführer Friedrich (Fritz) Herzig and the Motor Transport Sergeant (*Schirrmeister*) of the Company saw Jews packed together in a pit. Herzig and the Schirrmeister participated in the execution of the Jews, using submachine guns and hand grenades. SS-volunteer Ahti Pokela, also from the 3rd Company, was ordered to stand guard at the pit. The event was observed at close quarters by SS-Hauptsturmführer Yrjö Kaila. He commented in 1994 on the execution: "Unbelievable, but true. Many Finnish people would hardly want to believe this event today. What could I or should I have done? Guard Pokela was very upset by the massacre".[685]

THE BRIDGEHEAD OF DNIPROPETROVSK, AUGUST 1941: SHOOTING OF CIVILIANS

After the occupation of Dnipropetrovsk (now known as *Dnipro*; Russ. *Dnepropetrovsk*) and the destruction of the river bridges, the SS-Aufklärungs-Abteilung 5 held positions at the bridgehead on the eastern side of the River Dnieper. Some of the villagers had remained in the area and between five and ten unfortunate men were found in some sort of cellar. The Commander of the 3rd Company, SS-Hauptsturmführer Friedrich (Fritz) Hertzig, an Austrian by birth, sported an actively sadistic attitude towards civilians.[686] Hertzig suspected that these villagers had fired on SS-volunteers from behind. The Finnish volunteer Yrjö Kaila of the 3rd Company of the SS-Aufklärungs-Abteilung 5 remembered later that

(...) perhaps believing that the sounds of the shooting came from there, he ordered a man to shoot these unhappy villagers. We had prisoners, or rather a prisoner. In his polite way, Hertzig asked me to go ahead of the front line together with the prisoner to a corn field. I was asked to order the prisoner to shout to the enemy that they should come over to our side. The poor prisoner really tried to do this, but soon he was hit by a bullet from the rear. I do not know who shot in the darkness, but the bullet could just as well have hit me. Was this my misconception?[687]

ZHYTOMYR, MID-JULY 1941: THE DEATHBLOW OF A CITY

The City of Zhytomyr (Pol. *Żytomierz*, Ger. *Schytomyr*, Russ., *Yiddish Žitomir*) is situated approximately 80 km west of Kiev, and in the fall of 1939 it had around 95,000 inhabitants, of which around 35,000 were Ukrainians, some 30,000 Jews, about 13,000 Poles, and 4,000 Volkdeutsche. When Wehrmacht forces occupied the city on 9.7.1941, there were around 10,000 Jews there in a total of about 40,000 remaining inhabitants.[688] Shortly after the German tank and infantry forces broke through and entered Zhytomyr, SS-Einsatzkommando 4a arrived and summarily shot 187 "Soviet Russians and Jews".[689]

The Wiking round-ups

SS-Regiment Westland arrived in Zhytomyr on 15.7.1941 at 10 a.m. and continued its advance.[690] At least three units of SS-Regiment Nordland

Hanging of Soviet judges and Jews Moshe Kogan and Wolf Kieper at the market place in Zitomir, Ukraine 7.8.1941. Public hangings were commonly held as a warning to the locals. *WC.*

were also present in Zhytomyr: the 1st and 2nd Companies from 14.7.1941 until 22.7.1941, and the 12th Company which arrived from Radomyshl (Pol. *Radomyśl*) on 17.7.1941. SS-Division Wiking rounded up "the usual suspects".[691]

Einsatzkommando 4b

Einsatzgruppe C was present and active in Zhytomyr for a longer period. As a consequence, some Commissars and 31 Jews who were active Communists were killed. In the villages of Rudniya (*Rudnya-Horodyshche*) and Troyanov (*Troyaniv*), around 20 km south-west of Zhytomyr, twenty-six Jewish Commissars were hanged in front of 400 Jews forced to watch the execution. An additional 113 Jews were killed at Radomyshl around 50 km north-east of Zhytomyr. Einsatzkommando 4b pulled into Zhytomyr during 18.–19.7.1941. By then the city was heavily damaged by arson, and the population had declined from 95,000 to 40,000. Of those, about 5,000 are reported to have been Jews. The bulk of the local population in the summer of 1941 consisted of elderly and female agricultural workers of households with children. The many thousands of Jews living in Zhytomyr perished in the surroundings of the city during the summer of 1941. SS-Division Wiking was operating in the same sectors as Einsatzgruppe C and Einsatzkommando 4b.[692] In several municipalities, Wehrmacht forces took part in the killings.[693]

Einsatzkommando 4b reported to Berlin on 29.7.1941: "In Zhytomyr around 400 Jews, Communists, and supporters of the NKVD have been shot. Einsatzkommando 4b has carried out 2,531 executions".[694] In the broader Zhytomyr region, including cities like Vinnytsia, Berdychiv, and Zhytomyr itself, around 70,000 Jews have been estimated to have been killed by the German administration, police forces, and the SS in the first murderous sweep to find Jews in 1941.[695]

Cautionary hangings in the market square, 7.8.1941

On 7.8.1941, Einsatzkommando 4b publicly hanged two Soviet judges in the market square: Moshe Kogan and Wolf Kieper. They were both Jews. The German occupiers made this public execution a political demonstration. The judges were arrested in Cherniakhiv (Ger. *Tschernjachiw*) on 6.8.1941 and shortly afterwards the coming event was announced in Zhytomyr in German and Ukrainian with the help of loudspeakers supplied by the Propaganda Company of AOK 6. Thousands of spectators, among them several hundred German soldiers, watched the execution. Einsatzkommando 4a forced 402 Jewish men to watch the hangings; all of them were shot afterwards.[696] As far as is known, however, these hangings were not in any way related to the SS-Division Wiking.

KREMENTSUG, 12.8.1941: THE EXECUTION OF A SOVIET LIEUTENANT

In mid-August 1941, SS-Regiment Nordland passed through Krementsug (probably *Kremenchuk, Kremenčuk. Kremenchug, Krzemieńczuk*), west of Dnipropetrovsk (*Dnipro*). Here the Finnish volunteer Keijo Kääriäinen from the 2nd Company noted in his diary for 12.8.1941:

> Today I stood guard over a Russian Lieutenant, who had been captured in civilian clothes and condemned to death. I already believed that I would have to shoot him myself. Fortunately, this did not happen as the 'Jerries' (*saksmannit*) carried out the role of executioner. I do not have any particular desire to shoot an unarmed man.[697]

Dniprodzerzhynsk: Suspect Russians shot, 22.8.1941

In late August 1941, SS-Regiment Nordland entered the town of Dniprodzerzhynsk (now known as *Kamianske*), situated around 30 km west of Dnipropetrovsk (Dnipro). The number of inhabitants in 1939 was around 160,000, of whom around 4,900 were Jews. Most of the Jews left before the arrival of German troops on 22.8.1941.[698]

The city was occupied by the German forces from 22.8.1941, and the same day the volunteer Keijo Kääriäinen of the 2nd Company of SS-Regiment Nordland noted in his diary:

> [Today] the current commander of our platoon had two men in civilian clothes shot dead. The reason being that one of them wore Russian military-style boots and the other one a Russian military shirt. I watched the scene from a distance of 20–30 metres. In all, it took ten minutes before the 'Ivans' gave up their last breath. The slaughter was eventually carried out by hitting them over the head with a spade (…) A miserable scene (*Kurjaa katseltavaa*) (…).

The same evening, Kääriäinen also watched when two Russians were executed with a spade and a submachine gun. This act took 10–15 minutes.[699]

High representatives of the Finnish Defence Forces visited the Finnish Battalion of the SS-Division Wiking several times during 1941–1943. Lieutenant-General Hugo Österman (left) was known for his pro-German attitudes and he had actively supported the recruitment of Finnish volunteers to the Waffen-SS. Here he is seen watching an ongoing battle near Dnipropetrovsk in August 1941. *JT Coll., FWM.*

From early 1942, the Finnish SS-Volunteer Battalion arrived at the front. All the previous events are related to those "battle-ready" volunteers who served in the SS-Division Wiking from the beginning of the march eastwards, in the summer of 1941. From the presentation of the incident in the village near Donskoye onwards, the atrocities listed are related, in one way or another, to the men of the Battalion.

VILLAGE NEAR DONSKOYE, 18.1.1942: NECESSITY TO SHOOT THE IVANS

In January 1942, the Finnish SS-Volunteer Battalion reached Donskoye (*Donskoi, Donskoj*), a town about 250 km east of Dnipropetrovsk (*Dnipro*). Volunteer Taisto Kuuri of the 1st Company noted on 18.1.1942 in his diary:

Two days ago in Donskoi [sic] we got the urgent order to enter a village seven kilometres to the left. Russians there were holding positions in houses on the outskirts of the village (...) We cleared the village of Ivans and drove them back a few kilometres in the severe cold and storms from the steppe. We captured prisoners. As we left the village that evening, it became necessary to shoot the Ivans, because we could not take them with us.[700]

Kabardinskaya, 26.9.1942: All the deserters were shot and two Russians hanged

Volunteer Iivari Kemppinen of 1st Company, Finnish SS-Volunteer Battalion, noted on 29.6.1942 in Kabardinskaya (*Karabinskaja, Kabardinskaja*) west of Maikop in the Caucasus:

Deserters often arrive, even a couple of very handsome ones. Then the order was given that all deserters will be shot. It happened because local villagers had been shooting and organising sabotage. One hundred civilians equipped with pistols and hand grenades arrived in the area of the Battalion. Two Russians were hanged and left to dangle as a sign of warning to the villagers.[701]

TOLDZGUN, DECEMBER 1942: CLEARING THE VILLAGE

When questioned by the Finnish Security Police (Valpo) in 1947, SS-volunteer Paavo Merelä of 3rd Company, Finnish SS-Volunteer Battalion reported that in December 1942 the Finnish SS-Hauptsturmführer Karl-Erik Ladau had ordered the shooting of seven villagers in Tolskum [Toldzgun]

Himmler inspecting the troops of the SS-Division Wiking at the front in September 1942. *Bundesarchiv.*

and five Soviet deserters. The order had been carried out by a Finnish Pioneer platoon. Ladau was the Commandant of Tolskum [Toldzgun], a village between Nalchik and Vladikavkaz in what is now North Ossetia.[702] Volunteer Jaakko Hintikka was a member of that platoon and noted on 21.–22.12.1942 that the village of Toldzgun (*Tolskum, Toldsgun*) had been destroyed as "(…) the war had damaged the buildings and driven the people into the forests, where they lived until they dared re-enter the surroundings of their homes". In the last days of December 1942, Soviet forces attacked fiercely, and one evening a prisoner was taken just ahead of the positions: "Oh, what a miserable creature he was. He certainly cried when he was so well treated".[703]

However, shortly afterwards Hintikka added to his diary:

> The old year certainly did not end as [peacefully as] I imagined. Some small changes occurred in the very last hours. This was the end of a cruel (*raaka*) year, which I'll certainly remember also without notes. We unmasked five civilian spies and they were finished off. At sunset, they were brought to a hill and shot. There was also a couple of other prisoners. This was a brutal business as they begged for mercy. But the submachine gun did not recognise anything of that sort. The youngest was 17 years old and the second 20 years, the others old men with beards. The last one to be shot was the youngest. He covered the others first with earth and after that it was his turn. He was certainly a lad with strong nerves, as he met his death with honour.[704]

On the basis of Hintikka's information, it can be concluded that the incident reported by Merelä occurred in the evening of 31.12.1942. However, Ladau does not mention the event in his rather poor and somewhat insignificant memoirs, published in 2007, in which he does place himself as Commander of a Finnish Replacement Company in the area of Tšikola (*Chikola*) and Digora (both very close to Toldzgun) in December 1942. The unit participated in the ongoing defensive battles.[705]

METSENTINSKAYA, JANUARY-MARCH 1943: SHOOTING POWS

Volunteer Jaakko Hintikka of 12th Company, Finnish SS-Volunteer Battalion, noted on 25.1.1943 in his diary in Metsentinskaya (*Mechetinskaya*) in the Salsk area, around 200 km south-east of Rostov-on-Don:

> This village gives a rather peaceful impression, in spite of the sound of the distant thunder of guns. We've been here for a few peaceful days. Only a motorised patrol has gone out. The Russians intend to attack now really hard, with 7,000 men and tanks. It's good that we have aircraft, and the Stukas foiled the attempts of the Russians. We took many prisoners (…) but I do not know whether these have been shot as so much has happened.[706]

In early March 1943, Hintikka wrote: "Now we've set a minefield ahead. Immediately the following night a Russian patrol hit it. One of them was badly hurt; he was shot (…)".[707]

ATTITUDES TOWARDS JEWS AND REJECTION OF ATROCITIES

In this chapter, the attitudes towards the Jews detected among the Finnish SS-volunteers will be examined on the basis of observations made in the diaries, recollections, and writings by the volunteers. The presentation includes a set of different sub-sections: 1) the occurrence of anti-Jewish sentiments among the volunteers, 2) lessons on racial doctrines, 3) minor expressions of sympathy for the Jews, 4) attitudes of relative indifference to their plight, and 5) the rejection of atrocities. Finally, in order to get a comparative picture, there is also a sixth section on the corresponding attitudes found among Danish, Dutch, Norwegian, and Swedish volunteers.

Heinrich Himmler (left) and the Commander of the SS-Division Wiking, SS-Gruppenführer and Lieutenant-General of the Waffen-SS Felix Steiner. Steiner was a member of the NSDAP and the Sturmabteilung (SA), but not active in party politics. *OW Coll.*

ANTI-JEWISH SENTIMENTS AMONG THE FINNISH VOLUNTEERS

There is certainly an array of examples of anti-Jewish sentiments and statements in documents by the Finnish SS-volunteers. The first occurred at the time of their recruitment in April and May 1941. In the application form for the volunteers, a question on political opinions was included. Two of the applicants, Jouko Itälä and Heikki Mansala, answered "Anti-Semite".[708] Later, Itälä was promoted to become an SS-Hauptsturmführer and Mansala an SS-Obersturmführer. In 1945, one Signe Saarela, the cleaning lady of the Ratas Engineering Bureau – the front organisation for the Waffen-SS recruitment programme in Helsinki – told the Finnish Security Police (Valpo) of a conversation she had had with the wife of engineer Harry Backberg, the Ratas owner:

> And this Mrs. Engineer, she said that all of [the volunteers] should leave for Germany to attend the military school because we have no other possibility. In any case, the Russians (*Ryssä*) will come and take everything away from us and kill us. But with Hitler's help, we can survive, and she further thought that all the English are crazy. And the Jews should be killed...

Although this obviously was a kind of small talk, the wording of it may well illustrate the spirit of the Recruitment Office.[709]

SS-volunteer Vilho Kellokumpu mentioned that the Finnish volunteers arriving in Germany didn't know very much about the German attitude towards the Jews. However, the Finnish were soon told that they should have nothing to do with Jews. In Berlin and many other places, Kellokumpu observed signs with the text "Nicht für Jüden".[710] The volunteer Markus Käenmäki has for his part told of his experiences in Poland in the early summer of 1941. After reaching the River Weichsel, they went swimming and met five young Jewish males at the riverside. The Jewish boys walked fast, removed their caps, and bowed. The first impression of the volunteers was that the boys were joking. However, shortly afterwards they realised that the boys had to act in the way they did. According to Kellokumpu, they were told that: "a SS-man must not in any whatsoever make contact with the Jews, not even to chat with them".[711]

SS-Division Wiking reached the Lublin area on 20.6.1941. Here, for the first time, the SS-volunteers came into contact with local Jews, and later on a Finn among them reported that he participated in the maltreatment of Jews in the Lublin ghetto. However, the name of the Finnish SS-volunteer is not known.[712] SS-Untersturmführer Ahti Paikkala of the 6th Company of the SS-Regiment Westland noted on 20.6.1941 in Radomir, Poland, that among the Jews there were children in rags. They cried out for bread. The Jews wore yellow stars on their chests as well as on their backs and were not allowed to use the sidewalks. However, the Finnish SS-volunteers became uncomfortable when the younger German soldiers ordered Jews to take off their caps as they passed the rows of soldiers. The sides of the streets were crowded with ragged children and adults and every one of them cried the same words: "Bread, Bread, Bread" (*Brot, Brot, Brot*). In the municipality of Izbica, on 29.6.1941, Paikkala observed Jews, whom he now characterised as "a bad crowd" (*Der ewige Jude. Jo oli pahaista porukkaa*). The following day, SS-volunteer Martti Välimäki of the 11th Company of the same Regiment made similar observations in the Polish-Ukrainian border area. The Jews there wore a white sleeve badge and they also had to remove their caps when meeting Germans. Those who did not were shouted at and given fist-treatment.[713] From these diary notes, it seems as though the Finnish SS-volunteers may initially have been slightly confused over the German attitude to Jews. However, Välimäki appears to get accustomed to the spirit of the Regiment without much delay. On 11.7.1941, he was on guard in Proskurov and noted that "the Yids (*Juudakset*) had run away together with the Russians". By that stage his attitude towards the Jews was scornful.

SS-volunteer Jukka Tyrkkö writes in his memoirs on the impressions of the volunteers in a municipality east of Lemberg (*Lviv*) in the summer of 1941: "Some of us stopped in a small town entirely populated by Jews. The life of the inhabitants there appeared incredibly miserable. They wore tattered rags and the throwing of a cigarette butt caused a general scuffle." Tyrkkö also claims that the Jews of Ukraine "were commonly hated". He remembers how in July 1942 a Soviet partisan "with a Jewish look" about him was captured while attacking a German soldier and how the partisan was executed in the yard where the unit had its quarters.[714]

In October 1941, the Finnish citizen and SS-official Erik Nupnau was Chief of the Postal Censorship Office for the control of the letters by the Finnish volunteers in Berlin-Lichterfelde. His first advice to the newcomers at the Office

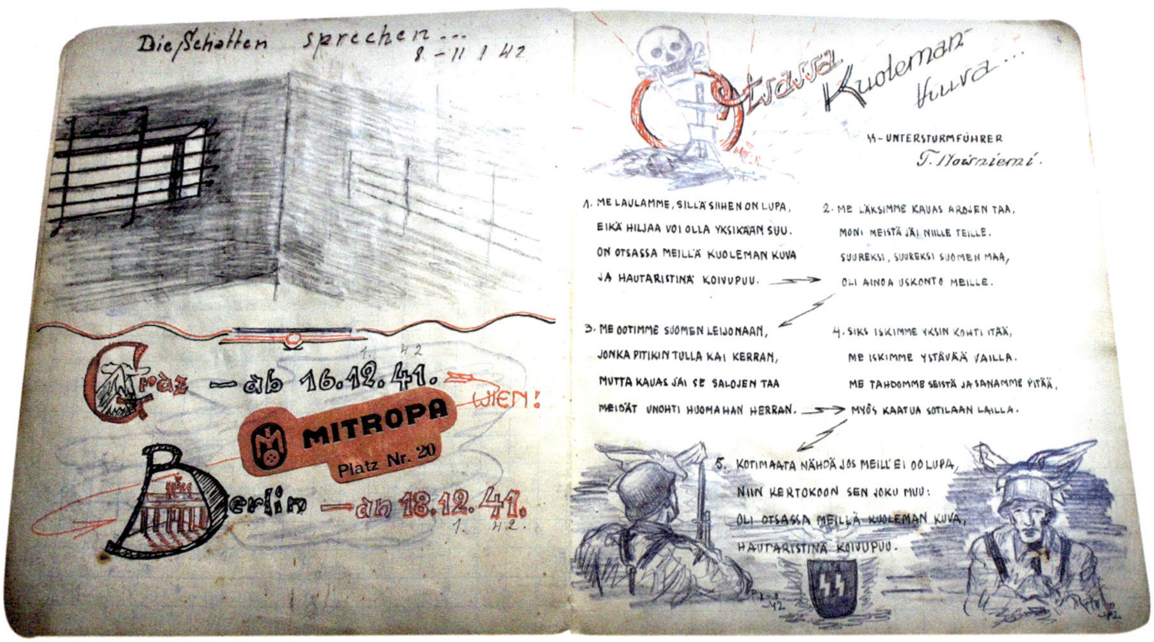

A Lamentation Poem in the diary of SS-volunteer Herkko Kosonen. *Private collection.*

Graves of Finnish SS-volunteers SS-Sturmmann Esa Meriö (+ 24.8.1941) and SS-Obersturmführer Lennart Wallén (+ 9.10.1942) in Ukraine and Caucasus. Lennart Wallén had been a member of the Swedish-speaking National Socialist association *Samfundet Folkgemenskap*, and he was one of the first officers to be ready to be recruited to the Waffen-SS from Finland. *OW Coll.*

was that they were not allowed to give up their seats in the trams to any Jew.[715] In mid-December 1941, the volunteers Matti Heikkilä and Esko Sonninen of the Finnish SS-Volunteer Battalion arrived in Kirovohrad (Russ. *Kirovograd*, now known as *Kropyvnytskyi*) and spotted the carcasses of dead horses along the road. There was also "a Jew cadaver" at the outskirts of the city: "The head was crushed, and the body was thrown naked into a grave, where it lay uncovered".[716] On 13.12.1941, in the village of Dobrovelitskovska not far from Krementsug (Ukr. *Kremenchuk*), volunteer Tauno Polón noted that Jewish houses were marked with small stars: "The German soldiers make them polish their boots. We Finns don't pay much attention to them (...) All Jews here are shot before long". A few days later, on 26.12.1941, Polón "(...) heard that 40,000 Jews have been killed so far, among them all men, women, children, and elderly". By 18.1.1942, Polón arrived in Dnipropetrovsk (*Dnipro*): "All the Jews have been taken away from here and at the moment I am staying in a Jewish home".[717]

In late 1941 and early 1942, volunteer Taisto Kuuri from the Finnish SS-Volunteer Battalion made a few diary notes on the Jews. On 10.12.1941, he arrived in the town of Haisyn (*Haysyn,* Pol. *Hajsyn*, Russ. *Gaysin, Gaisin*) and he noted that 70% of the population had been registered as Jews, of whom 5,000 had been shot, all stripped naked. Just 200 skilled workers had been saved. In Kirovograd, a German later told him in a bar that 25,000 local Jews had been shot. Whole families had been brought by truck to the fields away from the city and they were mowed down with machine guns.[718]

Volunteer Ensio Anttila from the Finnish SS-Volunteer Battalion passed through the main railway station in Prague at the beginning of 1942. On a track in a siding, he observed a train packed full of Jews. Aside from the Star of David on the chest, they were also wearing signs with numbers around their necks. Armed guards in green uniforms had been posted at the front and at the rear of the train. For Anttila, this was the first time he experienced such a spectacle and he started to ponder what fate awaited these poor human beings.[719] The SS-Untersturmführer Pekka Nummi of 5th Company, SS-Regiment Germania, was released in February 1942 and went back to Finland via Berlin. He noted Jews with a yellow star on their chest in the streets and shops. The service facilities had put up signs with the text: "Entry Prohibited For Jews" (Eintritt für Juden verboten) or "Jews Only" (Nur für Juden), thus signalling the prevailing racial segregation.[720]

A replacement intake of some 200 Finnish recruits arrived in Germany in the fall of 1942. Among them was Jaakko Hintikka of 12th Company, Finnish Volunteer SS-Battalion. In October 1942, he noted in his diary that the city of Kraków appeared a large and pleasant place. He wrote: "During the two days we spent here, those of our unit were billeted there. These Polish areas are still very dangerous for German soldiers. The Poles hate the Germans intensively and hate the SS-men far more. One doesn't dare to move around much at night because one will soon get a bullet or a razor-blade in the neck. These stories are no fairy-tales, because such things have really happened. The guys before us experienced the Polish hate in Kraków. Two boys got their throats cut as they were bringing in important information that night. Of more importance is that women are used as bait. A woman entices a soldier to some particular place, where the assassins are waiting, and then his life is cut off. Some guys disappeared without trace and nothing at all is known about [what happened to] them. But the guys certainly caroused in Kraków. One of them went driving a tram, very drunk as he was. The driver ran away and the guy drove through many stops. Another smashed all the windows of the streetcar and ran away. A third started to shoot in a dark street and ordered an old Jewish man to shout 'Heil Hitler'. I am sure that everybody wondered whether all Finns are as wild as these. Sure, all this was quite noisy when I really think about it".[721]

Volunteer Toivo Lemmetyinen of the Finnish SS-Volunteer Battalion had been transferred to the Replacement Company in Graz. On 14.4.1943, as he talked on Jews, Swedish-speaking volunteers from Finland, and the Freemasons, his fellow volunteer Toivo Tuomaala noted down his opinions. Lemmetyinen said: "Down with the Swedish-speakers (*Hurrit*) as well as the Yids (*Juudet*) and the Freemasons". Tuomaala characterised him as "a carefree boy who strongly hated the Swedish-speaking minority and the Jews". More generally, Tuomaala observed the spirit of the times: "Here by the way the propaganda (*brobaganda*) has risen up high against Jews (*jutkuja*), Freemasoners, and the Swedish-speakers".[722]

Hospital interior in Greiz. The Finnish volunteer Ari Vuokko far right together with other wounded fellows. *OW Coll.*

Many wounded SS-soldiers were sent to one of the many hospitals in the rear. Finnish SS-volunteer Ari Vuokko was sent to Reserve Military Hospital Greiz in Thuringia, Germany. *OW Coll.*

SS-INDOCTRINATION ON THE RACE ISSUE

The German leadership made at least some effort to teach the Finnish volunteers about basic racial doctrines. From its formation in late 1940, SS-Division Wiking already had an ideological training unit under an educational leader (*Schulungsleiter*). The task of this unit was to bring the racial and political ideas of the NSDAP to the Division members.[723] This was carried out by arranging classes on racial issues. Efforts targeting a tighter racial education appear to have been made in SS-Division Wiking with the issue of "Weltanschauliches Schulungsblatt Nr. 1." This didactic dispatch was an undated presentation of the topic "The SS-Division Wiking as the Common Destiny of the Free Germanic Kinfolk" (*Die SS-Division Wiking als der Schicksalsgemeinschaft der freien germanischen Stämme*). However, this document did not as such attack the Jews, but praised the Germanic people and the Division, which was regarded as an excellent expression of the community spirit

The inevitable outcome of the war began to be clear by June 1944, by the time General of the Waffen-SS Gottlob Berger visited the unveiling of a memorial to fallen Danish SS-volunteers at the Schalburg training site at Høveltegård near Helsingør, Denmark. *National Museum of Denmark.*

existing between these people.[724] Neither the author nor the date of the document is known. Finnish historian Mauno Jokipii made a note "Spring 1943" (*Keväällä 1943*) on his copy, but it appears possible that the text may have been written earlier than that. Historian André Swanström has for his part judged that the ideas of the Schulungsblatt rather accurately reflect the opinions held by the Division Commander Felix Steiner.[725]

Reichsführer-SS Heinrich Himmler arrived at SS-Junkerschule Bad Tölz on 23.11.1942 and spoke to the cadets for two hours. Tauno Polón noted: "He mentioned the current struggle on the basis of the racial doctrines and referred at the same time to the coming Europe, the new Germanic society (...)".[726] However, reflections of racial doctrines would also occur during physical training. Volunteer Konstantin (Kosti) Cande recalled that the drill sergeants used commands like: "Schweinerei! Hier ist wie im Judeschule".[727] This meant that the soldiers' discipline and order was as poor as was alleged in a Jewish school, i.e. swinishness.

A political lesson was given to 1st Company, SS-Volunteer Battalion on 25.6.1941, when volunteer Pekka Kurvinen was among the listeners. The lecturer explained that the Jews were of mixed racial origin and were "industrious", just as the superior races like Germans, Britons, Balts, Scandinavians, and Finns. Nevertheless, the Jew had inherited the bad qualities of various races. In Britain there was a Jewish government and Jewish attempts to gain power had occurred in Italy, whereas success in the Balkans had materialised only in part. In Russia the Jews had, however, been successful.[728] SS-volunteer Jaakko Saarela from the 4th Company, Finnish SS-Volunteer Battalion listened on 27.6.1941 to a lecture from his Company Commander. He said that it was the Jews who had caused the present situation, i.e. the outbreak of war between Germany and the Soviet Union. As Jews were deported from Germany, they migrated to France, Russia, and the USA, inciting propaganda against Germany.[729]

Eino Nevanlinna, another of the later replacements to the SS-Volunteer Battalion, participated in a political lesson on 22.12.1942 at SS-Junkerschule Bad Tölz. The teacher was a coarse former Catholic priest, who had become a political instructor. Music by Georg Friedrich Händel was played and hymns were sung. However, the words were not so subtly altered: "It is well when the knife-blade glints and Jewish blood splashes".[730]

In the Finnish Replacement Company in Graz, several lectures were given in 1942–1943 on the racial issue. The Company Commander SS-Obersturmführer Schröder gave a lecture on 9.2.1942 dealing with the laws of the Waffen-SS and racial doctrines. SS-Oberscharführer Mauno Alhainen lectured on 9.3. and 23.3.1943 on "The Jewish Issue".[731] Volunteer Toivo Tuomaala, who listened to Alhainen, noted in his diary: "He talked much sense".[732] In a letter to SS-Untersturmführer Unto Boman (later Unto Parvilahti) at the Finnisches Freiwilligen-Bataillon Verbindungsstelle in Berlin, Alhainen wrote:

> Furthermore I've been giving lectures, which have gained extraordinary popularity. Several comrades have talked to the Company Commander and asked for further lessons to the effect that there are by now four or five every week. And although the boys generally try to escape everything, all of them attend my les-

sons and they also listen very carefully. I've got the impression that there are very good political elements here".[733]

In the spring of 1943, Alhainen published an article in the right-wing radical activist newspaper *Ajan suunta* on his experiences of the Jews in Berlin. He wrote:

> When I arrived for the first time in Berlin in the fall of 1941, the Jews still appeared in the street with their badges. I must confess that then they were still numerous. However, since those days their number has essentially decreased, and it is now possible to state that Berlin is a clean city with regard to the Jews. They have been transferred eastwards, to the former Poland. There they have the possibility to engage in decent work. Nor are they now harming the Nordic race in this struggle for the rights of humanity and its living possibilities.[734]

According to a post-war report by the leftist Eino Salonen, Alhainen was nicknamed "Pikku-Göbbels" (Little Goebbels) during his SS-service, because of his fanatical National Socialist ideas.[735]

In another undated newspaper article in *Rintamamies* (The Frontman), a mouthpiece of the Finnish right-wing veterans of the 1918 Civil War (on the White side, naturally) and the 1939–40 Winter War, Alhainen dealt more extensively with the Jews:

> A new issue for you is the Jew of the East. You have seen Jews previously. Many were in Helsinki, putting their long noses in shop-doors along the former Heikinkatu.[736] There were certainly Jews also in Germany, but with yellow Stars of David on their breast. They have dedicated themselves to that symbol. That yellow mark, the color of plague, was chosen so that no white-skinned person would mistakenly become social with the Jews or have anything to do with them. However, as we entered the former Poland, Ukraine, and Russia a new Jewish type emerged. In Poland this was a proletarian Jew, who lived in miserable villages, in filthy and unclean buildings. They got their means of subsistence in various ways: by trading, by begging. No work was done, as that doesn't fit the Jewish character. However, the German principle was that those who did not work, should neither eat anything, and this was applied among others to the Jews. When one watched the work carried out by the Jews, that was surely hopeless and didn't earn the bread.[737]

Alhainen continued by stating that the behaviour of the SS-forces towards the natives in the various countries was unprejudiced and representative of men of culture. He continued that

> (...) we were anyway allowed to use Jews in all kinds of work for which casual assistance was needed. Such work could be the filling of the tyres of the cars with air or cleaning the vehicles, and for such jobs there were always Jews available. The natives in every village we entered would gladly report them, as they had long suffered from swindling by Jews. In carrying this out the Jews had benefited from all of the promises of the Talmud. Although the territory of the former Poland had been under Russian rule for only eighteen months, the Jews had risen to the surface everywhere as

lawyers, physicians, and bigwigs, not to mention the zealous Communists. Those holding top positions were predominantly Jews (...) The natives were pleased to share their [the Jews'] property with the permission of the Germans.[738]

The Finnish volunteer Leo Heikurainen attended an Officer Training Course at SS-Junkerschule Bad Tölz in 1943 where they had political lectures twice a week. The Lectures on the Jews made him feel sick, although he enjoyed the political classes.[739] A Finnish volunteer reported discussions on 10.3.1943 in a class about the Jewish question and the Freemasons.[740] The Liaison Officer and Bureau Chief Kim Lindberg gave a lecture on 16.4.1943 about the differences between race and nationality.[741]

However, there was also some opposition to the indoctrination. The Finnish SS-Obersturmführer Erik Lautia stated in early March 1942 that he would rather be incarcerated in prison than attend political lectures.[742] In 1944–45, the Finnish SS-Oberscharführer Thor-Björn Weckström gave political lessons three to four times every week on topics other than Jews in the SS-Schule Kongsvinger in Norway.[743] He acted on instructions of SS-Sturmbannführer Karl Leib of the Germanische Leitstelle in Oslo.[744] From June 1941, Weckström was a member of SS-Regiment Westland and was known for his firm commitment to National Socialist ideas. SS-Hauptsturmführer Jouko Itälä regarded after the war Weckström's talks as "Nazi nonsense" while SS-volunteer Veikko Häikiö said Weckström demonstrated "agitated opinions" on the Jews during his lessons. Volunteer Aimo Mäkitalo reported that Weckström blamed "Jewishness" for the concluding of the Finnish-Soviet Armistice in September 1944. In his lessons on National Socialism, he claimed that every human being in the world would become well-off if National Socialism were to triumph.[745]

FEELINGS OF SYMPATHY FOR THE SUFFERING JEWS

Several expressions of feelings of sympathy for the Jews among the Finnish SS-volunteers are known. On 12.5.1941, probably in Stettin, SS-volunteer Martti Koivula watched the anti-semitic Nazi propaganda movie *Der ewige Jude* ("The Eternal Jew", 1940)". In his diary, Koivula commented upon his impressions: "Most disgusting propaganda. Surely propaganda of this sort would not be accepted in Finland."[746] On 18.6.1941, SS-volunteer Jaakko Lakeala passed through the municipality of Wieluń in Poland and noted: "Here the Poles are marked with a yellow star. A humble crowd, with men who remove their hats". By "Poles", Lakeala probably means Polish Jews. Later, when participating in the march into the Soviet Union, he noted from 23.6.1941: "It was said that two German lorry drivers were shot in the night. Jews are suspected". However, Lakeala experienced shocking events, and he reported in the early entries of his diary, writing: "It is the biggest blunder in the world that I went on this journey. All that I have seen has opened my eyes on the world, but of all I have seen I will have to pay with my life and health".[747]

Also volunteer Olavi Liesinen of 16th Company, SS-Regiment Nordland passed through former Polish areas in June 1941. He has described his experiences:

The hostility against the Jews revealed itself. We were told about this problem as if the Jews were the beginning and end of all bad things and should be treated like dogs. To the other Finns, this was a most queer issue. We were in no way used to such things as this. However, I remembered when I myself visited South Africa aboard the *Suomen Joutsen* [a full-rigged sail training vessel belonging to the Finnish Navy]. A negro was completely isolated from the company of whites, and his existence was only fit for slave duty and something between a human and an animal. Now, here was the same style (...) Racial agitation was for once something foreign to us and inappropriate for adults. Arriving at the Polish side [of the former border], we were immediately aware of the rash behaviour of the Germans in occupied territory.[748]

Liesinen's narrative continued:

According to the Germans, the Poles lacked all of that nobility and idealism the Germans possessed in abundance. However, for myself I judged that idealism to be pure cruelty. The Finns found themselves in an exasperating position [between the Germans and the Poles] and none of us could accept those racial doctrines. Just watching how the Germans carried them out was disgusting. Young German SS-men acted like aggressors in their attitude to the civil population in the area. These youngsters didn't yet have any view of war other than that provided by propaganda. In that view the supposed enemy always perished. As we stopped at a village, enforced requirements continued. In order to avoid violence, the civilians delivered what they had at hand. Milk, eggs, and chickens were in demand. Directives on heating milk supplied by Poles reduced any risk of poisoning, and no one wanted Germans dying from the milk.[749]

Liesinen concluded:

The heroes of the New Europe [i.e. the SS-forces] let off volleys of gunfire as they pleased. In their opinion, it was necessary to kill a Jew with no distinction between men, women, and children. This was hard for us. In Finland we had been taught: thou shall not kill, and in peacetime we respected this. Not even during wartime did we accept murder. As our protests and our appeals appeared useless, we came up with a word which had an effect – *Du Jude*. This made our brothers-in-arms angry and they started to explain the qualities of pure blood. As a consequence, one or another Jew [was] successfully helped out unharassed.[750]

On 25.6.1941, the Finnish Liaison Officer SS-Obersturmführer Ensio Pihkala met the volunteers SS-Hauptsturmführer Yrjö Kaila and SS-Obersturmführer Erkki Puuperä of SS-Aufklärungs-Abteilung 5 in Hrubeshiv (Pol. *Hrubieszów*). They told him that the previous day a Jew had not properly greeted a German non-commissioned officer. The Jew had been "tortured, his beard and hair cut, and he was finally probably shot". In Bila Tserkva (Pol. *Biała Cerkiew*; Russ. *Belaya Tserkov*) on 15.7.1941, a few Finnish members of the SS-Aufkärungs-Abteilung 5 told Pihkala that they had "(...) ended up among crooks and murderers. The neighbours [= the Germans] readily snatched up goods and bravely killed un-

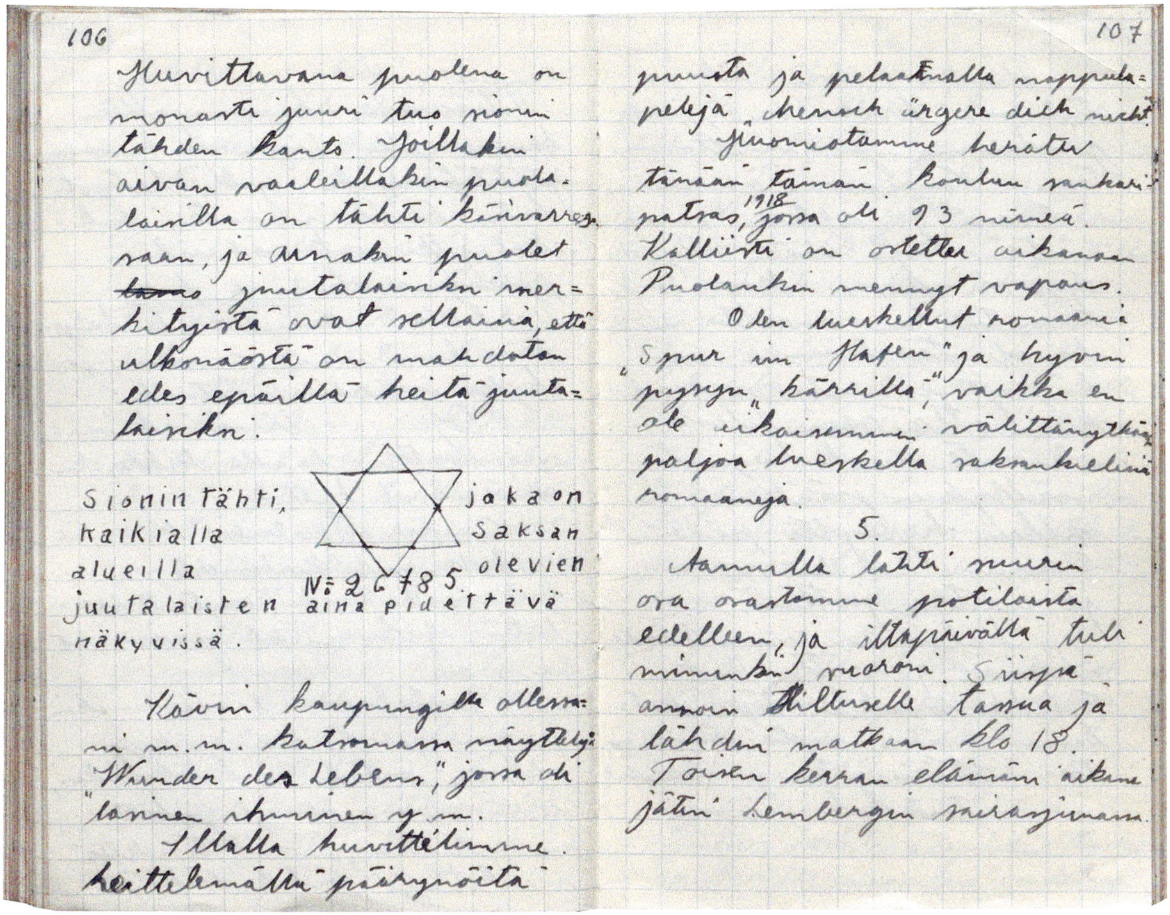
106

Huvittavana puolena on monasti juuri tuo nimen tähden kanto. Joillakin aivan vaaleillakin puolalaisilla on tähti käsivarressaan, ja monetkin puolet ~~tuos~~ juutalaisiksi merkityistä ovat sellaisia, että ulkonäöstä on mahdotonta edes epäillä heitä juutalaisiksi.

Sionin tähti, kaikialla alueilla juutalaisten näkyvissä. Jakaon Saksan olevien aina pidettävä N:o 26785.

Kävin kaupungilla ollessani m.m. katsomassa näyttelyä "Wunder des Lebens", jossa oli "lasinen ihminen y.m.

Illalla huvittelimme heittelemällä päärynöitä

107

puusta ja pelaamalla nappulapelejä "Mensch ärgere dich nicht".

Suomiotamme herätti tänään tämän koulun sankaripatsas, 1918 jossa oli 93 nimeä. Kalliista on otettu aikanaan Puolankin mennyt vapaus.

Olen lueskellut romaania "Spur im Hafen" ja hyvin pysyn kärryillä, vaikka en ole erikoisemmin välittänyt paljoa lueskella saksankielisiä romaaneja.

5.

Aamulla lähti meiden osa osastomme sotilaista edelleen, ja iltapäivällä tuli minunkin vuoroni. Sinne annoin Hiltuselle tassua ja lähdin matkaan klo 18. Toisen kerran elämäni aikana jätin Lembergin miraajinaan.

Finnish SS-volunteer Keijo Kääriäinen describes in his diary entry for 4.8.1942 the Jews of the Lemberg Ghetto wearing the yellow Star of David. He tells quite neutrally that this seems strange, as over half of those wearing the star are of pale complexion and do not differ from the rest of the population. There was no anti-Semitic legislation in Finland and Finnish Jews served in the Armed Forces just as did all the other male citizens.

armed prisoners and Jews. This = Glory. A most strange 'comradeship'".[751] The volunteer Reino Suonio passed through Lublin on 28.6.1941 and noted that the city was large, although very filthy. In a camp there were "a lot of Jews". After passing Rawa-Ruska (Ukr. *Rava-Ruska*, Yiddish *Rave*) and the old 1939 border on 30.6.1941 and on entering Soviet territory, he wrote: "Here one can see stark brutality, villages in ashes, dead horses, while tanks, cars, and other wrecks fill the sides of the roads. At the same time, I also watched Jewish refugees carrying bundles on their backs walking by the ruins of their houses. The life of Poles is not an easy one."[752]

Seppo Taivalmaa, a volunteer from 1st Company, Finnish SS-Volunteer Battalion, reported a train ride east of Lublin in the fall of 1941. In his recollections, he noted that at every stop dozens of boys under ten years approached the train asking: "Gentlemen, please bread!" (*Herren, bitte Brot!*). Taivalmaa wrote that they "(…) experienced watching this misery with great distaste and always when an opportunity allowed, we gave them bread and suchlike. This was surely strictly forbidden, but what could one do (…)". These boys may, however, have been ordinary Polish youths, as Taivalmaa does not expressively characterise them as Jews.[753]

By 19.3.1942, volunteer Uuno Ström from 1st Company of the Finnish SS-Volunteer Battalion was with his unit in Bachmutskij. In the same quarters there were also a few Finns from SS-Aufklärungs-Abteilung 5. Ström reported that "they told much about their tours last summer, in particular of the terrible destruction of the Jews".[754] Paavo Suutala of the Finnish SS-Volunteer Battalion also disliked the "dictate-command" in Germany and regretted in particular the German repressions against innocent people like the Jews.[755]

Volunteer Erik Savolainen from the same unit said in a post-war interrogation with the Finnish Security Police that from the beginning he felt sick because of the German command and oppression of Jews. Valpo noted for the record: "As a consequence of this he could not, in an intoxicated state, refrain from expressing his disgust towards this [behaviour] and was noted for it in Germany".[756]

The Finnish volunteer from SS-Nachschub-Abteilung 5 Markku Käenmäki wrote about his experiences of German policy towards Jews:

> The persecution and the repression of the Jews was a chapter of its own. In the opinion of the Germans, the Jews were an awful race, who blighted everyone who came into contact with them. For that reason, they had to be isolated from others. The racial ideologies thought the Jews were not even proper human beings, but sub-humans. The Jewish population in the countryside of Poland and Ukraine lived in really miserable conditions, and they had to experience bitterly the hatred and cruelties directed against them. They were abused and shot for little reason. For the Jews who met the columns of soldiers this meant death or at least a brutal and inhuman treatment. It was disgusting to watch this.

However, Käenmäki also wrote that all of the SS-men were not that brutal, but that "the bulk were decent and fair soldiers". He also concluded that the military discipline of SS-Division Wiking later improved and that the majority of "the known sad events happened in the very first initial phase of the attack.[757]

Käenmäki also reported on an occasion when he and his Finnish fellows were ordered to participate in the shooting of 24 Jews. An equivalent number of SS-soldiers were ordered to form the firing squad, one for each victim. The Jews were lined up at the edge of a large pit. Käenmäki reported:

> As we Finns got the order, we naturally could not refuse. If we had done that, there may perhaps have been two more to be shot. We prepared very slowly for the task and were even hurried up. Eventually there was nothing for it: we finally had to go to the place [of execution]. Luckily enough, two enthusiastic Germans offered themselves instead of us, and they were also accepted. We were not forced to shoot, and thus we avoided this very unpleasant task.[758]

However, Käenmäki does not mention either the place or the date of the event, but as he mentions that his unit passed through Lemberg, Zhytomyr, and Tarnopol, it may be presumed that the shooting took place somewhere along the marching route in the summer of 1941.

Volunteer Pauli Nummelin of the 1st Company, Finnish SS-Volunteer Battalion was wounded in the summer of 1942 and was brought to a military hospital in Lublin. An old Jewish Professor worked there as a cleaner and servant. Nummelin gave him ample amounts of bread and did not realise until afterwards that they both could have been severely punished.[759] Further, in an interview in 2016 the former member of the Finnish SS-Volunteer Battalion Sakari Haikala (formerly Sulinmaa) spoke about his experiences of the advance in 1941–43: "We certainly knew that the Jews were being pursued and killed, but in those days we couldn't do anything about it. We regarded anti-semitism as disgraceful and our sympathies were on the side of the Jews".[760] In his biography from 2016, Haikala recorded that he had an affair with a Jewish woman, who had converted to Christianity. As the Finnish SS-Volunteer Battalion on 4.12.1941 passed through Warsaw on 4.12.1941, heading for the front, he gave a girl of 7–9 years some bread and chocolate at the railway station. A German NCO had then – to the disgust of Haikala – told the girl to go away, put his pistol to her forehead, and threatened to shoot her. As Haikala objected, the NCO brushed him aside and claimed that Poles "don't want his food".[761] Haikala also stresses that he was warmly welcomed in a Jewish shop and that the Jews in his opinion were sympathetic. Nevertheless, Haikala's various statements must be set against a whole array of other belittling and retrospectively rationalising comments he makes. In this way, he denies that the Finnish volunteers would have committed any atrocities.[762]

Significantly, as the statements by Käenmäki, Nummelin, and Haikala are made respectively 62, 58, and 73 years after the events related, the stories are likely to have been influenced by opinions absorbed from the long post-war period. The statements do not thus necessarily document the attitude towards the Jews that the aforementioned volunteers entertained in the war-years themselves.

ATTITUDES OF INDIFFERENCE

A few of the notes on Jews in the diaries of the Finnish volunteers can be characterised as indifferent, as they merely record observations without any approving or disapproving remarks. Nevertheless, it is possible that by mentioning repressive German steps volunteers entertained an intent to draw attention to a policy they did not actually approve of. However, at least formally, these notes are registered as indifferent.

The Finnish SS-volunteer Keijo Kääriäinen from 2nd Company of the SS-Regiment Nordland arrived with his unit on 19.6.1941 in a little town in the General-Gouvernement, and he reported that Germans forced the local Jews to wash their vehicles. Kääriäinen experienced a miserable scene. Later, in August 1941 as he was considerably more experienced, he wrote when passing through Lemberg (*Lviv*): "The shop signs here show the conditions of [daily] life: *Nur für Deutsche*; *Nur für Deutsche und Verbundete*: *Juden und Hunden Eintritt verboten*; *Juden nich gewünscht*, etc. (Only for Germans and their Allies, Forbidden för Jews and Dogs, Jews Not Wanted Here). There are certainly plenty of Jews here, and they appear to even have some rights. Among other things I've seen some shops marked with the "Star of Sion". The wearing of that star is frequently amusing. Even some entirely fair [-complexioned] Poles wear the star on their sleeve. At least half of those marked as Jews are impossible to believe as being Jews by their looks".[763]

Also volunteer Aarno Nurmio of the 12th Company of the SS-Regiment Nordland recalled a negative experience from the march in the summer of 1941. His column of vehicles met long rows of POWs and escaping civilians on the road. A big Austrian threw stones from the platform body of the truck at Jews coming across.[764]

When the Finnish SS-Volunteer Battalion was transferred in December from Gross Born to the Eastern Front, it passed on 4.12.1941 through the railway station in Warsaw. A group of girls asked the volunteers for bread: "Not until quite some time later did they understand their having witnessed Jews on their way to the concentration camps".[765] This recollection by Ossian Leisimo of the Finnish SS-Volunteer Battalion seems to illustrate the initial naivety that characterised many of the Finnish volunteers. Some months later, perhaps in the winter of 1942, Seppo Taivalmaa (1st Company, Finnish SS-Volunteer Battalion) recalls a tram ride in Berlin:

> Opposite us in the streetcar stood a very nice girl. On her chest on the left side of her jacket was sewn a yellow star with the diameter of around eight centimetres, i.e. she was a Jew. I got the idea to start chatting with her, but talking to a Jew was strictly forbidden, and one never knew where monitors might be hiding. I would probably have gained nothing from a chat, but for her talking with me could have meant the final loss of her restricted freedom, so I rejected the idea.[766]

Finally, it can be noted that in the post-war period the chief Finnish recruiter of the SS-volunteers, Esko Riekki, played down the anti-Jewish actions of SS-Division Wiking: "Within this period there occurred no 'Jewish question' or anything else whatsoever. Certainly, some of the Finnish boys mentioned that they had heard that Jews were arrested when the Germans took Lemberg and other Jewish towns. They also said that

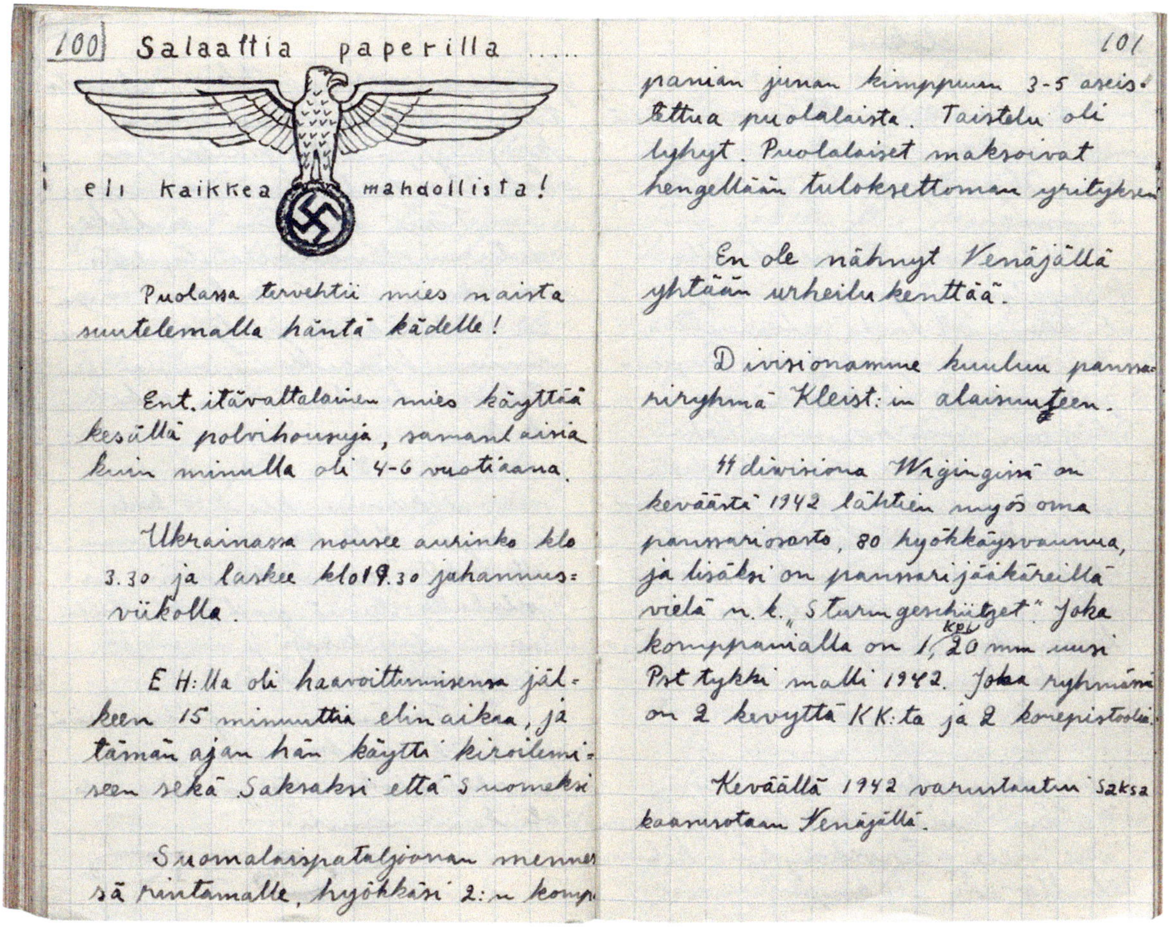
100 Salaattia paperilla .....

eli kaikkea mahdollista!

Puolassa tervehtii mies naista suutelemalla häntä kädelle!

Ent. itävaltalainen mies käyttää kesällä polvihousuja, samanlaisia kuin minulla oli 4-6 vuotiaana.

Ukrainassa nousee aurinko klo 3.30 ja laskee klo 19.30 juhannus=viikolla.

E H:lla oli haavoittumisensa jälkeen 15 minuuttia elinaikaa, ja tämän ajan hän käytti kiroilemiseen sekä saksaksi että suomeksi

Suomalaispataljoonan mennessä rintamalle, hyökkäsi 2:n komppanian junan kimppuun 3-5 aseistettua puolalaista. Taistelu oli lyhyt. Puolalaiset maksoivat hengellään tuloksettoman yrityksen

101

En ole nähnyt Venäjällä yhtään urheilukenttää.

Divisionamme kuului panssariryhmä Kleist:in alaisuuteen.

SS divisioona Wikingiin on keväästä 1942 lähtien myös oma panssariosasto, 80 hyökkäysvaunua, ja lisäksi on panssarijääkäreillä vielä n.k. „Sturmgeschütze". Joka komppanialla on 1 kpl 20 mm uusi Pst tykki malli 1942. Joka ryhmällä on 2 kevyttä KK:ta ja 2 konepistoolia.

Keväällä 1942 varustautui Saksa kaasusotaan Venäjällä.

Some random notes by Finnish SS-volunteer Keijo Kääriäinen in his diary, such as "I have not seen a single sports field in the Soviet Union" and that the German armed forces were prepared for gas war with the Red Army in the spring of 1942. He notes also that the SS-Division Wiking had received 80 new tanks and other armour. *Private collection.*

The central person in the recruiting of Finnish volunteers was the former Chief of the Finnish security police, Major of the Reserve Esko Riekki. He visited the volunteers in the winter of 1941–42, here hosted by SS-Obersturmführer Erkki Puuperä (center) from the reconnaissance Aufklärungs-Abteilung 5. *OW Coll.*

the conquest with tank forces in the Blitzkrieg was carried out with great ferocity".[767] However, Riekki simultaneously regarded German repressive actions against the Jews as entirely foolish. He reported that as far as he knew the mass arrests of the Jews and their extermination did not start until the beginning of 1942.

In spite of these remarks, Riekki was indubitably already aware that Jews were held in concentration camps before WWII. He may well have known further details, as he visited Dachau concentration camp himself in the early fall of 1937.[768] Of this visit, Riekki commented: "It was a hutted camp with good order, surrounded by barbed wire and guard towers. But it was no death factory". Dachau "(...) was a prison camp, in which Communists and other indisputable bad elements were held, perhaps several thousands of them. The camp was extraordinarily tidy with good order, and of course good German discipline. Himmler said that generally there were no escapes because his boys were good gunners

(*Meine Jungen schiessen gut*)".[769] Riekki visited the camp when attending a secret police meeting in Berlin between 30.8 and 13.9.1937. He was then in the company of Bruno Aaltonen, Deputy Chief of the Finnish Security Police. This meeting saw the participation of senior police officers from 15 semi-authoritarian, fascist, and strongly anti-Communist regimes. The Finnish delegates were the only representatives from a Nordic country. Neither Britain nor France took part in the meeting.[770]

REJECTION OF ATROCITIES AND LATENT ANTI-GERMAN VIEWS AMONG THE VOLUNTEERS

In this section, a review will be included on the critical attitudes among the Finnish SS-volunteers towards the atrocities against civilians, Jews, and Soviet POWs. Attitudes of this sort occurred among the other ethnic groups in the ranks of the Waffen-SS, although as it seems, these were rare and in individual cases. The purpose of the presentation is to accentuate that opinions among the volunteers were divided. There is no doubt that some of the volunteers, from Finland just as from the other Nordic countries, sided with the German-run massacres, and equally that a considerable number of the volunteers may have observed the atrocities with disdain and sorrow.

Volunteer Olavi Liesinen belonged to the 16th Company of SS-Regiment Nordland. From the beginning of the March to June 1941, he noted in his recollections that the 'Jewish problem' was explained to the unit as if the Jews had from the beginning all been bad and that they "should be treated like dogs without a master". As noted earlier above, as Liesinen's unit travelled through Poland, he looked upon razed villages that had certainly not been of any military value. In particular, the persecution of Jews left an impression of disgust, and he wrote:

> What we observed was difficult to believe. The racial hatred targeted against Jews verged on insanity. It is still today hard to believe that this was true, and I would be happy to regard it as a nightmare (...) We were unable to help. Holding discussions did not have any effect on the Germans, other than that they became even more agitated. For the Jews who ran towards our motorised columns, the encounter meant death or at least brutal, inhuman treatment. I remember how a Jewish man, woman, or a child could run in front of our cars like hunted animals. The men with the hats in their hand, bowing before the German soldiers as they ran. Scornful comments and threatening gestures with weapons terrified these people. The columns were long and the death following close upon their heels was terrible. The heroes of the New Europe [i.e. the SS-forces] let off volleys of gunfire as they pleased. In their opinion, it was necessary to kill the Jew, with no distinction between men, women, and children.[771]

On 3.7.1941, SS-volunteer Keijo Kääriäinen of 2nd Company, SS-Regiment Nordland was on the move together with other volunteers in the vicinity of Slowita. The unit had driven around 50 kilometres from Lemberg (*Lviv*) eastwards during the previous day. In his diary he mentions that the inhabitants of Nowiki (*Novyky*) village, 15 km northeast of Tarnopol (*Ternopil*), actually competed among themselves to bring them sandwiches, milk, and eggs. However, he observes that "as thanks and reward, the Germans shot several dark-complexioned Ukrainians, claiming that they were Jews. This was in my opinion the very height of swineish behavior!" (*Se oli minusta sikamaisuuden huippu!*).[772] The volunteer of 4th Company, Finnish SS-Volunteer Battalion Sakari Haikala has declared in a recent book (from 2016) that his attitude towards the Germans become a schizophrenic one: "simultaneously and equally with hate and admiration".[773]

Erik Liukkonen of the Finnish SS-Volunteer Battalion mentions that the Finnish volunteers were told to adapt to German norms of conduct shortly after arriving in Germany in the spring and early summer of 1941. Although the volunteers got fully acquainted with high-level German skills in war, they internalised all use of this, and adopted externally the extremely harsh military discipline. As Liukkonen put it bluntly, those elements who quickly realised what was going on "landed on their feet". However, in "their inner minds they always remained cold towards the Germans, towards German conduct in all its forms of expression. They become even more Finnish and it can be said that they actively rebelled against all that was German, to the extent that they started to hate their homeland because it was an ally of Germany. Nothing was ever discussed openly about these issues, but there were hints in half-spoken words; Germans were mistreated in suitable situations, they were scorned, and they were never trusted. The brutality of the Germans was hated and their behaviour was criticised very sharply, and in public". Liukkonen claims that this was the attitude most Finnish volunteers entertained, and that the committed National Socialists among the Finns were not looked upon favourably by the others.[774]

Volunteer Arvo Kokko of 5th Company, SS-Regiment Nordland recalled: "As the war started, opinions turned against the Germans".[775] But it was not until the summer of 1943 when the Finnish Army recalled the SS-Volunteer Battalion, at the end of its two-year service contract. This was against the wishes of the SS-Hauptamt (SS-HA), who wanted to prolong the service contract and the Waffen-SS cooperation with the Finns. Rather they sought to give service contracts to willing volunteers, to recruit new ones, and increase the numbers of volunteers.[776] The main Finnish recruiter for the SS-volunteers was Esko Riekki, who met Steiner at Helsinki Malmi Airport when he arrived in Finland on 31.5.1943. One of the first things Steiner asked him was why Finnish troops mistrusted the Germans (*Herr Riekki, Sie haben keine Vertauen zu uns. Weshalb, weshalb?*). Riekki tried to explain that the confidence in some respects had been shaken and that the Germans in a way had to again earn the trust of the Finnish soldiers. Steiner "did not like this, but as a gentleman he said nothing".[777]

In several cases, anti-German sentiments ended up in violent confrontations. One night in May 1941, some Finnish volunteers in the Heuberg training centre gave a few arrogant and malicious drill instructors among the German NCOs a good thrashing. Later there occurred a common wish among the Finnish volunteers to collectively whip the bullying German instructors.[778] As the Finnish SS-Volunteer Battalion in Gross Born was making preparations for transport to the front in November 1941, the German NCOs asked to transfer to another unit. It appears the reason was fear of being shot in revenge by the Finnish volunteers at a favourable moment at the front.[779] On 5.6.1943, two days after taking part in the *Waffenbruder* celebrations at the Pyynikki Stadium in Tampere to mark the volunteers' return to Finland, one former Finnish SS-volunteer met a German in the street in Jyväskylä. As he remembered old wrongs, he abruptly and without provocation stabbed the German with his knife. The wounded German had to be taken to hospital for treatment.[780]

Gladiaattori, the short-lived newsletter of the Replacement Company of the Finnish SS-Volunteer Battalion in Graz, was edited with a critical attitude towards the German leadership. The paper appeared in February-March 1942 and was abruptly terminated.[781] One expression of keeping their distance from German values was the participation of former SS-volunteers in the so-called Lapland War against the German forces under AOK 20 (*Armee Lappland/20. Gebirgs-*

The audience at the Tampere parade on 3.6.1943. In the first row, among others SS-General Felix Steiner, Lieutenant-General Lauri Malmberg, and the Rector of the University of Helsinki, Professor Rolf Nevanlinna. Nevanlinna was known for his pro-German sympathies and he chaired the support committee of the SS-volunteers. *OW Coll.*

Armee) in the fall of 1944. There is no particular study of the topic, but roughly 100 former SS-volunteers are believed to have fought the retreating German troops after the Finns and the Soviets ended hostilities and signed the Moscow Armistice in September 1944. Seven of the volunteers were killed in action in this seven-month conflict: the former SS-Rottenführers Keijo Koskelin and Niilo Sääskilahti in Ala-Tornio, 1. and 6.10.1944, Viljo Puotinen in Tornio, 7.10.1944, Kauko Kauppi in Rovaniemi, 12.10.1944, the former SS-Scharführers Sakari Kohola in Pudasjärvi, 2.10.1944 and Raine Ritari in Pudasjärvi, 27.10.1944, and SS-Obersturmführer Teuvo Hatara in Rovaniemi, 17.10.1944.[782]

Among the Norwegian volunteers, too, there seem to have been smouldering anti-German sentiments. Volunteer Eivind Reichelt, who served in an Ersatzkompanie of SS-Division Wiking, stated in a 1946 police interrogation:

> The Battalion Commander (Christian Frederik) von Schalburg (3rd Battalion Nordland) said after some Norwegians applied for release (*dimisjon*) that it was agreed that for the duration of their service the Norwegians would be sent to the rear for construction of 'shithouses' in German-occupied areas rather than fighting together with other Germanics. After this, I kept any anti-German inclinations to myself and regularly criticised sharply the Germanische SS Norwegen and the Reichskommissar for Norway Josef Terboven. I told my comrades that I liked the idea of deserting to the other side and fighting the Germans.[783]

It should be immediately obvious that on the one hand Reichelt writes that he kept his anti-German feelings to himself, but on the other hand he claims to have declared them loudly to his Norwegian fellows. The explanation for this stark contradiction is probably his split attitude to the Germans, or possibly the sense that such dangerous opinions might be "safer" with close comrades-in-arms. The juncture and context of these statements – a post-war police interrogation as part of the criminal prosecutions of volunteers in the "Germanic SS" – should also be considered.

Reichelt also said that during 1942 at the front he experienced many events that bolstered his attitude, and through his sister Eva he sent a letter to NS-Minister President Vidkun Quisling: In this he

> (...) pointed out the poor treatment of the Norwegians by the Germans and the Danish Battalion Commander, von Schalburg. Quisling and Riisnæs arrived at the front in April or May [1942] for a short visit. This gave me the opportunity to hand over a note to Riisnæs. In this note, I had made comments about various statements by German officers on the Norwegians. These statements were defamatory. Among others a German Obersturmführer said that he wished the Norwegians were on the other side, so he would have the opportunity to blow holes through our heads.[784]

Sverre Riisnaes was the Minister of Justice in the Nasjonal Samling collaborationist government, and he was also an SS-Standartenführer.

ANGRY AND UNDERSTANDING ATTITUDES TOWARDS THE JEWS AMONG DANISH, DUTCH AND NORWEGIAN SS-VOLUNTEERS

Similar anti-Jewish attitudes were to be found among the Danish, Dutch, Norwegian, and Swedish SS-volunteers. This appears from the following brief review.

The Danish SS-volunteers held generally anti-Jewish opinions, although no extensive review on the issue is known. In the newspaper of the Danish National Socialist movement *Faedrelandet* there are several pieces in which Danish volunteers expressed negative or dismissive opinions on Jews. In a letter to his family in October 1941, one Danish volunteer stated that he hoped to get to the front, and he mentioned: "simply getting permission to shoot a Jew or a Russian Commissar would bring great satisfaction, but that time will surely come". Frikorps Danmark was in 1941 deployed in Treskau in Poland for training. The Commander, SS-Obersturmführer Christian Peder Kryssing made use of Jews for his gardening work. In the winter months, they had to work in the garden with bare legs and without proper clothing.[785]

An expression of the hostile attitudes towards Jews is that open mass graves containing dead Jews were seen by some of the volunteers as more attractive than the prison camps.[786] A Danish volunteer wrote in a letter home: "Yes, we'll eradicate these Jews from the surface of the earth, because while there are Jews, there is also war. Now, I can imagine there are some who would say that the Jews are humans too. My answer would be that rats are also animals".[787] A Danish volunteer from the SS-Division Wiking and later attached to SS-Panzergrenadier-Regiment 24 Danmark, who was tried after the war, declared that he had twice tried to cancel his service contract. He had witnessed how Jewish women and children had been shot.[788] In the post-war trials, two Danish SS-volunteers of the Ersatz Company, Frikorps Danmark said that most of its members refrained from maltreating Jews – in spite of the anti-Jewish spirit among the volunteers.[789]

Anti-Jewish attitudes appear to have been present at least somewhat commonly among the Dutch SS-volunteers. In the summer and fall of 1941, Schütze Jan Olij served in 1st Company, SS-Regiment Westland. A piece of his nose was shot away in Tarashcha, he got a fragmentation wound in the shoulder in Dnipropetrovsk, and later similar fragmentation splinters in his backside, received in the vicinity of Rostov-on-Don, probably in mid-November 1941. He was cared for in a field hospital and transferred to a Recovery Company in Klagenfurt, Austria, in late 1941. From there, he sent his family an undated letter in which he wrote:

> I never saw so much trash and rottenness as in Russia. The people there die of hunger and misery. No W.C., no water supply, electricity, gas, streets, churches, cemeteries, doctors. Nothing but misery, dirt, and hunger. The children grow up without schooling and are wearing some old rags. If they get sick, there is no doctor and when they die, they are put in a pit in the ground and earthed over. There are no police, and the only thing Russia has to offer are bugs, lice, and Jews, which we finished off: the first two types by hand, the last with a pistol or a rifle. You see, your nephew has

> also become a killer, although my conscience is barely affected because of those few lousy Jews, who wring the poor Russian population dry by cheating and stripping them.[790]

Dutch historian Evertjan van Roekel has documented individual cases of anti-Jewish and anti-Semitic attitudes among the Dutch volunteers of the SS-Division Wiking. He made use of their letters home and diary notes on their involvement in hunts for and killing of Jews. Some of these stories were published in National Socialist newspapers like *Volk* and *Vaderland*. Partly based on the same diaries by Dutch volunteers, although more extensively, historian Cees Kleijn and journalist Stijn Reurs confirm the observations made by van Roekel.[791]

The anti-Jewish attitudes among the around 300 Norwegian members of the SS-Division Wiking have been studied by historian Sigurd Sørlie. Many of these volunteers entertained anti-Jewish ideas already before joining the Division, as anti-Semitism was one of central tenets of the far-right Nasjonal Samling movement. However, the German assault on the Soviet Union in the summer of 1941 gave oxygen to already existing anti-Jewish sentiments and strengthened them. The start of the war also launched an intensive propaganda campaign within the Wehrmacht and the Waffen-SS. As a consequence, the anti-Jewish attitudes flourished among the Norwegian volunteers and were expressed in numerous letters and writings in the newspapers in Norway. Hence the Jews were at least occasionally experienced as "weeds", "parasites", "leeches", "stinking individuals" and Zhytomyr could be called "a Jewish cave". The Jews were described as "worse than animals".[792]

After a visit to a prison camp, an anonymous volunteer wrote: "And if I've not previously been a hater of Jews, I have by now learned to become one.[793] The Norwegian SS-war correspondents Walter Fyrst (himself an SS-Hauptsturmführer), Egil Hartmann, Karl Holter, and Oswald Olsen published several anti-Jewish articles in the newspapers *Aftenposten* and *Fritt Folk* in 1941–43. According to these, the Jewish quarters in Kraków were stinking, and representatives of that disgusting race resided in Lublin.[794] Nevertheless, there was an assortment of opinions, as some of the volunteers did not share such aggressive attitudes towards the Jews, and some of the letters, diaries, and writings do not include tangible anti-Jewish opinions.[795] By contrast, the liquidation of the Jews also made some of the Norwegian SS-volunteers feel sick. Jan Taarneby of 9th Company, SS-Regiment Germania, witnessed the shooting of Jews and Soviet prisoners in Ukraine in late June 1941. Of his experiences, he said:

> We Norwegians reacted against this. Initially there were seven Norwegians in the Company (…) We swore that if we were spared from this hell, we would do anything in order to avoid the Germans, [but] we were under the obligation of duty for a year (…) The brutality of the Germans made a hard impact on the Norwegians. For my own part, I vomited the first time when I watched how the Germans could behave.

His compatriot Ørnulf Bjørnstad observed in late 1944 how German treatment of the Jews that summer was wrong: "Every Norwegian of our Battalion reacted against the ruthlessness of the Germans".[796] However, this statement was made in an internment camp in Sweden, and Bjørnstad may well by that stage have considered it in his interests to distance himself from the Germans.

The Norwegian SS-volunteer Olav Ingemar Tuff of SS-Regiment Nordland could not understand the German hatred towards Jews. According to Tuff's post-war recollections, in Rostov in the summer of 1942 a German officer ordered him to take part in the shooting of 16 Soviet POWs. Tuff refused and answered that he would not shoot unarmed men in that way, bluffing it was in direct contravention of Norwegian law. The officer was angry and threatened to also execute Tuff. However, he ultimately accepted his excuses and neither Tuff nor the POWs were shot.[797]

The Finns fully understood the difference between themselves and the volunteers who had come from Norway, Denmark, the Netherlands, and other occupied countries. Martti Koivula writes in his diary on 22.5.1941:

> Nice story from a bar. All kinds of shitheads are coming over grinning ear-to-ear and asking us 'Where're you from then, where you from?' and bragging all kinds of wonderful about themselves. And in the end, you know, all these types – the Norwegians, the Danes, the Dutch, the Yugoslavs – they are all here for completely different reasons from us. Now there was this Norwegian pushed in to our happy band and asked the same old question: 'Woher bist du?' Äimä [Nils Aejmelaeus] could not keep his mouth shut any longer, especially once he'd heard the fellow was from Norway, and he blurted out in fine Finnish fashion: 'Skriv upp det nu och komm ihåg, att vi äro inga Quistlingar, utan från fria Finnland' (*'Write it down now, and remember that we are no Quistlings [sic], but we're from Free Finland'*). It was an awful thing for Äimä to say, and a Finn would not have thought twice about re-arranging his face if the roles were reversed, but the Norwegian just gave us a funny look and left us alone.[798]

On 29.9.1941, the Swedish SS-volunteer Ragnar Linnér from SS-Regiment Nordland informed the Swedish Military Attaché Curt Juhlin Dannfelt of the atrocities he had experienced. He characterised the SS as a bunch of brutalised soldiers:

> The SS seldom took prisoners and only when larger units than a company surrendered. Otherwise they were shot on the spot. The prisoners were treated ruthlessly and were urged to move on with kicks and punches. 'Flintenweiber' [Soviet female soldiers] were shot immediately. But the SS were not alone, also 'Die Wehrmacht' acted in the same way with the exception that soldiers of Jewish origin were not directly separated out for execution. The explanation for this cold-blooded treatment among other things was the awful smell which the Russians spread, and their animal looks. In the occupied areas, local people willingly informed the 'SS-Sonderkommandos' about those who were Jews. These were quickly executed, including women and children.[799]

Both the Finns and the Swedes sent back early accurate information on the massive German murderous attacks on the Jews. However, the decision-makers in the Finnish and Swedish governments remained uncommunicative, indifferent, and passive.

THE FINNISH INVOLVEMENT

The purpose of this presentation has been to clarify the involvement of Finnish SS-volunteers in the atrocities in Ukraine and the Caucasus in the two years from 1941 to 1943. This project has been carried out by studying archival documents, personal recollections, and the published literature, but in particular by focusing on 76 diaries and some twenty recollections of the Finnish volunteers. To this end, the atrocities committed in 26 municipalities have been examined in the light of the diary notes and other personal information provided by the Finnish volunteers on their experience. However, these diaries, recollections, and interviews do not give a full or an appropriate view of the atrocities for two reasons. Firstly, they were produced predominantly on an occasional basis and secondly, they are often vague and frequently avoid precise details, especially on

A parade was held at the Pyynikki sports ground in Tampere on 3.6.1941. The volunteers lined up prior to inspection. *OW Coll.*

the identity of the perpetrators. Nevertheless, the information in these personal documents is useful, again for two reasons. In the first place, these documents are the only ones available on the personal experiences of the Finnish SS-volunteers. Secondly, in the course of 77 years since these acts took place, considerable additional information on the atrocities has been collected and today it is possible to place the experiences of the Finnish volunteers in context with other German atrocities.

In this concluding chapter, a set of crucial issues will be summarised. The first deals with the number of civilian and military victims along the route taken by SS-Division Wiking. The second issue is the pattern of perpetrators involved, and the third issue is explaining these perpetrator patterns. The last issue, and the most important from the perspective of the initial premise of the investigation, concerns Finnish involvement in the atrocities of SS-Division Wiking.

THE NUMBER OF VICTIMS

At the International Military Tribunal in Nuremberg, the lawyer Dr. Curt von Stackelberg mentioned that in the towns passed through by SS-Division Wiking from the outbreak of the war on 22.6.1941 until 21.9.1941 (Lemberg/Lviv, Złoczów/Zolochiv, Tarnopol/Ternopil, Płoskirów/Proskurov, Żytomierz/Zhytomyr, and Biała Cerkiew/Bila Tserkva) "more than six thousand civilians, Jews, were killed.[800] German historian Kai Struve has, for his part, estimated that units of SS-Division Wiking were directly involved in the killing of between 4,280 and 6,950 Jews and other civilians in Galicia in the summer of 1941. Of these, 350–500 were killed in Hrymailiv/ Grzymałów, 180–200 in Ozerna/ Jezierna, 250–400 in Skalat, 2,300–4,000 in Tarnopol, 600–850 in Zboriv/Zborów and 600–1,000 in Zolochiv.[801] Of the 7,290 to 11,308 killed in 54 different cities, municipalities, and villages listed by Struve, this would correspond to around 60%. However, the information given by the Tribunal and Struve is not fully inclusive, as of the ten municipalities only three are mentioned by both of them. Moreover, the figures given by Struve include predominantly Jews, but not non-Jewish locals or Soviet POWs. This means that the number of civilian victims along the route of the SS-Division Wiking must be considerably higher, by at least 2,000–3,000 deaths, provided the information from Nuremberg and Struve is accurate.

This study covers a set of municipalities not mentioned by von Stackelberg and Struve: the villages of Olszanica/Vilshanitsa, Nowosielce/Novosilky, Krzywicze/Krivichi and Slowita with a total of perhaps 150 civilians, the villages of Kurowice/Kurovychi, Nowiki, and Podhorodce/Pidhorodtsi with around 100 local people killed, the village of Urycz with perhaps some 300 civilian victims, the village of Mikulińce/Mykulyntsi with maybe about 50 people killed, and the village of Husiatyn where around 200 Jews were shot. In total there are an additional 700 civilians, at least, who were killed. From this it appears that a total of around 10,000 local people may well have been killed along the marching route of the SS-Division Wiking in 20 Ukrainian municipalities in July and August 1941.

Contrary to the situation with civilian victims, it is impossible to estimate the number of Soviet POWs shot dead by the Wehrmacht and SS-Division Wiking units. Some isolated figures, however, do give an indication: perhaps around 50 in the villages of Olszanica, Nowosielce, Krzywicze, and Slowita, around 180 in Kurowice, c. 100 in Tarnopol and about 300 in Mikulińce/Mykulyntsi. This would make a total of roughly 600, but the real number is probably considerably higher, as Soviet POWs were shot by the thousands in July and August 1941.

THE PATTERN OF PERPETRATORS

In the period from 1.–15.7.1941, based on the diaries and recollections of the Finnish volunteers, a total of 20 mass atrocities in Ukraine involved units of SS-Division Wiking. Other active and cooperating parties were Ukrainian nationalists in eight of the affected municipalities, the Einsatzgruppen (EG) in six, and Wehrmacht units in two of the municipalities. However, the overall pattern was not the same, because the actions occurred in locally shifting locations, which are presented in Table 2:

From the information in this Table, combined atrocity incidents were strongly represented on the local scene during the advance. A total of ten atrocity incidents were carried out as combined actions, particularly in municipalities where the absolute number of victims was greater. Beyond the ten atrocity events in which sub-units of SS-Division Wiking were the only perpetrator, they acted together with Ukrainian nationalists in seven cases. However, in a few municipalities three or four parties were involved in varying combinations: Ukrainian nationalists + Wehrmacht + SS-Division Wiking + EG (two cases) and Ukrainian nationalists + SS-Division Wiking + EG (one case). In one location, EG acted alone.

TABLE 2.
Pattern of perpetrators in Ukraine 1.–15.7.1941

PERPETRATORS	SITES OF ATROCITIES (N)
SS-Regiment Nordland	5
The SS-Division Wiking alone[802]	10
Ukrainian nationalists + SS-Division Wiking[803]	4
SS-Division Wiking + EG[804]	2
Ukrainian nationalists + Wehrmacht + SS-Division Wiking + EG[805]	2
Ukrainian nationalists + SS-Division Wiking + EG[806]	1
EG alone[807]	1
TOTAL	**20**

As a whole, these varying patterns may appear confusing, but there are operational as well as situational explanations for this. However, the crucial issue is why these six various combinations occurred? Another question is whether there was coordination between the efforts of the various actors, and if so, who organised or enforced the coordination?

Initially the Wehrmacht forces had the basic responsibility for the frontlines and carried out the breakthrough of Soviet defence lines. SS-Division Wiking was, until crossing the former Polish-Soviet border, a part of the second echelon behind the frontline forces, with the task of combing and securing the areas that had shortly before been passed through by Wehrmacht forces. Both the Wehrmacht and SS-Division Wiking aimed at a fast rate of progress. On clear roads, daily motorised advances of 30–50 kilometres were commonplace, and the Wiking forces made efforts to keep pace with the Wehrmacht troops: stops in the municipalities along the route of the advance were commonly of short duration, a few hours, a day and a night for bivouacking, or at most a few days. Pacifying and securing the rear areas along the route was done rapidly. In order to keep up with Wehrmacht units, the forces of SS-Division Wiking had to act quickly and in the most effective way. The tactical solution to this challenge was to paralyse the local communities by hitting them hard and fast and to then move on to the next municipality.

The atrocities in the Ukrainian village of Skalat on 5.7.1941 are illustrative. Whereas Wehrmacht troops treated the population, including the Jews, in a decent manner, the sub-units of the SS-Regiment Westland were issued orders to kill the local Jews and were given ten minutes to finish them off. In his recollection in 1945, the local Jew Abraham Weissbrod said: "The soldiers passed the order on to each other and quickly leaped from their automobiles, tanks, and other armoured vehicles and ran to the very centre of

Last memories with comrades. SS-volunteers looking at photo albums together, Hanko 1.6.1943. *OW Coll.*

town. Sweaty, begrimed from the long ride, in shirtsleeves with the cuffs rolled up, they ran about like wild wolves, firing their guns. First they assaulted those encountered on the streets. The first victim was Efraim Diener, whose beard they cut off along with part of his face (...) Peasant children and some of their elders ran after the raiders, pointing out *Jude! Jude!* Germans ran after the fleeing Jews, shooting at them constantly. They chased Mordechai Orenstein (the milkman) and his wife down to the river bank and drove them into the water. They fired at them until their bodies sank, leaving only red stains on the surface. Then some Germans, led by Ukrainian peasant children, ran among the houses, shooting at each Jew pointed out. Other soldiers raided homes: ostensibly searching for weapons and hidden Bolsheviks, while robbing, defacing, and destroying the contents of the homes. The allotted ten minutes sufficed to turn the town upside-down, to leave some twenty Jews killed and an equal number wounded. Some were slightly wounded and others seriously. The Jews sought to hide wherever they could. Their homes, now unguarded, fell prey to the Ukrainian peasants and Polish hoodlums, who rioted for hours afterwards. They stole whatever they could, and they beat unmercifully any Jew that they found".[808]

These atrocities were just the prelude of the savage violence. A full-scale pogrom was carried out on the following day, 6.7.1941, and a total 250–500 local Jews are estimated to have perished.[809] This documentation completely contradicts the claim by Division Commander Felix Steiner that units of SS-Division Wiking were so continuously engaged either in open firefights or in preparing operations that there was no time left for participating in the killings of local people. Weissbrod refers to a "Commander of the SS Brigade" who is said to have given the orders for the executions in Skalat on 5.7.1941. As these were carried out by SS-Regiment Westland, the commander in question would be SS-Oberführer Artur Phleps (Stolz) in as far as he was not acting on orders of the Division Commander himself, i.e. Felix Steiner. Also the Company Commander concerned must have been instrumental in the carrying out of the executions.

THE INTERLUDE OF THE UKRAINIAN NATIONALISTS

The Ukrainian nationalists were useful tools in the German occupation policy. Clandestine groups of Ukrainian nationalists in numerous municipalities were eagerly awaiting the German assault on the Soviet Union, which materialised on 22.6.1941. The readiness of these groups was of a broad character, as Ukrainian nationalist cadres planned strikes not only against the local units of the Soviet Army, but also against remaining Communist officials, fellow-travellers, and Jews. Furthermore, preparations were made for a Ukrainian takeover of local and national power as the Soviet forces were eliminated. The Norwegian volunteer Ørnulf Bjørnstad of 12th Company, SS-Regiment Germania, mentioned in his observations from July 1941 that Germans authorised the Ukrainian militias, called "Quislings" by Bjørnstad, to treat the Jews just as they pleased. He wrote: "The Jews were ordered to clean the streets of bodies, horse cadavers, and vehicles. In the midst of this, one could spot some of these Quislings hitting the Jews with sharp spades so that they fell down and remained on the ground".[810] German forces did permit the activities of the Ukrainian nationalists for a time, and their beating of local Jews remained an interlude with a duration of a few weeks from the start of hostilities.

In 1929, the Organisation of Ukrainian Nationalists (OUN, *Orhanizatsiya Ukrayins'kykh Natsionalistiv*) was founded in Vienna. Initially it operated in Western Ukraine as an alliance of the Ukrainian Military Organisation, smaller radical right-wing circles, and radical nationalists and intellectuals. In 1940, OUN was split into two factions: the moderate OUN-M (M for Andriy Melnik) and the radical OUN-B (B for Stepan Bandera).[811] The Ukrainian Legion (under German command and Bandera's control), divided into the Nachtigall and Roland Battalions, comprised 800 soldiers in arms. Also three so-called expeditionary groups (*pokhidni hrupy*) were formed, with the task of following the troops and establishing local administrations in the occupied areas, replacing the fleeing Soviets. Each of the groups comprised about 700 men, while the Ukrainian national leader Ivan Klymiv-Lehenda was the leader of the OUN underground on Soviet territory.[812] The U.S. historian Omer Bartov argues it is highly probable that OUN, in collusion with the Abwehr, triggered the strife between the nationalities through synchronised local coups, and for that purpose established local militias in Eastern Galicia. OUN groups attempted to foment uprisings in Lemberg (*Lviv*), Skole, Buchach (Pol. *Buczacz*), Sambir (Pol. *Sambor*), Pidhaitsi (Pol. *Podhajce*), and Monastyryska (Pol. *Monasterzyska*), and to present the arriving German forces with a fait accompli. However, the plans failed as the OUN-B leaders were arrested on

Some of the Finnish SS-volunteers joined the German SS-troops in Norway after Finland had signed the Moscow Armistice with Russia on 19.9.1944. They also recruited other volunteers from among the Finnish POWs taken by the Germans in Lapland during the short Lapland War fought to remove the German forces from Finnish soil. After World War II, many of those who went to Norway were incarcerated and some had to face trial for high treason - serving the German enemy forces of that time. One of them was SS-Obersturmführer Jouko Itälä, pictured in Tampere with a Finnish nurse attached to the SS-Division Wiking, Laine-Maire Kyöstilä. *OW Coll.*

9.7.1941 by a detachment of the Sicherheitsdienst (SD).[813]

Earlier, on 25.6.1941, OUN had attempted an uprising in Lemberg (*Lviv*) against the Soviet authorities. When Red Army forces started to withdraw, on 23. and 24.6.1941, the Ukrainian rebels mobilised and fired on the retreating troops in the streets from windows and roofs.[814] In his diary, the local resident Stanislaw Rózycki gives the date of 26.6.1941 for the failed OUN uprising in Lemberg (*Lviv*).[815] The rebellion, aimed at liberating Ukrainians imprisoned by the NKVD, failed and was brutally crushed by the NKVD. The Commander of Einsatzgruppe B, SS-Brigadeführer Dr Otto Rasch, reported on 2.7.1941 to the Chief of the Security Police: "The Ukrainian rebel movement in Lemberg was bloodily suppressed by the NKVD. Around 3,000 shot by the NKVD. The prison is burning". In a report dated 16.7.1941, Rasch wrote: "The reason for the attempted rebellion of the Ukrainians was to try to liberate their imprisoned people".[816] U.S. historian Alexander Dallin claims that in late June 1941 the Ukrainian Nationalists in Lemberg (*Lviv*) "staged a revolt that was savagely suppressed by the retreating Red Army and the NKVD. During the following days of chaos, it became obvious to the Germans that [Stepan] Bandera's followers, including those in the 'Nachtigal' Battalion, were displaying considerable initiative, conducting purges

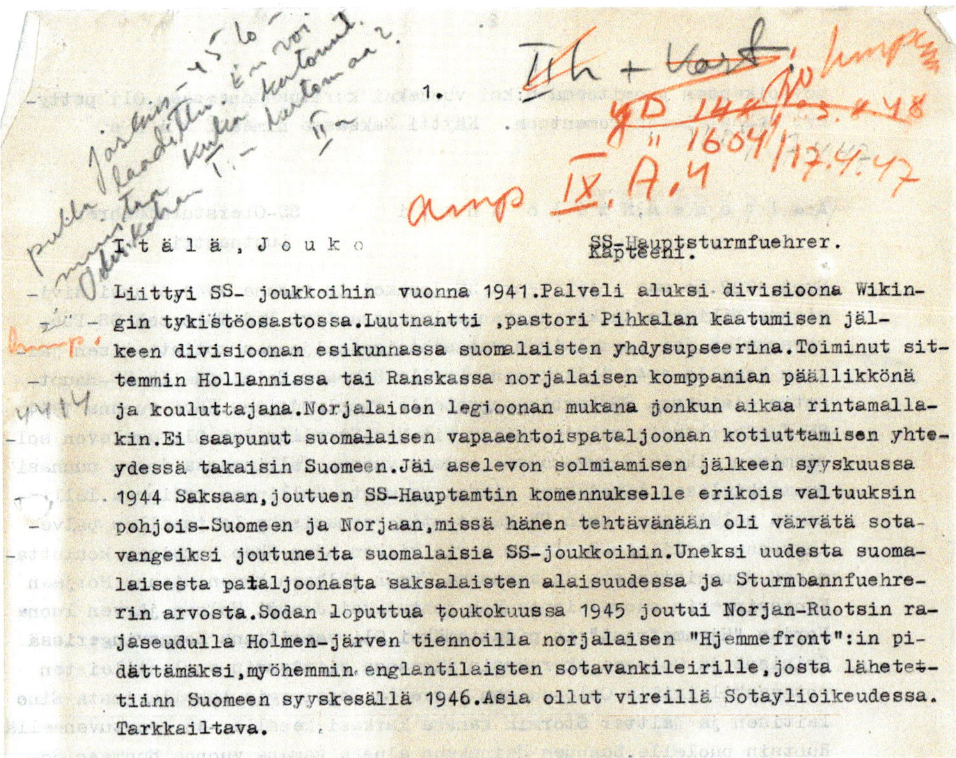

1.

Itälä, Jouko SS-Hauptsturmfuehrer. Kapteeni.

Liittyi SS- joukkoihin vuonna 1941.Palveli aluksi divisioona Wikingin tykistöosastossa.Luutnantti ,pastori Pihkalan kaatumisen jälkeen divisioonan esikunnassa suomalaisten yhdysupseerina.Toiminut sittemmin Hollannissa tai Ranskassa norjalaisen komppanian päällikkönä ja kouluttajana.Norjalaisen legioonan mukana jonkun aikaa rintamallakin.Ei saapunut suomalaisen vapaaehtoispataljoonan kotiuttamisen yhteydessä takaisin Suomeen.Jäi aselevon solmiamisen jälkeen syyskuussa 1944 Saksaan,joutuen SS-Hauptamtin komennukselle erikois valtuuksin pohjois-Suomeen ja Norjaan,missä hänen tehtävänään oli värvätä sotavangeiksi joutuneita suomalaisia SS-joukkoihin.Uneksi uudesta suomalaisesta pataljoonasta saksalaisten alaisuudessa ja Sturmbannfuehrerin arvosta.Sodan loputtua toukokuussa 1945 joutui Norjan-Ruotsin rajaseudulla Holmen-järven tiennoilla norjalaisen "Hjemmefront":in pidättämäksi,myöhemmin englantilaisten sotavankileirille,josta lähetettiinn Suomeen syyskesällä 1946.Asia ollut vireillä Sotaylioikeudessa. Tarkkailtava.

Finnish State Police (ValPo) report on Jouko Itälä written at the end of 1945. *NAF.*

and pogroms".[817] Lemberg (*Lviv*) resident Jacob Gerstenfeld-Maltiel reported that the Ukrainians, who were financially supported by the Germans, began "a diversion" on 25.6.1941: "They shot from garrets and roofs at the passing military trucks. Machine guns and even small cannon were stationed in the towers of the churches. The Russians took energetic steps to secure their rear. Without pause, armoured cars and tanks patrolled through the town. Simultaneously mobilisation started".[818]

The local NKVD instances received the order on 23.6.1941 to kill those political prisoners who could not be evacuated. However, the NKVD reprisals may explain only a part of the colossal piles of bodies in the prisons at Lemberg (*Lviv*). The bulk of the prisoners killed in Soviet custody were likely shot for the reason commonly given, that the Soviet authorities lacked the means to evacuate their prisoners. There is no accurate information of how many were killed in the putting down of the failed revolt. However, Soviet documents show a total of 2,464 prisoners were shot in Lemberg (*Lviv*) in late June 1941, 808 were released, and 1,546 remained in prison custody. German historian Kai Struve has estimated the number of those killed in the range of 2,358–2,752.[819]

On 30.6.1941, the OUN-B deputy leader Yaroslav Stetsko unilaterally proclaimed the creation of an independent Ukrainian state allied with Germany, and the formation of a government drawn from the Ukrainian National Committee. U.S. historian Alexander Dallin wrote that the Ukrainian leader

> (...) staged a sudden and unexpected coup in Lviv [Lemberg]. Just as the responsible Army Intelligence Officer, Prof. Hans Koch (...) had arranged a conference to establish a City Government in Lviv [Lemberg], he was taken to a rally, carefully staged in advance, where the OUN-B assembly proclaimed a 'Ukrainian State'. A move unforeseen both by the Abwehr and by Rosenberg's men [a reference to the Nazi chief ideologist Alfred Rosenberg, the recently-appointed head of the Reich Ministry for the Occupied Eastern Territories], the OUN proclamation was intended to present the Germans as well as the rival Ukrainian parties with a fait accompli.[820]

This step was, however, done without pre-approval from the German counterpart, and as a response Einsatzgruppe C created a Ukrainian political self-government for the city as a counterweight to the Stepan Bandera group, and on 4.7.1941 began to arrest Bandera's associates. The Stetsko government was dissolved on 5.7.1941. Later, the leading Ukrainian nationalists were arrested. Some of the members of the expeditionary groups were arrested and shot.[821]

A call was issued by OUN-B at the turn of the month June-July 1941: "Ukrainer! Bauer! Arbeiter!", which urged the founding of Ukrainian People's Militia in every village, town, and city. Among the tasks listed for the local militias were the destruction (*Vernichtung*) of Bolshevik partisans (*Diversanten*) in concert (*Einvernehmen*) with the German forces. Another task was taking an official grasp (*amtliche Erfassung*) of the Jews and isolating (*Absonderung*) them from the Aryan population stock in order to bring them to physical work.[822] As a consequence, pogroms occurred in 27 municipalities in Eastern Galicia, in 15 cases in places where a NKVD prison was located.[823]

Towards the end of July 1941, Reichsführer-SS Heinrich Himmler issued an order to establish collaborationist indigenous auxiliary police units composed of Ukrainians and other cooperative men of other nationalities. The number of men recruited to these new *Schutzmannschaften* all across the occupied territories (e.g. in the Baltic States, Belarus, and the Soviet Union) increased from about 33,000 to 300,000 by the end of 1942. In course of the war years, a total of approximately 100,000 Ukrainians are estimated to have served in these auxiliary police units subordinated to the SS. An estimated total of 30,000–40,000 Ukrainians in all the occupied areas are believed to have participated in German-administered mass killings of Jews.[824]

The locally-operated atrocities against Jews in Ukraine in the summer of 1941 have links back to earlier traditions in Ukraine and the so-called Pale of Settlement area (*Chertá osyédlosti*) for Jews in Russia, 1791–1917.[825] Anti-Jewish pogroms occurred in Ukraine on numerous occasions, in 1648–57, 1821, 1881–83, 1903–06, 1914, and in 1915.[826] After the Russian invasion in August 1914, Cossack forces were involved in several pogroms in Galicia, among other places in Lemberg (*Lviv*).[827] It has been estimated that at least 31,000 Jews perished in 1,236 pogroms and various offences in Ukraine in 1918–21. However, the real figures are probably higher.[828] The bulk of the pogroms were carried out in the Kiev area, but also in Lemberg (*Lviv*) in Galicia, Polish offenders killed some 300 Jews and Ukrainians on 21.–23.11.1918.[829] In March 1919, a total of 317 Jews were killed in Zhytomyr, and in November 1919 around 600 in Kiev.[830] On another occasion in 1918, the Jewish Quarter of Lviv was ransacked and 18 Jews were killed.[831] The Finnish Legation Chief in Kiev in 1918–19, Herman Gummerus, characterised the numerous Jews in Ukraine as "a definitely Russian-friendly and extremely German-hostile element". Gummerus, however, entirely avoided touching upon the atrocities against the Jews in 1918–19 just as in 1941–43.[832]

The involvement of Ukrainian nationalists may to some extent have been overstressed in the research literature. In any case, the atrocities committed by Ukrainians in Galicia varied strikingly by location. In Lemberg (*Lviv*) and Zboriv, the role of the OUN militia was quite apparent. In Zolochiv (*Złoczów*), too, the militia engaged in violent acts, although to a lesser degree. Nevertheless, in several municipalities the militia and Ukrainian locals took at least a minor role in the atrocities, as they were urged and encouraged by the arriving SS units.[833] As the Ukrainian nationalists may have killed thousands of Jews in July 1941[834], it can be concluded that the number of Jews slain by local Ukrainians in the period from 1918 to 1921 probably exceeded those killed by local Ukrainians in 1941–44. The reasons are that anti-Jewish outrages carried out by Ukrainian nationalists were of short duration, occurring primarily within just a few weeks in the summer of 1941.

THE ACCOMPANYING EINSATZGRUPPEN

The SS-Einsatzgruppe C following in the tracks of the SS-Division Wiking carried out their extermination tasks in an efficient way. The Einsatzgruppen were mobilised in the summer of 1941 as prime participants in the atrocities and emerged in a whole set of municipalities along the

Systematic mass liquidation of Jews continued in Ukraine in 1942. Einsatzgruppe troops committing mass murder of Jews in Ivanhorod, in what is now the Khrystynivka Raion. *WC.*

advance of the Wehrmacht and SS-Division Wiking in the first half of July 1941: the city of Lemberg/Lviv, the towns of Zboriv/Zborów, Hrymailiv/Grzymałów, the village of Urycz/Urych, the cities of Tarnopol (*Ternopil*) and Proskurov, the town of Bila Tserkva/Biała Cerkiew and the city of Zhytomyr. Although no precise figures exist for the civilians killed by the Einsatzgruppen, it is abundantly obvious these must have been considerable, and their activities systematically completed the initial sweep for Jews behind the advancing SS-Division Wiking. Further, the Einsatzgruppe C carried out 37 massacres in Western Ukraine in the space of a few weeks from 27.8.–30.9.1941 over and above the previous mass atrocities.[835]

THE DIVIDED ATTITUDE OF THE WEHRMACHT FORCES

In the onslaught on the Soviet Union in the summer of 1941, Wehrmacht units used the same brutal occupation policy formula as in Poland in 1939–41. Almost 22 million Poles came under the control of German forces in the fall of 1939, and far larger populations in the East experienced the same fate from June/July 1941. In consequence, around 40 million Soviet citizens, including 20 million people who became Soviet citizens in the period from 1939–41, and approximately 15 million in the Baltic area had to continue their lives in areas occupied by German troops. As these population masses were almost four times larger than the Poles who became German subjects in 1939, the scope for German occupation violence grew materially.

The significance of Wehrmacht occupation policy was summarised in the volume *Verbrechen der Wehrmacht: Dimensionen des Vernichtungskrieg 1941–1944*, published in Hamburg in 2002. An estimated total of ten million civilians were killed by Wehrmacht units – not in combat at the front, but in mass shootings, executions, and the burning of villages, towns, and entire areas. Moreover, it concluded that the Wehrmacht was not a misused tool, but an integral part of the National Socialist regime and that a considerable number of Wehrmacht officers and men were involved in the atrocities.[836] This was the situation in Ukraine and the Caucasus in 1941–43 when Finnish SS-volunteers were deployed in these areas. There is also acknowledgement of various Wehrmacht units participating in the atrocities along the line of advance during the summer of 1941: in the towns of Zolochiv/Złoczów and Zborów/Zboriv, and the cities of Tarnopol and Proskurov in the eight-day period of 3.–11.7.1941.

However, within Wehrmacht units there occurred a split attitude towards the atrocities against Jews, civilians, and Soviet POWs. Some rather weak attempts to halt the violence, which was seen as lacking military purpose, were made by Oberstleutnant Helmuth Groscurth and Colonel Otto Korfes in Zolochiv. The reason for their reluctance to sign off on the mayhem was not so much humanitarian concerns but rather that the atrocities caused an assortment of troubles: the violent acts distressed and offended the local population, and they eroded the potential support on the ground at the same time as the morale of the soldiers suffered from the shocking experiences. From the outset there also arose an awareness that information on the atrocities would in time leak out and reach those allied against Germany. As a result, parts of the Wehrmacht forces tried to deal with the atrocities by making attempts to thwart and restrict them, to conceal them and to destroy documents, and generally to direct them in forms that could be most easily hidden from outside eyes. For the very same reasons, the Commander of SS-Division Wiking Felix Steiner later acted in the same way

THE WIKING ATROCITIES AS MISSION-FOCUSED TACTICS

In the spring of 1941, the German Army was the most advanced military machine in the world. It was not fundamentally better equipped than the armed forces of other countries such as the British, French, Japanese, Soviet, or U.S. armies. However, the training and the operational models of the German troops were far more effective than in any other army. The German military leaders emphasised the creation of united primary groups characterised by military comradeship, strong loyalty, and common commitments. The training of the troops and guidance of the forces stressed the significance of the so-called *Auftragstaktik* (mission-focused tactics, mission command). This emphasised the carrying out of initiatives and independent tasks at the lowest possible level and individually.[837]

The *Auftragtaktik* schemes had a role also in the carrying out of the atrocities committed by the sub-units of SS-Division Wiking. Division Commander Felix Steiner and some of the Regiment and Battalion Commanders tried to maintain a certain distance from the atrocities, which were typically carried out in a decentralised way. Although the Regiment and Battalion Commanders must have been aware of them, and probably verbally suggested the actions, the executions were carried out by the minor units such as companies and individual platoons. The commanders of these smaller detachments are likely to have often acted at least semi-independently on the basis of their judgement of the local situation and current conditions.

There must have been some interactive communication with informative messages for coordination on the atrocities between the various participating parties: the Wehrmacht, the Ukrainian nationalists, and SS-Einsatzgruppen. However, it is impossible to point to any particular prime mover or coordinating institution, even though the role of SS-Division Wiking generally seems to have been pivotal. Such common action schemes appear to have followed a military breakthrough by Wehrmacht forces. These actions included subsequent combing, cleaning, and pacifying steps by SS-Division Wiking units, with less systematic violent interventions from Ukrainian nationalists and follow-ups from the SS-Einsatzgruppe. These various forces working together had the capacity to reasonably secure the municipalities and the surroundings of the route during the advance eastwards. It was of no greater significance whether one or another village or population centre remained untouched for a while. If a local danger emerged, either the Wehrmacht units in charge or SS-Division Wiking could send a motorised squad, a platoon, or some other small unit at hand to take care of the place. This was a kind of a self-driven order in accordance with *Auftragtaktik* methods, which were responsive, enterprising, innovative, and efficient.

The atrocities meshed fairly well with the regular conduct of SS-Division Wiking, with dispositions for skirmishes, front battles, troop movements, vehicle columns, and transport and supply efforts. As the violent events were included in the pattern of operational conduct, they did not delay the rapid advance any more than any other dispositions. The basic idea of the *Auftragstaktik* involved keeping an eye on the current situation, seizing opportunities and using time in a focused, forceful, and determined manner. In any event, the conduct of the SS-Division Wiking generally differed from the Army units operating in the second echelon and carrying out similar clearing and security tasks. These units appear to have got involved in atrocities to a lesser degree than SS-Division Wiking, which started the war on the Eastern Front by shooting Jews and Soviet POWs already in the days before any engagement in serious warfare. The main reason for this was obviously the more roused-up unit spirit and greater ideological commitment among the SS-soldiers. However, it must be noticed that none of the SS-Division Wiking members was sentenced in Court of Justice for atrocities and only 41 Wiking SS-members altogether.[838]

THE FINNISH VOLUNTEERS WERE WELL AWARE OF THE ATROCITIES

The sub-units and men of SS-Division Wiking engaged during the march into the Soviet Union and the drive through Ukraine and the Caucasus were involved in numerous atrocities. The diaries and the recollections by the Finnish volunteers show that practically everyone among them must, from the very beginning, have been aware of the atrocities and massacres. None of the volunteers are likely to have been able to grasp the full picture of these, but at least individual events witnessed and snippets of information about others were certainly common.

However, reporting on these is troubling. A small number of the volunteers kept diaries and made brief and often shocking or euphemistic notes on the violent acts, though written privately. This corresponds to the strong tendency of soldiers in general to attach themselves to various euphemisms for killing in their stories, and to avoid references to the 1907 Hague Convention on Land Warfare and the 1919 Geneva Convention on the treatment of POW:s.[839] The German Field Post censorship prevented the despatch of written notes on the atrocities to Finland. On the other hand, verbal information was spread eventually during home leaves and via letters forwarded without passing through the Censorship Office. There was a set of reasons that limited the spread of personal observations, in particular the emotional confusion of the volunteers and consequent psychological problems. The main reason for this was the psychological rupture within the volunteers. On the one hand, the violent acts were commonly seen as repugnant by the volunteers, but on the other hand the loyalty they felt for their German Commanders disturbed and complicated their reactions. The volunteer Sakari Haikala of the Finnish SS-Volunteer Battalion explained later that those moral dilemmas resulting from actions against the Jews were explained in this way: "We didn't talk about the issue as we could not quite grasp it. We rejected the matter, because if we had expressed an opinion, we would simultaneously have taken up a position against the Germans. For us, only the Finnish cause was important".[840]

In this respect, the volunteers did not all act in a uniform manner, as some condemned the atrocities, others were personally involved or sided with them, and the majority simply closed their eyes. Nevertheless, these events left an indelible trace in their minds and caused traumatic reactions, which the volunteers commonly tried to deal with through heavy drinking.

THE FINNISH INVOLVEMENT

The investigation of the large archival documentation and the literature has confirmed several cases in which the Finnish SS-volunteers engaged in violent acts against civilians and Jews. However, the documentation in diaries, recollections, notes, and documents is certainly vague and cannot really be confirmed in an entirely reliable way. Nevertheless, at least some of the cases show that Finnish volunteers did participate in carrying out atrocities against Jews and civilians: Thor-Björn Weckström in the village of Novosilky/Nowosielce on 2.7.1941, the two unknown Finnish volunteers who shot two civilians in the village of Podhorylce in the first week of July 1941, the participation of Ilmari Autonen in the killing of a Soviet Commissar in Dnipropetrovsk in August 1941, and the killings in Toldzgun on 31.12.1942 under the command of the Finnish SS-Hauptsturmführer Karl-Erik Ladau. Volunteers Olavi Karpalo and Unto Boman (later Parvilahti) are likely to have been involved in atrocities, and Boman may also have had a leading role in the burning of a chapel in either Ozerna or some other location in that area, on 3.7. or 4.7.1941. The documentation on the possible involvement of SS-Untersturmführer Kaj Laurell in alleged large-scale atrocities in the summer of 1942 is so vague and weak that no conclusions at all can be drawn. As the documentation on these events only occasionally mentions the number of civilians killed by Finnish volunteers, the real numbers are likely to be higher, perhaps at least a few dozens.

The readiness of the Finnish volunteers to shoot Soviet POWs was likely to have been much greater than that for killing civilians. There is a

A memorial ceremony for those who did not return, at Hietaniemi Cemetery in Helsinki, 19.9.1943. The man delivering the speech is Bank Manager Pehr. H. Norrmén. *OW Coll.*

whole set of vague documentation that indicates that it was not particularly uncommon to kill surrendered Soviet POWs in clear conflict with the norms of the Hague Convention of Land Warfare of 1907 and the Geneva Convention on the Treatment of Prisoners of War of 1929. One of the few clear cases documented by the volunteer Taisto Kuuri happened in a village near Donskoye on 18.1.1942. Although the documentation is poor, the Finnish volunteers are nevertheless likely to have participated in the deliberate killing of several hundred Soviet POWs in Ukraine and the Caucasus.

This investigation has been carried out using a considerable body of archival documents and literature. Although the SS-Investigation of the National Archives has not been able to access some diaries, letters, recollections and documents, new materials most likely will concern individual cases. This additional information will probably not change the picture presented in this report. After more than 75 years since the march of the SS-Division Wiking through Galicia and beyond, there are no longer any volunteers left to investigate as none of those individuals mentioned above are still living.

The first parliamentary elections in Finland since 1939 were held in March 1945, when World War II was still going on. The slogan of the Conservative Party (*Kokoomus*) declares (in a historical echo of pre-independence days): "We are not fascists, we do not want to be communists, let us be free Finns." *OW Coll.*

APPENDIX 1.

List of place names that have different spellings

COUNTRY	CURRENT NAME IN ENGLISH	UKRAINIAN NAME	POLISH NAME	RUSSIAN NAME	FORMERLY; OTHER KNOWN SPELLING
Ukraine	Amvrosiivka	Амвросіївка	-	Амвросиевка	Amvrosijevka; Ambrojewka
Ukraine	Arkhanhelivka	Архангелівка	-		Arkhangel'livka
Ukraine	Babi Yar	Бабин Яр, Babyn Jar	-	Бабий Яр, Babi Jar	Babi Yar
Russia	Novobakhmutskiy formerly Bachmutskij	-	-	Новобахмутский	Bachmutskij; Bachmutskij; Bahmutski
Ukraine	Barvinkove	Барвінкове		Барве́нково, Barvenkovo	-
Ukraine	Bila Tserkva	Бі́ла Це́рква	Biała Cerkiew	Белая Церковь Belaya Tserkov	Belaja Tserkov; Bila Tserkva; Bila Zerkwa; Biala Cerkiew; Belaja Zerkow; Bjelala Zerkow; Belaja Tserka
Ukraine	Berdychiv	Бердичів	Berdyczów	Берди́чев, Berdichev	*Yiddish:* וועשטידראַב, Bardichev
Ukraine	Khorostkiv	Хоростків	Chorostków	Хоростков, Chorostkow	Chorostkiv
Russia	Digora			Дигора́	*Ossetian:* Дигорæ, Digoræ
Ukraine	Dnipro, formerly Dnipropetrovsk	Дніпро formerly Дніпропетро́вськ		Днепр, Dnepr formerly Днепропетро́вск Dnepropetrovsk	*German (formerly):* Dnipropetrowsk; Djnepropetrowsk; Dnjepropetrovsk
Ukraine	Kamianske, formerly Dniprodzerzhynsk	Кам'янське		Каменское	Dneprodzerzinsk; Dobrowelitskowska; Kamjanske, formerly Dniprodzeržynsk
Ukraine	Donskoye	Донське			Donskoi; Donskoj
Ukraine	Haisyn or Haysyn	Га́йсин, Haysyn	Hajsyn	Га́йсин, Gaisin	
Poland	Hrubieszów	Грубешів Hrubeshiv			*Yiddish:* הריועשאוו
Ukraine	Hrymailiv	Грималів	Grzymałów		*Yiddish:* רימאלאוו, Rimalov; Hrymajliv; Hrymayliv; Grymailiv; Grimailov; Grymailov; Grzymalov; Grzymatów; Grzymatow
Ukraine	Husiatyn	Гусятин	Husiatyn	Гусятин, Gusjatin	*Yiddish:* הוסיאַטין, Husyatin; Husiatin; Husictyn; Gusiatin; Gusyatin; Gusatin; Usiatyn; Hysuatin
Poland	Izbica				*Yiddish:* איזשביצע Izhbitz, Izhbitze; Izbica
Ukraine	Kamianets-Podilskyi	Ка́м'яне́ць-Поді́льський	Kamieniec Podolski	Каменец-Подольский	*Yiddish:* קאמענעץ-פאדאלסק; Kamenets-Podolsky
Russia	Kabardinskaya			Кабардинская	Karabinskaja; Kabardinskaja
Ukraine	Kharkiv	Ха́рків, Chárkiv		Ха́рьков, Kharkov	*German:* Charkiw
Ukraine	Kropyvnytskyi (formerly Kirovohrad)	Кропивницький, Kropyvnyc'kyj (formerly Кіровогра́д)		Кировогра́д, Kirovograd	*German:* Kirowgrad; Kirowograd
Ukraine	Kremenchuk or Kremenchug	Кременчу́к, Kremenčuk	Krzemieńczuk	Кременчу́г, Kremenchug	Krementsug; Kremenets

COUNTRY	CURRENT NAME IN ENGLISH	UKRAINIAN NAME	POLISHNAME	RUSSIAN NAME	FORMERLY; OTHER KNOWN SPELLING
Ukraine	Kryvychi	Кривичі			Krivici Kryvychi; Krzwice; Krivitisji; Krywcza; Krziewice; Krzywice; Krywice
Ukraine	Kurovychi	Куровичі	Kurowice		Kurowich
Ukraine	Lviv	Львів, Lviv	Lwów	Львов, Lvov	*German:* Lemberg
Russia	Lineynaya			Линейная	Lineinaja
Russia	Majkop or Maykop			Майкоп	*German:* Maikop
Ukraine	Malgobek			Малгобе́к	*Ingush:* MarIалбике
Russia	Mechetinskaya			Мечетинская	Metsentinskaja
Russia	Mokrojelanchyk			Мокроєланчик	Mokrij Jalantschinskij; Mokryi Jelanschiki; Mokryij Jelantshik
Ukraine	Mykulyntsi	Микулинці	Mikulińce		Mykulynce; Mikolintza; Mikulincie; Mikulinie; Mikulinste; Mikulintza; Mykulinski; Mykulintsi; Mykulintse; Mykulinksi; Mykylinski
Ukraine	Nemyriv	Немирів	Niemirów	Немиров, Nemirow	*German:* Nemyriw
Ukraine	Novyky	Новики			Nowiki
Russia	Novomikhaylovskiy			Новомихайловский	Nowo Michailowka
Ukraine	Novohrad-Volynskyi	Новогра́д-Воли́нський, Novohrád-Volýns'kyj	Zwiahel	Новоград-Волынский, Novograd-Volynsky	*Yiddish:* ליווז, Zvil
Ukraine	Novosilky	Новосілки	Nowosielce		Nowosielki
Ukraine	Velyka Vil'shanytsya or Vilshanytsya	Велика Вільшаниця	Olszanica Wielka, Olszanica	Olshanitsa	Olszancia; Velyka Vilsanycja; Velika Vilyshanicya; Olszancica; Olszenica
Russia	Orlovskiy			Орловский	Orlowski; Orlowsky
Ukraine	Ostropol or Staryy Ostropil	Остропіль or Старий Остропіль		Старый Острополь, Stary Ostropol	
Ukraine	Ozerna	Озерна	Jezierna		
Ukraine	Pavlohrad, formerly Pavlograd	Павлогра́д		Павлогра́д	
Russia	Pavlodol'skaya			Павлодольская	Pavlodolskij
Ukraine	Pidhaitsi	Підгайці, Pidhajci	Podhajce		
Ukraine	Pidhirtsi	Підгірці	Podhorce		Podgorce
Ukraine	Pidvolochysk	Підволочиськ	Podwołoczyska	Подволочиск Podwoloczysk	*Yiddish:* Podvolitchisk, קסישטאָלאָוודאָפ,
Ukraine	Pidhorodtsi	Підгородці	Podhorodce	Подгородцы	Podgorodcy; Podhajce; Pidhorodce; Podhoroce; Podhorode; Podhorodche
Ukraine	Pohoril'tsi	Погорільці	Pohorylce	Погорельцы	Podhorylce
Ukraine	Khmelnytskyi, formerly Proskuriv	Хмельни́цький, Chmel'nyc'kyj formerly Проску́рів Proskuriw	Chmielnicki formerly Płoskirów	Хмельницкий Chmelnizki formerly Proskurow	Proskurow; Proskurov

COUNTRY	CURRENT NAME IN ENGLISH	UKRAINIAN NAME	POLISH NAME	RUSSIAN NAME	FORMERLY; OTHER KNOWN SPELLING
Poland	Radom				*Yiddish:* מעדאָר; Rodem; Radomir
Ukraine	Radomyshl	Радомишль, Radomyshl			Radomysl; Radomisl; Radomyzl
Ukraine	Rava-Ruska	Рава-Руська Rava-Rus'ka	Rawa Ruska		*Yiddish:* עוואר Rave; Rawa Russka
Russia	Rostov-on-Don			Ростóв-на-Донý, Rostov-na-Donu	Rostov-on-Don; Rostow-on-Don
Ukraine	Rudnya-Horodyshche	Рудня-Городище			Rudjina
Russia	Sagopshi			Сагопши	Sagopshi
Ukraine	Satanivka	Сатанівка			Satanovka-Kusmin
Ukraine	Skálat	Ска́лат	Skałat		
Russia	Skelyanskiy			Скелянский	Skeljanskij; Skeljanski
Ukraine	Slovita	Словіта			Slowita; Slowida
Ukraine	Sokal	Сокаль, Sokal			
Ukraine	Donetsk, formerly Stalino	Донецьк formerly Ста́ліно		Доне́цк formerly Сталино	
Russia	Staraya Russa			Старая Русса	
Russia	Taganrog			Таганрог	
Ukraine	Taranivka			Таранівка	Taranovka
Ukraine	Tarashcha or Tarascha	Тараща			*German:* Taraschtscha
Ukraine	Ternopil	Тернопіль, Ternopil'	Tarnopol	Тернополь, Ternopol'	*German:* Tarnopol; *Yiddish:* לפאָנראַט; לאָפענרעט; Ternepol; Tarnopl; Hebrew: לופונראט (לוֹפּוֹנְרַט); Tarnopol
Russia	Toldzgun			Толдзгун	*Ossetian:* Толдзгун; Tolskum; Toldsgun
Ukraine	Troyaniv	Троянів			Trojanov
Russia	Tšikola			Чикола́	*German:* Tschikola; *Ossetian:* Цикола, Цыкола; Chikola
Ukraine	Uman	Умань	Humań	Умань	
Ukraine	Urych	У́рич	Urycz	У́рыч	
Ukraine	Vynnyky	Ви́нники	Winniki	Ви́нники	*German:* Wynnyky
Ukraine	Vinnytsia	Вінниця, Vinnycja	Winnica	Ви́нница, Vinnica	*German:* Winniza; *Yiddish:* עציניוו; Vinitse; Vinnitsa
Ukraine	Zaporižžja or Zaporizhia or Zaporozhye	Запорі́жжя, Zaporizhzhya		Запоро́жье	Zaporozie
Ukraine	Zboriv	Зборів	Zborów	Зборов	Zborov; Zborob; Zbvorow
Ukraine	Zhytomyr	Жито́мир, Žytomyr	Żytomierz	Жито́мир, Žitomir	*Yiddish:* רימאָטישז; Žitomir; Schitomir; Zhytomir
Ukraine	Zolochiv	Золочів	Złoczów		*Yiddish:* וואָשטאָלז; Zlotchov; Zolotsjiv; Solotschew; Zlozcow; Zoltsjiv; Zlochiv

APPENDIX 2.

List of diaries by Finnish SS volunteers

WRITER OF DIARY	PROVENIENCE	UNIT	FORM OF DIARY	PERIOD	PAGE LENGTH
Aho, Matti	M. Jokipii Pk-2365/5; M. Jokipii Pk-1140/24	2/FFB	Typed copy	7.6.41–28.11.42	32 A4
Ala-Ilkka, Kauko	M. Jokipii Pk-1140/36-37	4/FFB, 3/FFB	Partial typed copy	23.1.43–6.4.43	6 A4
Duncker, Kaj	The Archive of SLS; K. Duncker, KDB 1941-44 Pk-1821/1-5	6/ART	Original and typed copy	3.2.41–2.4.43	-
Elmgren, Sven	M. Jokipii Pk-2365/5; M. Jokipii Pk-1140/24	1/FFB	Typed copy	3.12.41–9.8.43	163 A4
Gröndahl, Tapio	J. Kyösti priv. collect.	3/W, 1/W	Original, photographed	6.5.41–13.9.41	-
Haapaniemi, Kalevi	M. Jokipii Pk-1140/23; Veljesapu Assoc.	1/FFB	Partly typed copy; partly original	4.6.41–31.5.43	36 A4
Halinen, Anselm	M. Jokipii Pk-1140/15	2/FFB	Partial typed copy	29.4.42–10.10.42	7 A4
Hallavo, Veikko	M. Jokipii Pk-1140/36-37	2/Pz, 3/Pz, 2/FFB, 1/FFB	Original	15.5.41–12.2.42	-
Heikkilä, Matti	J. Saurio priv. collect.	1/FFB	Typed copy	31.10.41–28.1.42	18 A4
Heikurainen, Leo	M. Jokipii 78	1/FFB, Tölz	Original, photocopy	8.1.43–2.1.44	66 A4
Helminen, Eero	M. Jokipii Pk-1140/36-37; M. Jokipii Pk-2365/5; M. Jokipii Pk-1140/23	1/FFB	Original and 2 typed copies	6.1.42–31.12.42	4 A4
Hintikka, Jaakko	Veljesapu Assoc.	”200”, 12/FFB	Typed copy	30.8.42–28.5.43	22 A4
Hämäläinen, Esko	M. Jokipii Pk-2365/5; M. Jokipii Pk-1140/23	3/FFB	Typed copy	17.5.41–14.3.43	67 A4
Härkönen, Ilmari	J. Saurio priv. collect.	2/FFB	Typed copy	28.5.41–10.6.42	15 A4
Intke, Eino	J. Tyrkkö Pk-1618/5	4/FFB, 2/FFB	Original	21.11.41–19.4.42	-
Kallio, Esko	J. Saurio priv. collect.	2/FFB	Typed copy	6.5.43–15.10.43	17 A4
Kemppinen, Iivari	Veljesapu Assoc.	1/FFB	Typed copy	15.5.41–22.1.43	35 A4
Kihlström, Lennart	M. Jokipii Pk-1140/36-37	1/ART	Original	1.1.41–31.12.41	-
Koivula, Martti	M. Hakanpää priv. collect.	2/Flak	Original, photographed	4.5.41–16.9.41	98 ~A5
Korpela, Vilkas	M. Jokipii Pk-1140/23	1/Pz, 4/FFB	Typed copy	16.6.41–13.8.41	9 A4
Kurkiala, Kalervo	M. Jokipii Pk-1140/23; M. Jokipii Pk-1140/22	Staff	Typed copy	18.11.41–13.5.43	55 A4
Kurvinen, Pekka	M. Jokipii Pk-1140/36-37; M. Jokipii Pk-1140/23	1/FFB	Original and typed copy	4.6.41–28.10.41	43 A4
Kuuri, Taisto	M. Jokipii Pk-1140/23	1/FFB	Typed copy	3.6.41–15.4.43	51 A4
Kyrö, Oiva	M. Jokipii Pk-2365/5; M. Jokipii Pk-1140/23	4/FFB, 1/FFB	Typed copy	1.6.41–17.12.42	55 A4

WRITER OF DIARY	PROVENIENCE	UNIT	FORM OF DIARY	PERIOD	PAGE LENGTH
Kääriäinen, Keijo	M. Jokipii Pk-2365/5; Originals P. Kääriäinen priv. collect.	2/N, 1/FFB	Original and typed copy	20.5.41–9.4.43	146 A4
Lakeala, Jaakko	M. Hakanpää priv. collect.	Flak, Nachsch., 5/N	Original	22.5.41–11.10.41	59 ~A5
Lantto, Alvar	M. Jokipii Pk-1140/23	2/FFB	Typed copy	23.5.41–7.6.43	7 A4
Lapinjoki, Heikki	M. Jokipii Pk-1140/24; M. Jokipii Pk-2365/5	2/FFB, 10/FFB	Typed copy	20.5.41–1.6.43	77 A4
Latva-Panttila, Sakari	M. Jokipii Pk-1140/36-37; M. Jokipii Pk-1140/24; M. Jokipii Pk-2365/5	4/FFB, 1/FFB, 2/FFB	Original and 2 typed copies	7.1.42–12.5.43	6 A4
Lehtonen, Martti	Porvali, S. *Uskollisuus On Kunniamme.* 2008	4/FFB, 1/FFB	Typed copy	25.4.42–9.12.42	15 A4
Leppälä, Martti	M. Jokipii Pk-1140/36-37	1/Pz	Original and partly typed copy	23.5.41–2.1.42	-
Lummeranta, Kalevi	J. Tyrkkö Pk-1618/5	1/FFB	Original	10.1.42–24.3.42	-
Lähteenoja, Pauli	Porvali, S. *Uskollisuus On Kunniamme.* 2008	4/FFB, 1/FFB	Typed copy	9.11.42–20.11.42	-
Martikainen, Onni	J. Tyrkkö Pk-1618/5	3/FFB	Original	22.11.41–23.1.42	134 ~A5
Muilu, Eerikki	M. Jokipii Pk-1140/24; M. Jokipii Pk-2365/5	3/FFB, 11/FFB	Typed copy	3.8.41–22.9.42	109 A4
Mäkeläinen, Reino	M. Jokipii Pk-1140/24; M. Jokipii Pk-2365/5	1/FFB	Typed copy	1.12.41–26.4.42	27 A4
Mäki, Eino	O. Wikberg priv. collect.	2/FFB	Original, scanned	10.8.42–21.11.44	82 ~A5
Mörttinen, Aapo	J. Tyrkkö Pk-1618/5	3/FFB	Original	19.8.41–30.1.42	53 ~A5
Nahi, Antti	M. Jokipii Pk-1140/36-37	1/FFB	Original	5.6.41–20.1.42	-
Nevanlinna, Eino	M. Jokipii. Pk-2365/6	3/FFB, Tölz	Original, photocopy	1.10.42–13.7.43	220 ~A5
Nikkola, Pentti	O. Wikberg priv. collect.	9/N, 5/N	Typed copy	15.5.41–25.2.42	6 A4
Norvio, Viljo	M. Jokipii Pk-1140/24	6/W, 14/W	Typed copy	15.5.41–17.11.41	6 A4
Ojanen, Reino	J. Tyrkkö Pk-1618/5	2/FFB	Typed copy	4.6.41–1.6.42	67 ~A5
Paikkala, Ahti	M. Jokipii Pk-1140/2; M. Jokipii Pk-2365/5	6/W, 14/W	Typed copy	4.41–18.2.42	92 A4
Pihkala, Ensio	J. Tyrkkö Pk-1618/5	Staff	Original	17.6.41–19.7.41	102 ~A5
Pohjanlehto, Tauno	M. Jokipii Pk-1140/15	3/FFB, 2/FFB	Partial typed copy	18.1.42–16.10.42	3 A4
Polón, Tauno	M. Jokipii Pk-1140/24	3/FFB, Tölz	Typed copy	23.5.41–27.12.42	22 A4
Pyyhtiä, Yrjö	M. Jokipii Pk-1140/24	10/FFB	Typed copy	29.11.42–4.12.42	3 A4
Pöntinen, Risto	M. Jokipii Pk-1140/36-37; M. Jokipii Pk-1140/24	4/FFB, 2/FFB	Original and typed copy	11.11.41–10.7.42	10 A4
Pöyhönen, Sakari	J. Tyrkkö Pk-1618/5	6/W	Original	5.5.41–26.7.41	-
Raevaara, Heikki	O. Wikberg priv. collect.	1/FFB	Original, scanned	28.2.42–3.12.42	66 ~A5

WRITER OF DIARY	PROVENIENCE	UNIT	FORM OF DIARY	FORM OF DIARY	PAGE LENGTH
Rahikkala, Ahti	M. Jokipii Pk-1140/24	1/FFB	Typed copy	28.4.42–28.5.43	46 A4
Rautala, Simo	M. Jokipii 79; M. Jokipii Pk-1140/24; M. Jokipii Pk-2365/7	2/FFB	Partly original; Partly typed copy	27.10.41–29.9.42	-
Saarela, Jaakko	M. Jokipii Pk-1140/24; M. Jokipii Pk-2365/7	2/FFB, 4/FFB, 3/FFB	Typed copy	25.5.41–16.8.41	98 A4
Saarinen, Eino	O. Wikberg priv. collect.	1/FFB, 4/FFB	Original, scanned	1.6.41–2.1.42	18 A4
Sartio, Mauri	O. Wikberg priv. collect.	3/FFB, 1/FFB, 4/FFB	Typed copy	4.12.41–7.8.42	46 A4
Silanterä, Erkki	M. Jokipii Pk-1140/15	10/FFB	Typed copy	18.8.42–3.6.43	12 A4
Silfverberg, Alf	M. Jokipii Pk-1140/24	2/FFB	Typed copy	25.4.42–7.3.43	10 A4
Sinervo Martti	Sinervo's heirs	3/FFB	Original and partly typed copy	29.5.1941–18.5.1942	201 A4
Soila, Pekka	M. Jokipii Pk-1140/36-37; M. Jokipii Pk-1140/24; M. Jokipii Pk-2365/7	1/FFB	Original and 2 typed copies	28.4.42–3.4.43	18 A4
Soininen, Pentti	O. Wikberg priv. collect.	1/FFB, 3/FFB, 4/FFB	Original, scanned	4.6.41–31.1.42	64 ~A5
Somersalo, Olli	M. Jokipii Pk-1140/36-37; M. Jokipii Pk-1140/24; M. Jokipii Pk-2365/7	Med. Corps	Original and 2 typed copies	10.9.42–6.4.43	9 A4
Sonninen, Esko	J. Saurio priv. collect.	3/FFB	Typed copy	29.5.41–19.4.42	28 A4
Sormunen, Leo	M. Jokipii Pk-1140/24; M. Jokipii Pk-2365/7	3/FFB	Typed copy	21.1.42–14.12.42	22 A4
Ström, Uuno	M. Jokipii Pk-1140/25-26; M. Jokipii Pk-2365/7	1/FFB	Typed copy	26.4.41–25.8.43	578 A4
Sulosaari, Esko	M. Hakanpää priv. collect.	Flak,2/Pz, 1/Pz, 4/FFB	Original	3.7.42–2.10.42	43 ~A5
Suonio, Reino	M. Hakanpää priv. collect.	9/W	Original	14.5.41–16.2.42	104 ~A5
Suonto, Kauko	M. Jokipii Pk-1140/25-26; M. Jokipii 78	3/FFB	Typed copy	23.9.42–23.7.43	179 A4
Taivalmaa, Seppo	J. Saurio priv. collect.	1/FFB	Typed copy	3.6.41–14.1.42	16 A4
Tulonen, Eero	M. Jokipii Pk-1140/25-26	II/N, 3/FFB	Typed copy	1.10.42–5.2.43	13 A4
Tuomaala, Toivo	J. Saurio priv. collect.	3/FFB, 4/FFB	Original, scanned	1.2.1943–25.5.1943	-
Uusi-Jaakkola, Martti	M. Hakanpää priv. collect.	9/W	Original	8.5.41–16.12.42	420 ~A5
Viitala, Paavo	M. Jokipii Pk-1140/25-26	1/N	Typed copy	1.9.41–23.1.43	3 A4
Vuokko, Ari	Military Museum	2/FFB	Original	-	-
Vuolento, Paavo	M. Jokipii Pk-1140/25-26; M. Jokipii 78	2/FFB	Typed copy	1.1.42–13.2.43	40 A4
Välimäki, Martti	M. Jokipii Pk-1140/25-26; M. Jokipii 78	11/W	Typed copy	9.6.41–15.3.42	15 A4

STATISTICAL FIGURES

PROVENANCE:		
National Archives, Mauno Jokipii collection	44	58%
National Archives, Jukka Pellervo Tyrkkö private collection	7	9%
Military Museum, Helsinki	1	1%
Society of Swedish Literature in Finland (SLS)	1	1%
Private collections (including Veljesapu Association)	23	30%
Total	**76**	

FORM OF DIARY:		
Original (in whole, photocopy, scanned, photographed or at least partly original)	34	45%
Typed copy	42	55%
Total	**76**	

UNIT:		
Subunits of SS-Division Wiking	19	25%
Finnisches SS-Freiwilligen-Bataillon	54	71%
The Division Staff	3	4%
Total	**76**	

NOTES

1 Korhonen 1961, 1966–68, Upton 1965, 175–177, Jokipii 1996, 19–22.
2 Krosby 1966, 74–75, Hentilä-Jussila 1995, 178.
3 Krosby 1967, Manninen 1980, Jokipii 1988, Jokipii 1996, 71–72, Jokipii 2005, 56–58.
4 Jokipii 1996, 22–54, Jokipii 2005, 58–59, Westerlund 2017, 120–160.
5 Jokipii 1996, 55–57, Westerlund 2017, 220–224.
6 Mannerheim 1952, 263, 367.
7 Jokipii 1996, 77–105, Jokipii 2005, 59–66, Westerlund 2017, 156–160.
8 Jokipii 1968, 88–89, Manninen 1981, 696–705, Manninen 2011, 3–11, Manninen 2013, 240–49.
9 Westerlund 2017, 108–111.
10 Ibid., 129–131.
11 Ibid., 338–339.
12 The Archive of the SS-Investigation, The National Archives.
13 Westerlund 2017, 94–108.
14 Ibid., 98–102.
15 Immonen 1987, Karemaa 1998, Partanen 2005, Vihavainen 2013.
16 Hanski 2006.
17 Kemiläinen 1993, Kemiläinen 1998, Westerlund 2011, 136–157.
18 Nuremberg Laws. https://en.wikipedia.org/wiki/Nuremberg_Laws
19 Shaping the future: Indoctrinating Youth. https://encyclopedia.ushmm.org/contenct/en/article/indoctrinating-youth
20 SS-Division "Wiking" 1.1.1941–9.11.1942, SS-Panzergrenadierdivision "Wiking" 9.11.1942–22.10.1943 and 5. SS-Panzerdivision "Wiking" 22.10.1943–8.5.1945.
21 The diary of Kaj Duncker 31.5.1941, Kaj Duncker's Collection, Pk-1821/5, The National Archives.
22 5. SS-Panzer-Division Wiking. https://en.wikipedia.org/wiki/5th_SS_Panzer_Division_Wiking
23 Schön 2001, 62.
24 Estes 1984, 27. Ruotsalaiset Waffen-SS-miehet, jotka antoivat kaikkensa. Veikko Huuska. http://veikkohuuska.puheenvuoro.uusisuomi.fi/215960-ruotsalaiset-waffen-ss-miehet-jotka-antoivat-kaikkensa
25 Norwegian volunteers in the German Wehrmacht in WWII, by Marc Rikmenspoel & Jason Pipes. https://www.feldgrau.com/WW2-German-Wehrmacht-Norwegian-Volunteers.
26 Estes 1984, 26.
27 Statische Aufstellung der bei den Feld- und Ersatzeinheiten befindlichen germanischen Freiwilligen. Stand 6.2.1943. Attachment to Gottlob Berger's letter to Heinrich Himmler 10.2.1943, No-1486, Staatsarchiv Nürnberg, Strassner 1968, 433–434, information given by Cees Kleijn, Amsterdam, The Netherlands.
28 Estes 1984, 26.
29 Elo 2006, 22.
30 Estes 1984, 27, Struve 2015, 210–211, 563.
31 5. SS-Panzer-Division Wiking. https://sv.wikipedia.org/wiki/5._SS-Panzer-Division_Wiking (in Swedish)
32 SS-Division Wiking. Zustandsberich für Monat November 1941 (Stichtag 30.), The Archive of the SS-Investigation, The National Archives.
33 Ibid.
34 Westerlund 2017, 80–92.
35 Silvennoinen & Tikka & Roselius 2016, Swanström 2018, 45–84.
36 Westerlund 2017, 83–84.
37 Cande 2013, 22.
38 Divisioonan mies muistelee – SS-Rottenführer Arvo Kokon tarina osa 1. Recollection in Achtung 1.2016, 3.
39 The recollections by Olavi Liesinen 1969, The Archive of Mauno Jokipii, Pk-11450/27, The National Archives.
40 Christiansen 1950, Table 45, Christiansen & Poulsen & Smith 2001, 39, Christiansen& Poulsen & Smith 2014, 207.
41 Schön 2000, 16, Gyllenhaal-Westberg 2008, 256, 263, 295.
42 Svårt att få rekryter till Norska Legionen. Quisling lockar med ekonomiska fördelar. Artikel i Nu. *Världshändelserna inför världsopinionen* 22.8.1941, Blindheim 1978, 132–133, Gogstad & Grimnes & Røland 2005, 91, Brenden & Thomassen 2010, 13, Sørlie 2014, 183.
43 Ekberg 1991, 135–136.
44 Ekberg 1991, 105–107, Gunnar Lindqvist. https://fi.wikipedia.org/wiki/Gunnar_Lindqvist
45 Ekberg 1991, 101–102, Andersson 2015, Hjalmar von Bonsdorff. https://fi.wikipedia.org/wiki/Hjalmar_von_Bonsdorff
46 Ekberg 1991, 195.
47 Parvilahti 1959, 18–19.
48 Ekberg 1991, 107–111, Erkki Räikkönen. https://en.wikipe-

dia.org/wiki/Erkki_Räikkönen

49 Ekberg 1991, 2011–218.

50 Ekberg 1991, 190, 214.

51 Writing from the British Embassy in Washington D.C. to the Foreign Office 16.12.1942, Return of Finnish volunteers from Germany, Code 56 file 81, FO 371/36846, The National Archives, Kew.

52 Askey 2013, 543.

53 Weinberg 1994, 458.

54 Wegner 1990.

55 Westerlund 2017, 164–165.

56 Wikman 1992, 68, 84.

57 Askey 2013, 540.

58 Johnson 2006, 9, 11, 270–273, 293.

59 Goldsworthy 2007, 27.

60 Ibid. 540.

61 Was the Waffen-SS an elite force? https://history.stackexchange.com/questions/33415/was-the-waffen-ss-an-elite-force Was the Waffen-SS an extraordinarily effective fighting force? https://www.quora.com/Was-the-Waffen-SS-an-extraordinarily-effective-fighting-force-Why-Why-did-they-command-such-fear-and-respect-among-their-opponents-What-was-the-reason-behind-the-awe-and-fighting-efficiency-associated-with-the-Waffen-SS

62 Estes 1984, 211–212.

63 Pasher 2014, 260.

64 Bartov 1997, 327.

65 Quarrie 1984, 93.

66 Yrjö Kaila: SS-vaikutelmat/42. Yrjö Kaila's Collection, Pk-2356/9, The National Archives.

67 Alte Kameraden mollissa. Review of Felix Steiner's book "Die Freiwilligen der Waffen-SS" in *Helsingin Sanomat*, 28.8.1958, by Ypi (= Yrjö Kaila).

68 Ibid.

69 Estes 1984, 211.

70 Stein 1984, 250–251.

71 Goldsworthy 2007, 3, 58.

72 Stein 1966, 272.

73 Boll 2002, 75.

74 Tötung von Juden auf dem Gebiet der Strasse Lemberg-Zloczow, "Der Chef des Generalstabes" 3.7.1941, Ludwigsburger Zentrale Stelle.

75 Boll 2002, 75.

76 Kriegstagebuch des IV Armeekorps 2–3.7.1941, The Archive of the SS-Investigation, The National Archives.

77 Boll 2002, 75.

78 Angrick 2003, 582.

79 Larsson 2014, 37.

80 Stein 1966, 263–264.

81 Stein 1966, 264.

82 Goldsworthy 2007, 115, Waffen-SS in popular culture. https://en.wikipedia.org/wiki/Waffen-SS_in_popular_culture

83 Goldsworthy 2007, 114.

84 Ibid., 258–223, Werther 2004, 138, Fritz von Scholz. https://en.wikipedia.org/wiki/Fritz_von_Scholz

85 Waffen-SS in popular culture. https://en.wikipedia.org/wiki/Waffen-SS_in_popular_culture

86 Szlojme Mayer, ed. *Der Untergang fun Złoczów* The Destruction of Złoczów (Zolochiv, Ukraine). https://www.jewishgen.org/Yizkor/Zolochiv/Zolochiv.html

87 Geheime Kommandosache, Der Führer und oberste Befehlhaber der Wehrmach: Erlass über die Ausübung der Kriegsgerichstbarkeit im Gebiet "Barbarossa"13.5.1941, Der Chef des Oberkommandos der Wehrmacht Wilhelm Keitel, Ludwigsburger Zentrale Stelle, Schurig 1991, 160–161.

88 Hillgruber 1989, 94–96, Rhodes 2002, 15, Einsatzgruppen. https://en.wikipedia.org/wiki/Einsatzgruppen, Eduard Wagner (General). https://de.wikipedia.org/wiki/Eduard_Wagner _(General)

89 Ibid.

90 Einsatzgruppen (Mobile Killing Squads) https://encyclopedia.ushmm.org/content/en/article/mobile-killing-squads, List of Einsatzgruppen. https://en.wikipedia.org/wiki/List _of_Einsatzgruppen

91 Jokipii 1968, 191, 215, Jokipii 1996, 191, 215.

92 Yrjö Kaila's letter to Mauno Jokipii 12.10.1969, Mauno Jokipii's Collection, Pk-1140/34–35, The National Archives, Yrjö Kaila's recollection 1994, Yrjö Kaila's Collection, Pk-2356/9, The National Archives.

93 Goldsworthy 2007, 59, Carruthers 2014, 167.

94 Pidvoloschysk. https://en.wikipedia.org/wiki Pidvolochysk, Podwolocyska and its Surroundings (Podvolochisk, Ukraine) https://www.jewishgen.org/yizkor/podvolochisk/podvolochisk.html

95 Wykes 1974, 125.

96 "They really do smell like blood". Among Hitler's executioners on the Eastern Front. Interview with Anette Schücking-Homeyer in *Martyrdom & Resistance* March-April 2010 pp. 7–8, (also in *Spiegel Online*, see links), Novohrad-Volynskyi. https://en.wikipedia.org/wiki/Novohrad-Volynskyi

97 Ostropol. http://en.wikipedia.org/wiki/Ostropol

98 The diary of Pieter Willems, undated, NIOD, Amsterdam, Kleijn-Reurs 2018. The Archive of the SS-Investigation, The National Archives.

99 Mariupol. https://en.wikipedia.org/wiki/Mariupol

100 Mariupol. The Untold Stories. The Murder Sites of the

Jews in the Occupied Territories of the former USSR. https://www.yadvashem.org/untoldstories/database/index.asp?cid=493

101 Nikolai Dupak. https://iremember.ru/en/memoirs/others/nikolai-dupak/

102 Lower 2004, 114, Struve 2015, 566–585, 5. SS-Panzer-Division Wiking. https://www.axishistory.com/axis...germany.../germany.../1265-5-ss-panzer-division-wiking.

103 Lower 2005, 73–74, 79–83.

104 Trial testimony by Broer Wiesma 5.7.1977. Collection 461, Collectie proses, Inv. Nr. 21, NIOD, Kleijn-Reurs 2018. The Archive of the SS-Investigation, The National Archives.

105 Ibid.

106 Christian Frederik von Schalburg. https://fi.wikipedia.org/wiki/Christian_Frederik_von_Schalburg

107 Interrogation record N:o 28/46, Liukkonen (former Hildén), Erik Johannes, 20.5.1946, The Oulu branch of the Valtiollinen poliisi, The Valpo archive, The National Archives.

108 Jokipii 1968, 599–601.

109 Suomalaisten Waffen-SS -vapaaehtoisten matrikkeli 1941–1943 (2013), 147, Westerlund 2017, 109, Swanström 2018, 376, 406–407.

110 The diary of Jaakko Lakeala 9.10.1941, The Archive of the SS-Investigation, The National Archives.

111 Swanström 2018, 154.

112 André Swanström: Suomalaiset SS-miehet ja sotarikokset. http://www.skhs.fi/suomalaiset-ss-miehet-ja-sotarikokset/, Tämä kirje johti selvitykseen SS-vapaaehtoisten epäillyistä sotarikoksista. https://www.is.fi/kotimaa/art-2000005693915.html, Kuusela 2018, 7–11, Kääriäinen 2018, 11, Swanström 2018, 153–160.

113 The diary of Martti Leppälä 17. and 20.7.1941. Mauno Jokipii's Collection, Pk-1140/36–37, The National Archives.

114 Swanström 2018, 159.

115 Testimony by Hans Wilhelm Isenmann, The Archive of the SS-Investigation, The National Archives, Tarashcha. https://www.jewishgen.org/

116 Reenpää 1998, 191–192, Otavan arkisto. Interview with Heikki Reenpää by Kreeta Karvala in Iltalehti 9.12.2017.

117 Ibid.

118 Swanström 2018, 146–147.

119 Rostov-on-Don. http://www.yivoencyclopedia.org/article.aspx/Rostov-on-Don, Rostov-on-Don. The untold stories. https://www.yadvashem.org/untoldstories/database/index.asp?cid=798, Zmievskaya Balka. https://en.wikipedia.org/wiki/Zmievskaya_Balka, BBC: Russia row over Nazi massacre site in Rostov-on-Don. https://www.bbc.com/news/world-europe-16697485

120 Heikki Lemettinen's letter to his former teacher, 29.8.1942, The Archive of the SS-Investigation, The National Archives.

121 The diary of Kaj Duncker 27.2.1943, Kaj Duncker's Collection, Pk-1821/5, The National Archives.

122 Seppälä 1971, 34, 36.

123 Swanström 2018, 171-174.

124 Westerlund 2017, 20-21, 37, Swanström 2018, 174-176.

125 Swanström 2018, 176.

126 Westerlund 2017, 37, 260, Swanström 2018, 335-336.

127 Møller Hansen 2015, 106–107.

128 Christensen & Poulsen & Smith 2002, 100.

129 Larsen & Straede 2014, 224, Bay 2017, 164–165.

130 Information given by Lars Larsen, Copenhagen, Denmark.

131 Werther 2004, 142–143, Larsen & Straede 2014, 226–232.

132 Haaest 1998, 138–139, Christensen & Poulsen & Smith 2002, 162, "Ikke kammerat": forbrydelser mod sovjetiske krigsfanger. https://folkedrab.dk/artikler/ikke-kammerat-forbrydelser-mod-sovjetiske-krigsfanger

133 Werther 2004, 146–147.

134 Krabbe 1976, 120, Christensen & Poulsen & Smith 2002, 100.

135 Schön 2001, 165, Christensen & Poulsen & Smith 2002, 100.

136 Dagbok fra Østfronten 2012.

137 Werther 2004, 139–142, 148–149. "Ikke kammerat": forbrydelser mod sovjetiske krigsfanger. https://folkedrab.dk/artikler/ikke-kammerat-forbrydelser-mod-sovjetiske-krigsfanger, Werther 2004, 146–147.

138 Werther 2004, 142.

139 Sørlie 2015, 213.

140 Olav Tuff (91): Vi brente en kirke med sivilister. https://www.nrk.no/dokumentar/--nordmenn-deltok-i-drap-pa-sivile-1.11262316

141 Ilddåpen: Norsk frivillig skildrer boljsevikenes djevelske krigsførsel på Østfronten. Article by SS-Kriegsberichter Egil Hartmann in *Fritt Folk,* 19.7.1941, Westlie 2010, 53.

142 Og så bearer det videre - - ! En nordmann skildrer episode fra kampene på östfronten. Article by Olaf Wahlman in *Hirdmannen* 16.8.1941, Sørlie 2015, Ibid., 322, Ulateig 2006, 117–118, Bay 2017, 105.

143 Sørlie 2015, 337.

144 Ibid, Gyllenhaal & Westberg 2008, 280, 290, Gyllenhaal & Westberg 2010, 287, 289.

145 Gyllenhaal & Westberg 2008, 166–168.

146 Gyllenhaal & Westberg 2008, 290, Gyllenhaal & Westberg 2010, 286.

147 Gyllenhaal & Westberg 2008, 169–170, 293, Gyllenhaal

& Westberg 2010, 290, Kurt Lundin schildert der schwedischen Polizei am 24. Dezember 1943, wie die SS im Juli 1941 in Husiatyn Juden ermorderte. Die Verfolgung und Ermordung der europäischen Juden durch das nationalsozialistische Deutschland 1933–1945. Besetzte sowjetische Gebiete unter deutscher Militärverwaltung, Baltikum und Transnistrien, Band 8 2016, 503–505.

148 Gyllenhaal & Westberg 2008, 170, Kurt Lundin schildert der schwedischen Polizei am 24. Dezember 1943, wie die SS im Juli 1941 in Husiatyn Juden ermorderte. Die Verfolgung und Ermordung der europäischen Juden durch das nationalsozialistische Deutschland 1933–1945. Besetzte sowjetische Gebiete unter deutscher Militärverwaltung, Baltikum und Transnistrien, Band 8 2016, 503–505.

149 En f.d. nazist bekänner. Article in *Stockholms-Tidningen* 15.5.1963, Schön 2002, 187–200, 206–209.

150 Gyllenhaal & Westberg 2008, 294–295.

151 Gyllenhaal & Westberg 2008, 291, 288, information provided by Lennart Westberg, Sundsvall.

152 I.e. NS 19/63, NS 19/157, NS 19/247, NS 19/539, NS 19/745, NS 19/1539, NS 19/1777, NS 19/1991, NS 19/2150, NS 19/2260, NS 19/2485–2486, NS 19/ 2488, NS 19/3439, NS 19/3595, NS 19/3306, NS 19/ 3654, NS 19/3837, NS 19/3861, NS 19/3882, NS 19/3896, Persönliche Stab Reichsführer-SS, Bundesesarchiv, Lichterfelde.

153 Westberg 193, 580.

154 RS 4 Verbände und Einheiten der Feldformationen der Waffen-SS (überwiegend Reiterverbände) RS 4/1784 and RS 3–11/5, Militärarchiv-Bundesarchiv Freiburg.

155 Deutsche Dienststelle (WASt). https://de.wikipedia.org/wiki/Deutsche_Dienststelle_(WASt)

156 Suomalaisten Waffen-SS-vapaaehtoisten matrikkeli 1941–1943 (2013).

157 Die Zentrale Stelle der Landesjustizverwaltungen zur Aufklärung nationalsozialistischer Verbrechen. https://de.wikipedia.org/wiki/Zentrale_Stelle_der_Landesjustizverwaltungen_zur_Aufkl%C3%A4rung_nationalsozialistischer_Verbrechen

158 I.e. the collections B 162,B 162/6764, B 162/7185, B 162/7185, B 162/7993, B 162/8361, B 162/19140 and B 162/31429, Ludwigsburger Zentrale Stelle.

159 The diaries of Keijo Kääriäinen, Jaakko Lakeala, Pentti Nikkola, Eero Tulonen, and Paavo Viitala.

160 The diaries of Tapio Gröndahl, Viljo Norvio, Ahti Paikkala, Sakari Pöyhönen, Reino Suonio, Martti Välimäki and Martti Uusi-Jaakkola.

161 The diaries of Kaj Duncker and Lennart Kihlström.

162 The diaries of Veikko Hallavo, Vilkas Korpela and Martti Leppälä.

163 The diaries of Martti Koivula and Jaakko Lakeala.

164 The diary of Jaakko Lakeala.

165 The diaries of Kalervo Kurkiala, Ensio Pihkala, and Olli Somersalo.

166 The diaries of Matti Aho, Kauko Ala-Iikka, Sven Elmgren, Kalevi Haapaniemi, Anselm Halinen, Matti Heikkilä, Leo Heikurainen, Veikko Hallavo, Eero Helminen, Jaakko Hintikka, Esko Hämäläinen, Ilmari Härkönen, Eino Intke, Esko Kallio, Iivari Kemppinen, Pekka Kurvinen, Taisto Kuuri, Oiva Kyrö, Keijo Kääriäinen, Alvar Lantto, Heikki Lapinjoki, Sakari Latva-Panttila, Martti Lehtonen, Kalevi Lummeranta, Pauli Lähteenoja, Onni Martikainen, Eerikki Muilu, Reino Mäkeläinen, Eino Mäki, Aapo Mörttinen, Antti Nahi, Eino Nevanlinna, Reino Ojanen, Tauno Pohjanlehto, Tauno Polón, Yrjö Pyyhtiä, Risto Pöntinen, Heikki Raevaara, Ahti Rahikkala, Simo Rautala, Jaakko Saarela, Eino Saarinen, Mauri Sartio, Erkki Silanterä, Alf Silfverberg, Martti Sinervo, Pekka Soila, Pentti Soinen, Esko Sonninen, Leo Sormunen, Uuno Ström, Esko Sulosaari, Kauko Suonto, Seppo Taivalmaa, Eero Tulonen, Ari Vuokko, and Paavo Vuolento.

167 The diaries of Leo Heikurainen, Eino Nevanlinna, and Tauno Polón.

168 Yhdysupseerin tiedotuksia N:o 1 1.9.1941. The documents of K.E. Levälahti, The collection of Mauno Jokipii, Pk-1140/10, The National Archives.

169 Tauno Pohjanlehto: Muistelmia suomalaisesta SS-pataljoonasta and letter 17.6.1959, Mauno Jokipii's Collection, Pk-1140/28, The National Archives.

170 Swanström 2018, 417–418.

171 The diaries of Aarne Aarnio, Konstantin Cande, either Kalevi or Lauri Haapaniemi, either Erkki, Esko or Kaarlo Heiskanen, either Eino or Lauri Helenius, Simo Heliste, Toivo Hämäläinen, Jouko Ilkka, Matti Joki, Toivo Jokinen, Heikki Jämsänen, either Sulo or Toivo Kangaslampi, Osmo Kauppinen, Armas Kokkola, Pentti Koskenkanto, Aarne Kähärä, Sakari Lappi-Seppälä, Pentti Launonen, Ossian Leisimo, Jorma Liuhala, Björn Lönnblad, Esa Meriö, Pekka Nummi, Olavi "Olli" Partanen, Olavi Pellinen, Arvi Pyyhtiä, Yrjö Pyyhtiä, either Martti or Mikko Rautio, Paavo Sahari, either Pauli, Sulo or Veikko Silvennoinen, Teppo Tattari, Eero Tilus, Jukka Tyrkkö, either Paavo or Vilho Viitala, Kyösti Virtaniemi and Pertteli Yli-Harja.

172 The diaries of Ferdinand Frehé, Henri le Roux, Jan Olij, Martinus Rademacher, Martinus Weers and Pieter Willems.

173 Kleijn-Reurs 2018. The Archive of the SS-Investigation, The National Archives.

174 The diaries by Ørnulf Bjørnstad and Svein Lothe.

175 The diary by Helge Laerum.
176 The diaries by Kolbjørn Rogstadkjernet and Thor Sundby.
177 På Vikingeferd by Hans-Petter Hoff and Erindringer fra 1941–45 by Olav Tuff.
178 Lappi-Seppälä 1945, Kalas 1955, Parvilahti 1959, Tyrkkö 1960, Konttinen 1996, Lappalainen 1998, Jätinvuori 2000, Räsänen 2000, Ruusukallio 2007, Uskollisuus on kunniamme 2008, Cande 2013, Porvali 2014,Lempinen 2015, Ilkka 2016, Kyösti 2016 and Turunen 2016.
179 Lappi-Seppälä 1945, Nupnau 1946.
180 Westlie 2010, 22.
181 Die Waffen-SS. Eine Bilddokumentation 1994, 6.
182 Suomalaisten Waffen-SS-vapaaehtoisten matrikkeli 1941–1943 (2013), 38, 247, information given by Olli Wikberg, Helsinki.
183 Helsingin kaupungin raastuvanoikeuden 8 osaston 2 jaoston rikosasiain kirjavihko N:o 91/1958, The Magistrate's Court of Helsinki, The National Archives, Parvilahden juttu siirtyi lokakuulle. Mielenkiintoisia todistajalausuntoja. Article in *Suomen Sosialidemokraatti*, 12.9.1958.
184 Tauno Pohjanlehto: Muistelmia suomalaisesta SS-pataljoonasta and letter dated 17.6.1959, Mauno Jokipii's Collection, Pk-1140/28, The National Archives.
185 Information given by Olli Wikberg, Helsinki.
186 Brenden-Natedal 2017, 51–67, Regiment Nordland. https://no.wikipedia.org/wiki/Regiment_Nordland
187 Elo 2006, 22.
188 Engelhardt 1970, 4, Ruotsalaiset Waffen-SS-miehet, jotka antoivat kaikkensa. Veikko Huuska. http://veikkohuuska.puheenvuoro.uusisuomi.fi/215960-ruotsalaiset-waffen-ss-miehet-jotka-antoivat-kaikkensa
189 The diary of Kaj Duncker 31.5.1941, Kaj Duncker's Collection, Pk-1821/1, The National Archives.
190 Engelhardt 1970, 13,
191 Loppuun saakka. Kenr. von Scholz ja Everstil. Collani kaatuneet. Article in *SS-Aseveljet* 25.8.1944, Supplement to the journal *Rintamamies*.
192 List of awarded honours. Mauno Jokipii's Collection, Pk-1140/34–35, The National Archives.
193 Engelhardt 1970, 26.
194 Norwegian volunteers in the German Wehrmacht in WWII by Marc Rikmenspoel & Jason Pipes. https://www.feldgrau.com/WW2-German-Wehrmacht-Norwegian-Volunteers
195 Polewacz, Harry. https://prabook.com/web/harry.polewacz/2334954
196 List of awarded honours. Mauno Jokipii's Collection, Pk-1140/34–35, The National Archives.
197 Interview with Felix Steiner by Mauno Jokipii 27.6.1961. Mauno Jokipii's Collection, Pk-1140/33, The National Archives.
198 Engelhardt 1970, 23.
199 Regiment Westland. http://www.waffen-ss.nl/wikwest.php Panzer-Grenadier-Regiment 10 'Westland'/SS-Standarte 'Westland'. Nederlanders in de Waffen-SS. http://www.waffen-ss.nl/wikwest.php
200 The diary of Kai Duncker 25.6.1941, Kaj Duncker's Collection, Pk-1821/1, The National Archives.
201 Ruotsalaiset Waffen-SS-miehet, jotka antoivat kaikkensa. Veikko Huuska. http://veikkohuuska.puheenvuoro.uusisuomi.fi/215960-ruotsalaiset-waffen-ss-miehet-jotka-antoivat-kaikkensa
202 Elo 2006, 22.
203 Ulateig 2006, 106.
204 The diary of Kaj Duncker 27.9.1942, Kaj Duncker's Collection, Pk-1821/4, The National Archives.
205 Hilmar Wäckerle. https://en.wikipedia.org/wiki/Hilmar_Wäckerle
206 Dillon 2015, 35, 47–48, Hilmar Wäckerle. https://en.wikipedia.org/wiki/Hilmar_Wäckerle
207 Petropoulos 1996, 173–174, 204–205, 314, 317–318, Swanström 2018, 236–237, Karl Diebitsch. https://en.wikipedia.org/wiki/Karl_Diebitsch
208 Höhne 1996, 437, Mabire 1983, 13.
209 Gumz 1998, 33–50.
210 Bergel 1972, 106.
211 Arthur Phleps. https://en.wikipedia.org/wiki/Arthur_Phleps
212 Ulateig 2006, 106.
213 Ruotsalaiset Waffen-SS-miehet, jotka antoivat kaikkensa. Veikko Huuska. http://veikkohuuska.puheenvuoro.uusisuomi.fi/215960-ruotsalaiset-waffen-ss-miehet-jotka-antoivat-kaikkensa
214 Dieckmann, August https://de.wikipedia.org/wiki/August_Dieckmann_(SS-Mitglied)
215 The diary of Kaj Duncker 31.5.1941, Kaj Duncker's Collection, Pk-1821/, The National Archives, Joerchel, Wolfgang. https://hu.wikipedia.org/wiki/Wolfgang_J%C3%B6rchel
216 List of awarded honours. Mauno Jokipii's Collection, Pk-1140/34–35, The National Archives.
217 Ibid., Karl von Oberkamp.https://en.wikipedia.org/wiki/Karl_von_Oberkamp
218 Bernau 1991, 27–28.
219 Ulateig 2006, 106, Diary of Kaj Duncker 11.9.1941, Kaj Duncker's Collection, Pk-1821/2, The National Archives. Norwegian volunteers in the German Wehrmacht in WWII by Marc Rikmenspoel & Jason Pipes. https://www.

feldgrau.com/WW2-German-Wehrmacht-Norwegian-Volunteers
220 Herbert Gille. https://en.wikipedia.org/wiki/Herbert_Gille
221 Information given by Douglas Nash, Oregon, USA.
222 Weale 2010, 216.
223 List of awarded honours. Mauno Jokipii's Collection, Pk-1140/34–35, The National Archives.
224 SS-Gruppenführer Herbert Gille – en kompromissløs nasjonalsosialist. Den 12. soldat i den tyske forsvarsmakt som har mottatt jernkorsets ridderkors med sverd, eikelauv og briljanter. Article by the SS-Kriegsberichter Dr. Kristian Zarp in *Aftenposten* 29.4.1944.
225 Saksan entiset SS-miehet koolla. Article in Helsingin Sanomat 28.10.1952, Herbert Gille. https://en.wikipedia.org/wiki/Herbert_Gille
226 Ernst Otto Fick. http://jewiki.net/wiki/Ernst_Otto_Fick
227 List of awarded honours. Mauno Jokipii's Collection, Pk-1140/34–35, The National Archives.
228 Kausch, Paul-Albert. https://alchetron.com/Paul-Albert-Kausch
229 Westerlund 2017, 347.
230 Elo 2006, 22.
231 Norwegian volunteers in the German Wehrmacht in WWII by Marc Rikmenspoel & Jason Pipes. https://www.feldgrau.com/WW2-German-Wehrmacht-Norwegian-Volunteers
232 Olavi Karpalo's letter to Ensio Pihkala 28.7.1941, Mauno Jokipii's Collection, Pk-1141/8–10, The National Archives.
233 Hans-Albin Freiherr von Reitzenstein. https://de.wikipedia.org/wiki/Hans-Albin_Freiherr_von_Reitzenstein
234 Hans-Albin Freiherr von Reitzenstein. https://de.wikipedia.org//wiki/Hans-Albin_Freiherr_von_Reitzenstein
235 Elo 2006, 22.
236 Ulateig 2006, 106.
237 Yerger 1997 I, 205, Berthold Maack. https://de.wikipedia.org/wiki/Berthold_Maack
238 Berthold Maack. https://de.wikipedia.org/wiki/Berthold_Maack
239 Parvilahti 1959, Stein & Krosby 1966, 413–453, Jokipii 1968, 842, Tieke 1979, Jokipii 1996, Kuusela & Wikberg 1996, Wikberg 2001, Tieke 2002, Elo 2006, Suistola 2009, 326–346, Baryshnikov 2014, Westerlund 2017, Westberg 2017, 16–21, Finnish Volunteer Battalion of the Waffen-SS. https://en.wikipedia.org/wiki/Finnish_Volunteer_Battalion_of_the_Waffen-SS Finnish Volunteers in the Wehrmacht in WWII.
240 List of awarded honours. Mauno Jokipii's Collection, Pk-1140/34–35, The National Archives.
241 Interview with Felix Steiner by Mauno Jokipii 27.6.1961. Mauno Jokipii's Collection, Pk-1140/33, The National Archives, Loppuun saakka. Kenr. von Scholz ja everstil. Collani kaatuneet. Article in *SS-Aseveljet* 25.8.1944, Supplement to the journal *Rintamamies*.
242 Engelhardt 1970, 20.
243 Westerlund 2017, 380–385, Hans Collani. https://de.wikipedia.org/wiki/Hans_Collani, https://ipfs.io/ipfs/QmXoypizjW3WknFiJnKLwHCnL72vedxjQkDDP1mXWo6uco/wiki/Hans_Collani.html
244 Westerlund 2017, 253–257, 394–395.
245 Ibid., 11–12.
246 Freiwilligen-General Felix Steiner 1896-1966 (1998), Schütz 1999, Mathias 2001.
247 Gutmann 2017, 102.
248 Felix Steiner. https://en.wikipedia.org/wiki/Felix_Steiner
249 Ulateig 2006, 127.
250 Reitlinger 1956, 85, Wegner 1990, 44.
251 Felix Steiner. https://en.wikipedia.org/wiki/Felix_Steiner
252 Goldsworthy 2007, 42, 236.
253 Kadaverdiscipline. https://en.wiktionary.org/wiki/kadaver-discipline
254 Estes 1984, 25–26, 210.
255 Steiner 1947, 9.
256 Wegner 1990, 184–187.
257 Weale 2010, 213–214.
258 Mabire 1983, 427.
259 The diary of Kalervo Kurkiala 10.12.1941 and 29.5.1942, Mauno Jokipii's Collection, Pk-1140/23, The National Archives.
260 Tapola & Karjalainen 2012, 222, Westerlund 2017, 302.
261 The diary of J. Zachris Duncker 16.–25.5. and 20.–22.10.1942, J.Z. Duncker: På marskens specialuppdrag i krigens Europa, pp. 42–43, 51, unpublished manuscript, The Archive of Svenska Litteratursällskapet, Collection 898, Wikberg 2002, 1-5.
262 The report of Harald Öhquist 27.–29.8.1942, Mauno Jokipii's Collection, Pk-1140/29–30, The National Archives.
263 List of awarded honours. Mauno Jokipii's Collection, Pk-1140/34–35, The National Archives.
264 Ibid., 324–326.
265 "Isämme" ja komentajamme...". Article by the 'Erkki Olavi' in *SS-Aseveljet* N:o 23.1944, Supplement to the journal *Rintamamies*.
266 Tosi aseveljeyttä. Article in *Rintamamies* by Jukka Tyrkkö 25.8.1944.
267 Anlage 1. Felix Steiner: Bericht über den Besuch in Finnland von 31.5. bis 7.6.1943 and Anlage 2. Bericht des SS-Obergruppenführers Felix Steiner von Finnland,The Ar-

chive of the SS-Investigation, The National Archives.
268 SS-välikohtaus and Saksan entiset SS-miehet koolla. Articles in *Helsingin Sanomat* 27.8. and 28.8.1952, Freiwilligen-General Felix Steiner 1896–1966. Führer und Vater seiner Soldaten im Kampf gegen den Bolshewismus 1998, 24.
269 Freiwilligen-General Felix Steiner 1896–1966. Führer und Vater seiner Soldaten im Kampf gegen den Bolshewismus 1998, 24.
270 Parvilahti 1959, photos between pages 296 and 297, Virtanen 2018, 247.
271 Die finnischen Freiwilligen. Article in *Wiking-Ruf* 9/1956, 7.
272 Information given by Mika Hakanpää in Alahärmä.
273 Undated relation by Eero Helminen, the Archive of Veljesapu, The Parola Armour Museum.
274 I.e. Felix Steiner, Harry Polewacz, Hans-Joachim "Hajo" von Hadeln, Hilmar Wäckerle, Karl Diebitsch, August Dieckmann, Ernst Fick, Per-Albert "Peter" Kausch, Joachim Richter and Hans Collani.
275 Goldsworthy 2007, 31–32.
276 Cüppers 2005, 96.
277 I.e. Hilmar Wäckerle 2.7.1941, Alfred Schade 25.8.1941, Hans-Joachim "Hajo" von Hadeln 12.1.1943, Harry Polewacz 12.1.1943, Alois Braun 27.4.1943, August Dieckmann 10.10.1943, Arnold Stoffens 25.2.1944, Fritz von Scholz 28.7.1944, Arthur von Phleps (Stolz), Ernst Otto Fick 29.4.1945 and Wolfgang Joerchel 12.5.1945.
278 I.e. Hans Albin Freiherr von Reitzenstein + 30.11.1943, Hans Collani + 29.7.1944.
279 When all our brothers are silent 1983, 16, 17.
280 Yerger 1997 II and 1999.
281 August Dieckmann, Ernst Otto Fick, Hans-Joachim "Hajo" von Hadeln, Wolfgang Joerchel, Harry Polewacz, Felix Steiner, and Berthold Maack.
282 Arthur Phleps, Lebenslauf, SS-kartei, Bundesarchiv.
283 MacLean 1999 II, 278.
284 SS-Division-Wiking, Dienstalteliste 1.6.1941, Waffen-SS ja SS-Division-Wikingin asiakirjat, The Archive of the SS-Investigation, The National Archives.
285 Jokipii 1968, 132-147.
286 Swanström 2018, 178-179.
287 MacLean 1999 II.
288 I.e. Ploew, von Scholz and Steiner.
289 Parland 2012, 70.
290 Bernau 1991, 27.
291 Kurowski 2013, 53.
292 Rossino 2003, 227.
293 Gross 1979, 68, Lucas 1986, 3, 6, Rossino 2003, 13, m20–21, 68, 72, 77, 133–134, 157, 172–174, 186–190, 202–203, 232.
294 Garlinski 1985, 25, Kohniski 2012, 84, Invasion of Poland. https://en.wikipedia.org/wiki/Invasion_of_Poland
295 Kozlowski 1989, 7.
296 Lucas 1986, 5, 8–9.
297 Longerich 2010, 145.
298 Lucas 1986, 38–39, Latawski 2010, 132.
299 Matusak 1987, 21, Kulavig 2004, 135–136, Manley 2009, 32, 36–38.
300 Die Verfolgung und Ermordung der europäischen Juden durch das nationalsozialistische Deutschland 1933–1945. Besetzte sowjetische Gebiete unter deutscher Militärverwaltung, Baltikum und Transnistrien, Band 4 2011, 25.
301 Matusak 1987. 20.
302 Hartmann 2013, 76–78.
303 Wegner 1987, 299, An OSS Report on Wartime Population Changes in the Baltic.http://www.lituanus.org/1981_3/81_3_07.htm
304 World War II casualties of the Soviet Union. https://en.wikipedia.org/wiki/World_War_II_casualties_of_the_Soviet_Union
305 Ostarbeiter. https://en.wikipedia.org/wiki/Ostarbeiter, World War II casualties of the Soviet Union. https://en.wikipedia.org/wiki/World_War_II_casualties_of_the_Soviet_Union
306 Seppälä 1971, 34.
307 Kühnrich 1964,434.
308 Armeeoberkommando 11. Armeetagesbefehl 22 23.7.1941, Ludwigsburger Zentrale Stelle.
309 Divisionsbefehl SS-Division Wiking/Abt. Ia v. 11.6.1941, Betr.: Kampf gegen fdl. Heimtücke und Hinterlist. Sammelmappe mit Divisionsbefehlen und Befehlen aller Art der Abt. Ia, IIa. IIb, Ic, Ib mit Unterabteilungen 31.12.40 - Juni 1941, RS 3-5/3, BA-Militärarchiv, Freiburg.
310 The diary of Uuno Ström 22.9.1941, Mauno Jokipii's Collection, Pk-1140/38–39, The National Archives.
311 Krausnick & Buchheim & Broszat & Jacobsen 1968, 65.
312 Pohl 2008, 24.
313 Pohl 2008, 43.
314 Boll 2001, 73, Kruglov 2008, 273–274.
315 Matthäus 2004, 268.
316 Pohl 2008, 57, Lower 2011,15.
317 Browning 1998, xv, Arad 2009, 125, Larsen & Straede 2014, 96.
318 Arad 2009, 518–25, Kruglov 2008, 273, Lower 2012, 187.
319 Matthäus 2004, 245, Holmila 2013, 230.
320 Hartmann 2011, 64.
321 Boll 2001, 77, Hartmann 2011, 64.

322 MacLean 1999 I, 23–28.
323 Ereignismeldung UdSSR Nr. 24 16.7.1941, included in Die "Ereignismeldungen UdSSR" 1941 (2011), 132.
324 GK III. AK, Abt. Ic Nr. 478/41 geh. 2.10.1941, Anlage 214, p. 25, Auszugweise Abschrift aus Einzelanordnungen, RH 24-3/136, Bundesarchiv-Militärarchiv, Freiburg.
325 Evald O. Solbakken: Spesialrapport om tyskernes behandling av fanger og jöder 28.4.1945. S-1725 Legasjonen I Stockholm, del 1, serie Da, eske 453, Riksarkivet (Norge), Solbakken 1945, 131, Ulateig 2006, 158.
326 Evald O. Solbakken: Spesialrapport om tyskernes behandling av fanger og jöder 28.4.1945. S-1725 Legasjonen I Stockholm, del 1, serie Da, eske 453, Riksarkivet (Norge), Solbakken 1945. 132–133, Ulateig 2006, 158–159.
327 Falt for Norge. Hans Oppen Inn Memoriam. Article in an unknown newspaper 26.8.1941. The Archive of the SS-Investigation, File Bjørnstad-Taarneby, The National Archives.
328 Ibid., 135–137.
329 Sydnor 1990, 160.
330 Kûhnrich 1965, 74–75.
331 Slepyan 2006, 169.
332 Seppälä 1971, 48–49.
333 Ibid., 413.
334 Seppälä 1971, 162–167.
335 Overy 1997, 150.
336 Heaton 2001, 132.
337 Soviet partisans. https://en.wikipedia.org/wiki/Soviet_partisans
338 Gesin 2006.
339 Ereignismeldung UdSSR Nr. 14 6.7.1941, Nr. 24 16.7.1941, Nr 30 22.7.1941 and Nr. 37 29.7.1941, included in Die "Ereignismeldungen UdSSR" 1941, 84, 133, 163, 201.
340 Dallin 1957, 75.
341 Ibid., 76.
342 Eivind Reichelt. Avhort i Akebergsveiens fengsel den 5/10–1946, Oslo Politikammer, Landsviksavd., Riksarkivet (Oslo), Also the SS-Kriegsberichter Oswald Olsen mentions the same incident in his writing "Dagboksblader fra Sovjetsamveldet". Unknown paper and date. The Archive of the SS-Investigation, The National Archives.
343 Ibid., 138–140.
344 Recollection by Olavi Liesinen 21.12.1969. Mauno Jokipii's Collection, Pk-1140/27, The National Archives.
345 Ibid.
346 Kriegstagebuch des Finnisches-Freiwilligen-Bataillon der Waffen-SS 5.3.1942, SS-Aseveljet, Pk-1141/44–48, The National Archives, Suomalaisten Waffen-SS-vapaaehtoisten matrikkeli 1941–1943 (2013), 118.
347 The diary of Eino Mäki, The Archive of the SS-Investigation, The National Archives, Suomalaisten Waffen-SS-vapaaehtoisten matrikkeli 1941–1943 (2013), 156.
348 Heliste 2003, 3.
349 Heliste 2003, 3.
350 The diary of Kaj Duncker. Kaj Duncker's Collection, Pk-1821/4, The National Archives.
351 Turunen 2016, 130.
352 Kelin 2011, 6.
353 Mauno Jokipii's interview with Leo Heikurainen in 1959, Mauno Jokipii's Collection, Pk-1140/29–30, The National Archives.
354 The diary of Jaakko Hintikka 25.–26.11.1942, The Archive of the SS-Investigation, The National Archives.
355 Tyrkkö 1960, 159–160.
356 Berkhoff 2004, 11, 99, Liber 2016, 218.
357 Seppälä 1971, 34, Subtelny 2000, 460–461.
358 Berkhoff 2004, 102–103.
359 Christensen & Poulsen & Smith 2002, 98.
360 Berkhoff 2004, 106, 110, Liber 2016, 217.
361 Suomalaisia Ukrainan taisteluissa saksalaisten SS-joukkojen mukana. Rautaristejä suomalaisille vapaaehtoisille. Articles by Tk-rintamakirjeenvaihtaja Mauno P. Sjöstedt in the newspapers *Etelä-Suomen Sanomat* and *Länsi-Savo*, 10.1.1942, and in *Maaseudun tulevaisuus*,17.1.1942.
362 Tuomaala 2010, 65.
363 The recollection of Arvo Vidberg, the Archive of the SS-Investigation, The National Archives.
364 Kokemuksia ja tuntemuksia Saksan itärintamalta. Article by Markus Käenmäki in the newspaper *Ylä-Satakunta* 10.7.2003.
365 The diary of Martti Sinervo 13.9.1941, The Archive of the SS-Investigation, The National Archives.
366 Suomalaisten jääkärien 'tempauksia' Idän suurtaisteluissa. Article by Tauno Pajunen in *Hakkapeliitta*. No. 20, 1942.
367 Tyrkkö 1960, 95–96.
368 Porvali 2014, 101–102.
369 Korjus 1981, 92–93.
370 Scheurig 1991, 161, Römer 2008, Commissar Order. https://en.wikipedia.org/wiki/Commissar_Order
371 Hartmann 2011, 67.
372 Römer 2008, 576, 585, information given by Felix Römer, London.
373 Ulateig 2006, 232.
374 9. Panzer Division, Tätigkeitsberich (für die Zeit 22.6.1941–22.1.1942). Ludwigsburger Zentrale Stelle.
375 Hartmann 2010, 824.
376 Ilmari Autonen's letter to Unto Parvilahti 25.11.1941, Mauno

Jokipii's Collection, Pk-1141/1–3, The National Archives.

377 Jukka Tyrkkö's letter to Unto Boman 31.3.1942, Mauno Jokipii's Collection, Pk-1141/11–13, The National Archives, Swanström 2018, 162–164.

378 The diary of Kalervo Kurkiala 11.8.1942, Mauno Jokipii's Collection, Pk-1140/23, The National Archives.

379 Suomalaispataljoonan ensimmäinen taistelu Kaukasiassa. Nopealla hyökkäyksellä karkoitettiin kasakat asemistaan. Article by "T." (= Jukka Tyrkkö) in *Aamulehti*, 23.9.1942.

380 Vernehmungsniederschrift 4.3.1964 unterschrieben von Manfred Schönfelder, Ludwigsburger Zentrale Stelle.

381 Interview with Felix Steiner by Mauno Jokipii 27.6.1961. Mauno Jokipii's Collection, Pk-1140/33, The National Archives.

382 Yrjö Kaila: Recollections 1958, Yrjö Kaila's Collection, Pk-2356/8–9, The National Archives.

383 Lappi-Seppälä 1945, 91–93.

384 The diary of Ahti Paikkala, 22.6.1941, Mauno Jokipii's Collection, Pk-1140/24, The National Archives.

385 The diary of Martti Uusi-Jaakkola 22.6.1941, The Archive of the SS-Investigation, The National Archives.

386 The diary of Keijo Kääriäinen 23.6.1941, Mauno Jokipii's Collection, Pk-1140/34–35, The National Archives.

387 Recollection by Olavi Liesinen 21.12.1969. Mauno Jokipii's Collection, Pk-1140/27, The National Archives.

388 Konttinen 1996, 43.

389 Evald O. Solbakken: Spesialrapport om tyskernes behandling av fanger og jöder 28.4.1945. S-1725 Legasjonen I Stockholm, del 1, serie Da, eske 453, Riksarkivet (Norge), Solbakken 1945,129.

390 Amar 2015, 93, Sorlei 2015, 247.

391 Die Verfolgung und Ermordung der europäischen Juden durch das nationalsozialistische Deutschland 1933–1945. Besetzte sowjetische Gebiete unter deutscher Militärverwaltung, Baltikum und Transnistrien, Band 7 2011, 865–872, Band 8 2016, 739–744.

392 von Frijtag Drabbe Künzel 2015, xiii.

393 Kriegs-Tagebuch – II./SS.Rgt. Westland 1.7.1941, The Archive of the SS-Investigation, The National Archives.

394 Amar 2015, 94.

395 Rhodes 2002, 59, Hartmann 2010, 672.

396 Jokipii 1996, 238–239, Rhodes 2002, 64–66, Verbrechen der Wehrmacht 2002, 94–99, Deutscher Osten 1939–1945 (2003), 79–84, Kruglov 2008, 273, Hartmann 2010, 672, Longerich 2010, 194, Himka 2011, 209–245, Polonsky 2012, 425, Amar 2015, 95, Sørlie 2015, 246, Lviv. https://en.wikipedia.org/wiki/Lviv, Lviv pogroms. http://en.wikipedia.org/wiki/Lviv_pogroms

397 Struve 2015, 376–379, information given by Kai Struve, Halle.

398 Yones 2004, 75–76, 79.

399 Yones 2004, 77.

400 Ibid. 78, Struve 2015, 298–304.

401 Yones 2004, 80, Antisemitism. An Annotated Bibliography 2002, 336.

402 Jokipii 1996, 190, Struve 2015, 253–255, 260, 354–360.

403 Kochanski 2012, 260.

404 Mick 2016, 291.

405 Gerstenfeld-Martiel 1993, 53.

406 Ibid., 53–54.

407 Struve 2015, 307–322.

408 Ibid., 323–336.

409 Ibid., 336–343.

410 Ibid., 350–353.

411 Information given by Kai Struve, Halle, Germany.

412 Ibid., 54–55.

413 The Encyclopedia of the Jewish Diaspora, Poland Series: Lwów Volume (Lviv, Ukraine. https://www.jewishgen.org/yizkor/lviv/lviv.html

414 Erwin Schulz. https://en.wikipedia.org/wiki/Erwin_Schulz

415 Yones 2004, 78.

416 Testimony by Hans Wilhelm Isenmann, The Archive of the SS-Investigation, The National Archives. Struve 2015, 363, Lower 2005, 235, Ulateig 2006, 80.

417 Struve 2015, 361–362.

418 Krausnick & Wilhelm 1981, 186-187, Dean 2000, 20–21, Yones 2004, 78, Rossolinski-Liebe 2013, 220–236, Aman 2015, 94–101.

419 Struve 2015, 253.

420 Pohl 2009, 244–245, Struve 2015, 255–256.

421 Ereignismeldung UdSSR Nr. 13 5.7.1941, Included in Die "Ereignismeldungen UdSSR" 1941 (2011), 82, Struve 2015, 369.

422 Pohl 2009, 244–245.

423 Felix Landau beschreibt Anfang Juli 1941, wie er als Mitglied einers Einsatzkommandos in Lemberg Exekutionen teilnimmt. Die Verfolgung und Ermordung der europäischen Juden durch das nationalsozialistische Deutschland 1933–1945. Besetzte sowjetische Gebiete unter deutscher Militärverwaltung, Baltikum und Transnistrien, Band 8 2016, 155–157.

424 Kochanski 2012, 292, The Encyclopedia of the Jewish Diaspora, Poland Series: Lwów Volume (Lviv, Ukraine), https://www.jewishgen.org/yizkor/lviv/lviv.html

425 Boll 2001, 77.

426 Mick 2016, 290–292, Struve 2015, 307–309.

427 Interview with Edmond Henri le Roux, DANS, The Haag,

Kleijn-Reurs 2018. The Archive of the SS-Investigation, The National Archives.

428 Med Divisjon "Wiking". Fra Lublin til Kaukasus. Newspaper writing in the Norwegian SS-paper *Germaneren* 1944 by SS-Rottenführer Per Pedersen, The Archive of the SS-Investigation, The National Archives.

429 Emberland & Kott 2012, 238.

430 Halle 1972, 15, Ulateig 2006, 185, Olav Tuff (91): Vi brente en kirke med sivilister. https://www.nrk.no/dokumentar/--nordmenn-deltok-i-drap-pa-sivile-1.11262316 , En krig for livet. https://www.dt.no/nyheter/en-krig-for-livet/s/2-2.1748-1.3177758?service=print , Olav Tuff memories. https://universalcuriosity.wordpress.com/2016/06/

431 Ulateig 2006, 136.

432 Information given by Sigurd Sørlie, Oslo, Norway.

433 Ulateig 2006, 130–133.

434 The diary of Helge Laerum, The Archive of the SS-Investigation, The National Archives.

435 Sørlie 2015, 212, information given by Sigurd Sørlie, Oslo, Norway.

436 Ulateig 2006, 80.

437 "Vi i NS bør gjøre alt vi kan for å støtte Tyskland i dets kamp, for nå gjelder det Europas være eller ikke være". SS-man Josef Hansen førteller om sine upplevelser I det røde "paradis". Hansen's writing in *Vestfold Presse* 10–1.1942.

438 Sørlie 2015, 332.

439 Jokipii 1996, 191.

440 The diary of Martti Uusi-Jaakkola 1.7.1941, The Archive of the SS-Investigation, The National Archives.

441 The diary of Reino Suonio. The Archive of the SS-Investigation, The National Archives.

442 Kokemuksia ja tuntemuksia Saksan itärintamalta. Article by Markus Käenmäki in the newspaper *Ylä-Satakunta* 10.7.2003.

443 Kaj Duncker's diary 1.7.1941, Kaj Duncker's Collection, Pk-1821/1, The National Archives.

444 Diary of Pentti Nikkola 1.7.1941, The Archive of the SS-Investigation, Norway. The National Archives.

445 Ensio Pihkala's diary 1.7.1941, Mauno Jokipii's Collection, Pk-1618/5, The National Archives.

446 Parvilahti 1959, 71.

447 The diary of Keijo Kääriäinen 1.7.1941, Mauno Jokipii's Collection, Pk-1140/34–35, The National Archives.

448 Jokipii 1996, 189.

449 Lappi-Seppälä 1945, 91–92.

450 Ibid., 92.

451 The diary of Ahti Paikkala 1.7.1941, Mauno Jokipii's Collection, Pk-1140/24, The National Archives.

452 Parvilahti 1959, 70.

453 The diary of Jaakko Lakeala 3.7.1941, The Archive of the SS-Investigation, The National Archives.

454 The diary of Martti Koivula 12.5.1941, The Archive of the SS-Investigation, The National Archives.

455 The diary of Jaakko Lakeala 3.7.1941, The Archive of the SS-Investigation, The National Archives.

456 The diary of Sakari Pöyhönen 1.7.1941. Mauno Jokipii's Collection, Pk-1618/5, The National Archives.

457 Struve 2015, 223, 564.

458 The diary of Kaj Duncker 2.7.1941, Kaj Duncker's Collection, Pk-1821/1, The National Archives.

459 The diary of Jan Olij 2.7.1941, CABR, Den Haag, Kleijn-Reurs 2018. The Archive of the SS-Investigation, The National Archives.

460 "That's Not The Germans" (report of Olszanica/Vilshanitsa atrocities, in a Lviv online paper). https://zaxid.net/to_ne_ti_nimtsi_n1266107

461 The diary of Martti Uusi-Jaakkola 2.7.1941, The Archive of the SS-Investigation, The National Archives.

462 The diary of Kaj Duncker 2.7.1941, Kaj Duncker's Collection, Pk-1821/1, The National Archives, Struve 2015, 564.

463 The diary of Martti Uusi-Jaakkola 2.7.1941, The Archive of the SS-Investigation, The National Archives.

464 Muuan "arvostelu". Article by Sakari Lappi-Seppälä in *Vapaa Sana,* 28.11.1945.

465 Parvilahti 1959, 67, Strassner 1968, 38, Schütz 1999, 83–84, Mathias 2001, 142, van Roekel 2011, 136–137,Gyllenhaal & Westberg 2008, 292, Holmila 2013, 234–237, Swanström 2018, 236–238.

466 Lappi-Seppälä 1945, 86, Steiner 1992, 92.

467 The diary of Kaj Duncker, Kaj Duncker's Collection, Pk-1821/1, The National Archives.

468 Kriegs-Tagebuch – II./SS-Rgt. Westland 2.7.1941, The Archive of the SS-Investigation, The National Archives.

469 The diary of Pieter Willems 2.7.1941, NIOD, Kleijn-Reurs 2018. The Archive of the SS-Investigation, The National Archives.

470 The diary of Martinus Weers 2.7.1941, NIOD, Kleijn-Reurs 2018. The Archive of the SS-Investigation, The National Archives.

471 The diary of Ensio Pihkala 13.6.–27.7.1941, Jukka Tyrkkö's Collection Pk-1618/5, The National Archives.

472 The diary of Ahti Paikkala, April 1941–18.2.1941, Mauno Jokipii's Collection, Pk-1140/24, The National Archives.

473 The diary of Kaj Duncker 2.7.1941, Kaj Duncker's Collection, Pk-1821/1, The National Archives.

474 Carlheinz Behnke: Geschichte der 5. SS-Artillerie Messbatterie, The Archive of the Truppenkameradschaft

5. SS-Panzer-Division "Wiking", B 436, Bundesarchiv-Militärarchiv, Freiburg.
475 Sarasalo 2000, 4.
476 Yrjö Kaila: Recollections 1958. Yrjö Kaila's Collection, Pk2357/9, The National Archives.
477 The diary of Martinus Rademaker 2.7.1941, NIOD, Amsterdam, Kleijn-Reurs 2018. The Archive of the SS-Investigation, The National Archives.
478 The diary of Martti Uusi-Jaakkola 2.7.1941, The Archive of the SS-Investigation, The National Archives.
479 Recollection by Ludwig Ergert 29.3.1995, Tod Wäckerle, The Archive of the SS-Investigation, The National Archives.
480 Trigg 2015, 91–92.
481 Information given by Kai Struve, Halle, Germany.
482 Sørlie 2015, 315, 329.
483 Strassner 1968, 38.
484 The diary of Martinus Rademaker and Ferdiand Frehé 2.7.1941, NIOD, Amsterdam, Kleijn-Reurs 2018. The Archive of the SS-Investigation, The National Archives.
485 Christensen & Poulsen & Smith 2001, 94, 446–447.
486 The diary of Martti Koivula 12.5.1941, The Archive of the SS-Investigation. Vol. SS-vapaaehtoisten päiväkirjat (lisäykset), The National Archives.
487 Holmila 2013, 235, 237.
488 Jokipii 1996, 192, 759–760.
489 Holmila 2013, 234–237, Swanström 2018, 239.
490 Strassner 1968, 38, Krabbe 1976, 41.
491 Struve 2015, 563.
492 Kriegs-Tagebuch – II./SS-Rgt. Westland 1.7.1941, The Archive of the SS-Investigation, The National Archives.
493 Ibid. 353, information given by Cees Kleijn and Stijn Reurs, Amsterdam, the Netherlands.
494 Nederlandse nazi's vermoordden boere. Article in *Limburgsch Dagblad* 30.5.1986, De Zevene Kompagnie schoot 22 Russische burgers dood in 1941: de versewgen misdaad van Nederlandse SS-ers. Article in *Het Vrije Volk* 30.5.1986.
495 Russen vragen Lubbers SS'e rs ti berechten. Article in *Het Vrije Volk* 20.6.1986.
496 The diary of Ferdinand Frehé 1.7.1941, NIOD, Amsterdam, Kleijn-Reurs 2018. The Archive of the SS-Investigation, The National Archives, van Roekel 2011, 136.
497 Ibid.
498 Elo 2006, 63–77.
499 The diary of Sakari Pöyhönen 2.7.1941. Mauno Jokipii's Collection, Pk-1618/5, The National Archives.
500 Emberland & Kott 2012, 239, Struve 2015, 563.
501 Larsson 2014, 37.
502 De Zevene Kompagnie shoot 22 Russische burgers dood in 1941: de versewgen misdaad van Nederlandse SS-ers. Article in *Het Vrije Volk* 30.5.1986.
503 Recollection by Landoald Stücker 7.10.1987, The Archive of the SS-Investigation, The National Archives.
504 Elo 2006, 23.
505 Butler 1979, 45, Heinz Fanslau. https://de.wikipedia.org/wiki/Heinz_Fanslau
506 Investigation record with Thor-Björn Weckström 662/1947 24.11.1947, ValPo II, Vol. 46 SS-miehet, The National Archives, Teloittiko "Kurre" juutalaisia? Article by Pasi Lehtinen in *Ilta-Sanomat* 26.3.2014.
507 Ibid, Holmila 2013, 232–233.
508 Suomalaiset vapaaehtoiset SS:n teloitusoperaatiossa itärintamalla. Article in *Demari* 11.2.1998 by Boris Salomon.
509 Westberg 1983, 581.
510 Ptk. N:o 636/47 Sakari Lappi-Seppälä, ValPo II, Vol. 46, The National Archives, Lappi-Seppälä 1945, 86–87.
511 Lappi-Seppälä 1945, 88.
512 Ibid. 89, Holmila 2013, 232.
513 Lappi-Seppälä 1945, 89–90.
514 Ibid. 86–91.
515 Ptk. N:o 636/47 Sakari Lappi-Seppälä, ValPo II, Vol. 46 SS-miehet, The National Archives.
516 Elo 2006, 23, 63–77.
517 Mauno Jokipii's interview with Christian Rosenbrjöijer, Mauno Jokipii's Collection, Pk-1140/29–30, The National Archives.
518 The diary of Veikko Hallavo,5. or 6.7.1941, Mauno Jokipii's Collection, Pk-1140/36–37, The National Archives.
519 Ibid., diary note 8.7.1941.
520 Boll 2002,62–63.
521 Struve 2015, 584–585, 669, Ein angehöriger der 295. Infanteridivision schreibt Anfang Juli 1941 die Ermordung Hunderter Ukrainer in Zloczow debn Juden zu. Bericht über Zloczow, gez. Wittke, o.D. Die Verfolgung und Ermordung der europäischen Juden durch das nationalsozialistische Deutschland 1933–1945. Besetzte sowjetische Gebiete unter deutscher Militärverwaltung, Baltikum und Transnistrien, Band 8 2016, 159.
522 Tannenbaum 1986, 165.
523 Szlojme Mayer, ed. *Der Untergang fun Złoczów* The Destruction of Złoczów (Zolochiv, Ukraine). https://www.jewishgen.org/Yizkor/Zolochiv/Zolochiv.html
524 Ibid.
525 Tennenbaum 1986, 167–168.
526 Szlojme Mayer, ed. *Der Untergang fun Złoczów* The Destruction of Złoczów (Zolochiv, Ukraine). https://www.jewishgen.org/Yizkor/Zolochiv/Zolochiv.html

527 Ibid, Struve 2015, 570.
528 Boll 2002, 67–69; The City of Złoczów (Zolochiv, Ukraine). https://www.jewishgen.org/Yizkor/Zolochiv1/Zolochiv1.html#TOC
529 Ibid. 69–70, Emberland & Kott 2012, 239–240, The City of Złoczów (Zolochiv, Ukraine). https://www.jewishgen.org/Yizkor/Zolochiv1/Zolochiv1.html#TOC, The Destruction of Złoczów (Zolochiv, Ukraine). https://www.jewishgen.org/Yizkor/Zolochiv/Zolochiv.html
530 Altman, S.: Haunting Memories, Zolochiv, Ukraine, https://jewishgen.org/Yizkor/Zolochiv1/zole029.html, Bartov 2007, 174, Struve 2015, 576.
531 The City of Złoczów (Zolochiv, Ukraine). https://www.jewishgen.org/Yizkor/Zolochiv1/Zolochiv1.html#TOC The Destruction of Złoczów (Zolochiv, Ukraine). https://www.jewishgen.org/Yizkor/Zolochiv/Zolochiv.html
532 Information given by Kai Struve, Halle, Germany.
533 Ibid., The City of Złoczów (Zolochiv, Ukraine). https://www.jewishgen.org/Yizkor/Zolochiv1/Zolochiv1.html#TOC, Helmuth Groscurth. https://en.wikipedia.org/wiki/Helmuth_Groscurth, Struve 2015, 578.
534 Szlojme Mayer, ed. *Der Untergang fun Złoczów* The Destruction of Złoczów (Zolochiv, Ukraine). 1947, 14. https://www.jewishgen.org/Yizkor/Zolochiv/Zolochiv.html
535 Boll 2002, 70–71, 75, Bartov 2007, 170, Longerich 2010, 194, Emberland & Kott 2012, 238, Polonsky 2012, 426–427, Zolochiv, https://en.wikipedia.org/wiki/Zolochiv The City of Złoczów (Zolochiv, Ukraine) https://www.jewishgen.org/Yizkor/Zolochiv1/Zolochiv1.html#TOC
536 Kriegs-Tagebuch – II./SS-Rgt. Westland 3.7.1941, The Archive of the SS-Investigation, The National Archives, Struve 2015, 571.
537 Ibid., 74–75.
538 Struve 2015, 566.
539 Boll 2002, 69–71
540 The City of Złoczów (Zolochiv, Ukraine). https://www.jewishgen.org/Yizkor/Zolochiv1/Zolochiv1.html#TOC
541 Boll 2002, 71, 75, 77.
542 Information given by Kai Struve, Halle, Germany.
543 Ereignismeldung UdSSR Nr. 24 16.7.1941, included in Die "Ereignismeldungen UdSSR" 1941 (2011), 133.
544 Boll 2002, 72.
545 "Zlosczow" – Encyclopedia of Jewish Communities in Poland, Volume II (Zolochiv, Ukraine). The City of Złoczów, (Zolochiv, Ukraine). https://www.jewishgen.org/Yizkor/Zolochiv1/Zolochiv1.html#TOC
546 Ereignismeldung UdSSR Nr. 19 11.7.1941, Records of the Reich Leader of the SS and Chief of the German Police, Part 1, RG 242, T175, Microfilm, Roll 223, The National Archives and Records Administration of the United States (NARA), Reitlinger 1956, 157, Stein 1966, 272–273, Gyllenhaal & Westberg 2008, 292, Ibid., 240, Zboriv. https://en.wikipedia.org/wiki/Zboriv, Jewish Families from Zborov, Ukraine, https://www.geni.com/projects/Jewish-Families-from-Zborov-Ukraine/29340
547 Struve 2015, 568–569.
548 Boll 2002, 73.
549 Ibid.
550 Ereignismeldung UdSSR Nr. 19 11.7.1941, included in Die "Ereignismeldungen UdSSR" 1941 (2011), 104, Struve 2015, 569.
551 The diary of Martinus Rademaker 2.7.1941, NIOD, Amsterdam, Kleijn-Reurs 2018. The Archive of the SS-Investigation, The National Archives.
552 The diary of Jan Olij, CABR, Den Haag, Kleijn-Reurs 2018. The Archive of the SS-Investigation, The National Archives.
553 Sørlie 2015, 337.
554 The diary of Ensio Pihkala 3.7.1941, Pk-1618/5, The National Archives.
555 The diary of Kaj Duncker 3.7.1941, Kaj Duncker's Collection, Pk-1821/1, The National Archives.
556 The diary of Sakari Pöyhönen 1.7.1941. Mauno Jokipii's Collection, Pk-1618/5, The National Archives.
557 Ereignismeldung UdSSR Nr. 19 11.7.1941, Records of the Reichs Leader of the SS and Chief of the German Police, Part 1, RG 242, T175, Microfilm, Roll 223, The National Archives and Records Administration of the United States (NARA), also included in Die "Ereignismeldungen UdSSR" 1941 (2011), 104, Reitlinger 1956, 157, Stein 1966, 272–273, Gyllenhaal & Westberg 2008, 292, Struve 2015, 588.
558 Struve 2015, 588, 669.
559 "Zborow" – Encyclopedia of Jewish Communities in Poland, Volume II (Ukraine). https://www.jewishgen.org/yizkor/pinkas_poland/pol2_00202.html
560 "Zborow" – Encyclopedia of Jewish Communities in Poland, Volume II (Ukraine). https://www.jewishgen.org/yizkor/pinkas_poland/pol2_00202.html
561 Struve 2015, 586–587, Zboriv. https://en.wikipedia.org/wiki/Zboriv, Jewish Families from Zborov, Ukraine, https://www.geni.com/projects/Jewish-Families-from-Zborov-Ukraine/29340
562 Struve 2015, 587–588.
563 The diary of Ferdinand Frehé, NIOD, Amsterdam, Kleijn-Reurs 2018. The Archive of the SS-Investigation, The National Archives.
564 The diary of Jaakko Lakeala 4.7.1941, The Archive of the

SS-Investigation, The National Archives.

565 Struve 2015, 589–590.

566 Ibid.

567 The diary of Martti Uusi-Jaakkola, The Archive of the SS-Investigation, The National Archives.

568 Helsingin kaupungin raastuvanoikeuden 8 osaston 2 jaoston rikosasiain kirjavihko N:o 91/1958, The Magistrate's Court of Helsinki, The National Archives.

569 Helsingin kaupungin raastuvanoikeuden 8 osaston 2 jaoston rikosasiain kirjavihko N:o 91/1958, The Magistrate's Court of Helsinki, The National Archives, Parvilahden juttu siirtyi lokakuulle. Mielenkiintoisia todistajalausuntoja. Article in *Suomen Sosialidemokraatti,* 12.9.1958.

570 Lappi-Seppälä 1945, 105–106.

571 Struve 2015, 590.

572 Helsingin kaupungin raastuvanoikeuden 8 osaston 2 jaoston rikosasiain kirjavihko N:o 91/1958, The Magistrate's Court of Helsinki, The National Archives, Parvilahden juttu siirtyi lokakuulle. Mielenkiintoisia todistajalausuntoja. Article in *Suomen Sosialidemokraatti* 12.9.1958.

573 Unto Boman: Selostus toiminnastani Saksassa 1941–1944. ValPo II, Y.D. 1893/18.8.47 and interrogation with "20a" (= Matti Tamminen), ValPo's personal dossier on Parvilahti (Boman), Unto Ilmari, The Archive of ValPo, The National Archives.

574 The diary of Keijo Kääriäinen 4.7.1941, Mauno Jokipii's Collection, Pk-1140/34–35, The National Archives.

575 The diary of Pentti Nikkola 2.–3.7.1941, The Archive of the SS-Investigation, The National Archives.

576 The diary of Keijo Kääriäinen 4.7.1941, Mauno Jokipii's Collection, Pk-1140/34–35, The National Archives.

577 The diary of Pentti Nikkola 2.–3.7.1941, The Archive of the SS-Investigation, The National Archives.

578 Yrjö Tenomaa's letter to his mother 12.10.1941, Mauno Jokipii's Collection, Pk-1140/36–37, The National Archive, Jokipii 1996, 196.

579 Polish roots. http://polishroots.org/GeographyMaps/SlownikGeograficzny/tabid/61/Default.aspx

580 Pidhorodtsi. http://nl.wikipedia.org/wiki/Pidhorodtsi

581 "Podhajce" – Encyclopedia of Jewish Communities in Poland, Volume II (Ukraine). https://www.jewishgen.org/yizkor/pinkas_poland/pol2_00410.html,
The Destruction of our City - Podhajce https://jewishgen.org/Yizkor/Podhajce/pod209.html

582 Pidhirtsi. https://en.wikipedia.org/wiki/Pidhirtsi

583 Trial testimony by Hendrikus Valks 1.6.1977. Collection 461. Collectie process, Inv. Nr. 21, NIOD, Kleijn-Reurs 2018. The Archive of the SS-Investigation, The National Archives.

584 Information given by Cees Kleijn, Amsterdam, The Netherlands.

585 Ibid., Vier Duitsers en twee Finnen voerden executies uit. Article by Mari de Henk in *De Telegraaf,* 9.6.1977, Kleijn-Reurs 2018. The Archive of the SS-Investigation, The National Archives.

586 Ibid.

587 Elo 2006, 63–77.

588 Vier Duitsers en twee Finnen voerden executies uit. Article by Mari de Henk in *De Telegraaf,* 9.6.1977

589 Ibid.

590 Pohl 1996, 70.

591 Struve 2015, 486, The Encyclopedia of Jewish Life Before and During the Holocaust 2001, 1363, The Jewish Community of Urycz. https://dbs.bh.org.il/place/urycz, Enter 'The Dutchman' Pieter Menten. https://www.jewishgen.org/yizkor/Galicia3/gal122.html

592 Trial testimony by Hendrikus Valks 1.6.1977. Collection 461. Collectie proces, Inv. Nr. 21, NIOD, Kleijn-Reurs 2018. The Archive of the SS-Investigation, The National Archives.

593 Trial testimony by Jan Henri Albert Keuter 27.6.1977. Collection 461. Collectie proces, Inv. Nr. 21, NIOD, Kleijn-Reurs 2018. The Archive of the SS-Investigation, The National Archives.

594 Vier Duitsers en twee Finnen voerden executies uit. Article by Mari de Henk in *De Telegraaf,* 9.6.1977, Kleijn-Reurs 2018. The Archive of the SS-Investigation, The National Archives, O'Neil 2016, 73–74.

595 Rhodes 2002, 59, Ulateig 2016, 165, Struve 2015, 591.

596 Verbrechen der Wehrmacht 2002, 100–122, Bartov 2007, 153, Longerich 2010, 194, Tarnopol Ghetto. https://en.wikipedia.org/wiki/Tarnopol_Ghetto, "Tarnopol" – Encyclopedia of Jewish Communities in Poland, Volume II (Ternopil, Ukraine). https://www.jewishgen.org/Yizkor/pinkas_poland/pol2_00234.html
Ternopil. https://en.wikipedia.org/wiki/Ternopil

597 Bartov 2007, 154, Kruglov 2008, 274.

598 Strassner 1968, 38, Krabbe 1976, 41, Mathias 2001, 143, Kurowski 2013, 30.

599 Struve 2015, 592, 603–611.

600 Ulateig 2006, 172–173, Struve 2015, 292–593.

601 Struve 2015, 602.

602 Tarnopol" – Encyclopedia of Jewish Communities in Poland, Volume II (Ternopil, Ukraine). https://www.jewishgen.org/Yizkor/pinkas_poland/pol2_00234.html

603 Ibid.

604 Tarnopol" – Encyclopedia of Jewish Communities in Poland, Volume II (Ternopil, Ukraine). https://www.jewish-

gen.org/Yizkor/pinkas_poland/pol2_00234.html
605 Information given by Kai Struve, Halle, Germany.
606 Emberland–Kott 2012, 240.
607 Ereignismeldung UdSSR Nr. 14 6.7.1941, Nr. 19 11.7.1941 and Nr. 24 16.7.1941, included in Die "Ereignismeldungen UdSSR" 1941 (2011), 84, 104, 133, Struve 2015, 596–597, 601–602.
608 The diary of Ferdinand Frehé 3.7.1941, NIOD, Amsterdam, Kleijn-Reurs 2018. The Archive of the SS-Investigation, The National Archives.
609 The diary of Martinus Rademaker 2.7.1941, NIOD, Amsterdam, Kleijn-Reurs 2018. The Archive of the SS-Investigation, The National Archives.
610 The diary of Martinus Weers 4.7.1941, NIOD, Amsterdam, Kleijn-Reurs 2018. The Archive of the SS-Investigation, The National Archives, van Roekel 2011, 153.
611 Christensen & Poulsen & Smith 2002, 96, 447.
612 The diary of Pieter Willems ca 4.7.1941, NIOD, Amsterdam, Kleijn-Reurs 2018. The Archive of the SS-Investigation, The National Archives, van Roekel 2014, 154–155.
613 Ulateig 2006, 170.
614 Ibid., 154.
615 The diary of Pentti Nikkola 5.7.1941, The Archive of the SS-Investigation, The National Archives.
616 The diary of Reino Suonio 5.7.1941, The Archive of the SS-Investigation, The National Archives.
617 The diary of Jaakko Lakeala 5.7.1941, The Archive of the SS-Investigation, The National Archives.
618 Kriegs-Tagebuch – II./SS-Rgt. Westland 4.7.1941, The Archive of the SS-Investigation, The National Archives.
619 The diary of Ensio Pihkala 4.7.1941, Jukka Tyrkkö's Collection, Pk-1618/5, The National Archives.
620 The diary of Ahti Paikkala, Mauno Jokipii's Collection, Pk-1140/24, The National Archives, The German Army and Genocide 1999, 82–83.
621 The diary of Sakari Pöyhönen 1.7.1941. Mauno Jokipii's Collection, Pk-1618/5, The National Archives.
622 Konttinen 1996, 42–43.
623 Ibid.
624 The diary of Martti Koivula 12.5.1941. The Archive of the SS-Investigation, Vol. SS-vapaaehtoisten päiväkirjat (lisäykset), The National Archives.
625 Recollection by Olavi Liesinen 21.12.1969, Mauno Jokipii's Collection, Pk-1140/27, The National Archives, Jokipii 1968, 213, Kokemuksia ja tuntemuksia Saksan itärintamalta. Article by Markus Käenmäki in the newspaper *Ylä-Satakunta* 10.7.2003.
626 Ibid.
627 Mauno Jokipii's interview with Christian Rösenbröijer, Mauno Jokipii's Collection, Pk-1140/29–30, The National Archives.
628 Struve 2015, 570.
629 Records of the Militärgerichtshof Nr. II, Fall IV 2.9.1947, Staatsarchiv Nürnberg.
630 Erwin Tschenstscher. https://de.wikipedia.org/wiki/Erwin_Tschentscher
631 Records of the Militärgerichtshof Nr. II, Fall IV 2.9.1947, Staatsarchiv Nürnberg.
632 File Walter Braunagel (5. SS-Div. Wiking) AR-Z 70/1968, Ludwigsburger Zentrale Stelle.
633 Rhodes 2002, 63, Ulateig 2006, 77–79, 198–200, Struve 2015, 570.
634 File Walter Braunagel (5. SS-Div. Wiking) AR-Z 70/1968, Ludwigsburger Zentrale Stelle.
635 Records of the Militärgerichtshof Nr. II, Fall IV 2.9.1947, Staatsarchiv Nürnberg.
636 Mikulince, Milkulintsy, Ukraine. https://kehilalinks.jewishgen.org/suchostaw/sl_mikulince.htm
637 Information repeated by Manfred Schönberger 4.5.1964 to the Landeskriminalamt Baden-Württemberg. Vernehmungsniederschrift unterschrieben von Manred Schönberger, Ludwigsburger Zentrale Stelle, Struve 2015, 670, information given by Kai Struve, Halle, Germany.
638 Emberland-Kott 2012, 241, information given by Kai Struve, Halle, Germany.
639 Nusia Schweizer Horowitz: My Town During the Second World War, The Life of Horrors of Mrs. Klars Reich-Schrenzel. Recorded and written down by Mr. Schmulevic on January 19th, 1955, Pelz, Zalmand: A Baby Girl Captured by the Gentiles. The Tragedy of our town Mikulince and the Pelz family, and Kleinman, N., A Page in Jewish History. Mikulince, Mikulintsy, Ukraine. https://kehilalinks.jewishgen.org/suchostaw/sl_mikulince.htm, Mikulince Yizkor Book (Mikulintsy, Ukraine), https://www.jewishgen.org/yizkor/mikulintsy/mikulintsy.html
640 Ibid.
641 Ulateig 2006, 151–152, Nusia Schweizer Horowitz: My Town During the Second World War. Mikulince, Mikulintsy, Ukraine. https://www.jewishgen.org/yizkor/Mikulintsy/miko49.html
642 Horowitz: My Town... https://www.jewishgen.org/yizkor/Mikulintsy/miko49.html
643 Leon M. Kahane: Mikulince – Our Friendly Town, ibid.
644 Information given by Kai Struve, Halle, Germany.
645 Ibid.
646 Evald O. Solbakken: Spesialrapport om tyskernes behandling av fanger og jöder 28.4.1945. S-1725 Legasjonen

I Stockholm, del 1, serie Da, eske 453, Riksarkivet (Norge), Solbakken 1945, 129–130, Ulateig 2006, 159, Emberland & Kott 2012, 240.

647 Ulateig 2006, 162.

648 Ibid., 163.

649 Kriegs-Tagebuch – II./SS-Rgt. Westland 5.7.1941, The Archive of the SS-Investigation, The National Archives.

650 Hrymayliv (Grymailiv, Grimailov, Grymailov, Grzymalov). https://yahadmap.org/#village/hrymailiv-grymailiv-grimailov-grymailov-grzymalov-ternopil-ukraine.85

651 Emberland & Kott 2012, 241, Struve 2015, 626–628.

652 The diary of Ferdinand Frehé 5.7.1941, NIOD, Amsterdam, Kleijn-Reurs 2018. The Archive of the SS-Investigation, The National Archives, van Roekel 2014, 157.

653 The diary of Ensio Pihkala 5.7.1941, Jukka Tyrkkö's Collection, Pk-1618/5, The National Archives.

654 Ibid.

655 Struve 2015, 621–625, 669.

656 Struve 2015, 541, information given by Kai Struve, Halle, Germany.

657 Recollection by Yitzchak Goldflies "Survival in Camp" and Abraham.Witoff "Ukrainians and Poles Helped to Murder the Jews". Chorostków, Ukraine. https://www.jewishgen.org/yizkor/khorostkov/Khorostkov.html#TOC, information given by Kai Struve, Halle, Germany.

658 The diary of Kaj Duncker 5.7.1941, Kaj Duncker's Collection, Pk-1821/1, The National Archives.

659 Information given by Kai Struve, Halle, Germany.

660 Kriegs-Tagebuch – II./SS-Rgt. Westland 5.-6–7.1941, The Archive of the SS-Investigation, The National Archives.

661 The diary of Ferdinand Frehé 6.7.1941, NIOD, Amsterdam, Kleijn-Reurs 2018. The Archive of the SS-Investigation, The National Archives, van Roekel 2014, 148–149.

662 van Roekel 2011, 149.

663 Ibid., 154–155.

664 Ibid., 156.

665 van Roekel 2011, 150.

666 The diary of Kaj Duncker 5.7.1941, Kaj Duncker's Collection, Pk-1821/1, The National Archives.

667 The diary of Martti Koivula 12.5.1941, The Archive of the SS-Investigation, Vol. SS-vapaaehtoisten päiväkirjat (lisäykset), The National Archives.

668 Lower 2005, 53–54, 225. Mick 2016, 295.

669 Mathias 2001, 143–144.

670 Bartov 2007, 106, Emberland & Kott 2012, 242.

671 Kurt Lundin schildert der schwedischen Polizei am 24. Dezember 1943, wie die SS im Juli 1941 in Husiatyn Juden ermorderte. Die Verfolgung und Ermordung der europäischen Juden durch das nationalsozialistische Deutschland 1933–1945. Besetzte sowjetische Gebiete unter deutscher Militärverwaltung, Baltikum und Transnistrien, Band 8 2016, 503–505.

672 Solbakken 1945, 293, Schön 2001, 170, Gyllenhaal 2008, 293.

673 Hartmann 2010, 824.

674 Proskurov 2012, 1449–1452, Proskurov. The Untold Stories. The Murder of Jews in the Occupied Terriories of the Former USSR. http://www.yadvashem.org/untoldstories/database/index.asp?cid=748

675 Kruglov 2008, 274.

676 The diary of Ensio Pihkala 11.7.1941, Pk-1618/, The National Archives.

677 The diary of Reino Suonio, The Archive of the SS-Investigation, The National Archives.

678 The diary of Martti Uusi-Jaakkola 11.7.1941, The Archive of the SS-Investigation, The National Archives.

679 The diary of Martti Välimäki 11.7.1941, Mauno Jokipii's Collection Pk-1140/24, The National Archives.

680 The diary of Jaakko Lakeala 12.7.1941, The Archive of the SS-Investigation, The National Archives.

681 Belaja Tserkov – pieni ukrainalaiskaupunki. Undated newspaper writing by Mauno Olavi Alhainen, Mauno Jokipii's Collection, Pk-1140/15, The National Archives.

682 Belaya Tserkov. http://jewua.org/belaya_tserkov/ Bila Tserkva. https://sv.wikipedia.org/wiki/Bila_Tserkva, 1941 Bila Tserkva massacre. https://en.wikipedia.org/wiki/1941_Bila_Tserkva_massacre

683 Oberstleutnant Helmuth Groscurth informiert Generalfeldmarschall Walter von Reichenau am 21. August 1941 über das Schicksal der jüdischen Kinder von Belaja Cerkov. Die Verfolgung und Ermordung der europäischen Juden durch das nationalsozialistische Deutschland 1933–1945. Besetzte sowjetische Gebiete unter deutscher Militärver waltung, Baltikum und Transnistrien, Band 8 2016, 253–257, Helmuth Groscurth. https://en.wikipedia.org/wiki/Helmuth_Groscurth

684 Walter von Reichenau. https://de.wikipedia.org/wiki/Walter_von_Reichenau

685 Yrjö Kaila's recollection 1994. Yrjö Kaila's Collection, Pk-2356/9.

686 Yrjö Kaila's recollection 1994. Yrjö Kaila's Collection, Pk-2356/9, Yrjö Kaila's recollection 1958, The collection of Mauno Jokipii, Pk-1140/34–35, The National Archives.

687 Ibid.

688 Ereignismeldung UdSSR Nr.27 19.7.1941, including Die "Ereigninsmeldungen UdSSR" 1941 (2011), 147.

689 Ereignismeldung UdSSR Nr. 30 22.7.1941, including Die "Ereignismeldungen UdSSR" 1941 (2011), 163.

690 Kriegs-Tagebuch – II./SS-Rgt. Westland 15.7.1941, The Archive of the SS-Investigation, The National Archives

691 Radomyshl, Ukraine. https://www.jewishgen.org/communities/community.php?usbgn=-1051928

692 Butler 1979, 45–46, Zhytomyr. https://en.wikipedia.org/wiki/Zhytomyr Radomyshl, Ukraine. https://www.jewishgen.org/communities/community.php?usbgn=-1051928

693 Pohl 2008, 34–35, The Wiking Division, The SS-Ahnenerbe and Einsatzgruppe D. https://forum.axishistory.com/viewtopic.php?t=135203&star=75

694 Ereignismeldung UdSSR Nr.37 29.7.1941, included in Die "Ereignismeldungen UdSSr" 1941 (2011), 201.

695 Lower 2008, 234.

696 Rhodes 2002, 123–124, 146–149, Lower 2005, 14,36, 79–81, 234–235, Ereigningsmeldung UdSSR Nr. 44 6.8.1941, Nr.47, 9.8.1941, Nr. 50 12.8.1941 and Nr. 58 20.8.1941 and, included in Ergeinigsmeldungen UdSSR" 1941 (2011), 250, 266, 271, 320–321.

697 The diary of Keijo Kääriäinen 10.8.1941, Mauno Jokipii's Collection, Pk-2365/5, The National Archives.

698 Dneprodzershinsk (Kamenskoye). The Untold Stories. https://www.yadvashem.org/untoldstories/database/index.asp?cid=337

699 The diary of Keijo Kääriäinen 23.4.1941–25.7.1943, Mauno Jokipii's Collection, Pk-1140/34–35, The National Archives.

700 The diary of Taisto Kuuri 18.1.1942, Mauno Jokipii's Collection, Pk-1140/23, The National Archives.

701 The diary of Iivari Kemppinen 26.9.1942, The Archive of the SS-Investigation, The National Archives.

702 Ilm. N:o 303 14.2.1947, Asia: Kapteeni Ladau, ValPo, Sotilasluonteiset järjestöt, SS-miehet, Vol. 46. The National Archives, Tyrkkö 2014, 1–8, Vertanen 2005, 19–20, Swanström 2018, 165–166.

703 The diary of Jaakko Hintikka 28.–31.12.1942, The Archive of the SS-Investigation, The National Archives.

704 ibid.

705 Ruusukallio 2007, 74.

706 The diary of Jaakko Hintikka 25.1.1943, The Archive of the SS-Investigation, The National Archives.

707 Ibid., diary note 6.–12.3.1943.

708 Hakemukset SS-joukkoihin 1941. The archive of SS-Aseveljet, Pk-1141/25–29, 75–80, The National Archives.

709 ValPo's personal dossier on Harry Backberg, Card 25.7.45 Y.D. 17/20/20.7.1945, The Archive of ValPo, The National Archives.

710 Tuomaala 2010, 65, 99.

711 Kokemuksia ja tuntemuksia Saksan itärintamalla. Article by Markus Käenmäki in the newspaper *Ylä-Satakunta,* 8.7.2003.

712 Emberland & Kott 2012, 236.

713 The diaries of Ahti Paikkala 20. and 29.6.1941 and Martti Välimäki 30.6.1941, Mauno Jokipii's Collection, Pk-1140/24, The National Archives.

714 Tyrkkö 1960, 69, 126, 208.

715 Olavi Alsta: Aseellisen SS:n kenttäpostin sensuuri. Recollection by Mauno Alhainen (after the war, Alhainen wrote as a journalist in *Helsingin Sanomat* and other newspapers as Olavi Alsta) 1962. Mauno Jokipii's Collection, Pk-1140/27, The National Archives.

716 The diaries of Esko Sonninen and Matti Heikkilä 14.12.1941, The Archive of the SS-Investigation, The National Archives.

717 The diary of Tauno Polón 26.12.1941 and 18.1.1942. Mauno Jokipii's Collection, Pk-1140/24, The National Archives.

718 The diary of Taisto Kuuri 10.12.1942, Mauno Jokipii's Collection, Pk-1140/25.

719 Mauno Jokipii's interview with Ensio Anttila. Mauno Jokipii's Collection, Pk-1140/29–30, The National Archives.

720 The recollection of Pekka Nummi. The Archive of the SS-Investigation, The National Archives.

721 The diary of Jaakko Hintikka 7.–13.10.1942, The Archive of the SS-Investigation, The National Archives.

722 The diary of Toivo Tuomaala 14.4.1943, The Archive of the SS-Investigation, The National Archives.

723 Records of the Militärgerichtshof Nr II, Fall IV 2.9.1947, Staatsarchiv Nürnberg, Smith–Poulsen–Christansen 1999, 73–96.

724 Weltanschaulischen Schulungsblatt Nr. 1, Mauno Jokipii's Collection, Pk-1140/19, The National Archives.

725 Swanström 2018, 119.

726 The diary of Tauno Polón 23.11.1942. Mauno Jokipii's Collection, Pk-1140/24, The National Archives.

727 The recollections of Konstantin Cande, The Archive of the SS-Investigation, The National Archives.

728 The diary of Pekka Kurvinen 25.7.1941, Mauno Jokipii's Collection, Pk-1140/36–37, The National Archives.

729 The diary of Jaakko Saarela 27.6.1941, Mauno Jokipii's Collection, Pk-2365/7, The National Archives.

730 The diary of Eino Nevanlinna 22.12.1942. Mauno Jokipii's Collection, Pk-2365/6, The National Archives, Swanström 2018, 342.

731 The diary of Uuno Ström. 9.3.1943. The collection of Mauno Jokipii, Pk-1140/25, The National Archives, Jokipii 2001, 8, Westerlund 2017, 284–286, Swanström 2018, 131–136.

732 The diary of Toivo Tuomaala 9.3.1943. The Archive of the SS-Investigation, The National Archives.

733 Mauno Alhainen's letter to Unto Boman (Parvilahti)

14.3.1943, EK-ValPo, the personal dossier on Unto Parvilahti, The National Archives.

734 Ibid., 9.3.1941, Mauno Alhainen: Berliinin totaalisessa sodassa. Article in *Ajan suunta,* March - May 1943. Mauno Jokipii's Collection, Pk-1140/10 and Pk-1140/19, The National Archives.

735 Eino Salonen's pro memoria "SS-miehet" 26.10.1945, I B SKP, Vol. 29, Kansan Arkisto.

736 The Helsinki thoroughfare was renamed Mannerheimintie on 4.6.1942.

737 Välähdyksiä. SS-vuosien varrelta III. Undated newspaper by Mauno Alhainen writing in *Rintamamies* ca. 1943. Mauno Jokipii's Collection, Pk-1940/15, The National Archives.

738 Ibid.

739 Mauno Jokipii's interview with Leo Heikurainen in 1959, Mauno Jokipii's Collection, Pk 1140/29–30, The National Archives.

740 The diary of Kauko Suonto 10.3.1941. Mauno Jokipii's Collection, Pk-1140/25–26, The National Archives.

741 The diary of Uuno Ström 16.4.1943. The collection of Mauno Jokipii, Pk-1140/25, The National Archives.

742 Obersturmführer Lautia noudettu pois junasta sekä pidätetty. Article in *Gladiaattorin* lisälehti N:4, around 3.3.1942, The Archive of the SS-Investigation, The National Archives.

743 Ptk. N:o 662/47, Thor-Björn Weckström and Ptk. N:o 26/46 Gunnar Koskenkorva, ValPo II, Vol. 46 SS-miehet, The National Archives.

744 Actually, the name is spelled Loeb in the interrogation with Weckström by ValPo, but the proper name is Leib. Karl Leib. https://en.wikipedia.org/wiki/Karl_Leib

745 Jouko Itälä: Promemoria toiminnastani vuosina 1939–1946, 8.7.1946, Ptk. N:o 102/46 Veikko Alfred Häikiö, laadittu 13–16.3.1946 and Ptk. N:o 92/46, Aimo Johannes Mäkitalo, ValPo II, Vol. 46 SS-miehet, The National Archives.

746 The diary of Martti Koivula 12.5.1941, The Archive of the SS-Investigation. Vol. SS-vapaaehtoisten päiväkirjat (lisäykset), The National Archives.

747 The diary of Jaakko Lakeala. The Archive of the SS-Investigation, The National Archives.

748 Undated recollection by Olavi Liesinen. Mauno Jokipii's Collection, Pk-1140/27, The National Archives.

749 Ibid.

750 Ibid.

751 The diary of Ensio Pihkala 25.6. and 15.7.1941. Jukka Tyrkkö's Collection, Pk-1618/5, The National Archives, Swanström 2018, 228.

752 The diary of Reino Suonio 28.6.1941, The Archive of the SS-Investigation, The National Archives.

753 Recollection by Seppo Taivalmaa, The Archive of the SS-Investigation, The National Archives.

754 The diary of Uuno Ström 19.3.1942, Mauno Jokipii's Collection, Pk-1140/25–26, The National Archives.

755 Akp. N:o 331/747, Paavo Ilmari Suutala. ValPo II SS-miehet, Vol. 46, The National Archives.

756 Er.Sal. V.R.K.D. N:o 3/10 1944 Saap. 11/1 1944. Pro memoria eräiden kansallissosialismia tai Saksaa muuten lähellä olevien piirien toiminnasta, 8.1.1945. Vol. 46 SS-miehet, The National Archives.

757 Kokemuksia ja tuntemuksia Saksan itärintamalta. Article by Markus Käenmäki in *Ylä-Satakunta* 10.7.2003.

758 Kokemuksia ja tuntemuksia Saksan itärintamalta. Writing by Markus Käenmäki in the newspaper *Ylä-Satakunta,* 10.7.2003.

759 Nummelin 2000, 4.

760 SS-miehenä Suomen vuoksi. Interview with Sakari Haikala in *Itä-Savo* by Annamari Haimi 23.10.2016, "Koko Skandinavia alistettaisiin Suomelle". Interview with Sakari Haikala in *Etelä-Suomen Sanomat* 21.7.2007.

761 Turunen 2016, 92–93, 101–102.

762 Ibid., 131, 134, 164, 185–193.

763 The diary of Keijo Kääriäinen 19.6. and 4.8.1941, Mauno Jokipii's Collection, Pk-2365/5, The National Archives.

764 SS-Unterscharführer Aarno Nurmio muistelee 2012, 10.

765 Räsänen 2000, 75–76.

766 Recollection by Seppo Taivalmaa, The Archive of the SS-Investigation, The National Archives.

767 Interview with Esko Riekki 10.12.1964, L.A. Puntila's Collection, Vol. 25, The National Archives.

768 Esko Riekki's letters to Mauno Jokipii 24.11.1958 and in autumn 1961, Mauno Jokipii's Collection, Pk-1140/29–30, The National Archives.

769 Interview with Esko Riekki 10.12.1964, L.A. Puntila's Collection, Vol. 25, The National Archives.

770 Borgersrud 2017, 206.

771 Recollection by Olavi Liesinen, 21.12.1969. Mauno Jokipii's Collection, Pk-1140/27, The National Archives.

772 The diary of Keijo Kääriäinen 3.7.1941, Mauno Jokipii's Collection Pk-1140/34–35, The National Archives, Jokipii 1996, 193.

773 Turunen 2016, 259.

774 Interrogation record N:o 28/1946. Liukkonen (former Hildén), Erik Johannes 20.5.1946, The Oulu branch of the Valtiollinen poliisi, The ValPo Archive, The National Archives.

775 The recollections of Arvo Kokko. The Archive of the SS-Investigation, The National Archives.

776 Westerlund 2017, 396–405.
777 Interview with Esko Riekki 10.12.1964, L.A. Puntila's Collection, Vol. 25, The National Archives.
778 Kyösti-From 2016, 45, 88.
779 Westerlund 2017, 277.
780 The diary of Uuno Ström, early June 1943. The collection of Mauno Jokipii, Pk-1140/25, The National Archives, Westerlund 2017, 330–331.
781 Westerlund 2017, 282–285, Swanström 2018, 127–129.
782 Suomalaisten Waffen-SS -vapaaehtoisten matrikkeli 1941–1943 (2013), 60, 103, 110, 117, 195, 208, 235.
783 Eivind Reichelt. Avhørt i Åkebergsveiens fengsel den 5/10–1946, Oslo Politikammer, Landsviksavd., Riksarkivet (Oslo).
784 Ibid.
785 Information given by Lars Larsen, Copenhagen, Denmark.
786 Larsen & Straede 2014, 291–292.
787 Goldsworthy 2007, 169.
788 Information given by Lars Larsen, Copenhagen, Denmark.
789 Larsen & Straede 2014, 291.
790 Undated letter from Jan Olij to his family in early 1942, CABR, Den Haag, Kleijn-Reurs 2018. The Archive of the SS-Investigation, The National Archives.
791 van Roekel 2012, 153–169, von Frijtag Drabbe Künzel 2015, 121, Kleijn-Reurs 2018. The Archive of the SS-Investigation, The National Archives.
792 Sørlie 2015, 266–271, 331, 471.
793 Bay 2017, 104.
794 Westlie 2010, 52–66, 79–80, 88–90, 104.
795 Sørlie 2015, 272.
796 Evald O. Solbakken: Spesialrapport om tyskernes behandling av fanger og jöder 28.4.1945. S-1725 Legasjonen I Stockholm, del 1, serie Da, eske 453, Riksarkivet (Norge)
797 Olav Tuff (91): Vi brente en kirke med sivilister. https://www.nrk.no/dokumentar/--nordmenn-deltok-i-drap-pa-sivile-1.11262316, En krig for livet. https://www.dt.no/nyheter/en-krig-for-livet/s/2-2.1748-1.3177758?service=print
798 Diary of Martti Koivula. Private collection of Mika Hakanpää.
799 Schön 1999, 134–135, Schön 2001, 145.
800 Records of the Militärgerichtshof Nr. II, Fall IV 2.9.1947, Staatsarchiv Nürnberg.
801 Struve 2015, 668–669.
802 i.e. the atrocities in the villages of Olszanica 2.7.1941, Nowosielce 2.–3.7.1941, Krivichi 2.2.1941, Slowita 2.7.1941, Kurowice 3.7.1941, and Nowiki 3.–4.7., the towns of Ozerna 3.–5.7.1941, Chorostków 5.7.1941, and Husiatyn 6.7.1941, and in the village of Podhorodce 7.7.1941.
803 i.e. atrocities in Zborów/Zboriv, 4.7.1941, Mykulyntsi, 5.7.1941 and Hrymailiv 5.7.1941, and in Urycz 7.7.1941.
804 i.e. the atrocities in Proskurov, 11.7.1941 and Bila Tserkva, 15.7.1941.
805 i.e. the atrocities in Lemberg and Zolochiv 3.–4.7.1941, 1.7.1941.
806 i.e. the atrocities in Tarnopol, 4.–5.7.1941.
807 i.e. Zhytomyr, mid-July 1941.
808 Skalat, Memorial Volume of the Community which perished in the Holocaust (Ukraine). https://Jewishgen.org/yizkor/skalat/skalat.html
809 Struve 621–625, Swanström 2018, 150.
810 Evald O. Solbakken: Spesialrapport om tyskernes behandling av fanger og jöder 28.4.1945. S-1725 Legasjonen I Stockholm, del 1, serie Da, eske 453, Riksarkivet (Norge).
811 Organization of Ukrainian Nationalists. https://en.wikipedia.org/wiki/Organization_of_Ukrainian_Nationalists
812 Subetlny 2000, 464–465, 200–265, Boll 2001, 65, Mick 2016, 290, 292.
813 Bartov 2002, 66.
814 Struve 2015, 247.
815 Die Verfolgung und Ermordung der europäischen Juden durch das nationalsozialistische Deutschland 1933-1945. Besetzte sowjetische Gebiete unter deutscher Militärverwaltung, Baltikum und Transnistrien, Band 8 2016, 150.
816 Ereignismeldung UdSSR Nr. 10 2.7.1941 and Ereignismeldung UdSSR Nr.24 116.11.1941, included in "Die Ereignismeldungen UdSSR" 1941 (2011), 65, 131.
817 Dallin 1957, 119.
818 Gerstenfeld-Maltiel 1993, 49.
819 Struve 2015, 214–216, Struve 2018, 15.
820 Dallin 1957, 119, Struve 2015, 288–298.
821 Ibid., 120, Subtelny 2000, 463–464, Lviv, Kohanski 2012260, Lower 2012, 204, https://en.wikipedia.org/wiki/Lviv Stepan Bandera. https://en.wikipedia.org/wiki/Stepan_Bandera, Yaroslav Stesko. https://en.wikipedia.org/wiki/Yaroslav_Stetsko
822 Die Organisation Ukrainiser Nationalisten sicht im Sommer 1941 die Aufgabe einer neuen ukrainischen Verwaltung auch darin, die Juden von der übrigen Bevölkerung zu abzusondern" (Ende Juni order Anfang July 1941). Die Verfolgung und Ermordung der europäischen Juden durch das nationalsozialistische Deutschland 1933-1945. Besetzte sowjetische Gebiete unter deutscher Militärverwaltung, Baltikum und Transnistrien, Band 8 2016, 138–139.
823 Golczewski 2008, 137.
824 Gesin 2006, 48, Liber 2016, 215–216.
825 Pale of Settlement. https://en.wikipedia.org/wiki/Pale_of_

Settlement
826 Pogrom. https://en.wikipedia.org/wiki/Pogrom, Antisemitism and Pogroms in the Military (Russian Empire). https://encyclopedia.1914-1918-online.net/article/antisemitism_and_pogromsin_the_military_russian_empire
827 Budnitskii 2012, 236,
828 Gergel 1951, 237–252, Motta 2017, 177–19.
829 Kenes 1992, 293–315, Jewish Pogroms in Ukraine, 1918-1921. Fond FR-3050 Kiev District Commission of the Jewish Public Committee for the Provision of Aid to Victims of Pogroms; Opis'1-3. https://www.bsb-muenchen.de/mikro/lit485.pdf Lwów pogrom (1918). https://en.wikipedia.org/wiki/Lwów_pogrom_(1918)
830 An Account of Firsthand Testimonies of an Unknown Holocaust during the Russian Civil War, from the archives of the KGB, Jewish Pogroms in the Ukraine and Byelorussia (1918-1921) 1994, 6, 47–49.
831 Budnitskii 2012, 245.
832 Gummerus 1931, 32, Gummerus 1943, 2.
833 Information given by Kai Struve, Halle, Germany.
834 Matthäus 2004, 268.
835 Pohl 2008, 36.
836 Verbrechen der Wehrmacht 2002.
837 Däniker 1940, Hornborg 1941, 109–11, Däniker 1942, Däniker 1941 II, Hornborg 1944, 191–193, van Crevald 1983, 33–37, 74–76, Bartov 1991, 30–31, Zetterling 2003, Fritz 2011, 234–237.
838 https://www.expostfacto.nl/junsv/brd/dstst01.html
839 Rintala 1975, 179, Kivimäki 2006, 197, Neitzel & Welzer 2011.
840 SS-miehenä Suomen vuoksi. Interview with Sakari Haikala by Annamari Haimi in *Itä-Savo*, 23.10.2016, Turunen 2016, 102.

ARCHIVES

Bundesarchiv, Berlin-Lichterfelde, Germany
NS 19
SS-Kartei
Verleihungsliste des Eisernen Kreuzes, SS-Division Wiking, Heerespersonalamt, RH 7/1353, S. 1–171
Verleihungsliste für Verleihung des Kriegsverdienstkreuzes, SS-Division Wiking, Heerespersonalamt, RH 7A/643

Bundesarchiv-Militärarchiv, Freiburg, Germany
Nachlass Wolfgang Vopersal
Personal file on Felix Steiner
RH 24-3/136, GB III. AK, Anlagen zum Tagebuch Ic Bd:3: 23.9.-12.12.-41
RS 3-5/3 Sammelmappe mit Divisionsbefehlen und Befehlen aller Art der Abt. Ia, IIa, IIb, Ic, Ib mit Unterabteilungen 31.12.40-Juni 1941
Truppenkameradschaft 5. SS-Panzer-Division "Wiking", B 436
RS 3–4

Centraal Archief van de Bijzondere Rechtspleging (CABR), Den Haag
Diary of Edmond Henri le Roux

Data Archiving and Networked Services (DANS), Den Haag
Jan Henri Albert Keuter, trial testimony
Pieter Nicolaas Menten, trial testimony
Edmond Henri le Roux, interview
Hendrikus Arnoldus Valks, trial testimony
Broer Wiersma, trial testimony

Die Zentrale Stelle der Landesjustizverwaltungen zur Aufklärung nationalsozialistischer Verbrechen, Ludwigsburg, Germany
B 162/7183 verb. Vg. AR 591/71 betr. SS-Panzer-Division "Wiking"/Rgmt. Westland 1971–72
B 162/7185 verb. Vg. AR 1.058/71 betr. SS-Panzerdivision "Wiking"/Rgmt. Westland 1971, 1975
B 162/7993 Ermittlungen gg. Angehörige der 5. SS-Panzerdivision "Wiking" wg. des Vorwurfs der Beteiligung an Einzelvervrechen im Raum Zhitomir u.a.O. 1941, 1967–71
B 162/8361 Ermittlungen gg. Angehörige der 5, SS-Panzerdivision "Wiking" wg. Beteiligung an zahlreichen Einzelverbrechen an verschiedenen Orten in Galizien und in der Ukraine im Verlauf des Jahres 1941, 1968–72
B 162/31429 Eingabe des niederländischen Landesstataastanwalts betr. der Tötung von 180 Juden durch niederländischen Angehörige der SS-Division "Wiking" im Juli 1941 in Tarnopol (Ukraine) 1981–82, 1986

Kansan Arkisto (The People's Archive), Helsinki
SS-miehet. Eino Salosen's pro memoria, 1 B SKP Uttmp IV, Vol. 29

National Archives, Kew, London
FO 371/36846, Return of Finnish volunteers from Germany 1943, Code 56, file 81

Nederlands Instituut voor Oorloogsdocumetatie (NIOD), Amsterdam
Collection 244 – Europese dagboeken en egodocumenten
Nr 1251. Diary of Antoon Ferdinand Frehé
Nr 991. Diary of Martinus Rademaker
Nr 1073. Diary of Martinus Johannes Weers
Nr 1254. Diary of Pieter Albertus Gerardus Willems
Collection 461 – Collectie process Menten (Pieter Nicolaas Menten, 1899–1987)
Inv.nr 21: Henrikus Arnoldus Valks

Riksarkivet, Oslo, Norway
Interrogation record, Eivind Reichelt, Oslo Politikammare 1946
Utrikesdepartementet, S-1725 Legasjonen i Stockholm, del 1, serie Da, eske 453

Staatsarchiv Nürnberg (Germany)
KV-Prozesse. Fall 4
NO-1486
NO-1783
NO-2215

Stiftelsen norsk Okkupasjonshistorie, SNO (online)
Numerous writings

The Archive of the Veterans' Association *Veljesapu r.y.*, The Parola Armour Museum, Finland
Single documents and prints

The Archive of the Svenska Litteratursällskapet (The manuscript department of the Helsinki University Library)

Kaj Duncker's diary 1941–43, Collection 894

J. Zacharias Duncker's diary 1942–44, Collection 894

The National Archives (Finland)

Helsingin Raastuvanoikeuden 8 osaston 2 jaoston Rikos-asiain Kirjavihkot 1958, No.s 86-98 (Crime case records of the Helsinki City Magistrate's Court)

Johnny Bode, the personal file of ValPo

Kaj Duncker diary 1941–43, Pk-1821/1–6, copy, the original in the Archive of Svenska Litteratursällsällskapet, The collection of Kai Duncker, Vol. 23–27 (The Manuscript and Rare Books Department of Helsinki University)

Mauno Jokipii Collection, Pk-1140 and Pk-2365

T.M. Kivimäki Collection

Jukka Pellervo Tyrkkö Collection Pk-1618/5

L.A. Puntila Collection

SS-aseveljet ry 1943–44, Pk-1141

ValPo II, Vol. 46 SS-miehet

Yrjö Paavo Ilmari Kaila Collection, Pk-2356

ValPo, Volume 198, Skandinavia ja Baltian maat, Taantumus, fascismi Ruotsissa

The Archive of the SS-Investigation

The National Archives and Records Administration of the United States (NARA)

Records of the Reichs Leader and the German Police, Part 1, RG 242, T 175, Microfilm, Roll 223

RG 319, Entry ZZ-5, IRR Personal Name Files (Selected Printouts), Box 15, File: Steiner, Felix (D185547)

Unpublished manuscripts

Aro, Tuija: Suomalaisten rotu saksalaisissa ja pohjoismaisissa tietosanakirjoissa. Master's thesis in history. Helsingin yliopisto/University of Helsinki 1982

Duncker, J.Z.: På marskens uppdrag I krigens Europa. The Archive of Svenska Litteratursällskapet, Collection 894

Engelhardt, Poul Ranzow: Regiment Nordland I Division Wiking. Manuskript 1970 (Stiftelsen norsk Okkupasjonshistorie, SNO, online)

Kleijn, Cees & Reurs, Stijn: Report on Dutch sources concerning the involvement of the SS-Division "Wiking" in war crimes and crimes against humanity in Ukraine in the Summer of 1941, commissioned by The National Archives of Finland (Kansallisarkisto) 20.7.2018 (Kleijn-Reurs 2018)

Partanen, Tanja: Elias Simojoki ryssänviha-ideologian kehittyminen vuoden 1923 mennessä. Jyväskylän yliopiston historian pro gradu -tutkielma. Jyväskylä 2005

Steiner, Felix: Tactics of Mobile Units. Operations of the 5th SS Panzergrenadier Division "Wiking" at Rostov and the Maripol Oilfields (Summer 1942). NARA 1947

Weintraub, Daniel: "Suomen juutalaisten vapauksia ja oikeuksia ei millään tavoin ole loukattu". Juutalaisvastaisuuden Suomen juutalaisissa herättämät tunnot ja reaktiot 1930-luvulta jatkosodan päättymiseen. Helsingin yliopisto/University of Helsinki. Master's thesis 1997

Vertanen, Anu: Rintamalta Ratakadulle. Suomalaiset SS-miehet kommunistisen ValPon kohteina 1945–1948. Jyväskylän yliopisto/Jyväskylä University. Master's thesis in history 2005

Westlie, Bjørn: Norske krigskorrespondenter på Østfronten 1941–45. Masteroppgave i historie. Institut for arkeologi, konservering og historie. Universitetet i Oslo 2010

Informants

Hakanpää, Mika, Jalasjärvi, Finland

Kleijn, Cees, Amsterdam, The Netherlands

Moore, John P., Oregon, USA

Nash, Douglas, Oregon, USA

Natedal, Tommy, Jevnaker, Norway

Reurs, Stijn, Amsterdam, The Netherlands

Römer, Felix, London, UK

Struve, Kai, Halle, Germany

Söderlund, Ake, Mariehamn, Finland

Trang, Charles, France

Tyas, Stephen, St Albans, UK

Westberg, Lennart, Sundsvall, Sweden

Wikberg, Olli, Helsinki, Finland

Web Sites

An OSS Report on Wartime Population Changes in the Baltic. http://www.lituanus.org/1981_3/81_3_07.htm

André Swanström: Suomalaiset SS-miehet ja sotarikokset. http://www.skhs.fi/suomalaiset-ss-miehet-ja-sotarikokset/

Antisemitism and Pogroms in the Military (Russian Empire). https://encyclopedia.1914-1918-online.net/article/antisemitism_and_pogromsin_the_military_russian_empire

Arnold Stoffers http://military.wikia.com/wiki/Arnold_Stoffers

Belaya Tserkov. http://jewua.org/belaya_tserkov/

Berthold Maack. https://de.wikipedia.org/wiki/Berthold_Maack

Bila Tserkva. https://sv.wikipedia.org/wiki/Bila_Tserkva

Chorostków (Ukr. Khorostkiv), Ukraine: https://www.jewishgen.org/yizkor/khorostkov/Khorostkov.html#TOC

Commissar Order https://en.wikipedia.org/wiki/Commissar_Order
Die Feldpost: Zemnsur 1939/45. https://www.forum-der-wehrmacht.de/index.php?thread/2616-die-feldpost-zensur-1939-45/
Die Zentrale Stelle der Landesjustizverwaltungen zur Aufklärung nationalsozialistischer Verbrechen https://de.wikipedia.org/wiki/Zentrale_Stelle_der_Landesjustizverwaltungen_zur_Aufklärung_nationalsozialistischer_Verbrechen
Deutsche Dienststelle (WASt) https://en.wikipedia.org/wiki/Deutsche_Dienststelle_(WASt)
Dneprodzershinsk (Kamenskoye). The Untold Stories. The Murder Sites of the Jews in the Occupied Territories of the former USSR https://www.yadvashem.org/untoldstories/database/index.asp?cid=337
Eduard Wagner (Gen.) https://de.wikipedia.org/wiki/Eduard_Wagner_(General)
Einsatzgruppen. https://en.wikipedia.org/wiki/Einsatzgruppen
Einsatzgruppen (Mobile Killing Squads). https://encyclopedia.ushmm.org/content/en/article/mobile-killing-squads
En krig for livet. https://www.dt.no/nyheter/en-krig-for-livet/s/2-2.1748-1.3177758?service=print
Encyclopedia Judaica: Gaisin. https://jewishvirtuallibrary.org/gaisin
Enter 'The Dutchman' Pieter Menten. https://www.jewishgen.org/yizkor/Galicia3/gal122.html
Erich von Manstein. http://en.wikipedia.org/wiki/Erich_von_Manstein
Erkki Räikkönen. https://en.wikipedia.org/wiki/Erkki_Räikkönen
Ernst Otto Fick. https://www.jewiki.net/wiki/Ernst_Otto_Fick
Erwin Schulz. https://en.wikipedia.org/wiki/Erwin_Schulz
Erwin Tschentscher. https://de.wikipedia.org/wiki/Erwin_Tschentscher
Felix Steiner. https://en.wikipedia.org/wiki/Felix_Steiner
Finnish Volunteer Battalion of the Waffen-SS. https://en.wikipedia.org/wiki/Finnish_Volunteer_Battalion_of_the_Waffen-SS
Finnish Volunteers in the Wehrmacht in WWII. https://www.feldgrau.com/WW2-German-Wehrmacht-Finnish-Volunteers
Fritz von Scholz. https://en.wikipedia.org/Fritz_von_Scholz
Gunnar Lindqvist. https://fi.wikipedia.org/wiki/Gunnar_Lindqvist
Hans Collani. https://ipfs.io/ipfs/QmXoypizjW3WknFiJnKLwHCnL72vedxjQkDDP1mXWo6uco/wiki/Hans_Collani.html
Herbert Gille. https://en.wikipedia.org/wiki/Herbert_Gille
Heinz Fanslau. https://de.wikipedia.org/wiki/Heinz_Fanslau
History of Taganrog. https://en.wikipedia.org/wiki/History_of_Taganrog
Hjalmar von Bonsdorff. https://fi.wikipedia.org/wiki/Hjalmar_von_Bonsdorff
Hrymayliv (Grymailiv, Grimailov, Grymailov, Grzymalov). https://yahadmap.org/#village/hrymailiv-grymailiv-grimailov-grymailov-grzymalov-ternopil-ukraine.85
"Ikke kammerat": forbrydelser mod sovjetiske krigsfanger. https://folkedrab.dk/artikler/ikke-kammerat-forbrydelser-mod-sovjetiske-krigsfanger-
Introduction to Feldpost. https://axis101.bizland.com/Feldpost.html
Invasion of Poland https://en.wikipedia.org/wiki/Invasion_of_Poland
Jewish Families from Zboriv, Ukraine. https://www.geni.com/projects/Jewish-Families-from-Zborov-Ukraine/29340
Jewish Pogroms in Ukraine 1918–1921. Fond FR-3050 Kiev District Commission of the Jewish Public Committee for the Provision of Aid to Victims of Pogroms; Opis'1-3. https://www.bsb-muenchen.de/mikro/lit485.pdf
Johnny Bode. https://en.wikipedia.org/wiki/Johnny_Bode
Kadaverdiscipline. https://en.wiktionary.org/wiki/kadaverdiscipline
Kirovograd. https://www.jewishvirtuallibrary.org/kirovograd
Karl von Oberkamp https://en.wikipedia.org/wiki/Karl_von_Oberkamp
Kroessel, Yosef: From Podhajce to Soviet Russia. https://jewishgen.org/Yizkor/Podhajce/pod209.html#Page218
List of Einsatzgruppen. https://en.wikipedia.org/wiki/List_of_Einsatzgruppen
Lothar Rendulic. https://en.wikipedia.org/wiki/Lothar_Rendulic
Lviv. https://en.wikipedia.org/Lviv
Lviv pogroms. https://en.wikipedia.org/wiki/Lviv_pogroms
The Encyclopedia of the Jewish Diaspora, Poland Serie https://en.wikipedia.org/wiki/Karl_von_Oberkamp:
Lwów Volume (Lviv, Ukraine). https://www.jewishgen.org/yizkor/lviv/lviv.html
Manfred Schönfelder. https://en.rightpedia.info/w/Manfred_Schönfelder
Mariupol. https://en.wikipedia.org/wiki/Mariupol
Mariupol. The Untold Stories. The Murder Sites of the Jews in the Occupied Territories of the former USSR. https://www.yadvashem.org/untoldstories/database/index.asp?cid=493
Mikulince, Mikulintsy, Ukraine. https://kehilalinks.jewishgen.org/suchostaw/sl_mikulince.htm
Mikulince Yizkor Book (Mikulintsy, Ukraine). https://www.

jewishgen.org/yizkor/mikulintsy/mikulintsy.html
Nesterov. http://en.wikipedia.org/wiki/Nesterov
Nikolai Dupak. https://iremember.ru/en/memoirs/others/nikolai-dupak/
Norwegian Volunteers in the German Wehrmacht in WWII, by Marc Rikmenspoel & Jason Pipes. https://www.feldgrau.com/WW2-German-Wehrmacht-Norwegian-Volunteers
Novohrad-Volynskyi. https://en.wikipedia.org/wiki/Novohrad-Volynskyi
Olav Tuff (91): Vi brente en kirke med sivilister. https://www.nrk.no/dokumentar/--nordmenn-deltok-i-drap-pa-sivile-1.11262316
Olav Tuff memories. https://universalcuriosity.wordpress.com/2016/06/
Organization of Ukrainian Nationalists. https://en.wikipedia.org/wiki/Organization_of_Ukrainian_Nationalists
Ostarbeiter. https://en.wikipedia.org/wiki/Ostarbeiter
Ostropol. https://en.wikipedia.org/wiki/Ostropol
Pale of Settlement. https://en.wikipedia.org/wiki/Pale_of_Settlement
Panzer-Grenadier-Regiment 10 'Westland'/SS-Standarte 'Westland'. Nederlanders in de Waffen-SS. http://www.waffen-ss.nl/wikwest.php
Pidhirtsi. https://en.wikipedia.org/wiki/Pidhirtsi
Pidhorodtsi. https://nl.wikipedia.org/wiki/Pidhorodtsi
Pidvoloschysk. https://en.wikipedia.org/wiki/Pidvolochysk
"Podhajce" – Encyclopedia of Jewish Communities in Poland, Volume II, (Ukraine). https://www.jewishgen.org/yizkor/pinkas_poland/pol2_00410.html
Podwolocyska and its Surroundings (Podvolochisk, Ukraine) https://www.jewishgen.org/yizkor/podvolochisk/podvolochisk.html
Polish roots: Wyżniany (now Vyzhnyany, Ukraine) http://polishroots.org/Geography/S%C5%82ownikGeograficzny/SGKP-Wy%C5%BCniany/tabid/458/Default.aspx
Pogrom. https://en.wikipedia.org/wiki/Pogrom
Proskurov. The Untold Stories. The Murder Sites of the Jews in the Occupied Territories of the former USSR. http://yadvashem.org/untoldstories/database/index.asp?cid=748
Radomyshl, Ukraine. https://www.jewishgen.org/communities/community.php?usbgn=-1051928
Records of U.S. Army Commands, 1942–. https://www.archives.gov/research/captured-german-records/us-army.html
Rostov-on-Don. http://www.yivoencyclopedia.org/article.aspx/Rostov-on-Don
Rostov-on-Don. The Untold Stories. The Murder Sites of the Jews in the Occupied Territories of the former USSR. https://www.yadvashem.org/untoldstories/database/index.asp?cid=375
BBC: Russia row over Nazi massacre site in Rostov-on-Don. https://www.bbc.com/news/world-europe-16697485
Ruotsalaiset Waffen-SS-miehet, jotka antoivat kaikkensa. Veikko Huuska. http://veikkohuuska.puheenvuoro.uusisuomi.fi/215960-ruotsalaiset-waffen-ss-miehet-jotka-antoivat-kaikkensa
Skalat, Memorial Volume of the Community which perished in the Holocaust (Ukraine). https://Jewishgen.org/yizkor/skalat/skalat.html
Stepan Bandera. https://en.wikipedia.org/wiki/Stepan_Bandera
Soviet partisans. https://en.wikipedia.org/wiki/Soviet_partisans
Taganrog during World War II. https://en.wikipedia.org/wiki/Taganrog_during_World_War_II
Tarashcha. https://www.jewishgen.org/ukraine/GEO_town.asp?id=157
"Tarnopol" – Encyclopedia of Jewish Communities in Poland, Volume II (Ternopil, Ukraine). https://www.jewishgen.org/Yizkor/pinkas_poland/pol2_00234.html
Tarnopol Ghetto. https://en.wikipedia.org/wiki/Tarnopol_Ghetto
Ternopil: https://en.wikipedia.org/wiki/Ternopil
The City of Złoczów (Zolochiv, Ukraine) https://www.jewishgen.org/Yizkor/Zolochiv1/Zolochiv1.html#TOC
The Destruction of Złoczów (Zolochiv, Ukraine). https://www.jewishgen.org/Yizkor/Zolochiv/Zolochiv.html
The Jewish Community of Urycz. https://dbs.bh.org.il/place/urycz
The Wiking Division, The SS-Ahnenerbe and Einsatzgruppe D. https://forum.axishistory.com/viewtopic.php?t=135203-&star=75
"They really do smell like blood" http://www.spiegel.de/international/europe/they-really-do-smell-like-blood-among-hitler-s-executioners-on-the-eastern-front a-674375.html
"That's not the Germans" https://zaxid.net/to_ne_ti_nimtsi_n1266107
Tämä kirje johti selvitykseen SS-vapaaehtoisten epäillyistä sotarikoksista. https://www.is.fi/kotimaa/art-2000005693915.html
Waffen-SS in popular culture. https://en.wikipedia.org/wiki/Waffen-SS_in_popular_culture
Walter von Reichenau. https://de.wikipedia.org/wiki/Walter_von_Reichenau
Was the Waffen-SS an elite force? https://history.stackexchange.com/questions/33415/was-the-waffen-ss-an-elite-force
Was the Waffen-SS an extraordinarily effective fighting force? https://www.quora.com/Was-the-Waffen-SS-an-extraordinarily-effective-fighting-force-Why-Why-did-they-command-such-fear-and-respect-among-their-opponents-What-

was-the-reason-behind-the-awe-and-fighting-efficiency-associated-with-the-Waffen-SS
Wilhelm Bittrich. https://en.wikipedia.org/wiki/Wilhelm_Bittrich
World War II casualties of the Soviet Union. https://en.wikipedia.org/wiki/World_War_II_casualties_of_the_Soviet_Union
Yaroslav Stetsko. https://en.wikipedia.org/wiki/Yaroslav_Stetsko
Zboriv. https://en.wikipedia.org/wiki/Zboriv
"Zborow" – Encyclopedia of Jewish Communities in Poland, Volume II (Ukraine). https://www.jewishgen.org/yizkor/pinkas_poland/pol2_00202.html
Zhytomyr. https://en.wikipedia.org/wiki/Zhytomyr
Zmievskaya Balka. https://en.wikipedia.org/wiki/Zmievskaya_Balka
"Zlosczow" – Encyclopedia of Jewish Communities in Poland, Volume II (Zolochiv, Ukraine). https://www.jewishgen.org/yizkor/pinkas_poland/pol2_00217.html
Zolochiv. https://en.wikipedia.org/wiki/Zolochiv
5. SS-Panzer-Division Wiking. https://www.axishistory.com/axis...germany.../germany.../1265-5-ss-panzer-division-wiking
5. SS-Panzer-Division Wiking. https://sv.wikipedia.org/wiki/5._SS-Panzer-Division_Wiking
26. Waffen-Grenadier Division der SS "Hungaria" (ungarische Nr.2) – 26. Dywizja Grenadierów SS "Hungaria" (2. weglerska). http://www.dws-xip.pl/reich/waffen/26dgren.html
1941 Bila Tsekva massacre. https://en.wikipedia.org/wiki/Bila_Tserkva_massacre

LITERATURE

Ahonen, Paavo: Antisemitismi Suomen evankelis-luterilaisessa kirkossa 1917–1933. Suomen kirkkohistoriallinen seura. Helsinki 2017

Amar, Tarik Cyril: The Paradox of Ukrainian Lviv. A Borderland City between Stalinists, Nazis, and Nationalists. Cornell University Press. Ithaca, New York 2015

Among Hitler's Executioners on the Eastern Front. Interview with Anette Schücking-Homeyer in *Martyrdom & Resistance*, March-April 2010 pp. 7-8 (Note, also in *Spiegel Online*, see links)

Andersson, Martin: Hakkorset på vikingaseglet. Nazismens kopplingar till Svenskfinland 1932-48. Paipis. Sipoo 2015

Angrick, Andrej: Besatzungspolitik und Massenmord. Die Einsatzgruppe D in der südlichen Sowjetunion, 1941-43. Hamburger Edition. Hamburg 2003

Antisemitism. An Annotated Bibliography. Ed. by Susan Sarah Cohen. Volume 18. Saur. München 2002

Arad, Yitzhak: The Holocaust in the Soviet Union. University of Nebraska Press. Lincoln, Nebraska 2009

Askey, Nigel: Operation Barbarossa. The Complete Organisational and Statistical Analysis, and Military Simulation. Volume IIA. Nigel Askey. Morrisville, North Carolina 2013

Bartov, Omer: Hitler's Army. Soldiers, Nazis and war in the Third Reich. Oxford University Press. New York 1991

Bartov, Omer: A View from Below. Survival, Cohesion and Brutality on the Eastern Front. Article in: Wegner, Bernd (Ed.): From Peace to War. Germany, Soviet Russia and the World, 1939-1941. Berghahn Books. Oxford 1997, pp. 325–338

Bartov, Omer: Erased. Vanishing Traces of Jewish Galicia in Present-Day Ukraine. Princeton University Press. Princeton, New Jersey 2007

Baryshnikov, V.N.: Finni na sluzje v vojskah SS v gody vtoroj mirovoj voiny. Vtoroje izdanie i ispravlennoje i dopolnennoje. Sankt-Petersburg 2014

Bay, Eirik Gripp: Himmlers valkyrjer. Frontsøstrene på østfronten. Cappelen Damm. Oslo 2017

Bergel, Hans: Würfelspiele des Lebens. Vier Porträts bedeutender Siebenbürger. Conrad Haas, Johann Martin Honigberger, Paul Richter, Artur Phleps. Meschendörfer. München 1972

Berkhoff, Karel: Harvest of Despair. Life and Death in Ukraine under Nazi Rule. Belknap Press of Harvard University Press. Cambridge, Massachusetts 2004

Bernau, Günter: SS-Panzer-Artillerie-Regiment 5 in der Panzer-Division Wiking. Wupperthal 1991

Blindheim, Svein: Nordmenn under Hitlers fane: Dei norske frontkjemparane. Noreg. Oslo 1977

Boll, Bernd: Złoczów, July 1941. The Wehrmacht and the Beginning of the Holocaust in Galicia. Article in: Bartov, Omer & Grossmann, Anita & Mary Nolan: Crimes of War. New Press (W.W. Norton & Co.). New York 2002 pp. 61–99

Borgersud, Lars: Wollweber-organisasjonen i Norge. Lars Borgersrud. Oslo 2017

Brenden, Geir & Thomassen, Arne Håkon: SS-Schijäger-Bataillon "Norge". Norska skidjägare på östfronten 1941-44. Leandoer & Ekholm. Stockholm 2010

Brenden, Geir & Natedal, Tommy: Norske frivillige i Waffen-SS. Vega Forlag. Oslo 2017

Browning, Christopher R.: Ordinary Men. Reserve Police Battalion 101 and the Final Solution in Poland. Harper Perennial. New York 1998

Budnitskii, Oleg: Russian Jews Between the Reds and the Whites, 1917-1920. University of Pennsylvania Press cop. Philadelphia, Pennsylvania 2012

Butler, Rupert: The Black Angels. A History of the Waffen-SS. St. Martin's Press. New York 1979

Cande, Konstantin: SS-miehen muistikuvia sodasta ja siviilistä. Ed. & pub. Johan Salo. Tuusula 2013

Carruthers, Bob: The SS on Trial: Evidence from Nuremberg. Pen & Sword Military. Barnsley, South Yorkshire 2014

Christensen, Claus Bundgård & Poulsen, Niels Bo & Smith, Peter Scharff: Under hagekors og Dannebrog. Danskere i Waffen SS 1940-45. Aschehoug. København 2001

Christensen, Claus Bundgård & Poulsen, Niels Bo & Smith, Peter Scharff: Germanic Volunteers from Northern Europe. Article included in: The Waffen-SS. A European History. Ed. by Jochen Böhler & Robert Gerwath. Oxford University Press. Oxford 2017 pp. 42–75

Christiansen, Karl O.: Mandlige landssvigere I Danmark under besaettelsen. G. E. C. Gads. København 1950

Christiansen, Claus Bundgård, Poulsen, Niels Bo & Smith, Peter Scharff: Dänen in der Waffen-SS 1940-1945: Ideologie, Integration und Kriegsverbrechen im Vergleich mit anderen "germanischen" Soldaten. Article in: Die Waffen-SS. Neue Forschungen (Krieg in der Geschichte). Schulte, Jan Erik, Lieb, Peter, Wegner, Bernd (Ed.). Verlag Ferdinand

Schöningh. München 2014, pp. 196–215
van Creveld, Martin L.: Fighting Power. German and U.S. Army Performance, 1939-1945. Arms and Armour Press. London 1983
Cüppers, Martin: Wegbereiter der Shoah: die Waffen-SS, der Kommandostab Reichsführer-SS und die Judenvernichtung 1939-1945. Wissenschaftliche Buchgesellschaft. Darmstadt 2005
Dallin, Alexander: German Rule in Russia, 1941-1945. A Study of Occupation Policies. St. Martin's Press. London 1957
Dean, Martin: Collaboration in the Holocaust. Crimes of the Local Police in Belorussia and Ukraine, 1941-1944. Macmillan. Basingstoke 2000
Der Prozess gegen die Hauptkriegsverbrecher vor dem Internationalen Militärgerichtshof. Volumes 1-23. Nürnberg 1947-49
Der Untergang fun Złoczów. Red. von Szlojme Mayer. Ibergang. Münich 1947
Deutsche Besatzungsherrschaft in der UdSSR 1941-1945. Dokumente der Einsatzgruppen in der Sowjetunion II. Angrick, Andrej & Mallmann, Klaus-Michael & Matthäus, Jürgen & Cüppers, Martin (Ed.). WBG. Darmstadt 2015
Deutscher Osten 1939-1945. Der Weltanschauungskrieg in Photos und Texten. Mallmann, Klaus-Michel & Riess, Volker & Pyta, Wolfram (Ed.). WBG. Darmstadt 2003
Die "Ereignismeldungen UdSSR" 1941. Dokumente der Einsatzgruppen in der Sowjetunion I. Klaus-Michael Mallmann & Andrej Angrick & Jürgen Matthäus & Martin Cüppers (Ed.). WBG. Darmstadt 2011
Die Finnische Freiwilligen. Article in *Wiking-Ruf*, 9/1956, pp. 7–10
Die Waffen-SS. Eine Bilddokumentation. von Herbert Walther mit Beiträgen von Generalfeldmarschall v. Manstein, Generalleutnant a. D. Hasso V. Manteuffel und Heinz Höhne. Podzun-Pallas. Oldenburg 1994.
Die Verfolgung und Ermordung der europäischen Juden durch das nationalsozialistische Deutschland 1933-1945.
Band 4. Polen September 1939 – July 1941. Bearbeitet von Klaus-Peter Friedrich. Oldenbourg. München 2011
Band 7–8. Sowjetunion mit annektierten Gebieten I & II. Bearbeitet von Bert Hoppe et al. Oldenbourg. München 2011 and 2016
Dillon, Christopher: Dachau and the SS. A Schooling in Violence. Oxford University Press. Oxford 2015
Divisioonan mies muistelee – SS-Rottenführer Arvo Kokon tarina osa 1. Recollection in Achtung. Veljesapu Perinneyhdistys ry:n jäsen- ja tiedotuslehti 1.2016 pp. 1, 3–12.
Däniker, Gustav: Gelände, Feuerwirkung und Waffeneinsatz. Verlag von Huber. Frauenfeld 1940
Däniker, Gustav: Saksan sodanjohto ja saksalainen sotilas. Saksan lähetystön sanomalehtiosasto. Helsinki 1941
Däniker, Gustav: Saksalainen strategia. Otava. Helsinki 1942
Ekberg, Henrik: Führerns trogna följeslagare. Den finländska nazismen 1932-1944. University of Helsinki. Helsinki 1991
Elo, Veikko: Pantin lunastajat. Apali oy. Hämeenlinna 2006
Emberland, Terje & Kott, Matthew: Himmlers Norge. Nordmenn i det storgermanske prosjekt. Aschehoug. Oslo 2012
Ertel, Heinz & Schulze-Kossens, Richard: Europäische Freiwillige Im Bild. Nation Europa Verlag. Coburg 2000
Ertel, Manfred: Blond mit braunen Wurzeln. Article in *Der Spiegel* Nr 51/1999, pp. 152–156
Eräs vuositaival. Uuden jääkäripataljoonan komentaja kertoo. Interview with Hans Collani by Jukka Tyrkkö in *Suomi-Saksa, Saksalais-suomalainen kulttuurilehti* 31/32, 1942, p. 19
Estes, Kenneth William: A European Anabasis. Western European Volunteers in the German Army and SS, 1940-1945. University of Maryland. College Park, Maryland 1984
Felix Steiner, eräs uuden Euroopan sodanjohtaja. Article by SS-Oberscharführer Jukka Tyrkkö in *Suomen Kuvalehti*, 32/1942 (8.8.1942)
Freiwilligen-General Felix Steiner 1896-1966. Eine Biographie. Führer und Vater seiner Soldaten im Kampf gegen den Bolschwismus. Kameradenwerk Korps Steiner (Selbstverlag). Melbeck 1998
von Frijtag Drabbe Künzel, Geraldien: Hitler's Brudervolk. The Dutch and the Colonization of Occupied Eastern Europe, 1939-1945. Routledge. New York 2015
Fritz, Stephen G.: Frontsoldaten. Den tyske soldaten under andra världskriget. Fischer & Co, cop. Stockholm 2011
Garlinski, Józef: Poland in the Second World War. Macmillan Press. London 1985
Gergel, Nahum: The Pogroms in the Ukraine in 1918-1921. Article in *YIVO Annual of Jewish Social Science*, New York 1951 pp. 237–252
Gerstenfeld-Maltiel, Jacob: My Private War. One Man's Struggle to Survive the Soviets and the Nazis. Vallentine Mitchell. London 1993
Gesin, Michael: The Destruction of the Ukrainian Jewry During World War II. Lewiston. New York 2006
Gogstad, Anders Chr. & Grimnes, Ole Kr. & Rødland, Kjartan: Der veiene skiljes. Hvorfor opplevde vi krigen so forskjellig? Eide. Bergen 2005
Goldsworthy, Terry: Valhalla's Warriors. A History of the Waffen-SS on the Eastern Front 1941-1945. Dog Ear Publishing. Indianapolis, Indiana 2007
Gross, Jan Tomasz: Polish Society under German Occupation. The Generalgouvernement, 1939-1944. Princeton University Press. Princeton, New Jersey 1979

Gummerus, Herman: Orostider i Ukraina. Minnen från min verksamhet som legationschef i Kiev. Söderström. Helsinki 1931
Gummerus, Herman: Ukraina under bolsjevikoket. Svenska tysklandsvänner i Finland. Turku 1943
Gumz, Jonathan: German Counterinsurgency Policy in Independent Croatia, 1941-1944. Article in *The Historian* Vol. 61/1 (1998), pp. 33–50
Gutmann, Martin R.: Building a Nazi Europe. The SS's Germanic Volunteers. Cambridge University Press. Cambridge 2017
Gyllenhaal, Lars & Westberg, Lennart: Svenskar i krig 1914-1945. Historiska media. Lund 2008
Gyllenhaal, Lars & Westberg, Lennart: Swedes at War. Willing Warriors of a Neutral Nation, 1914-1945. The Aberjona Press. Bedford, Pennsylvania 2010
Haaest, Erik: Intet nyt fra Østfronten. Beretningen om Regiment 24 Dänemarks sidste Kommandør. Bogan. Lynge 1998
Halle, Frode: Fra Finland til Kaukasus: Nordmenn på Østfronten 1941-1945. Dreyer. Oslo 1972
Hanski, Jari: Juutalaisvastaisuus suomalaisessa aikakauslehdissä ja kirjallisuudessa, 1918–1944. Kirja kerrallaan. Helsinki 2006
Harten, Hans-Christian: Himmlers Lehrer. Die Weltanschauliche Schulung in der SS 1933-1945. Ferdinand Schöningh. Paderborn 2014
Hartmann, Christian: Wehrmacht im Ostkrieg. Front und militärisches Hinterland 1941/42. Oldenbourg. München 2010
Hartmann, Christian: Unternehmen Barbarossa. Der deutsche Krieg im Osten 1941-1945. C.H. Beck, cop. München 2011
Hartmann, Christian: Operation Barbarossa. Nazi Germany's War in the East, 1941-1945. Oxford University Press. Oxford 2013
Hatheway, Jay: In Perfect Formation. SS Ideology and the SS-Junkerschule-Tölz. Schiffer Publishing. Atglen, Pennsylvania 1999
Heaton, Collin: German Anti-Partisan Warfare in Europe 1939-1945. Schiffer Publishing. Atglen, Pennsylvania 2001
Heliste, Simo: Hyökkäystä ja perääntymistä Wiking tiedustelupataljoonassa. Writing in *Achtung* 3/2003, pp. 1–5
Hillgruber, Andreas: War in the East and the Extermination of the Jews. Article in Marrus, Michael Robert (Ed.): The Nazi Holocaust. Part 3: The Final Solution. The Implementation of Mass Murder. Vol 1. De Gruyter. Westpoint, Connecticut 1989, pp. 85–114
Himka, John-Paul: The Lviv Pogrom of 1941. The Germans, Ukrainian Nationalists, and the Carnival Crowd. Article in *Canadian Slavonic Papers – Revenue canadienne des slavistes* 53(2), 2011, pp. 209–243
Hinsley, E.H.: British Intelligence in the Second World War. Vol. 2. H.M.S.O. London 1979
Holmila, Antero: "*Soldaten wie andere auch*". Finnish Waffen-SS Volunteers and Finland's Historical Imagination. Included in: Muir, Simo & Worthen, Hana: Finland's Holocaust. Silences of History. Palgrave Macmillan. Basingstoke 2013, pp. 218–244
Hornborg, Eirik: Blixtkrigets mysterium. Artikel I *Nya Argus* 9.1941, pp. 109–111, signed E.H.
Hornborg, Eirik: Blixtkrigets fiasco. Artikel I *Nya Argus* 13.1944, pp. 191–193, signed E.H.
Höhne, Heinz: Hitlers SS och Gestapo. Del 1 och 2. Bergh. Stockholm 1977
Höhne, Heinz: Der Orden unter dem Totenkopf. Die Geschichte der SS. Weltbild. Augsburg 1996
Ilkka, Jouko: Jouko Jaakko Ilkan sotatie. Isän muistelmia sota-ajalta. Pertti Ilkka. Nurmo 2016
Immonen, Kari: "*Ryssästä saa puhua…*" Neuvostoliitto suomalaisessa julkisuudessa ja kirjat julkisuuden muotona 1918–39. Otava. Helsinki 1987
Isaksson, Pekka: Kumma kuvajainen. Rasismi rotututkimuksessa, rotuteorioiden saamelaiset ja suomalainen fyysinen antropologia. Kustannus-Puntsi. Inari 2001
Isaksson, Pekka & Jokisalo, Jouko: Kallonmittaajia ja skinejä. Rasismin aatehistoriaa. Suomen rauhanpuolustajat (Hakapaino). Helsinki 1998
Johnson, Paul Louis: Horses of the German Army in World War II. Schiffer Publishing. Atglen, Pennsylvania 2006
Jokipii, Mauno: Panttipataljoona. Suomalaisen SS-pataljoonan historia. Veljesapu (Gummerus). Helsinki 1996 (First published in 1968).
Jokipii, Mauno: Propaganda Waffen-SS:ssä. Writing in *Achtung* 2/2001, pp. 6–9
Jokipii, Mauno: Hitlerin Saksa ja sen vapaaehtoisliikkeet. Waffen-SS:n suomalaispataljoona vertailtavana. Suomalaisen Kirjallisuuden Seura. Helsinki 2002
Jätinvuori, Leo: Sotavuodet, täydennysmiehen (200) omakustannemuistelmat. Privately published book 2000
Kalas, Helmer: Kymmenen vuotta seikkailujen tiellä. Nide oy. Hämeenlinna 1955
Karemaa, Outi: Vihollisia, vainoojia, syöpäläisiä. Venäläisviha Suomessa, 1917–1923. Suomen historiallinen seura. Helsinki 1998
Kelin, Åke: Miukselta Terekille. Former SS-Scharführer writing in *Achtung* 3/2011, pp. 1–7
Kemiläinen, Aira: Suomalaiset, outo Pohjolan kansa. Rotuteoriat ja kansallinen identiteetti. Suomen historiallinen seura. Helsinki 1993

Kemiläinen, Aira: Finns in the shadow of the "Aryans". Race theories and racism. Finnish Historical Society. Helsinki 1998
Kenez, Peter: Pogroms and White Ideology in the Russian Civil War. Article in: Pogroms. Anti-Jewish Violence in Modern Russian History. ed. by John D. Klier & Shlomo Lambroza. Cambridge University Press. Cambridge 1992, pp. 293–315
Kirchhoff, Hans: Holocaust i Danmark. Syddansk Universitetsforlag. Odense 2013
Kivimäki, Ville: Sotilaan työ, siviilin taakka. "Vihollisen tuhoamisen" dynamiikasta, kokemuksesta ja muistosta. Article in: Ihminen sodassa. Suomalaisen kokemuksia talvi- ja jatkosodasta. Tiina Kinnunen & Ville Kivimäki (eds.). Minerva. Helsinki 2006 pp. 191–208
Kochanski, Halik: The Eagle Unbowed. Poland and the Poles in the Second World War. Harvard University Press. Cambridge, Massachusetts 2012
Konttinen, Penna: Elämässä mukana. Sotainvalidien veljesliitto. Helsinki 1996
Korjus, Jaakko: Otsassa kuoleman kuva. Raportti suomalaisesta SS-vapaaehtoisjoukosta. Vaasa oy. Vaasa 1981
Kozlowski, Eugeniusz: Article in: Pietrowski, Wlodzimierz & Stolarski, Mieczyslaw: Poland in World War II, 1939-1945. Polish Agency Interpress. Warszawa 1989, pp. 1–8
Krabbe, O.: Danske soldater i kamp på Østfronten, 1941-1945. Odense Universitetsforlag. Odense 1976
Krausnick, Helmut & Wilhelm, Hans-Heinrich: Die Truppe des Weltanschauungskrieges. Die Einsatzgruppen der Sicherheitspolizei und des SD, 1938-1942. Deutsche Verlags-Anstalt. Stuttgart 1981
Krausnick, Helmut & Buchheim, Hans & Broszat, Martin & Jacobsen, Hans-Adolf: Anatomy of the SS State. Collins. London 1968 (Original in German 1965)
Krosby, Hans Peter: Nikkelidiplomatiaa Petsamossa 1940-1941. Translated by Markku Järvinen. Kirjayhtymä. Helsinki 1966
Krosby, Hans Peter: Suomen valinta 1941. Translated by Erkki Ihanainen. Kirjayhtymä. Helsinki 1967
Kruglov, Alexander: Jewish Losses in Ukraine, 1941-1944. Article in: Brandon, Ray & Lower, Wendy (eds.): The Shoah in Ukraine. History, Testimony, Memorialization. Indiana University Press (United States Holocaust Memorial Museum). Bloomington, Indiana 2008 pp. 272–290
Kulavig, Erik: Stalins hjemmefront 1941-1945. Syddansk Universitetsforlag. Odense 2004
Kurowski, Franz: SS-Obersturmbannführer Paul-Albert Kausch. Vom Artillerist zum Kommandeurs des Waffen-SS-Panzerregiments 11 "Hermann von Salza". Flechsig, Verlagshaus Würzburg GmbH & Co. KG. Würzburg 2013
Kuusela, Kari: Helsingin kerholla saksalaisvieraita. Article in *Achtung* 3/2001, p. 7
Kuusela, Kari: Suomalaiset SS-miehet ja juutalaiset. Article in *Achtung* 1/2008, pp. 7–11
Kuusela, Kari & Wikberg, Olli: Wikingin suomalaiset. Suomalaiset SS-miehet kuvissa. Finnish Volunteers of SS-Division Wiking. Wiking-Divisioona Oy. Helsinki 1996
Kühnrich, Heinz: Der Partisanenkrieg in Europa 1939-1945. Dietz. Berlin 1965
Kyösti, Jukka & From, Synnöve: Suomalaisena SS-miehenä itärintamalla. Herkko Kosonen aseveljineen Wiking-divisioonassa. Minerva Kustannus Oy. Helsinki 2016
Kääriäinen, Pekka: Arvoisa Tasavallan Presidentti. Letter in *Achtung* 1/2018, p. 11
Lappalainen, Niilo: Vaarallisilla teillä. Viimeiset suomalaiset SS-miehet. WSOY. Porvoo 1998
Lappi-Seppälä, Sakari: Haudat Dnjeprin varrella. SS-miehen päiväkirjan lehtiä. Aa osakeyhtiö. Helsinki 1945
Larsen, Dennis & Straede, Therkel: En skole i vold - Bobruisk 1941-44 - Frikorps Danmark og det tyske besættelsesherredømme i Hviderusland. Gyldendal. København 2015
Larsson, Lars T.: Hitler's Swedes. A History of the Swedish volunteers in the Waffen-SS. Helion & Co. Solihull, West Midlands 2014
Latawski, Paul: Foreword to an article included in: War in a Twilight World. Partisan and Anti-Partisan Warfare in Eastern Europe, 1939-45. Ed. by Ben Shepherd & Juliette Pattinson. Palgrave Macmillan. Houndmills, Basingstoke, Hampshire 2010, pp.131–136
Lempinen, Olavi: Pääkallosotilas. SS-vapaaehtoiseksi 16-vuotiaana. Otava. Helsinki 2018
Liber, George O.: Total Wars and the Making of Modern Ukraine 1914-1954. University of Toronto Press. Toronto 2016
Longerich, Peter: Holocaust. The Nazi Persecution and Murder of the Jews. Oxford University Press. Oxford 2010
Lower, Wendy: "Anticipatory Obedience" and the Nazi Implementation of the Holocaust in the Ukraine. A Case Study of the Central and Peripheral Forces in the Generalbezirk Zhytomyr, 1941-1944. Article in *Holocaust and Genocide Studies* Vol. 16 1/2002, pp. 1–22
Lower, Wendy: Nazi Empire-Building and the Holocaust in Ukraine. University of North Carolina. Chapel Hill, North Carolina 2005
Lower, Wendy: "On Him Rests the Weight of the Administration". Nazi Civilian Rulers and the Holocaust in Zhytomyr. Article in: The Shoah in Ukraine. History, Testimony, Memorialization. Ed. by Ray Brandon and Wendy Lower. Indiana University Press. Bloomington,

Indiana 2008, pp. 224–247
Lower, Wendy: The Diary of Samuel Golfard and the Holocaust in Galicia. Altamina Press in association with the U.S. Holocaust Memorial Museum. Lanham, Maryland 2011
Lower, Wendy: Axis Collaboration, Operation Barbarossa, and the Holocaust in Ukraine. Article in: Nazi Policy on the Eastern Front, 1941. Total War, Genocide, and Radicalization. Ed. by Alex J. Kay, Jeff Rutherford & David Stahle. Boydel & Brewer, University of Rocherster. New York 2012, pp. 186–219
Lucas, Richard C.: Forgotten Holocaust. The Poles Under German Occupation, 1939-1944. Hippocrene Books. Lexington, Kentucky 1986
Löb, Ladislaus: Dealing with Satan. Rezsö Kasztner's daring rescue mission. Jonathan Cape. London 2008
Mabire, Jean: Die SS-Panzer-Division "Wiking". Germanische Freiwillige im Kampf für Europa. K.W. Schutz. Oldendorff 1983
MacLean, French L.: The Field Men: The SS Officers Who Led the Einsatzkommandos – the Nazi Mobile Killing Units. Schiffer Military History. Atglen, Pennsylvania 1999 (MacLean 1999 I)
MacLean, French L.: The Camp Men: The SS Officers Who Ran the Nazi Concentration Camp System. Schiffer Military History. Atglen, Pennsylvania 1999 (MacLean 1999 II)
Manley, Rebecca: To the Tashkent Station. Evacuation and Survival in the Soviet Union at War. Cornell University Press. Ithaca, New York 2009
Mannerheim, Carl Gustaf Emil: Minnen D. 2, 1931-1946. Norstedt. Stockholm 1952.
Manninen, Ohto: Suomalaisen SS-pataljoonan syntyvaiheet. Article in Sotilasaikakauslehti 1981 pp. 696–705
Manninen, Ohto: Ajanuksena uusi jääkäripataljoona 27. Suomalaisen SS-pataljoonan syntyvaiheet. Article in Parole. Jääkärisäätiö Jääkäripataljoonan 27:n perinneyhdistyksen jäsen lehti 2.2011 pp. 3–11
Manninen, Ohto: Panttijääkärit - suomalaisen SS-pataljoonan syntyvaiheet. Article included in: Vaiettu totuus. Salattuja ja vähän tunnettuja tapauksia sotavuosilta. Kauko I. Rumpunen (toim). Valitut Palat. Helsinki 2013 pp. 241–249
Mathias, Karl-Heinz: Felix Steiner. General der Waffen-SS und seine europäischen Freiwilligen. Eine umfassende Darstellung. DS-Verlag. Riesa 2001
Matthäus, Jürgen: Operation Barbarossa and the Onset of the Holocaust, June-December 1941. Article in: Browning, Christopher R.: The Origins of the Final Solution. The Evolution of Nazi Jewish Policy, September 1939-March 1942. William Heinemann. London 2004, pp. 244–308
Matusak, Piotr: The Resistance in Poland. Article in: Polish Resistance Movement in Poland and Abroad, 1939-1945. Ed. by Stanislaw Okeki. Polish Scientific Publishers. Warszawa 1987, pp. 11–157
Mehner, Kurt (Ed.): Die Waffen-SS und Polizei 1939-1945. Schriftenreihe Führung und Truppe. Militair-Verlag Klaus W. Patzwall. Norderstedt 1995
Messenger, C.R.M.: Hitler's Gladiator. The Life and Times of Oberstgruppenführer and Panzer-Generaloberst der Waffen-SS Sepp Dietrich. Brassey´s Defence Publishers. Exeter 1988
Mick, Christoph: Lemberg, Lwów, L'viv, 1914-1947. Violence and Ethnicity in a Contested City. Purdue University Press. West Lafayette, Indiana 2016
Motta, Giuseppe: The Great War against Eastern European Jewry 1914-1920. Cambridge Scholars Publishing. Cambridge 2017
Moxter, Hans G.: Die Postzensur in Finnland – Suomen postisensuuri – Finska postcensuren – Finsk postcensur – Finnish mail censorship – Censura postal de Finlandia. Forschungsgemeinschaf Nordische Staaten im Bund Deutscher Philatelisten. Niedernhausen 1975
Moxter, Hans G.: Finnland – Feldpost, Suomi – Kenttäpostia, Finland – Fältpost, Finland – Field Post. Forschungsgemeinschaf Nordische Staaten e. V. im Bund Deutscher Philatelisten. Niedernhausen 1978
Neitzel, Sönke & Welzer, Harald: Sotilaat. Taistelemisesta, tappamisesta ja kuolemisesta. Gummerus. Jyväskylä 2011. Originally in German: Soldaten. Protokolle vom Kämpfen, Töten und Sterben. Fischer. Frankfurt am Main 2011
Neumann, Peter: The Black March. The Personal Story of an SS Man. Bantam Books. Toronto 1985
Nummelin, Pauli: Markamme varrelta. Writing in *Achtung* 3/2000, p. 3
Nupnau, Eric: Farligt spel. Två års upplevelser i Tyskland efter kriget. Holger Schilds förlag. Helsingfors 1946
O'Neil, Robin: Jewish Genocide in Galicia. Robin O´Neil. Raleigh, North Carolina 2016
Overy, Richard James: Russia's War, 1941-1945. TV Books. London 1997
Parland, Mark: Pahoja natsi-kenraaleita joita ei teloitettu. Mark Parland. Helsinki 2012
Parvilahti, Unto: Terekille ja takaisin. Suomalaisen vapaaehtoisjoukon vaiheita Saksan itärintamalla 1941–43. Otava. Helsinki 1959
Pasher, Yaron: Holocaust versus Wehrmacht. How Hitler's "Final Solution" Undermined the German War Effort. University Press of Kansas. Lawrence, Kansas 2014

Petropoulos, Jonathan: Art as Politics in the Third Reich. University of North Carolina Press. Chapel Hill, North Carolina 1996
Pohl, Dieter: Nationalsozialistische Judenverfolgung in Ostgalizien 1941-1944. Organisation und Durchführung eines staatlichen Massenverbrechen. Oldenbourg Wissenschaftsverlag. München 1996
Pohl, Dieter: The Murder of Ukraine's Jews under German Military Administration and in the Reich Commissariat Ukraine. Article in: The Shoah in Ukraine. History, Testimony, Memorialization. Ed. by Ray Brandon & Wendy Lower. Indiana University Press. Bloomington, Indiana 2008 pp. 23–76
Pohl, Dieter: Die Herrschaft der Wehrmacht. Deutsche Militärbesatzung und einheimische Bevölkerung in der Sowjetunion 1941-1944. Oldenbourg Wissenschaftsverlag. München 2009
Polonsky, Antony: The Jews in Poland and Russia. Volume III, 1914 to 2008. Littman Library of Jewish Civilization. Oxford 2012
Porvali, Seppo: Rautaristi. SS-mies Yrjö Pyyhtiän tarina. Revontuli. Tampere 2014
Proskurov. Article in: Encyclopedia of Camps and Ghettos 1933-1945, Vol 2 Ghettos in German-Occupied Eastern Europe. Ed. by Martin Dean. Indiana University Press. Bloomington, Indiana 2012 pp. 1449–1452
Quarrie, Bruce: Hitler's Samurai. The Waffen-SS in action. Patrick Stephens. Wellingborough, Northants 1984
Ragnarök. SS-divisionen Nordlands pansarspaningsavdelningens kamp och undergång i Pommern, Brandenburg och Berlin, berättad av en svensk Waffen-SS-frivillig. Nordland Arkiv. Linköping 1996 (This is a recollection by the Swedish SS-volunteer Erik Wallin, first published under the pseudonym Jerk Viking in 1945)
Reenpää, Heikki: Pojanpoika. Otava. Helsinki 1998
Reitlinger, Gerald: The SS: Alibi of a Nation, 1922-1945. Heinemann. London 1956
Rhodes, Richard: Masters of Death. The SS-Einsatzgruppen and the Invention of the Holocaust. Perseus. Oxford 2002
Rintala, Paavo: Sotilaiden äänet – Kannaksen läpimurtotaisteluista 1944. Uusi kirjakerho. Helsinki 1975
van Roekel, Evertjan: Jongens van Nederland. Nederlandse vrijwilligers in de Waffen-SS. Spectrum. Antwerpen 2012
Rossino, Alexander B.: Hitler strikes Poland. Blitzkrieg, Ideology, and Atrocity. University Press of Kansas. Lawrence, Kansas 2003
Rossolinski-Liebe, Grzegorz: Der Verlauf und die Täter der Lemberger Pogroms vom Sommer 1941. Article in: *Jahrbuch für Antisemitismusforschung* Vol. 22, 2013, pp. 207–243
Ruusukallio, Pekka: Suomen puolesta. Kahden armeijan taistelija Karl-Erik Ladau. Pirkanmaan sotilaspiirien perinneyhdistys. Hämeenlinna 2007
Räsänen, Liisa: Ossianin Laulut. Atena. Jyväskylä 2000
Römer, Felix: Der Kommissarbefehl. Wehrmacht und NS-Verbrechen an der Ostfront 1941/42. Schöningh. Paderborn 2008
Sarasalo, Juhani: Päivän tapahtumat, 1.7.1941. Writing in *Achtung* 3/1998, pp. 4–5
Sauer, Karl: Die Verbrechen der Waffen-SS. Eine Dokumentation. Hrsg. im Auftrag des Präsidiums der VVN - Bund der Antifaschisten. Röderberg-Verlag. Frankfurt am Main 1977
Scheurig, Bodo: Alfred Jodl. Gehorsam und Verhängnis. Propylän. Berlin 1991
Schütz, Waldemar (Ed.): General Felix Steiner. Befehlshaber der europäischen Freiwilligen in der Waffen-SS im Kampf gegen den Kommunismus. DVG, Deutsche Verlagsgesellschaft. Preussisch Oldendorf 1999
Schön, Bosse: Svenskarna som stred för Hitler. Ett historiskt reportage. Månpocket. Stockholm 1999
Schön, Bosse: Där järnkorsen växer. Ett historiskt reportage. Månpocket. Stockholm 2001
Seppälä, Helge: Neuvostopartisaanit toisessa maailmansodassa. WSOY. Porvoo 1971
Silvennoinen, Oula & Tikka, Marko & Roselius, Aapo: Suomalaiset fasistit. Mustan sarastuksen airuet. WSOY. Helsinki 2016.
Smith, Peter Scharff & Poulsen, Niels Bo & Christensen, Claus Bundegård: The Danish Volunteers in the Waffen-SS and German Warfare at the Eastern Front. Article in: *Contemporary European History* Vol. 8 1/1999, pp. 73–96
Snyder, Timothy: Bloodlands: Europe between Hitler and Stalin. Vintage. New York 2019
Solbakken, Evald O.: I fengsel og landflyktighet. Tiden. Oslo 1945
SS im Einsatz. Eine Dokumentation über die Verbrechen der SS. Deutscher Militärverlag. Berlin 1964
SS-Unterscharführer Aarno Nurmio muistelee. Osa 2. ed. Jussi Kaisla. Article in *Achtung* 1/2012, pp. 8–13
Stein, George H.: The Waffen SS. Hitler's Elite Guard at War. Cornell University Press. Ithaca, New York 1966
Stein, Georg H. & Krosby, H. Peter: Das Finnische Freiwilligen-Bataillon der Waffen-SS. Article in *Vierteljahrshefte der Zeitgeschichte* 4/1966, pp. 413–453
Steiner, Felix: Die Freiwilligen der Waffen-SS. Idee und Opfergang. Deutsche Verlagsgesellschaft. Rosenheim 1992 (first published in 1958)
Steiner, Felix: Die Armee der Geächteten. Plesse Verlag.

Göttingen 1963
Strassner, Peter: Europäische Freiwillige. Die Geschichte der 5. SS-Panzerdivision Wiking. Munin. Osnabrück 1968
Struve, Kai: Deutsche Herrschaft, ukrainischer Nationalismus, antijüdische Gewalt. Der Sommer 1941 in der Westukraine. De Gruyter Oldenburg. Berlin 2015
Struve, Kai: Der Sowjetische Massenmord an Gefängnisinsassen in Lemberg Ende Juni 1941: Orte und Opferzahlen, pp. 1–16. Article published in Ukrainian: *Ukraina moderna* 9.9.2018 (http://uamoderna.com/md/struvelonckoho)
Subtelny, Orest: Ukraine. A History. University of Toronto Press. Toronto 2000 (First published in 1988)
Suistola, Jouni: Suomalaiset Waffen-SS:n palveluksessa. Article in: Stein, Georg: Waffen-SS. Hitlerin eliittikaarti sodassa 1939–1945. Atena. Jyväskylä 2009, pp. 326–346
Suomalaisten jääkärien 'tempauksia' Idän suurtaisteluissa. Article by Tauno Pajunen in *Hakkapeliitta*, the mouthpiece of the Finnish White Guard (or Civil Guard) militia from 1925-1944, when the Guard was disbanded following pressure from the Soviet Union. Issue No. 20, 1942
Swanström, André: Hakaristin ritarit. Suomalaiset SS-miehet, politiikka, uskonto ja sotarikokset. Atena. Helsinki 2018
Sydnor, C.W.: Soldiers of Destruction. The SS Death's Head Division 1933-1945. Princeton University Press. Princeton, New Jersey 1990
Sørlie, Sigurd: Solkors eller hakekors. Nordmenn I Waffen-SS, 1941-1945. Dreyers forlag. Oslo 2015
Tapola, Päivi & Karjalainen, Mikko: Mannerheimin haastaja. Kenraali Harald Öhquist. Otava. Helsinki 2013.
Tennenbaum, Samuel Lipa: Złoczów Memoir, 1939-1944. A Chronicle of Survival. Authors Choice Press. New York 1986
The German Army and Genocide. Crimes Against War Prisoners, Jews, and Other Civilians in the East, 1939-1944. New Press. New York 1999
The Memorial (Yizkor) Book of Podhajce, Ukraine. JewishGen. New York 2013
The Shoah in Ukraine. History, Testimony, Memorialization. ed. by Ray Brandon & Wendy Lower. Indiana University Press. Bloomington, Indiana 2008
The SS on Trial. Evidence from Nuremberg. The Illustrated Edition., ed. and introduced by Bob Carruthers. Pen & Sword Military. Barnsley, South Yorkshire 2014
Tieke, Wilhelm: Das Finnische Freiwilligen-Bataillon der Waffen-SS: III. (finn.)/ "Nordland". Munin Verlag. Osnabrück 1979
Tieke, Wilhelm: Das Ende zwischen Oder und Elbe. Der Kampf um Berlin 1945. Motorbuch-Verlag. Stuttgart 1981
Tieke, Wilhelm: Tragedy of the Faithful. A History of the III. (Germanisches) SS-Panzer-Korps. J J Fedorowicz Pub. Winnipeg 2001
Tieke, Wilhelm: Suomalainen SS-pataljoona. Das Finnische Freiwilligen-Bataillon der Waffen-SS. Gummerus. Helsinki 2002
Trigg, Jonathan: Hitlers vikingar. Historien om det skandinaviska Waffen-SS. Den Norske Legion, Frikorps Danmark, Wiking och Nordland. Fischer & Co. Stockholm 2015
Tuomaala, Ritva: Kunniani on uskollisuus. Veteraanin elämäkerta. Viljo Kellokummun muistojen tallentajana Ritva Tuomaala. Ritva Tuomaala. Rovaniemi 2010
Turunen, Mirja: Koska kotimaa meidät lähetti. SS-mies Sakari Haikala Hitlerin eliittijoukoissa. Docendo. Jyväskylä 2016
Tyrkkö, Jukka: Suomalaisia suursodassa. SS-vapaaehtoisten vaiheita jääkäreiden jäljillä 1941–43. WSOY. Porvoo 1960
Tyrkkö, Jukka: Joulumme Kaukasuksella 1942. Article in *Achtung* 4/2014, pp. 1–8 (reprint of an article with the same title in *Rintamamies* No. 50–51 from 1942)
Tyrkkö, Jukka: Felix Steiner, eräs uuden Euroopan sodanjohtaja. Article in *Achtung* 3/2018, pp. 1, 3–7 (Reprint of an article with the same title in *Suomen Kuvalehti*, 8.8.1942)
Ulateig, Egil: Jakten på massemorderne. En dokumentarbok. Forlaget Reportasje. Oslo 2006
Uskollisuus on kunniamme. Koonnut Seppo Porvali. Apali. Tampere 2008
Vassiltchikov, Marie "Missie": Berlin Diaries, 1940-1945. Knopf. London 1987
Weale, Adrian: The SS: A New History. Little, Brown. London 2010
Wegner, Bernd: The Tottering Giant: German Perceptions of Soviet Military and Economic Strength in Preparation for Operation Blau (1942). Article in: Intelligence and International Relations, 1900-1945. ed. by Christopher Andrew & Jeremy Noakes. University of Exeter. Exeter 1987, pp. 293 311
Wegner, Bernd: The Waffen-SS. Organization, Ideology, and Function. Blackwell. Oxford 1990
Weinberg, Gerald L.: A World at Arms. A Global History of World War II. Cambridge U.P. Cambridge 1994
Verbrechen der Wehrmacht. Dimensionen des Vernichtungskrieges 1941-1944. Ausstellungskatalog. Hamburger Institut für Sozialforschung (Hg.). Hamburg 2002
Werther, Steffen: Dänische Freiwillige in der Waffen-SS. Wiss. Verlag. Berlin 2004
Westberg, Lennart: Krigsförbrytarprocesser i Västtyskland. Article in *Svensk Juristtidskrift* 8/1983, pp. 578–583
Westberg, Lennart: Finländarna som stred i Waffen-SS. Article in *Militärhistoria* 2/1997, pp. 16–21
Westerlund, Lars: Avioliitot ja kihlaukset rotupolitiikan varjossa. Saksalaisten sotilaiden ja suomalaisten naisten avio-

liitto- ja kihlausilmoitukset sanomalehdissä 1941-1944. Article included in: Saksalaisten sotilaiden lapset. Ulkomaalaisten sotilaiden lapset Suomessa 1940-1948, Osa I – The Children of German Soldiers. Children of Foreign Soldiers in Finland 1940-48, Vol. I. Kansallisarkisto. Helsinki 2011 pp. 116–185

Westerlund, Lars: Cirkus Collani. De finländska SS-frivilliga 1941-1943. En sedeskildring baserad på de frivilligas egna berättelser. BoD - Books on Demand. Helsingfors 2017

Vihavainen, Timo: Ryssäviha. Venäjän-pelon historia. Minerva. Helsinki 2013

Wikberg, Olli: Dritte Nordland. Suomalainen SS-vapaaehtoispataljoona kuvissa. The Photo History of the Finnish Volunteer Battalion of the Waffen-SS, 1941-1943. Gummerus. Helsinki 2001

Wikman, Leo: Liten kugge I stort spel – en stabsofficers minnen. Schildt. Helsingfors 1992

Virtanen, Elina: Schwester, lotta ja maanpetturi. Ruth Munckin (1886-1976) muistot ja tulkinnat elämänsä kulusta. Sigillum. Turku 2018

Wykes, Alan: Hitler's Bodyguards. SS Leibstandarte. Ballantine Books. New York 1974

Yerger, Mark C.: Allgemeine-SS. The Commands. Units and Leaders of the General SS. Schiffer. Atglen, Pennsylvania 1997 [Yerger 1997 I]

Yerger, Mark C.: Waffen-SS Commanders. The Army, Corps and Divisional Leaders of a Legend. Augsberger to Kreutz (Vol. 1), Krüger to Zimmermann (Vol. 2). Schiffer Pub. Atglen, Pennsylvania 1997 [Yerger 1997 II] and 1999

Yones, Eliyahu: Smoke in the Sand: The Jews of Lvov in the War Years 1939-1944. Gefen Publishing House. Jerusalem 2004

Zetterling, Niklas: Blixtkrig! 1939-1941. Krigsvetenskapliga institutionen, Försvarshögskolan. Stockholm 2003

NEWSPAPER ARTICLES

Alte Kameraden mollissa. Review of Felix Steiner's book "Die Freiwilligen" in *Helsingin Sanomat*, 28.8.1959 by 'Ypi' (= Yrjö Kaila)

De Zevende Kompagnie schoot 22 Russische burgers dood in 1941: de verzegen misdaad van Nederlandse SS-ers. Article in *Het Vrije Volk*, 30.5.1986 (The Seventh Company killed 22 Russian civilians in 1941: The Concealed Crime of Dutch SS-men)

Den smygande nynazistiska faran. Article by Mark Parland in *Vasabladet*, 20.4.1988 (The Sneaking Danger of Neo-Nazism)

"Emme tienneet tuhoamisleireistä". Writing by Timo Kiiski in *Iltalehti*, 8.4.2007

Falt for Norge. Hans Oppen In memoriam. Clipping from an unknown newspaper, 26.8.1941 (Included in the archive of the SS-Investigation of the National Archives, File Bjørnstad-Taarneby)

"He halusivat näyttää, että juutalaiset voivat hyvin". Writing by Brynolf Palmgren in *Helsingin Sanomat*, 6.1.2007

Hitlers specialorganisation för död och förintelse. Article by Mark Parland in *Vasabladet*, 26.1.1988 (Hitler's special organisation for death and annihilation)

Ilddåpen: Norsk frivillig skildrer bolsjevikenes djevelske krigsførsel på Østfronten. Writing by SS-Kriegsberichter Egil Hartmann in *Fritt Folk*, 19.7.1941

"Isämme" ja komentajamme ... Piece written by 'Erkki Olavi' in *SS-Aseveljet* 23/1944, (a supplement to the journal *Rintamamies*)

Kokemuksia ja tuntemuksia Saksan itärintamalta. Articles by Markus Käenmäki in the newspaper *Ylä-Satakunta*, 3.7., 8.7., 10.7. and 15.7.2003

"Koko Skandinavia alistettaisiin Suomelle". Interview with Sakari Haikala in *Etelä-Suomen Sanomat* by Tuomo Komulainen, 21.7.2007

Loppuun saakka. Kenr. von Scholz ja everstil. Collani kaatuneet. Writing in *SS-Aseveljet*, 25.8.1944, (a supplement to the journal *Rintamamies*)

Muuan "arvostelu". Writing by Sakari Lappi-Seppälä in *Vapaa Sana*, 28.11.1945

Nazibrott i efterljus. Article by Mark Parland in *Vasabladet*, 13.5.1941 (Nazi crime [viewed] in later light)

Nederlandse nazi's vermoorden boeren. Article in *Limburgsch Dagblad*, 30.5.1986 (Dutch Nazis killed farmers)

Og så bearer det videre - - ! En nordmann skildrer episode fra kampene på østfronten. Article by Olaf Wahlman in *Hirdmannen*, 16.8.1941

Oppgjør med en svindler. "SS-offiseren Peter Neumann", som I sin bok "Dødens drabanter" retter grove beskyldningen mot Waffen-SS och Regiment Nordland. Slik ser det ut bak hetspropagandans kulisser. Anonymous writing by Ole Kristian Brunaes in *Folk og land*, 16.1.1960

Otavan arkisto. Interview with Heikki Reenpää by Kreeta Karvala in *Iltalehti*, 9.12.2007

Parvilahden juttu siirtyi lokakuulle. Mielenkiintoisia todistajanlausuntoja. Article in *Suomen Sosialidemokraatti*, 12.9.1958

Russen vragen Lubbers SS'ers te berechten. Article in *Het Vrije Volk*, 20.6.1986 (Russians ask Lubbers to try SS-men)

Saksan entiset SS-miehet koolla. Article in *Helsingin Sanomat*,

28.10.1952
Sjöstedt, Mauno P.: Suomalaisia Ukrainan taisteluissa saksalaisten SS-joukkojen mukana. In the newspapers *Etelä-Suomen Sanomat* and *Länsi-Savo*, 10.1.1942 and in *Maaseudun tulevaisuus*, 17.1.1942.
SS-Gruppenführer Gille – en kompromissløs nasjonalsosialist. Den 12. soldat i den tyske forsvarsmakt som har mottatt jernkorsets ridderkors med sverd, eikelauv og briljanter. Piece by SS-Kriegsberichter Dr. Kristian Zarp in *Aftenposten*, 29.4.1944
SS-man Josef Hansen førteller om sine upplevelser I det røde "paradis". Hansen's piece in *Vestfold Presse*, 10.1.1942
SS-miehenä Suomen vuoksi. Interview with Sakari Haikala in *Itä-Savo* by Annamari Haimi, 23.10.2016
SS-välikohtaus. Ramcke leimaa liittoutuneet "sotarikollisiksi". Article in *Helsingin Sanomat*, 27.10.1952
Suomalaiset vapaaehtoiset SS:n teloitusoperaatiossa itärintamalla. Article in *Demari*, 11.2.1998 by Boris Salomon
Suomalaispataljoonan ensimmäinen taistelu Kaukasissa. Nopealla hyökkäyksellä karkoitettiin kasakat asemistaan. Writing by "T." (= Jukka Tyrkkö) in *Aamulehti* 23.9.1942.
Svårt att få rekryter till Norska Legionen. Quisling locker med ekonomiska fördelar. Article in *Nu. Världsopinionen inför världsfrågorna*, 22.8.1941
Teloittiko "Kurre" juutalaisia? Writing by Pasi Lehtinen in *Iltalehti*, 26.3.2014 (Did "Kurre" execute Jews?)
Tosi aseveljeyttä. Piece in *Rintamamies*, 25.8.1944 by Jukka Tyrkkö.
Vier Duitsers en twee Finnen voerden executies uit. Article by Mari de Henk in *De Telegraaf*, 9.7.1977 (Four Germans and two Finns carried out executions)

INDEX

Aalto, Keijo 122, 123
Aaltonen, Bruno 28, 183
Aarni, Tauno 59
Adler, Meir 134
Aejmelaeus, Nils (Äimä) 189
Alhainen, Mauno Olavi (later Olavi Alsta) 119, 173, 174
Alkio, Paavo 57
Allerhand, Maurycy 104
Alsta, Olavi *see* Alhainen, Mauno Olavi
Altman, Solomon 127–129
Angrick, Andrej 37
Anttila, Ensio 170
Anttonen, Erkki 57
Asikainen, Pauli 86
Autonen, Ilmari 91, 202

Backberg, Harry 167
Bandera, Stepan 99, 195–197
Bartov, Omer 35, 195
Behnke, Carlheinz 114
Berger, Gottlob 18, 19, 21, 36, 69, 172
Berger, Salomon 134
Bjørnstad, Ørnulf 81, 82, 95, 151, 188, 189, 194
Blobel, Paul 103
Boll, Bernd 37, 130, 131
Boman, Unto (from 1944 Unto Parvilahti) 31, 43, 58, 59, 73, 91, 108, 110, 136, 139, 173, 203
Bonsdorff, Hjalmar von 30
Brauchitsch, Walther von 39
Braun, Alois 106, 152
Braunagel, Walter 147
Brenna, Olof 105

Cande, Konstantin (Kosti) 27, 173
Christensen, Claus Bundgård 116
Collani, Hans 67, 68, 70
Cüppers, Martin 73

Dallin, Alexander 196, 197
Dannfelt, Curt Juhlin 189
Diebitsch, Karl 63, 70, 120
Dieckmann, August 64, 105
Diener, Efraim 194
Dietrich, Josef "Sepp" 67
Duncker, Kaj 86, 108, 111, 112, 114, 119, 133, 154, 155
Dupak, Nikolai 41

Eisen, Moses 128
Ellenberg (Rabbi) 128
Engelhardt, Poul Rantzow 61, 62
Engelmann, Josef 86
Ergert, Ludwig 114, 115
Estes, Kenneth 34, 36, 69

Fagerholm, Lars 119
Fanslau, Heinz 120
Fick, Ernst 65
Frehé, Ferdinand 118, 119, 134, 135, 144, 153–155
Freimann, Luisa 128
Friedman, Philip 103
Frydman, Sara 142
Fyrst, Walter 188

Gerstenfeld-Maltiel, Jacob 100, 197
Gille, Herbert 64, 65, 70, 74, 75, 139
Goldberg, Mojzez 40
Goldflies Yitzchak 154
Goldsworthy, Terry 37, 38
Grandell, Leonard 16
Groscurth, Helmuth 129, 130, 159, 200
Gröndahl, Aulis 123, 156
Gummerus, Herman 198

Hadeln, Hans-Joachim "Hajo" Freiherr von 62, 63
Haikala, Kauko 57
Haikala, Sakari (formerly Sakari Sulinmaa) 57, 86, 179, 184, 202
Hakkarainen, Aarne 120
Hallavo, Veikko 124
Hansen, Josef 106
Hartmann, Egil 52, 188
Hatara, Teuvo 47, 186
Hautala, Eino 139
Heck, Walter 63
Heder, Eberhardt 106
Heikkilä, Matti 169
Heikurainen, Leo 86, 175
Heim, Wilhelm 136
Heinz, Franz Josef 63
Heldmann, Constantin 66
Heliste, Simo 86
Hellemaa, Mika 57
Hemmo, Unto 123
Herold, Ulrich 118
Herrmann, Günther 103, 133, 143
Hertzen, Gunnar von 32
Herzig, Friedrich (Fritz) 160
Hetiyev, S. 112
Heydrich, Reinhard 23, 39
Himmler, Heinrich 19, 21, 30, 36, 54, 63, 65, 69, 71, 74, 75, 79, 164, 166, 173, 182, 198
Hintikka, Jaakko 86, 16, 170
Hitler, Adolf 15, 38, 40, 50, 53, 65, 67, 69, 85, 99, 104, 108, 167, 170
Holmila, Antero 116
Holter, Karl 188
Horn, Walter 18, 47
Hukari, Veijo 123
Husen, Heinrich 50
Häikiö, Veikko 175
Häkli, Olavi 29
Händel, Georg Friedrich 173
Höglund, Elis 53

Ilkama, Tapio 139
Isenmann, Hans Wilhelm 47, 101, 102, 106
Itälä, Jouko 29, 167, 175, 195, 196

Joerchel, Wolfgang 64
Johansen, Bernhard 105
Johansson, Per-Olof "Pärre" 42

Johansson, Sulo 42
Jokipii, Mauno 39, 55, 74, 107, 116, 117, 173
Jopaks (brothers, nickname) 125

Kahane, Leon M. 150
Kaila, Niilo 120
Kaila, Yrjö 35, 36, 40, 92, 114, 120, 160, 176
Kaiser Friedrich der Grosse ("Alte Fritz") 61
Kallia, Rauno 33
Kalsta, Arvi 32
Kaniuk, Wladyslaw 141
Kari, Väinö 33
Karinen, Antti 146
Karpalo, Olavi 44–46, 139, 203
Kauhanen, Aarne 28
Kauppi, Kauko 186
Kausch, Paul-Albert "Peter" 65, 66, 70, 74
Kelin, Åke 86
Kellokumpu, Vilho 88, 167
Kemppinen, Iivari 164
Keuter, Jan Henri Albert 139, 140
Khrushchev, Nikita 82
Kieper, Wolf 161, 162
Kiperman, Zipora 154
Kitzinger, Karl 88
Kivi, Risto 139
Kleijn, Cees 58, 188
Kleist, Ewald von 24
Kluge, Günther von 37
Klymiv-Lehenda, Ivan 127, 195
Koch, Hans 197
Kochalty, Helmut 147
Kogan, Moshe 161, 162
Kohanski, Halik 99
Kohola, Sakari 186
Koivisto, Pentti 90
Koivula, Martti 111, 116, 146, 155, 156, 175, 189
Kokko, Arvo 27, 184
Konttinen, Penna 95, 145
Korfes, Otto 130–132, 200
Korjus, Jaakko 90
Koskelin, Keijo 186
Koskimies, Eino 85
Kosonen, Herkko 42, 60, 168
Kotilainen, Väinö 16
Krabbe, Oluf 51
Kroeger, Erhard 103
Kronisch, Lejd 134
Kryssing, Christian Peder 187
Kujala, Pekka 119
Kurkiala, Kalervo 43, 58, 70, 72, 91
Kuronen, Eero 41
Kurvinen, Pekka 173
Kuuri, Taisto 163, 169, 204
Kuusinen, Otto Ville 13
Kyöstilä, Laine-Maire 195
Käenmäki, Markku 89, 108, 167, 178, 179
Kärki, Antti 120
Kääriäinen, Keijo 57, 93, 109, 137, 152, 162, 177, 180, 181, 183
Könönen, Kalevi 89

Laakkonen, Toivo 46
Labbart, Rolf 66
Ladau Karl-Erik 164
Laerum, Helge 106
Lakeala, Jaakko 45, 111, 135, 145, 159, 175
Landau Felix 103
Lantto, Alvar 59
Lapinjoki, Heikki 90
Lappi-Seppälä, Sakari 39, 58, 59, 92, 109, 112, 121–123, 136
Larsson, Lars T. 37, 120
Launonen, Pentti 120
Laurell, Kaj 47, 203
Lautia, Erik 175
le Roux, Edmond Henri 104
Lehto, Matti 123
Leib, Karl 175
Leisimo, Ossian 180
Lemettinen, Heikki 48
Lemmetyinen, Toivo 170
Leppälä, Martti 46, 109
Levälahti, Kustaa Eemil 56, 58
Liesinen, Olavi (Veikko) 27, 85, 93, 146, 175, 176, 183
Lindberg, Kim 175
Lindqvist, Gunnar 30, 32
Linnér Ragnar 52, 189
Liukkonen, Erik 41, 43, 45, 184
Longerich, Peter 76
Lower, Wendy 41
Lundin, Kurt 52, 53, 157
Lundqvist, Gösta 119
Lwow, Dovid 131
Lähtimäki, Matti 27

Maack, Berthold 66
MacLean, French L. 74
Madsen (Danish volunteer) 61
Malmberg, Lauri 71, 185
Mannerheim, Carl Gustaf Emil 17, 70, 71
Mansala, Heikki 167
Manstein, Erich von 90
Mathias, Karl-Heinz 157
Mattelmäki, Auvo see Nieminen, Auvo
Matti, Elias 86
Maunula, Paavo 90
Mayer, Szlojme 130
Merelä, Paavo 164, 165
Meriö, Esa 169
Miklos, Fred. (Alfred) 138, 155
Molotov, Vyacheslav 13
Munck, Ruth 73
Mustakallio, Martti 32
Müller, Heinrich 23
Mäkinen, Antti 119
Mäkitalo, Aimo 175

Nakari, Pentti 46
Neumann 41
Nevanlinna, Eino 173
Nevanlinna, Rolf 71, 185
Nieminen, Auvo (later Auvo Mattelmäki) 139
Nikkola, Pentti 108, 136, 137
Noisniemi, Torkel 120
Norberg, Curt Birger 53
Norrmén, Pehr H. 30, 203
Nummelin, Pauli 179
Nummi, Pekka 170
Nupnau, Erik 58, 168
Nurmi, Unto 46
Nurmio, Aarno 180
Nyberg, Aarne 57

Oberkamp, Karl Ritter von 64, 152
Olij, Jan 112, 133, 187
Olsen, Oswald 188
Orenstein, Mordechai 194
Otto, Günther 147, 148
Overy, Richard 83

Paasonen, Aladár 47
Paikkala, Ahti 93, 110, 112, 114, 145, 167
Pajari, Aaro 70
Pajunen, Tauno 89
Parland, Mark 47
Parvilahti, Unto *see* Boman, Unto
Pasher, Yaron 35
Pedersen, Per 104
Phleps, Artur Gustav Martin (also Artur Stolz, Martin Stolz) 63, 64, 74, 194
Pihkala, Ensio 40, 44, 45, 108, 112, 133, 145, 153, 159, 176
Plöw, Walter 62
Pohl, Dieter 139
Pokela, Ahti 160
Polewacz, Harry 62, 63, 70
Polón, Tauno 169, 173
Porttinen, Kalevi 119
Porttinen, Leo E. 46
Poulsen, Niels Bo 116
Preng, Wilhelm 118
Puotinen, Viljo 186
Puuperä, Erkki 176, 182
Pyyhtiä, Yrjö 89
Pääkkönen, Jussi 119
Pöyhönen, Sakari 111, 119, 134, 145

Quisling, Vidkun 15, 28, 186, 194

Rademaker, Martinus 114, 133, 143, 144
Rahola, Heikki 120
Ramsay, Henrik 70, 71
Rangell, J.W. 47
Rantanen, Reino 139
Rasch, Otto 196
Rau (German) 156
Reedijk, Meeuwis 139
Reenpää, Heikki 47
Reenpää, Heikki A. 47
Reichel, Erwin 71
Reichelt, Eivind 84, 186
Reichenau, Walther von 159
Reitzenstein, Hans-Albin Freiherr von 66
Renner, Fritz 102
Renner, Hermann 102
Rentz, Maximilian 103
Ressler, Walter 118, 119
Reurs, Stijn 58, 188
Riedweg Franz 69
Rickki, Esko 180, 182, 184
Riekki, Tero 63
Riisnaes, Sverre 186
Rijksen, Hans 118
Rijsdijk, Jan 155
Rintala, Pentti 46
Ritari, Raine 186
Roekel, Evertjan van 155, 188
Roques, Karl von 157
Rosberg, John 30
Rosenberg, Alfred 197
Rosenbröijer, Christian 123, 146, 147
Rosenqvist, Helge 123
Rossino, Alexander B. 76
Rundstedt, Gerd von 24
Ryti, Risto 70, 71
Räihä, Timo 123
Räikkönen, Erkki 31, 32
Röhm, Ernst 66

Saarela, Jaakko 173
Saarela, Signe 167
Sahari, Paavo 119
Salonen, Eino 174
Sander, Erwin 141
Sarasalo, Juhani 113, 114
Savolainen, Erik 178
Schade, Alfred 74, 120, 122, 123
Schalburg, Christian Frederik von 41, 51, 61, 186
Scheffer (Officer) 62
Schmidt, Johan 50
Schmulevic (Mr., local man at Mykulyntsi) 149
Schobert, Eugen Ritter von 78
Schoenfeld, H. F. Arthur 33
Scholz, Fritz von ("Alte Fritz") 24, 41, 61, 62, 70
Schröder (SS-Obersturmführer) 173
Schultze, Heinz 129
Schulz, Erwin 101, 103
Schweizer Horowitz, Nusia 149
Schön, Bosse 52, 53
Schönfelder, Manfred 92, 150
Schöngarth, Eberhard 103
Seppälä, Helge 49
Setälä, Ahti 120
Sinervo, Martti 89
Sjöstedt, Mauno P. 88
Slepyan, Kenneth 83
Smith, Peter Scharff 116
Somersalo, Olli 136
Sonninen, Esko 169
Stackelberg, Curt von 147, 191
Stalin, Joseph 13
Stein, George H. 37, 38
Steiner, Felix 25, 35, 36, 40, 61, 62, 65–71, 73–76, 78, 92, 115, 118, 147, 148, 151, 152, 157, 166, 173, 184, 185, 194, 200, 201
Stetsko, Yaroslav 197
Stolz, Artur *see* Phleps, Artur
Stolz, Martin *see* Phleps, Artur
Struve, Kai 99, 131–134, 154, 191, 197
Ström, Uuno 78, 178
Stücker, Landoald 120
Stülpnagel, Carl-Heinrich von 24
Sulinmaa, Sakari *see* Haikala, Sakari
Suonio, Reino 107, 145, 159, 178
Suutala, Paavo 178
Swanström, André 45, 46, 74, 173
Swat, Gerard de 133
Sääskilahti, Niilo 186
Sørlie, Sigurd 188

Taarneby, Jan 81, 82, 95, 151, 188
Taivalmaa, Seppo 178, 180
Talvela, Paavo 70
Tamminen, Matti 59, 135, 136, 139
Tennenbaum (Tenenbaum), Samuel Lipa 126, 127
Tenomaa, Yrjö 137
Terboven, Josef 15, 186
Terkel, Anna 142
Teschmann (SS soldier) 133
Tiainen, Esko 120
Trigg, Jonathan 115
Tschentscher, Erwin 147, 148
Tuff, Olav Ingemar 51, 105, 189
Tuomaala, Toivo 170, 173
Tyrkkö, Jukka 55, 57–59, 72, 86, 89, 91, 168

Ulateig, Egil 141, 143, 151, 152
Uusi-Jaakkola, Martti 93, 107, 112, 114, 135, 159

Wagner, Eduard 39

Wahlman, Olaf 52, 106
Walden, Karl Rudolf 70
Valks, Hendrikus 138, 139
Wallén, Lennart 31, 169
Vauhkonen, Veijo 120
Weale, Adrian 69
Weckström, Thor-Björn 112–113, 120–123, 175, 202
Weers, Martinus 114, 144
Wegman (Officer) 78
Wegner, Bernd 33
Veikkola, Juha 57
Weinberg, Gerald L. 33
Weissbrod, Abraham 193, 194
Vesenne, Jorma 88
Vidberg, Arvo 89
Wiersma, Broer 41
Wietersheim, Gustav von 141, 157
Wikberg, Olli 60
Wikman, Leo 33
Willems, Pieter 40, 113, 144, 155
Wintergerst, Karl 102
Witoff, Abraham 154
Witting, Rolf 17
Voinovsky, Peter 159
Wolff, Karl 65
Wolkowicz, Shlomo 131
Vopersal, Wolfgang 54
Voutilainen, Erkki 86
Vuokko, Ari 171
Vuolento, Paavo 119
Wykes, Alan 40
Wäckerle, Hilmar 63, 74, 113–117, 119–123, 136, 138, 139, 147
Välimaa, Eino 139
Välimäki, Martti 139, 159, 167, 168

Yerger, Mark 74
Yones, Eliyahu 99

Zephorah, Namen 134
Zimmer, Joseph 128

Äimä *see* Aejmelaeus, Nils

Öhquist, Harald 70, 71
Østenby, Erik 106
Österman, Hugo 71, 163